Judging in a Therapeutic Key

Judging in a Therapeutic Key

Therapeutic Jurisprudence and the Courts

Edited by

Bruce J. Winick

David B. Wexler

Carolina Academic Press

Durham, North Carolina

ISBN: 0-89089-408-6
LCCN: 2003104168

Carolina Academic Press
700 Kent Street
Durham, North Carolina 27701
Telephone (919) 489-7486
Fax (919) 493-5668
www.cap-press.com
Email: cap@cap-press.com

Printed in the United States of America

To Judges Bill Schma, Peggy Hora, and Randy Fritzler, who started us off on this journey.

CONTENTS

Part II
From Description to Prescription:
Emerging Principles and Proposals

FOREWORD

By Judge (rtr.) William F. Dressel
President, The National Judicial College, Reno, Nevada

This work brings together scholarly analysis and examples of practical application to an evolving judicial role and concept of justice. The Introduction succinctly describes the history and nature of problem-solving courts, including the integral role of therapeutic jurisprudence to the effectiveness of these courts. The text describes specific approaches and the therapeutic principles, which are the foundation for this jurisprudence.

Every generation has had judges who believed there had to be a better way to dispense justice. I have heard it said many times that there had to be more to judging than finding the truth and deciding between two positions, especially in certain cases. "Offenders" kept coming back on revocation or new charges taking more and more court time and services. Thus, judges began to look to the social sciences and to direct court officers to use the expertise of mental health, medical, and other professionals. These judges wanted solutions that would make an impact on the causes of behavior so they could do more than just punish the act. Thus, you have seen judges take a different approach in juvenile cases as they sought to fashion orders to change behavior, living conditions, or care received. In criminal cases, conditions were imposed and jurisdiction maintained to enforce compliance. The relevance of therapeutic jurisprudence became apparent when judges started asking if the conditions or programs required made any difference. Judges were becoming "problem solvers" and that role increased as courts began to receive more cases arising out of recurring behavior that while legally defined as criminal was symptomatic of societal problems (i.e., homelessness, mental illness, substance abuse, etc.). This is a different role, and one can understand why jurists would be more comfortable in turning over the "why" of behavior to someone else. It is time, however, for judges of all courts to challenge their comfort level and seek solutions within the parameters of their jurisdiction to address the causes of behavior which brought the person before the court—time for judges to be problem solvers.

This publication is important and timely since the appropriateness of creating or maintaining problem-solving courts is being questioned. Responsible members of the judicial system raise the concern that resources are being diverted away from traditional adjudication responsibilities in a time of scarce resources. They also question whether judges should expand their jurisdictions beyond resolving disputes framed by pleadings. Understanding the value of judicial problem solving to address a court's business and the impact of therapeutic jurisprudence will be invaluable in addressing those concerns. Whatever may be the fate of these courts, an important lesson to be gleaned from this work is that the principles of therapeutic jurisprudence can be applied by judges whenever they engage in addressing societal problems, no matter how framed on a docket.

ACKNOWLEDGMENTS

We are once again delighted to publish with Carolina Academic Press, and thank its President, Keith Sipe, for giving us this opportunity and for, as always, being so easy to work with. And we heartily thank Tim Colton, Linda Lacy, and Jay Stallings for expertly sheparding the book through the entire process. The secretarial and administrative work regarding the book was performed at the University of Miami School of Law, and we thank Eileen Russell, secretary to Bruce Winick, and work study/assistant Jessica C. Serrano, for feats of cybergymnastics in preparing the book for submission to the publisher. For research assistance, we are most grateful to Adi Martinez, of the University of Puerto Rico School of Law, and to Abby Meltzer of the University of Miami School of Law. David Wexler gives special thanks to his two deans: Toni Massaro of the University of Arizona, and Efren Rivera of the University of Puerto Rico. He is also grateful to the Dean's Council of the University of Arizona James E. Rogers College of Law for a summer research grant to work on this book, and to the University of Puerto Rico for a sabbatical semester to do so. Bruce Winick gives special thanks to Dean Dennis O. Lynch of the Univeristy of Miami. We also thank the authors and journals that allowed us to reprint relevant articles and excerpts in this book, and thank those authors who have written essays expressly for this collection: Judges Carmen Lopez and J. Richardson Johnson, Professors Barbara Babb, Carrie Petrucci, and Stephanos Bibas, and psychologist Charles Kennedy. And we are, above all, appreciative of all the judges who have guided our work over the last several years. Many have been enormously helpful and supportive. The efforts and help of three of them—Bill Schma (Kalamazoo, Michigan), Peggy Hora (Alameda County, California), and Randy Fritzler (Clark County, Washington)—have been extraordinary, to us personally and to the development of the therapeutic jurisprudence perspective and its application to judging. It is our pleasure to dedicate this book to them.

Judging in a Therapeutic Key

Introduction

I. A Transformation in the Judicial Role

In the past dozen or so years, a remarkable transformation has occurred in the role of the courts. Courts traditionally have functioned as governmental mechanisms of dispute resolution, resolving disputes between private parties concerning property, contracts, and tort damages, or between the government and the individual concerning allegations of criminal wrongdoing or regulatory violation. In these cases, courts typically have functioned as neutral arbiters adjudicating controversies about historical facts or supervising juries engaged in the process of doing so.

In recent times, a range of new kinds of problems have been brought to the courts. Many are social and psychological in nature. They present the need for the courts not only to resolve disputed issues of fact, but also to attempt to solve a variety of human problems that are responsible for bringing the case to court. Traditional courts limited their attention to the narrow dispute in controversy. These newer courts, however, attempt to understand and address the underlying problem that is responsible for the immediate dispute, and to help the individuals before the court to deal effectively with the problem in ways that will prevent recurring court involvement.

Increasingly known as problem solving courts, these are specialized tribunals established to deal with specific problems, often involving individuals who need social, mental health, or substance abuse treatment services. These include criminal cases involving individuals with drug or alcoholism problems, mental health problems, or problems of family and intimate violence.

In many respects, the roots of this new judicial approach can be traced back to indigenous and tribal justice systems, including noteworthy examples in what today constitutes the United States, Canada, Australia, and New Zealand—and a serious effort is now underway to learn from those systems and to introduce some of their perspectives and techniques into western judicial structures.

In terms of western judicial machinery, the forerunner of today's specialized problem solving courts is the juvenile court, started in Chicago in 1899 as an attempt to provide a rehabilitative approach to the problem of juvenile delinquency. The juvenile court system received a major due process wake-up call in 1967 when the United States Supreme Court in *In re* Gault recognized the importance of not dropping the due process guard simply because of governmental "good intentions," such as a goal of rehabilitation rather than punishment. *Gault* is a message that modern problem solving courts and judges must always heed in their work.

The "modern" antecedents of the problem solving court movement can be traced to drug treatment court, founded in Miami in 1989. Drug treatment court was a response to the recognition that the processing of drug possession charges not involving violence in the criminal courts and sentencing the offender to prison did not succeed in changing the offender's addictive behavior. Criminal court dockets became swollen with these drug cases, and the essentially retributivist intervention of the criminal court and prison seemed to do little to avoid repetition of the underlying problem. The result was a revolving door effect in which drug offenders typically resumed their drug-abusing behavior after release from prison. Instead of relying on the traditional criminal justice approach, drug treatment court emphasized the rehabilitation of the offender and cast the judge as a member of the treatment team. Offenders accepting diversion to drug treatment court or pleading guilty and agreeing to participate in drug treatment court as a condition of probation agreed to remain drug-free, to participate in a prescribed course of drug treatment, to submit to periodic drug testing to monitor their compliance with the treatment plan, and to report periodically to court for judicial supervision of their progress.

The success of these courts in helping many addicts to end their addiction and to avoid re-involvement with the criminal court led to a tremendous growth in the number of drug courts nationally and internationally. Indeed, there are now juvenile drug treatment courts, specializing in dealing with drug abuse problems on the part of juveniles, and dependency drug treatment courts, dealing with drug problems on the part of families charged with child abuse or neglect.

Another well-known problem solving court, which was loosely modeled after drug treatment court, is domestic violence court. Domestic violence courts attempt to protect the victims of domestic violence, to motivate perpetrators of domestic violence to attend batterers' intervention programs, and to monitor compliance with court orders and treatment progress.

One of the most recent types of problem solving court to emerge is mental health court, started in 1997 in Broward County, Florida. Mental health court is a misdemeanor criminal court designed to deal with people arrested for minor offenses whose major problem is mental illness rather than criminality. This is a revolving door category of patients who periodically are committed to mental hospitals, treated there with psychotropic medication, experience sufficient improvement to be discharged from the hospital, and then fail to take needed medication in the community. As a result, they frequently decompensate, sometimes committing minor offenses that result in their arrest. Mental health court seeks to divert them from the criminal justice system and to persuade them to accept treatment voluntarily in the community, linking them with treatment resources, and providing social service support and judicial monitoring to ensure treatment compliance.

A number of other specialized tribunals have emerged in recent years that have a treatment orientation and that apply, in varying degrees, many of the principles and techniques of drug treatment court and these other courts. They include teen court (or youth court), which deals with juveniles charged with very minor offenses. Teen court functions by having teenage volunteers, as well as teen court "graduates," serve as jurors and, with some special training, as teen court prosecutors and defense counsel.

Other specialized courts include reentry court, designed to assist offenders who have been released from prison to effect a successful reintegration into society, and an emerging application of this approach for sex offenders, in the form of a sex offender reentry court. These courts also include dependency court, frequently a branch of family or juvenile court, which deals with issues of child abuse and neglect, and which often involves the provision of services designed to teach parenting skills and avoid the repetition of abusive behavior.

These courts and others like them grow out of a recognition that traditional judicial approaches have failed, at least in the areas of substance abuse, domestic violence, certain kinds of criminality, child abuse and neglect, and mental illness. These are recycling problems, the reoccurrence of which traditional interventions did not succeed in bringing to a halt. The traditional judicial model addressed the symptoms, but not the underlying problem.

In response to these failings, new judicial approaches were needed. These new approaches involve a collaborative, interdisciplinary approach to problem solving in which the judge plays a leading role. Not only is the judge a leading actor in the therapeutic drama, but the courtroom itself becomes a stage for playing out crucial scenes, and the judge assumes the role of director, coordinating the roles of many of the actors and providing a needed motivation for how they will play their parts and an inspiration to play them well.

The new problem solving courts and approaches are all characterized by active judicial involvement and the explicit use of judicial authority to motivate individuals to accept needed services and to monitor their compliance and progress. They are concerned not merely with processing and resolving the court case, but in achieving a variety of tangible outcomes associated with avoiding reoccurrence of the problem.

Problem solving courts and approaches thus represent a significant new direction for the judiciary. It is a new direction, moreover, that has proved to be highly satisfying and rejuvenating to many judges. And this more holistic approach has now spilled out from problem solving courts to influence the role and work of judges in trial courts of general jurisdiction and appellate courts as well.

Judge Roger K. Warren, President of the National Center for State Courts, has crisply and effectively captured the comparison between the "traditional" and the "transformed" court processes:

A Comparison of Transformed and Traditional Court Procedures

Traditional Process	Transformed Process
Dispute resolution	Problem-solving dispute avoidance
Legal outcome	Therapeutic outcome
Adversarial process	Collaborative process
Claim- or case-oriented	People-oriented
Rights-based	Interest- or needs-based
Emphasis placed on adjudication	Emphasis placed on post-adjudication and alternative dispute resolution
Interpretation and application of law	Interpretation and application of social science
Judge as arbiter	Judge as coach
Backward looking	Forward looking
Precedent-based	Planning-based
Few participants and stakeholders	Wide range of participants and stakeholders
Individualistic	Interdependent
Legalistic	Common-sensical
Formal	Informal
Efficient	Effective

In a related endeavor, Chief Deputy Magistrate Jelena Popovic, of Melbourne, Victoria, Australia, is working on a similar comparison of the qualities of 'traditional' versus 'therapeutic jurisprudence' judicial officers. At press time, hers is a work in progress that notes illustrative traditional qualities such as dispassionate, impersonal, limited communication, and autonomous decision-making, compared to therapeutic jurisprudence qualities such as warm, personal, open communication, and a team approach to decision-making.

Part I of our anthology tries to bring this new judging to life by reprinting short and punchy journalistic descriptions of several types of problem solving courts. Using Judge William Schma's essay, "Judging in the New Millennium," originally written as an introduction to a special therapeutic jurisprudence issue of *Court Review*, the official journal of the American Judges Association, Part I illustrates how the new judging can be used not only in specialized courts, but also in general civil and criminal cases.

Curiously, until recently, the problem solving courts revolution and the new judging has been largely atheoretical. Drug treatment court originated as an experiment, by frustrated judges and practitioners, to facilitate the substance abuse treatment process. When the drug treatment court approach seemed promising, it was transplanted to other judicial settings. But *why* these programs seem to work has, until recently, remained largely unexamined.

II. Therapeutic Jurisprudence as a Theoretical Foundation for These New Judicial Approaches

Here is where therapeutic jurisprudence may be profitably brought into the picture. Therapeutic jurisprudence is an interdisciplinary perspective that can provide a grounding for the new judicial movement, for therapeutic jurisprudence specifically asks *what* legal arrangements work and *why*.

Therapeutic jurisprudence began in the area of mental health law, criticizing various aspects of mental health law that seemed, curiously, to produce antitherapeutic consequences for the people that the law was designed to help. Although it originated in the area of mental health law, therapeutic jurisprudence soon found easy application to other areas of the law—criminal law, juvenile law, family law, personal injury law—and has now emerged as a therapeutic approach to the law generally.

Therapeutic jurisprudence focuses our attention on the traditionally under-appreciated area of the law's considerable impact on emotional life and psychological well-being. Its essential premise is a simple one: that the law is a social force that can produce therapeutic or antitherapeutic consequences. The law consists of legal rules, legal procedures, and the roles and behaviors of legal actors, like lawyers and judges. Therapeutic jurisprudence proposes that we use the tools of the behavioral sciences to study the therapeutic and antitherapeutic impact of the law, and that we think creatively about improving the therapeutic functioning of the law without violating other important values, such as *Gault*-like due process concerns.

Therapeutic jurisprudence can thus be regarded as a theoretical foundation for problem-solving courts and approaches. It has much to offer judges concerning how they treat the people before them, and has insights regarding how courts might be structured so as to maximize their therapeutic potential.

In a joint resolution adopted in the year 2000, the Conference of Chief Justices and the Conference of State Court Administrators endorsed the notion of problem-solving courts and calendars and the use by such courts of principles of therapeutic jurisprudence to improve judicial functioning. Therapeutic jurisprudence can thus provide principles or what Professor Robert Schopp has called "instrumental prescriptions" for how courts might perform their problem solving functions.

Just as judges dealing with antitrust cases need to understand basic principles of economics, and judges dealing with patent cases need to understand basic principles of engineering, judges performing in a problem-solving capacity, dealing as they do with human problems, need to understand some principles of psychology, the science of human behavior. They must be aware that they are functioning as therapeutic agents, and that how they interact with the individuals appearing before them will have inevitable consequences for the ability of those individuals to be rehabilitated or otherwise to deal with their underlying problems.

The people appearing in problem-solving courts—and often in general criminal, civil and family courts—are there because they have problems that they have not recognized or had the ability to deal with effectively. They may have alcoholism or substance abuse problems, and these may contribute to repetitive criminality, domestic violence, or child abuse and neglect. They may be repetitive perpetrators of domestic violence or child abuse as a result of cognitive distortions concerning their relationships with their spouses or children or because they lack the social skills to manage their anger or to resolve problems other than through violence. They may suffer from mental illness that impairs their judgment about the desirability of their continuing to take needed medication. They may be in denial about the existence of these problems, refusing to take responsibility for their wrongdoing, rationalizing their conduct, or minimizing its negative impact on themselves and others. Many of these are problems that will respond effectively to available treatment, but only if the individual perceives that he or she has a problem and is motivated to deal with it.

Problem-solving courts and judges applying a therapeutic jurisprudence approach in more general courts make the resolution of these problems an important goal of the judging enterprise. Part II of the book is designed to offer judges functioning in these ways the tools that are necessary to play their new roles effectively. Emerging principles of therapeutic jurisprudence shed light on how court structures and the conduct of individual judges can help people solve crucial life problems. Judges can interact with individuals in ways that will induce hope, for example, and will motivate them to consider availing themselves of treatment programs. Judges can use techniques that will encourage offenders to confront and solve their problems, to comply with rehabilitative programs, to develop law-abiding coping skills, and the like. Judges functioning in these ways need to develop enhanced interpersonal skills, to understand the psychology of procedural justice, to learn how to serve as effective risk managers, and to learn about the other approaches that therapeutic jurisprudence has to offer. Part II of the book focuses on these emerging principles of therapeutic jurisprudence—principles that can be used in specialized problem-solving courts and in courts in general. Indeed, the final portion of the book even looks at how *appellate* courts might use principles of therapeutic jurisprudence in crafting opinions and in formulating legal doctrine.

In many ways, the problem-solving court movement, and the use of therapeutic jurisprudence in an enhanced and transformed judicial role, may be regarded as a type of 'public health' approach to the judicial system. The public health approach seeks to tackle problems such as addiction, delinquency, domestic violence, and mental illness, and to do so through systemic ways that will make serious inroads in preventing or otherwise reducing the incidence of those problems.

Public health deals with prevention at three different levels: primary, secondary, and tertiary. Very loosely speaking, primary prevention is pure prevention, secondary prevention is early intervention, and tertiary prevention is treatment or rehabilitation.

By the time problems reach the courthouse door, the focus often is on rehabilitation, or tertiary prevention, as it is, for example, in drug treatment courts. But, in some of the problem-solving court settings, other earlier levels of prevention are also in play.

For instance, teen court can be viewed as a type of secondary prevention. Since the delinquent behavior triggering the teen court system is typically quite minor, and the defendant a first offender at that, teen court actually serves as prompt intervention in the early expression of delinquent behavior. And dependency drug court, which serves as tertiary prevention—rehabilitation—for drug abusing parents, may serve as *primary* prevention—pure prevention—when looked at from the perspective of the lives—and the health, future behavior, and well-being—of the *children* at stake. If dependency drug court works to get the parents back on track, effective parenting may steer the children in a healthy and law-abiding direction. Primary prevention is also at work in unified family court settings which seek to minimize the trauma to the children of divorcing parents.

This transformation in the judiciary, then, seeks to create judicial structures, and also to focus the work and behavior of the individual judge, so as to treat and prevent serious problems. It views these problems from a public health-type perspective, and recognizes the importance of using therapeutic jurisprudence principles to help people solve problems that otherwise would likely produce repeated court involvement.

We hope the book as a whole will advance the overall enterprise of judging with an ethic of care. We encourage the reader to participate in the dialogue that is already taking place. An international and interdisciplinary listserv already exists. Further information, a detailed bibliography, upcoming activities, and relevant links can be found on the web site of the International Network on Therapeutic Jurisprudence at http://www.therapeuticjurisprudence.org/.

References

Atwood, Barbara, *Tribal Jurisprudence and Cultural Meanings of the Family*, 79 Neb. L. Rev. 577 (2000).

Center for Disease Control, A Framework for Assessing Effectiveness of Disease and Injury Prevention (1992).

Chase, Deborah J., & Hora, Peggy F., *The Implications of Therapeutic Jurisprudence for Judicial Satisfaction*, 37 CT. REV. 12 (Spring, 2000).

Conference of Chief Justices & Conference of State Court Administrators, *Resolution in Support of Problem-Solving Courts*, 2 J. CENTER FOR FAMS., CHILD., CTS. 2 (2000) (CCJ RESOL. 22 & COSCA RESOL. 4).

Court Review, *Special Issue on Therapeutic Jurisprudence*, 37 Ct. Rev. 1–68 (2000).

Gilbert, Janet, Grinam, Richard & Parnham, John T., *Applying Therapeutic Principles to a Family-Focused Juvenile Justice Model (Delinquency)*, 52 ALA. L. REV. 1153 (2001).

In re Gault, 387 U.S. 1 (1967).

Johnny, Ronald Eagleye, *The Duckwater Shoshone Drug Court 1997–2000: Melding Traditional Dispute Resolution With Due Process*, 26 AM. INDIAN L. REV. 261 (2001).

Levine, Murray, *The Family Group Conference in the New Zealand Children, Young Persons and Their Families Act of 1989* (CYP & F): REV. & EVAL., 18 BEHAV. SCI. & L. 517 (2000).

Scheff, Thomas J., *Community Conferences: Shame and Anger in Therapeutic Jurisprudence*, 67 REV. JUR. U.P.R. 97 (1998).

Schma, William G., *Judging for the New Millennium*, 37 Ct. Rev. 4 (2000).

Schopp, Robert F., *Therapeutic Jurisprudence: Integrated Inquiry and Instrumental Prescriptions*, 17 BEHAV. SCI. & L. 589 (1999).

Special Issue on Therapeutic Jurisprudence, 37 CT. REV. 1 (2000).

STOLLE, DENNIS P., WEXLER, DAVID B. & WINICK, BRUCE J., EDS., PRACTICING THERAPEUTIC JURISPRUDENCE: LAW AS A HELPING PROFESSION, (2000).

Warren, Roger K., *Reengineering the Court Process* (September 24–25,1998), *in* Presentation to Great Lakes Court Summit.

WEXLER, DAVID B. & WINICK, BRUCE J., eds., LAW IN A THERAPEUTIC KEY: DEVELOPMENTS IN THERAPEUTIC JURISPRUDENCE, (eds.) (1996).

Zion, James W., Navajo Therapeutic Jurisprudence, 18 Touro L. Rev. 563 (Spring 2002).

Part I
The New Judicial Approaches

A. The Revolving Door

The following newspaper account of the release from prison of Nando, a drug offender, paints a graphic portrait of the deficiencies in the ways our existing criminal justice system handles drug offenses. While the story ends too early for us to learn whether Nando will re-offend, we are left with the sad feeling that this eventuality is quite likely, and with a nagging concern that our criminal justice system can do more to help him to avoid this outcome. A recent study by the Justice Department's Bureau of Justice Statistics shows that 66.7 percent of drug offenders were re-arrested for at least one serious new crime within a three-year period following their release. *Criminal Justice Drug Letter*, p.4 (Sept. 2002). Drug offenders represented 32.6 percent of those released from prison, and another 3.3 percent had been incarcerated for driving while intoxicated. *Id.* Thus, in the way it deals with drug offenders, the existing criminal justice system is a revolving door.

Out of Jail, Into Temptation: A Day in a Life
by Alan Feuer
(February 28, 2002, PA1, Col 3; Copyright 2002
by The New York Times, reprinted with permission)

Nando came home from jail to a small apartment in the Bronx that stank like a backed-up toilet.

He had been gone eight months, behind bars for selling crack, and as he came through the door from Rikers Island, he wrinkled his nose at the smell. His spider plant was dead. Its blackened leaves crumpled under his touch. His telephone was dead. He blew in the receiver, but the line was out.

The bathroom faucet spewed brown water. A bag of chips in the kitchen was covered in dust.

"It's like a garbage dump," he said. "I've got a lot of work to do."

The work would not be easy. What lay ahead for Nando, a 20-year-old man who agreed to spend his first day out of jail with a reporter and photographer as long as his last name did not appear in print, would prove to be a veil of dark temptation, a toxic mix of the traps and troubles that sent him off to prison to begin with.

Each year, more than 20,000 inmates are released from the C-76 jail on Rikers Island, which houses those serving terms of a year or less. Unlike state prisoners, these city convicts have no probation or parole officers to report to once they are released. They are free to find jobs, or buy drugs, without the authorities watching.

Nando was released at 5 a.m. on Feb. 4. By 7 a.m., he had learned that his best friend had just been arrested on a crack charge. By 9 a.m., he was languishing in a welfare office. By 10, he had been offered a joint. By 10:15, he had been offered his old job back, selling crack and marijuana.

By the end of the day, he had watched an old friend try to hide her drug habit from her curious toddler son. He had stood at the hospital bed of his catatonic mother. He had sorted through the mail that had piled up for months. The electric company was threatening to shut his power off.

He chose to return to his fifth-floor walk-up in the Morrisania section of the Bronx. His girlfriend and his old pals were still in the neighborhood; so was his past as an addict and a dealer. Though home seemed the natural place to go, it was also where his problems had started. Nando knew that in advance. He knew it the moment he stepped off the Rikers Island bus in northern Queens at 5:16 a.m.

It was still dark and the other men ran for the subway. Nando sniffed the air and smiled. "It's good to be out," he said.

Nando, short for Fernando, is a skinny man with scruff on his chin and Chinese characters tattooed along his neck. He started peddling drugs at 14, started using them at 15. He was jailed last June for selling 200 grams of crack to an undercover officer.

The city releases Rikers Island inmates on a squalid street corner in Queens Plaza every day between 3 and 5:30 a.m. Each one carries a $3 MetroCard provided by the prison and his jailhouse chattel in a paper bag. Nando got off the bus with a Hermann Hesse novel in his bag and an ambitious to-do list in his head: Reconnect with family. Stay off drugs. Enroll in college. Find a job.

His first stop was his father's apartment in Co-op City. He arrived about 6. His younger brother, David, hugged him in the kitchen, still wearing his pajamas. His father, Fernando Sr., handed him a winter coat, a videotape of the Super Bowl and a couple of $20 bills.

"I never expected any kid of mine to wind up where he wound up," the father said. "I ain't never going back, not even on a visit. Don't know about him, but I ain't never going back."

It was a brief reunion. Nando's father was due at the factory where he works and his brother was due at school. His father gave Nando keys to the apartment. Nando mused that he might just buy a dog.

It was a terrible idea, his father said. "No dogs," he ordered. "Right now, you can't afford to feed yourself."

East Tremont Avenue cuts through the Bronx like a swollen femoral artery. It is a wide urban boulevard of barber shops and Spanish greasy spoons. But to Nando, it might as well have been the only road in a tiny town.

He knew everyone. The woman walking by was the manager of a grocery store, he said. The crumpled man on the corner was a crackhead. An unmarked Chevrolet rolled by and, out of instinct, Nando ducked; it was a prowling team of undercover cops.

"I don't want to be here, but there's nowhere else to go," he muttered as the car drove by. "Lots of us end up right back in the same damn place. It makes me want to blow up the 'hood."

Bad News About a Friend

He turned down Boston Road until he came to a dim apartment house on Crotona Park East. Nando put his hands to his mouth and hooted like an owl. "Hey yo, Chuckie!" he yelled. "Hey yo, where's Chuck?"

A woman appeared in a fourth-floor window and shouted for him to come inside. The lobby smelled like feces. Its ceiling light was smashed. The walls looked like a notebook, covered in graffiti. The scrawl praised murder and masturbation.

The woman in the window was Nando's former girlfriend, Jackie, who quickly gave him the news: Chuckie—her brother and Nando's friend—had been arrested the day before.

Nando was crushed. He had just left Rikers Island, and now Chuckie might be headed there himself.

Five minutes later, Nando left. "The ghetto of all ghettos," he said as he walked toward home.

At his old apartment, the stench got up to meet him. It smelled like a stadium men's room on a hot summer's day. Dirty dishes were piled in the sink; a box of Cheerios stood open on the table. He turned on the television, and the screen looked like a finger-painting. The picture tube was blown.

It was starting to dawn on him, he said: he was out of jail, responsible for himself, alone. He popped a compact disc in the player and sat down on his rocking chair. "I used to sit here for hours getting high," he said, rocking slowly, staring at his hands. "I can feel the whole thing pulling at me. What am I going to do?"

On the walk home from Jackie's, he had called his girlfriend, Mery, and set a date for 9 a.m. He needed to clean himself, but first he had to clean the shower. A thick layer of scum had settled in the tub.

He went to the bathroom with a toilet brush. There, on the sink, were his mother's false teeth.

A Reminder of His Mother

Six months ago, a guard woke him to say, "Your mother's had a heart attack. She's in the hospital in Brooklyn." The jail allowed him a visit. He went and stared at his mother. All she could do was twitch her head.

Nando ignored the teeth. He cleaned the tub and showered. Then he looked for clothes in the bedroom his mother had used before she had fallen ill. The bed was stripped of sheets and gave the impression of a vacant lot. Nando ignored that, too.

Three hours earlier, after getting off the prison bus, Nando had laughed at a movie billboard with the slogan, "Behind every good man, there is a woman kicking his butt." At 9 a.m., Mery was waiting for him on the corner of Suburban Place and Boston Road. Her smile lit up the sidewalk two full blocks away.

They hugged. They kissed. She touched his hair, grown long on Rikers Island. They kissed again and didn't care who watched.

Mery is going to college while living in a homeless shelter. She is Nando's one good thing, and Nando freely admits it. Still, he sometimes finds her loving attention hard to take.

They walked down Boston Road to the subway station so Mery could head to school. She scooted up the stairs, then turned around. "Yo, behave!" was all she said.

At the welfare office across the street, Nando filled out forms for Medicaid. It was 9:15, and the room was already packed. Telephones rang. Babies cried. Nando put his name on the list. He was 21st in line.

The form asked, "Do you have any of these problems?" Nando checked the boxes next to "Urgent Personal or Family Problems" and "No Food."

Thirty minutes later a clerk informed him that he had come to the wrong place. The office he needed was on 138th Street, 40 blocks away.

He was mad at the clerk. He was mad at himself. He stormed outside to a pay phone and punched in a number. "Yeah," he said. "What up? I'm on the block. I'm home."

Minutes later, a bony man in a baggy sweatshirt came walking down the block. His name was Rob, and he was a member of Nando's former drug crew. On Boston Road, the two old friends bumped chests. Rob made fun of Nando's hair.

"What you up to, son?" Nando asked.

Rob did not waste time. "I'm smoking a blunt with you."

Everywhere, Temptation

Suddenly, a choice: Go to the welfare office or get high with Rob. The choice got harder when Rob's cell phone began to ring. The call was for Nando. It was his old crack boss, asking if he wanted to go back to work.

According to city officials, 80 percent of Rikers Island's inmates test positive for drug use, and drugs are why most end up on the island to begin with. In the past, Nando had taken drugs and sold drugs. Now, within 60 seconds, he'd had offers to do both again.

"No, I'm straight," he told the boss, "but I'll let you know." Then he turned down Rob's joint. But as he stood there talking, his old crack customers walked by. They waved and nodded. It was as if he'd never left.

With Rob in tow, Nando went back to Jackie's place. He wanted someplace quiet to use the phone. He wanted the address of his mother's hospital in Brooklyn. It had been six months; he wanted to see her face.

When Jackie opened the door, the marijuana smoke enveloped him like a blanket. He called information for the hospital's address, trying to ignore the smell. Jackie ran through the rooms, opening windows, spraying a can of air freshener. Her little boy, Aaron, came down the hallway. Aaron is 3. Jackie is 18.

Nando headed for the door and as he went out, Rob came in. He had bought a cheap cigar and stuffed it full of dope.

Nando unloaded on him on the street.

"Keep doing that and you'll wind up on Rikers Island," he said. Rob brushed him off. Nando let out a cold laugh at his buddy. "You best make sure you don't wind up in jail," he said.

The trip to the hospital took an hour. As Nando approached his mother's room, an orderly stopped him in the hall.

"Who are you?" she asked. She was baffled by the answer. "Her son?" the woman said. "Why don't you ever visit? Where have you been the last six months?"

His mother's limbs were frozen, her eyes so empty of emotion they looked like dirty glass. Her face twitched uncontrollably, and Nando stood there, wordless. The orderly told him if he pinched her fingers she would feel it. But other than that, she would not respond.

Nando stared at his mother for 30 minutes, trying to fight back tears. On the nightstand was the fake red rose he had bought on the way to see her.

"A day in my life," he said on the street again, his voice gone soft. "Anyone want it?" It was 2:15 p.m.

A Reminder in the Mail

Back at home, he planned his week. Hit the job center. Hit the right welfare office.

Then he went downstairs to get his mail.

On Rikers, he had taken a writing class, and his last assignment was to write a letter to himself as a happy 70-year-old man. He was to describe that happy life, writing from the future, to himself as he was now, at 20. He had to describe the choices he had made.

The letter was in his mailbox.

Dear Nando,

I remember those days we spent on Rikers Island. Pretty rough, huhh! Well, as for me, I made the best of it. I chose to change a couple of things about myself in order to get where I'm at now. Let's just say I'm at a place where it's always sunny and hot and when it rains, it really rains. I got a few kids now and a beautiful wife with a handful of grandchildren. What I chose to do was leave all the drugs and negative things alone. It was really rough at first, but I never gave up. I always knew I could do more.

Sincerely,
Nando

He sat on the rocking chair and read the letter, twice. Then he lay down on his mother's bed.

It was 4 p.m. and he wasn't sleepy. Tomorrow was only eight hours away.

––––––––––

Nando's story provides a glimpse of a judicial system that does not reflect the therapeutic jurisprudence approach to judging that this book describes and commends. The judicial process dealt with Nando's offense, but neglected his underlying problems. Imprisonment provided him with an opportunity to reflect upon his life and to resolve to change it. But neither the court nor the prison system provided him with the tools to deal with his problem, and he was simply released to the community with a subway card and little more. Some offenders in Nando's situation will have the social support and inner resources needed to turn their lives around, and we hope that Nando is among them. But many do not, and will succumb to the peer pressure, economic exigencies, and stress of life in their old environment by reoffending. They will recycle through the criminal justice system, receiving longer terms of imprisonment but not the help they may need to make any real change. They will contribute to the revolving door effect that all too often characterizes our existing judicial processes.

Instead of seeing Nando as a case, we envision a world in which the judge and the judicial process will view him as a person with a problem, and will help him to identify his problem and offer him the help he may need to resolve it. Our vision is not one of paternalistic courts that coerce people to accept treatment or other services. We are skeptical about whether anyone can be coerced into rehabilitation. Rather, we think that rehabilitation must start with the individual and build on his or her own strengths and desire to effect change. Criminal accusation or involvement in other court processes can be catalysts to change. They provide opportunities for people to confront their problems and to consider whether to deal with them. We think that judges can help in this process, but only if they look beyond the presenting symptoms that the case before them may reflect and try to understand and address the individual's underlying problems.

We envision judges possessing a heightened sensitivity to human problems and an understanding of the clinical, counseling, and educational tools that may help to resolve them. We envision judges who care deeply about the people appearing before them. We envision judges who, in a collaborative way, can assist them to understand when an underlying psychological or behavioral problem contributes to their court involvement and can provide the help they may need to face it. This is a new model for judging, one that sees judges as problem solvers who understand many of the insights and techniques of such other disciplines as psychology and social work. Accordingly, this book is about how judges can, in appropriate circumstances, be therapeutic agents. It seeks to raise the consciousness of judges concerning their potential as healers, and to acquaint them with the therapeutic jurisprudence principles and techniques that they will need to play this role effectively.

We thus envision a judicial world quite different from the one experienced by Nando. We recognize that not everyone will share our vision, and that some judges will abuse the power that the new role we contemplate will give them. *See e.g.,* James L. Nolan, Jr. *Reinventing Justice: The American Drug Court Movement.* (2001); Morris B. Hoffman, *The Drug Court Scandal,* 78 N. C. L. Rev. 1437 (2000); Morris B. Hoffman, *Therapeutic Jurisprudence, Neo-Rehabilitationism, and Judicial Collectivism: The Least Dangerous Branch Becomes the Most Dangerous.* 29 Ford. Urb. L. J. 2063, (2002). Such abuses are always possible, of course, especially by judges who fail to heed the lessons of *In re Gault,* 387 U.S. 1 (1967), that we underscore in our Introduction to this book. We need to be on guard to prevent these abuses, and to caution judges to avoid coercion and a heavy-handed paternalism. We thus share some of the criticisms that have been made of problem solving courts and problem solving judges, but hasten to note that in evaluating these criticisms, we must compare the model of judging we propose not to some non-existent utopian ideal, but to the judicial system we now have—the one that Nando experienced.

* * *

Let us now examine the new judicial models that have been emerging in recent years. What are these new problem solving courts, and how do they function? After brief introductory notes, we use newspaper accounts and short essays written by some of the judges who have served in these courts to tell their stories.

B. Drug Treatment Court

The following two newspaper accounts describe Drug Treatment Court, an approach pioneered in 1989 in Miami that has spread across the country. Contrast this approach with the traditional punitive criminal justice model applied to Nando, the drug offender sentenced to eight months imprisonment in the prior excerpt, and then simply released.

Breaking the Cycle of Addiction: Officials Seek to Spread the Word on Drug Treatment Courts

by Gloria Hayes
(November 15, 2000; Vol. 223, No. 96,
The Legal Intelligencer, Copyright 2000 by
American Lawyer Media, reprinted with permission).

On a recent afternoon, a defendant stood before Judge Louis J. Presenza for her monthly status hearing in the Philadelphia Treatment Court program.

Months earlier in this same courtroom, the woman had waived the right to trial and enrolled in a voluntary program that would help her to overcome her addiction. If the program is successful, her record will be rendered as clean as her bloodstream—all charges dismissed. However, on this day the report of her progress was not a good one. The defendant had tested positive for cocaine use, and in addition she had skipped several group-therapy sessions.

"What do you have to say for yourself, ma'am?" the judge asked, attempting, as is customary, to elicit an explanation for the relapse.

But in the face of incontrovertible evidence against her, the defendant repeatedly denied the allegations, shaking her head in the negative throughout the questioning process. The volume of the judge's voice mounted with his anger. Already amplified by a microphone, his questions now reverberated throughout the courtroom.

"Do you expect me to believe that somebody forced it down your throat?" Judge Presenza asked her with obvious disbelief. "Or did they inject it into you against your will?"

The occupants of the jury box paid rapt attention to the exchange, but not because they would be called on to decide this individual's guilt or innocence. They were present because they were relatively new to the program and had been sanctioned to observe and learn from the day's proceedings.

21

Their fate, like the woman's standing before the bench, rested exclusively in the hands of the judge.

The woman being questioned by Presenza was not the first on this day to have a relapse on record, but she was the first and only participant to deny accountability. Earlier, the judge had sanctioned one to write an essay about what recovery meant to her. Another had been referred to a structured residential treatment program. A third would repeat addiction assessment after admitting he had initially reported a lesser quantity of drug consumption than he had actually been using. His level of treatment would then be adjusted accordingly.

Few were surprised when the judge ordered an armed Philadelphia police officer to take the defendant immediately into custody where she would serve a week in jail. This type of "wake-up call" is not intended to be punitive, but to break the protective shell of denial that keeps addicts hooked even while they claim to be invested in their recovery. Many who have completed the program admit that this hurdle often proves to be the most difficult to overcome and rarely happens without being forced to face the consequences of their actions.

"Most of them call me and thank me after their week is over," Presenza said afterward.

For the past three years, the drug court movement in Pennsylvania has experienced steady growth and increasing interest from many jurisdictions searching for solutions to clogged dockets and overcrowded prisons. In April 1997, the Philadelphia Treatment Court was the first in Pennsylvania to open its doors, and by the end of the year, Chester and York counties had also opened drug courts. There are now seven operating drug courts in Pennsylvania and two in the planning stages, one of those being Delaware County.

Current programs are showing signs of success. Among Philadelphia Treatment Court graduates, 6 percent have been re-arrested with a resulting 3 percent reconviction rate. In Chester County, the rate of re-arrest was 5 percent, and their retention rate in the program was slightly above the national average of 70 percent. Nearly 72 percent of participants stayed enrolled or have successfully graduated. That number is double the retention rate for traditional drug-rehab programs.

Still, the drug court programs in Pennsylvania and New Jersey have reached a critical point, as program advocates seek permanent commitments and long-term funding for the programs.

In September, the Pennsylvania Commission on Crime and Delinquency sponsored a second annual workshop in State College, Pa. During that meeting, drug court personnel from around the state formed the Pennsylvania Association of Drug Court Professionals to promote collaboration among the individual courts and to further their common objectives.

"One of our goals is to spread the gospel and to inform the public what drug courts are and what successes we've achieved both statewide and nationally," Presenza said. In addition to his role as president judge of the

Philadelphia Municipal Court, Presenza was unanimously elected president of the PADCP at the recent workshop. "We also want to share information and resources and to encourage others to plan and implement drug courts."

A National Trend

Eleven years ago, Janet Reno, then district attorney of Dade County Fla., founded the first drug court in Miami. Although it was considered controversial at the time, more than 20 other jurisdictions followed suit in the next two years. This created the impetus for a national trend; all 50 states currently have at least one drug court and half have 25 or more.

Despite the U.S. government's "War Against Drugs," substance abuse continues to be a problem both nationally and locally. The number of prison inmates serving time for drug-related offenses has risen more than 1,000 percent since 1980 while the federal drug-control budget has skyrocketed from $1.53 billion to $17.77 billion nationally. Philadelphia experienced a 141 percent increase in drug arrests in the last decade, while the Court of Common Pleas saw a 1,526 percent increase in drug case dispositions.

Drug court programs provide an alternative to prosecution for nonviolent drug offenders. And the savings in terms of costs are significant, supporters point out. Incarceration of drug-using offenders costs a minimum of $25,000 per year—and as much as $50,000. In comparison, the most comprehensive drug court system costs an average of $3,000 annually for each offender.

Instead of prosecution and incarceration, the goal of drug courts is to treat the underlying addiction that can compel drug users to commit theft or sell drugs to support their addiction. Prosecutors and public defenders assume a collaborative rather than an adversarial role, and they individualize treatment plans to each defendant under close supervision of the drug-court judge.

In Philadelphia, treatment plans may include anything from attending drug treatment and group therapy to getting job training and completing a GED. Participants—whose identities are not disclosed to the public—are strictly supervised and required to report to the judge regularly. Clients are also assigned case managers who assist them to respond more appropriately to situations that cause them to "use."

Participants remain on the program for a minimum of a year. Each defendant must remain drug-free during four phases of increasing length, ranging from 30 to 120 days. Failure to do so results in termination from the program—and they serve the sentence for the offense for which they were initially arrested.

Lengths of treatment vary from state to state and county to county. But each drug court program in the country must adhere to 10 requirements in order to be eligible for federal funding through the U.S. Department of Justice.

In New Jersey, the judiciary recently gave its support to expanding drug courts to encompass all 21 counties in that state. In May, the Conference of Criminal Presiding Judges issued a report favoring the expansion. However, it is unclear how the Legislature will respond to its recommendation. Earlier this year, the Administrative Office of the Courts began a study of a possible statewide system, which the office is due to issue later this Fall, including a detailed section on costs and funding.

Funding has become an issue of increasing concern now that the programs are moving out of the pilot stage. Virtually all drug courts have existed on grants either in part, or entirely, at some stage of their operation. The U.S. Department of Justice has made implementation and enhancement grants to local drug courts provided they operate within the 10 standards laid out by the NADCP and make matching funds available. For the most part, federal grants are available only during the first two years of a court's operation, regardless of the success of the program.

Making the Case

Early results indicate that treatment programs successfully break the cycle of addiction and recidivism. According to a report prepared by the Justice Department's Office of Justice Programs called, "Looking at a Decade of Drug Courts," nearly half of all defendants convicted of a felony drug offense will recidivate within two to three years, and many will escalate to committing violent crimes as their addictions worsen.

Despite the daunting statistics, some legislators have been reluctant to support the drug court programs. Chester County Judge Jacqueline Carroll Cody said that the county commissioners in Chester County at first declined to match funds required to receive a Justice Department implementation grant. However, when the public defender, prosecutor, judge and other court personnel agreed to volunteer their time without financial compensation, the DOJ considered the combined manpower to be "in-kind contributions." The court opened, and the commissioners have since come on board.

"There are still those who believe that anybody involved with drugs should be in jail," Cody said. The judge said she has invited several legislators to witness drug court in action, after which they expressed enthusiasm for the program. "After all," she said, "this is a new way of treating a serious problem."

Both Presenza and Cody conceded that until long-term statistics become available, it is unlikely that permanent funding will be granted. Currently, only 20 states have dedicated state funding. Others have procured funds from diverse sources to keep drug courts in operation. These include proceeds from drug asset forfeiture, tobacco settlement funds, sales tax surcharges, contributions from private foundations and revenues from fines, to name only a few.

"We have to be creative in the way we deal with this issue," Presenza said. "Treatment Court is a philosophy, and once you believe in a philosophy you find a way to adopt and implement it."

Terry Emphasizes Counseling in San Jose

by Shannon Lafferty
(May 22, 2001; No. 99, The Recorder, Copyright 2001
by American Lawyer Media, reprinted with permission).

SAN JOSE—When defendant Cynthia Davis remorsefully appeared in Santa Clara's drug court Wednesday to report a drug relapse, Judge Lawrence Terry gave her a pep talk and then tightened control of her treatment and supervision.

"Don't give up. You are doing OK. These relapses are part of recovery," Terry explained. "But remember one step back and two steps forward is called progress. You have to be patient."

For Terry, understanding the cycle of addiction is as important as knowing the nuance of the drug laws. And part of understanding addiction means being a cheerleader as well as a jurist and acknowledging that part of recovery is navigating setbacks.

"It's about progress. It's about growth. It's not about perfection," Terry says.

Davis' willingness to admit her relapse and continue treatment met with a round of applause.

Another defendant, Patricia Baldovinos, had more positive news to report to the court. She's stayed clean and sober 168 days. Terry, encouraged by her progress, stayed her nine-month jail sentence. Another smattering of applause erupted.

Terry is one of the pioneering judges of Santa Clara County's drug court, held in the refurbished Levi Strauss warehouse in downtown San Jose. Terry and four other judges see 5,000 drug cases a year, handling every aspect of the case except trial. Terry's and the other drug court judges' approach has earned Santa Clara County a reputation for its emphasis on counseling rather than just incarcerating drug offenders.

Judges say the court, which has already tapped into community resources for treating addiction, will have fewer missteps when implementing Proposition 36—the controversial drug initiative passed in November—and could be a model for other counties.

Terry said he and Judge Stephen Manley first started an informal drug court in the mid-1990s, because they saw how drug addicts repeatedly cycle through the court systems. Simply convicting and sentencing drug offenders was not fixing the larger problem of addiction.

Terry said he took notice when outside counselors would appear in court for defendants and advocate treatment as opposed to jail time for nonviolent drug offenses. The judge familiarized himself with rehabilitation treatment options and started substituting them for jail sentences.

While Judge Manley often receives top billing for his work pursuing state and federal funding for Santa Clara's drug court, Terry, who works more independently, has been crucial to its success.

Attorneys compliment Terry on his knowledge and understanding of addiction and say his approach balances pressure and compassion.

"What he tells people, and it's the truth, is he's going to push them, shove them, box them by using the threat of incarceration to get them to start down a path of 12-step recovery," said Deputy District Attorney Eugene Baldwin. "But the message isn't delivered with a heavy hand."

"It's part a court with sanctions, and it's part trying to positively reinforce to people to make positive changes in their life," said Deputy District Attorney David Angel. "He really speaks from the heart, and he brings incredible insight to this."

Terry takes more time addressing defendants than judges handling other criminal calendars do, which has mixed results, attorneys say. While to some defendants he can sound preachy, others seem to appreciate the encouragement.

Terry knows that his approach can be perceived as going easy on drug offenders, but said the war on drugs won't be won simply with a crime and punishment mentality.

"A lot of people might equate that to being warm and fuzzy and a pushover. So be it," Terry said. "What you are trying to do is to have people take action in their lives. You can't go out there yelling."

Attorneys say Terry is congenial, not overly formal and has a good relationship with attorneys—most of whom appear before him several days a week.

"It's not a place for intense litigation. Attorney passions don't flow over [in drug court], so there is no real collision between attorneys and judge," Baldwin said.

Terry said he appreciates attorneys who take seriously their role in a recovering addict's life.

"Their role as an attorney can be a very strong influence on the positive outcome beyond protection of constitutional and legal rights," Terry said. "They realize they have an opportunity to contribute to their client's life."

Terry, who is technically retired, says he has vowed to stick around for the implementation of Prop 36.

"We want to use it as an opportunity to get more people into recovery," Terry said.

The drug court model has spread rapidly throughout the United States, and there also now are drug treatment courts in a number of jurisdictions internationally, including Canada, Australia, New Zealand, England, Ireland, and Scotland. There also are a number of courts internationally that use therapeutic jurisprudence in dealing with other kinds of problems. Articles relating to these international developments are set forth in the References section of this Part under Recent International Developments.

Does drug treatment court work? Is drug treatment administered as part of the drug treatment court process more efficacious than drug treatment delivered without court involvement? Is drug treatment court more effective than the traditional criminal justice punishment model? These are important empirical questions that have not yet been fully answered. Although there is much anecdotal evidence of drug treatment court's success, as well as a good many studies pointing in this direction, serious questions have been raised concerning the research methodology that often is used in attempting to answer these questions. How success should be measured is itself a perplexing question. The following selection presents what we think is a fair and measured analysis of what we know and don't know at this point concerning the effectiveness of the drug treatment court model.

Research on Drug Courts:
A Critical Review, 2001 Update
by Steven Belenko, Ph.D.
(The National Center on Addiction and Substance Abuse at
Columbia University, Copyright 2001 by Center on Addiction
and Substance Abuse (CASA), reprinted with permission)

Executive Summary

This is a critical review of 37 published and unpublished evaluations of drug courts (including seven juvenile drug courts, one DUI court, and one family drug court) produced between 1999 and April 2001. The conclusions drawn from this research are generally consistent with those of previous reviews published by the author in June 1998 and December 1999. Drug courts have achieved considerable local support and have provided intensive, long-term treatment services to offenders with long histories of drug use and criminal justice contacts, previous treatment failures, and high rates of health and social problems. Program completion rates are generally consistent with previous findings, with an average of 47% of participants graduating. Drug use and criminal activity are relatively reduced while participants are in the program.

Less clear are the long-term post-program impacts of drug courts on recidivism and other outcomes. In this critical review of drug court research, four of the six studies that examined one-year post-program recidivism found a reduction, but the size of the reduction varied across courts. None of the studies reported post-program drug use, employment, or other outcomes for all drug court participants, so these impacts remain largely unknown. Three studies used random assignment to drug court or control conditions and all found a reduction in recidivism for the drug court participants; however, none of these studies distinguished between in-program and post-program rearrests, and sample sizes were small in two of the studies. Several studies that examined program costs found that average per-client drug court costs are lower than standard processing, primarily due to reduced incarceration. However, straight diversion may be less expensive and intrusive for low-risk offenders and achieve similar outcomes as drug courts.

This review suggests a continuing need for better precision in describing data sources, measures, and time frames for data collection. Data quality and information systems problems continue to affect the quality and utility of drug court evaluations. Despite the importance of looking inside the "black box" of drug court treatment, relatively few evaluations included data on program services, either because of lack of data or because service delivery was not included in the evaluation design. Findings from several evaluations suggest that drug court impacts may fluctuate over time, indicating the importance of multi-year or replication studies to gauge the long-term impacts of drug courts. Finally, research on juvenile and family drug courts is still in its very early stages, making conclusions about their impacts impossible. Qualitative analyses suggest that a number of juvenile courts have faced implementation or operational problems.

Several of the evaluations included detailed and useful descriptions of operational components, including the screening and referral process. A fuller understanding of the impacts of drug courts in the context of the larger criminal justice system requires more research on the targeting, referral, screening, and admission process. The use of experimental designs to test program impacts in several of the evaluations is another encouraging trend. The findings from several evaluations that drug court clients have high rates of mental health problems suggest that programs need to consider inclusion of services for co-occurring disorders. Future research on drug courts needs to examine the client, operational, and treatment delivery characteristics that affect outcomes, so that drug courts can maximize their impacts and cost effectiveness, and the relative effectiveness of the various elements of the drug court model can be better understood.

———————

Plainly more research is needed. Given the high recidivism rates prevalent in our traditional criminal justice model, we should be willing to try new approaches. But when we do so, we should build in research to see what works, and be willing to make appropriate modifications and improvements in light of what that research shows. We should strive to identify promising developments in offender rehabilitation and clinical practice, and to see how they can be brought into the legal-judicial system. In many ways, this is what we attempt to do in Part II of this book. We do not pretend to have the answers, but think we have identified some promising developments that can be adapted to the judicial process and applied by judges embracing the problem solving approach we suggest. What is called for is a collaborative effort by scholars, judges, court administrators, and social science researchers to develop, test, and revamp new approaches to help the courts to face the complex human problems with which they increasingly must deal.

C. Juvenile Drug Treatment Court

The drug treatment court model, described in the above section, has been adapted in a variety of other contexts. The following two selections describe its application to juveniles accused of drug offenses.

Crucial, Caring Attention: A New Juvenile Drug Court 'Team' Deals with Everything from Tattoos to Marijuana in an Effort to Turn Wayward Kids Around

by Susan D. Etkind
(July 20, 1998, Vol. 24, No. 30,
The Connecticut Law Tribune, Copyright 1998 by
American Lawyer Media, reprinted with permission).

Not many judges spend a lot of time worrying about tattoos. But Hartford Superior Court Judge H. Maria Cone, who presides over the state's only juvenile drug session, is worrying one recent day about 15-year-old Jennifer's tattoos.

Jennifer (not her real name) is one of the stars of the five-month-old drug session. She tests negative for drug use, faithfully attends group counseling sessions and is excelling at her community service assignment in juvenile court.

But the tattoos continue to bedevil Cone. "My concern is that they're so permanent and so large," she says. She's also angry that the tattoo artist did them without the consent of Jennifer's mother.

Tattoos are just one of the wide-ranging items on the agenda of the drug session, which seeks to help young offenders—the average age is 15—turn their lives around at an early stage. Like its older cousins, the state's three drug sessions for adults, the program uses a coordinated team approach. (The adult drug sessions are in New Haven, Bridgeport and Waterbury.)

In the juvenile session, the "drug team" is generally made up of a judge, prosecutor, public defender or private defense attorney, lead probation officer, a social worker from the public defender's office and a treatment provider.

"It's good, caring attention," says Antonio L. Coles, a treatment provider and substance abuse counselor who works for Connecticut Junior Republic, a youth program that is involved in the drug session. The kids in the program crave that kind of attention, he says, and it's key to their success.

31

And members of the drug team may come together to offer support in ways unheard of in a conventional court setting. For example, Deputy Assistant Public Defender Robert J. Meredith, Juvenile Prosecutor Brian L. Casinghino and Lisa Corcoran, a social worker with the public defender's office, recently took Jennifer out to lunch.

"We just wanted to let her know we were proud of her," says Meredith.

Taking Jennifer out for lunch, says Casinghino, let her know that "we have regard for her...People look at her as an individual who deserves to be treated with kindness and with respect."

That's important, he adds, because "she lives in a caustic environment."

If a participant successfully completes the program, which spans six to nine months and includes regular courtroom meetings with the drug team, counseling, urinalysis and other requirements, criminal charges are dismissed.

"We have different expectations for each kid," says Casinghino.

The session is being funded through a $230,000 one-year federal grant from the U.S. Department of Justice, says Brooks C. Campion, court planner with the Office of Alternative Sanctions, who has been involved in planning and implementing the juvenile drug session. The grant is used primarily to fund a range of programs through Connecticut Junior Republic.

Campion says the Judicial Branch, which applied for the original grant, has applied for a continuation grant in the same amount for 1999.

The juvenile session is still in its infancy—12 kids have been admitted and there are seven active cases—but a recent meeting on July 14 demonstrates how it works.

At 2 p.m. Cone meets with Meredith, Casinghino, Corcoran, Coles and a few visitors. Lead Probation Officer and liaison to the Probation Department Michele Hall, a regular member of the team, is out that day.

The group sits in a circle in Courtroom A in the juvenile court and detention center on Broad Street. The purpose of the weekly meeting is to assess the kids' progress over the past week (are their urine tests clean, have they been meeting curfew, etc.) and review potential new participants.

One Day's Docket

On the docket today are six active cases and two possible newcomers.

Referrals can come from attorneys, judges, juvenile detention or the probation office following an arrest, usually for a drug-related crime, such as possession of marijuana, or another nonviolent offense, such as larceny or violation of probation. Once a referral is made, treatment provider Coles assesses the teenager and makes a recommendation to the team.

He recommends that the first candidate, a young man with a history of violent behavior, be turned down for admission. After discussion, the team concurs that the boy would be better off in a structured residential setting.

"I don't want to put anyone in the program at risk, either the other kids or the staff," says Cone.

They agree they'll talk to the other potential candidate at the 3 o'clock court session to gauge his commitment.

"The child has to want to be in drug court," Meredith, the public defender, says later. "The judge is pretty much running your life, telling you what to do seven days a week."

"If he doesn't want to make a real commitment, I don't want him to be in the program because it's going to be hard enough for him," Cone says.

The others are making—or not making—various degrees of progress. Jennifer is doing great and Cone wonders aloud whether they can find some money to pay her for her community service in the court.

But even her experience shows just how difficult drug court can be. Jennifer was assigned to work in the court after a probation officer saw her on the street with a beer in her hand. The assignment was a sanction and Cone recalls Jennifer's anger at the time. "I hate her," she recalls her saying. "I hate that judge."

Others are having mixed success. Trevor (not his real name) has been missing his curfew and his family has been evasive when the probation officer calls. There is a discussion about what to do, ranging from cutting his curfew back from 6 p.m. to 5 p.m. to putting him under house arrest. The final decision will be made shortly, when court convenes.

Another participant, Scott (also not his real name), tested positive for marijuana use and is completing a stint in detention. "Since the middle of June, he's been using marijuana continuously," Cone says, displeased.

After the weekly meeting ends, the chairs are reconfigured in rows, Cone dons a black robe over her periwinkle suit and, one by one, the participants and their parents (usually the mother) take their seats at the long table in front of the judge's bench.

"The power of a judge, when you talk to a judge, is extraordinary," says Meredith. "There's a certain respect that's commanded."

Praise and Power

Cone dispenses praise or asks pointed questions. She points out to one young man, for example, that the results of the most recent drug tests will show whether he's telling the truth about not smoking marijuana. Meredith whispers to his clients and other members of the drug team supply information as needed.

For the most part, the kids speak briefly and quietly. They seem somewhat intimidated by the setting.

The boy who has missed his curfew, however, launches into a convoluted speech about why he was not available to come to the phone when his probation officer called. Marlene Tyson, the probation officer who provides intensive supervision, is not sold on the explanation and neither is the prosecutor.

"That doesn't sound good, your honor," Casinghino says. "It's not right, as Ms. Tyson says, to try to dupe the court and court officials."

But the boy's doing well otherwise and the judge strikes a middle course—avoiding house arrest but cutting his curfew back an hour.

Another girl reports to the court that she didn't show up for her job at Taco Bell one day because she was still angry over a fight she'd had with her sister.

"That's something you really have to work on," says Cone. "If you're mad, you've got to find a way to deal with it, rather than not going to work."

The prescription: anger management and conflict resolution programs for the girl and in-home therapy for the family, including the sister.

Although it's far too early to gauge the Hartford program's success, recent studies of the Santa Clara County Drug Treatment Court and the Delaware Juvenile Drug Court Diversion Program—the first two published studies of juvenile drug courts, according to their authors—indicate that juvenile programs have the potential to be successful.

The introduction to the studies, which their authors acknowledge are small-scale and short-term, reads: "Both evaluations suggest that juvenile drug courts are providing a positive impact on the recidivism and retention rates of substance abusing juvenile offenders."

Across the country, there are 91 juvenile drug courts in 33 states, says Lolita R. Curtis, vice president of the National Association of Drug Court Professionals, in Alexandria, Va. The first juvenile program was established in 1995 in California, she says.

A Deliberate Start

Cone says the drug team is deliberately starting off slowly and its members are learning as they go along. And while the adult sessions provide a helpful blueprint, there are also major differences. For example, adults are presumed to have control over their lives while adolescents are necessarily bound up with their families.

Also, participants in the adult drug session may have seen their lives spin hopelessly out of control, losing jobs, families, self-respect, money and property because of an addiction.

"Hopefully, the children we see in this drug court will never hit rock bottom," says Meredith.

Among teen-agers, the drugs of choice are marijuana and alcohol. In some cases, teens use a drug called "wet," an intoxicating stimulant that is a mix of marijuana and formaldehyde. Members of the drug team say they have not seen evidence of other drugs, such as heroin or cocaine.

"I don't see any of them as addicts," says Coles.

Casinghino agrees that staying clean is not often a problem. The kids have a tougher time staying in school, he says. But no one minimizes the drug use they do see. Meredith says it "could be catastrophic down the road" if it's not dealt with at this stage.

The focus of the drug team and the drug session, however, is on the kids' entire lives.

To provide wide-ranging support, entities ranging from the youth organization to probation to social workers, offer programs that include group counseling, art therapy, social skills, assistance in finding jobs and substance abuse counseling and education.

But participants — and their families — must follow the drug session's requirements.

"We try to keep it as real as possible," says Coles, explaining that they make a clear connection between actions and consequences. "We're going to do what we say we're going to do."

For now, it appears that incremental steps — clean urine tests, successful work experiences, reports from mothers that their children are staying home and being cooperative around the house — are the building blocks of the juvenile drug session.

"Each kid," says Casinghino, "is doing a little bit better than they were doing a few months ago."

'You Earn Your Freedom' Juvenile Drug Court Keeps Youths on Track

by Xiao Zhang
(April 26, 2002, Copyright 2002 by Grand Forks
Herald, reprinted with permission).

In this courtroom, you can hear laughter sometimes. You even can hear applause sometimes.

Twelve young people between the ages of 14 and 18 were watched by their parents and a team of social workers and legal professionals Thursday afternoon, as one by one, they did their weekly report in front of Judge Deb Kleven.

This is the Juvenile Drug Court at the Northeast Central District Court in Grand Forks. As a pilot program, Juvenile Drug Courts were set up in Grand Forks and Fargo in May 2000 to help young offenders who have substance abuse problems stay clean, sober and crime-free. The program also aims at teaching juveniles that they are accountable for their actions and giving them tools to better handle life.

Young people who have been diagnosed with drug or alcohol problems and have committed nonviolent crimes may be recommended for the Juvenile Drug Court program, where they go through 10 to 12 months of intensive supervised probation. Instead of being put in jail, they live their regular life—go to school—and take scheduled and random drug and alcohol tests, receive counseling on their drug/alcohol problems, participate in community work and report to the judge on a regular basis.

On completion of the program, the participant's current offense will be dismissed. If the participants stay drug and offense-free for a two-year period, they may be entitled to dismissal of their juvenile records.

National trend

Juvenile drug courts are among a national trend to handle people with substance abuse problems with an emphasis on treatment rather than punishment. In Bismarck, an adult drug court run by the state's Department of Corrections was established under the same philosophy.

It costs $80,000 to $90,000 per year to run the Juvenile Drug Court in Grand Forks, compared to $40,000 per year to keep each juvenile in jail, said Marilyn Moe, coordinator for the state's juvenile drug courts.

The Juvenile Drug Courts, started by the state Supreme Court Justice Mary Maring, are supported by federal grants and matching grants from the state Supreme Court. When in court, participants answer a list of questions ranging from their grades and performances at school to what family activities and good deeds they did for the week.

The judge asks them some questions and then gets feedback on the young person's performance by speaking with their family members who are present in the courtroom. He's been excellent, sometimes a parent would say.

The audience claps when they hear a young person has done really well. The atmosphere is like friends and family talking and catching up.

With these guys you see them every week, said Judge Kleven about how the Juvenile Drug Court is different from a regular court. You see the family, so you feel like you know them. It's harder when they fail. You are rooting for them.

The parents can feel that. It's been great, said the mother of a teenage girl, who has been in the program since August. She requested the judge to put a curfew of 7 p.m. on her daughter, which she said prevented her daughter from seeing some of her friends, who get her to use drugs.

The girl used to skip school for up to a quarter of the school year and had been caught for possession of methamphetamines.

She has been drug-free since August, and in the past three weeks, she has never been late or skipped school.

Asked if she feels going through the program limits too much of her freedom, she said, You earn your freedom.

By being disciplined, the young people in the program may earn a night of late curfew to go to the prom, removal of electronic monitoring, or become a platinum participant, who has the opportunity to enter a drawing for prizes.

Support group

A team of more than a dozen people forms the support group for these young people: addiction counselors, a probation officer, prosecuting and defense attorneys, school representatives, a law enforcement officer, a school representative and social services.

Each Thursday before court, the team meets to review the past week regarding each participant. Mike got an A in English; Julie got into a car accident; Jerry will graduate next month. Every little improvement, every little change is discussed and strategies designed for these individuals. The program has served more than 60 individuals in both courts in Grand Forks and Fargo. Some 40 people have graduated from the program in both cities.

Impressive track record

Some graduates have really impressed the Juvenile Drug Court team.

Peter Welte, assistant state's attorney on the team, said even though he was skeptical when the program first started, the results of the program were impressive. At the County Bar Association luncheon on Thursday, he proudly gave the group examples of successful graduates: a girl who stayed nine months drug free and gave birth to a drug-free baby, boys who have placed in the state's wrestling meet.

It's remarkable, he said.

The state's First Lady Mikey Hoeven attended the luncheon and later toured the addiction treatment facility.

Not everyone abandons drugs forever after being through such a program. But a study on the group done by Kevin Thompson, a sociology professor at North Dakota State University, showed that participants of this program are less likely to commit an offense again than juveniles in similar situations. As the mother of the teenage girl puts it, It's up to her whether she relapses or not. I can't make her not use (drugs). But for the girl, graduating from the program in July won't be the end of her drug-free life. I don't want to use it again, she said.

D. Juvenile Dependency Drug Treatment Court

The drug treatment court model also has been adapted for application in Dependency Court, a division of Family Court that deals with issues of child abuse and neglect, including the termination of parental rights when appropriate. In a high percentage of these cases, one or both parents has a substance abuse problem. The Dependency Court's focus is not on criminal charges, but rather on protecting the welfare of children. As the following two selections show, these courts are now making use of the drug treatment court model in an attempt to deal with the underlying problems, including substance abuse, that seem to precipitate abuse and neglect. If these problems can be successfully dealt with, future acts of abuse and neglect can be prevented and the child can remain at home with the family, rather than being placed in foster care or in a state institution.

The Juvenile Dependency Drug Treatment Court of Santa Clara County, California
by Judge Leonard P. Edwards
(Excerpted from 10 Juv. & Fam. Just. Today 16–17 (2001),
Copyright (2001) by National Council of Juvenile and
Family Court Judges, reprinted with permission).

My first experience with a drug court occurred one evening three years ago when I attended an adult drug court graduation. It was a festive affair with two judges presiding over a courtroom packed with clients, professionals, families, and well-wishers. Each graduate received a diploma, made a short speech and was roundly applauded. Of the approximately 20 graduates there were two women, one of whom I recognized from my court system (I am a juvenile court judge and work exclusively with child abuse and neglect cases). Both women fully participated in the proceedings, graduated, and made short speeches about their recovery.

Out of curiosity I returned to my court to investigate what had happened in the juvenile dependency court and found that both women had lost their children to the child welfare system. One had her parental rights terminated and the other's child was placed in a permanent guardianship at about the same time they had become involved in the adult drug court. Halfway through the drug court process, they had already lost their children. There was no mention of their children in the drug court graduation.

I concluded that something was wrong with a court system that celebrated treatment success but failed to include reunification with one's children as a part of that success. When I took this back to the members of the juvenile dependency court system, everyone agreed that we should start our own drug court, a juvenile dependency drug treatment court, and that we should coordinate with the adult drug treatment court.

The process we started resembled the creation of most drug courts. Key professionals, including attorneys, the court clerk, social service workers, and substance abuse providers met and discussed substance abuse treatment in the juvenile dependency system. Substance abuse is the most frequently occurring presenting problem in juvenile dependency court, one in which the court and social service agencies should be experts. We were not and soon learned a great deal about how to improve what we do in the treatment of substance abusing parents. A site visit to the family Drug Court in Washoe County (Reno), Nev., including a meeting with Presiding Judge Charles M. McCee, gave us great guidance.

At our initial meetings we determined that we needed a better assessment process, additional in-patient treatment beds for mothers and their children, additional outpatient programs for mothers and a dedicated court calendar where we could meet each week and discuss both administrative and cast [court] issues. The critical first step was approaching the politicians as a team and asking for additional services for mothers and children. Ordering treatment with no services or services with a six-month waiting list would be counter-productive. We pointed out that substance abuse service resources had been designed primarily for the men its [in] our community, and we demonstrated that the services we requested would actually save the county money by reducing the time children spent in foster care.

We got what we wanted: a court-based substance abuse assessor and increased inpatient and outpatient services for women. Our plan was for all parents with substance abuse allegations to participate in an assessment at their first contact with the juvenile court and for the treatment plan to be based upon that assessment. For such an early assessment, the client had to agree, but with strong support from their attorneys, almost all of the parents participated in these assessments within the first few days of coming to the court.

Then we had to find clients for the court. We discovered that there were two distinct categories of substance abusing clients—those who had a parallel criminal case in the criminal justice system (and who may be in the adult drug court) and those who had no involvement in the criminal justice system. The difference was significant because our county already had several adult drug courts, and we did not want to create conflicting orders between the two courts. The judges in the adult drug court made it clear that they wanted their treatment plans and court orders to take precedence over ours. We agreed, but pointed out that they were getting a late start on many cases. In light of the federal and state timelines governing permanency placement in the juvenile dependency court, we knew that if the adult drug court started late, the parents would lose their children.

Since participation in the juvenile dependency drug treatment court is voluntary, we had a very slow start. After six months we had five clients in the treatment court. Parents (95 percent have been mothers) were reluctant to volunteer for the juvenile dependency drug treatment court probably because they did not know what it would entail. But the parents' attorneys were strong supporters of the court, believing that involvement would maximize their clients' chances to regain custody. Both participating parents would sign a contract which agreed to submit to sanctions (including jail) should the parent fail to follow the advancement plan. The court's infrastructure has developed over time to include protocols and procedures, forms, a mission statement, and a budget.

The juvenile dependency drug treatment court has met on Wednesdays since October 1998. First we consider applications by parents to participate in the court and then discuss the progress that clients in the court are making. Social workers with specialized drug court assignments supervise the cases. Substance abuse treatment providers send reports on each client's progress, and the team talks with each client for up to 15 minutes at each court appearance.

We learn something new from almost every client. We learn about the details of recovery, about housing difficulties, the problem of accessing mental health services for dual diagnosis parents, and about the problems that many of the men in the clients' lives present for them. We also learn about how much these mothers want to become clean and sober so that they can regain custody of their children.

We have also learned about success. Watching the transformation of the mother has been inspirational. In a few short months most of them looked like new people—healthier, happier, and with increased self-esteem. They have taken control of their lives and suddenly have realistic goals. In most cases, the court has been able to return their children and assist them in transitioning to the community.

Additionally, those in the court and those who have graduated have developed a strong supportive relationship with each other, one that enables them to turn to each other for support while in the community. The most innovative development came from the law office which represents the parents. They hired two of the first graduates and asked them to counsel new clients about the drug court and its advantages. These "Mentor Moms," support parents as they participate in treatment. Their success led to a national award last year from the Model Court project of the National Council of Juvenile and Family Court Judges.

After completing our second year in October, 75 clients have participated in our juvenile dependency drug treatment court. Thirty-two have graduated and 10 have left the program. Interestingly, half of those who have left the program have reunited with their children. They were successful but followed a slightly different path. In all cases, the decisions concerning the children's permanent placement have been made more quickly than in those cases not in the drug treatment court. The success is so great that we have decided to start a second juvenile dependency drug treatment court.

The drug court philosophy we utilize is not new. Judges have always known that compliance with court orders is increased when the client must appear before the court at a review. Not only does it work, but judges, court personnel, probation, and substance abuse professionals find working in drug courts satisfying. It is particularly satisfying when that work benefits parents and their children.

Fighting for Families
by Patty Fisher
(May 12, 2002, Copyright 2002 by San Jose Mercury News, reprinted with permission).

SHELLY Zwijsen has been planning this Mother's Day weekend for a long time. A trip to the park, "Spider-Man" and Chinese food. The hard part will come after dinner, when she'll kiss her children goodbye and check herself back into the halfway house where she's working to kick her drug addiction.

Next Mother's Day, she plans to be clean, sober and living with her family full-time. If she makes it, she'll be another success story in Santa Clara County's family drug court.

Studies show that when parents abuse or neglect their children, four times out of five either Mom or Dad has a substance-abuse problem. For years, courts have routinely taken children away from drug-abusing parents, usually forever. But when parents lose their kids, everyone loses. Kids wind up in foster care or are adopted by strangers. Parents are left with feelings of loss and failure. And the already overburdened child welfare system gets more cases.

There's a better way: Help parents get off drugs and deal with the problems they took drugs to forget, such as violent relationships, childhood trauma or mental illness. It won't always work. But even if it works some of the time, it will save money on foster care, which is very expensive. And it will save families, which are priceless.

That's the philosophy behind Santa Clara County's Juvenile Dependency

Drug Court, run by Superior Court Judge Leonard Edwards. It is one of about 30 family drug courts in the country. Only highly motivated parents are chosen. Since it opened in 1998, more than 150 parents, mostly mothers, have participated. About 75 have graduated. Ten dropped out and the rest are still in the program. About 70 percent who stick with it get their children back, compared with fewer than 50 percent of those outside drug court.

When Zwijsen showed up in Edwards' courtroom last October, she was about to lose custody of her two kids, now ages 4 and 6. Police had found her using PCP while the kids were in the house. Under a 1997 federal law, parents have one year to get clean or face termination of their parental rights. If the child is younger than 3, the parents only get six months.

The law was intended to save kids from years of custody limbo. But a year isn't much time to kick a drug habit, so the court has to work quickly, throwing a team of professionals at each case.

The team gathers for a brown-bag lunch before court each week to discuss the 40 or so cases on the calendar. There are social workers, mental health counselors, domestic violence counselors, drug treatment counselors, welfare caseworkers, attorneys for the kids, attorneys for the parents and attorneys for the social workers.

In court, Edwards is the supportive father figure to the clients, praising them for clean drug tests and regular attendance at 12-step meetings, gently chastising them for missteps, urging them not to give up on themselves. "You've made so much progress," he tells a woman who's discouraged because she can't find an apartment. "These problems we're talking about are a lot better than the problems you used to have."

Watching it all are the "mentor moms," veterans who graduated from drug court, got their kids back and now help other addicts.

Barbara Bond is Zwijsen's mentor. She's been clean for nearly four years, and still grapples with how much her addiction cost her.

"My kids used to say I was like Medusa when I was using," she said. "I tell the women to do this while their kids are little, so they won't miss out on so much."

The beauty of the drug-court concept is that it's not just about drugs. Edwards recognizes that drug treatment is just the front door, the way to get to the other problems that tear families apart. "Sobriety and parenting are not necessarily consistent with each other," he said. "But parenting will flow after you've taken care of yourself."

Sometimes parenting doesn't flow. Some people unsuccessfully fight addiction their whole lives, others don't bother to fight. We can't let kids spend childhood waiting for sober parents. But if the alternative is broken families and more children in foster care, then it makes sense to give parents a fighting chance.

———

E. Sentencing Circles

Criminal sentencing typically is decided on by the sentencing judge, based largely on the nature of the crime for which the defendant has been convicted and partially on facts concerning the defendant's prior record and social history. Increasingly, the sentencing judge's discretion is limited by sentencing guidelines that specify a range within which sentencing may occur. The sentencing process certainly provides the offender with an opportunity to confront his or her wrong-doing and to undertake behavioral change, including participation in a rehabilitative program or adoption of a relapse prevention plan, when appropriate. In recent years, an alternative approach to sentencing—indeed, an alternative vision of sentencing and punishment—has begun to penetrate our thinking and sentencing practices, particularly in the juvenile area. This approach, known as Restorative Justice, grew out of aboriginal and tribal practices in Australia, New Zealand, Canada, and the United States. The following news account describes a Canadian application of this approach in a juvenile context, a dramatic contrast with our typical practices of sentencing criminal offenders.

Teen Bully Finds Justice, Healing and the Courage to Apologize: Sentencing Circle Requested by Mother of Suicide Victim
by Daniel Girard
(May 15, 2002, News Section, Copyright 2002 by
The Toronto Star, reprinted with permission).

The 17-year-old girl was crying too hard to speak each time the eagle feather came her way during her sentencing circle.

But, finally, at the end of the day, she gathered herself enough to apologize for the bullying that led to the suicide of another girl.

Clutching the hand of her grandfather who held the feather, she walked across the floor of the crowded room and stood before the mother of her victim.

"I'm sorry for everything that I have done to Dawn-Marie and your family," she said, handing Cindy Wesley a letter she had written.

Cindy Wesley replied: "All I ask of you is: Be a better person."

The two then held each other, crying.

The girl had been convicted of criminally harassing Dawn-Marie Wesley, 14, who later committed suicide.

At a sentencing circle requested by Cindy Wesley, who is married to a native man, a group of native elders, family members and court and school officials gathered here yesterday to pass judgment.

For more than three hours, 20 people took turns holding an eagle feather in their hands and telling what was in their hearts — sorrow, hope, pride in their heritage and, most of all, a desire to stop the destructiveness that comes with bullying in our schools.

The girl, 17, a native who cannot be identified under the Young Offenders Act, was sentenced to 18 months probation, told to write a 750-word essay on the dangers of bullying and told to speak on the subject in high schools.

Following the sentencing, Cindy Wesley said she was very pleased with it because she got the healing she wanted and "I got the remorse I was looking for."

More was accomplished than by a typical court sentencing because "in a court of law, her and I couldn't have talked," Wesley said.

"I didn't see her (Dawn-Marie) but I know she was there today," Wesley told reporters. "I know that right now, as this sun shines down on us, her and the creator are shining with us.

"She's at peace with the way this was handled."

Native sentencing circles are not common in British Columbia but are being used more and more. It's crucial to have the community participate for it to work.

Provincial Court Judge Jill Rounthwaite found in March that the girl threatened to beat up Dawn-Marie Wesley for "talking about her" and shouted over the phone that "You are f---ing dead."

Wesley hanged herself with her dog's leash in the basement of her home in nearby Mission.

She left behind a note saying she could no longer take the bullying of three girls — one of whom was convicted, another acquitted and a third who is yet to stand trial in the case.

It's one of the first cases in Canada to lead to criminal charges over schoolyard threats.

Addressing the sentencing circle, Rounthwaite, a mother of two young girls, said she hoped this case would make everyone take bullying more seriously.

"My hope is that all of us can work within our own family and with those children within our reach to help them understand that what they say off the cuff can be harmful and hurtful," she said.

All members of the sentencing circle, held in the room of a retreat and conference centre in this community 75 kilometres east of Vancouver, said they would heed the judge's call by making the girl recognize what she'd done wrong and use it to help others. They would also, as a community, endeavour to make sure she never strayed again.

"She made a mistake and she's sorry about it," said the girl's uncle.

"It's time for her to make amends and move on and become a better person."

Looking at Cindy Wesley, who has become a crusader against schoolyard bullying and recently appeared on the American talk show Oprah, he said: "As you've gone on to do things positively with this, hopefully (she) can go on to do things positively."

Bill Bertschy of the Sliammon First Nation, the keeper of the circle overseeing the proceedings, called on all to use the event to begin the healing.

"We're here today to learn to live in harmony and to learn how to do things in a good way," Bertschy said.

Randy Huth, principal of Mission Secondary School where the girls attended, called on the girl sentenced to turn the story into something that could "help our young people" who may be bullies or bullied.

"It's part of growing up but it's also something we need to address more and more," Huth said. "And, (she), I think, could really help us out."

F. TEEN COURT OR YOUTH COURT

Teen court, or youth court as it often is known, bears some similarities to the sentencing circles discussed above. It is a form of peer justice—and positive peer pressure—in which a teenager, accused of a very minor offense, is permitted to opt out of juvenile court and instead be tried before a jury composed of other teenagers who have been through the teen court process. The teens also get to play the role of prosecutor and defense attorney. The following two newspaper accounts show how the process works and describe the benefits that many teenagers involved in teen court have experienced. (Teen court is also described in Part II, F, in a selection by Wexler devoted to how the judiciary can help offenders develop problem-solving skills.)

Youths Face a Jury of their Peers: Teen Court Offers a Chance to Clear Records of Minor Offenses

by Julie Elliott
(April 14, 2002, Denton County Section, 2d ed., pg. 1T, Copyright 2002 by The Dallas Morning News, reprinted with permission).

LEWISVILLE—Seventeen-year-old Joey DuBiel and Cody Haefele, 18, huddled together on their side of the Lewisville courtroom and tried to determine if they should put their 16-year-old client on the stand to defend herself against a charge of underage drinking.

The two youths, who volunteer to present real cases in the Lewisville Teen Court, determined that it was best to keep her off the stand—despite a surprise move by teen prosecutors who called the girl's mother as a witness against her.

The facts were clear: the 16-year-old smelled of alcohol and was visibly sick when a Lewisville officer ticketed her. And she had already admitted her guilt.

But both defense attorneys wanted her to have a second chance.

"[The defendant] was responsible enough to not get behind the wheel," said Joey, a senior at Lewisville High School. "She used responsibility to protect herself and to protect others. She knew her limits."

In the end, the teen jury sentenced the defendant to 53 hours of community service and three jury terms in teen court—essentially serving on the jury three nights. The sentence is between the minimum and maximum penalties for underage drinking.

This is just one of the many cases that teens present each year in the Lewisville Teen Court, a program designed to give first-time juvenile offenders the opportunity to keep their records clear of Class C misdemeanors such as theft under $50, traffic tickets and alcohol possession citations.

The court, which was founded in 1994, is an alternative to the adult justice system that allows teen defense and prosecution attorneys to present a case to a jury of the defendants' peers. Other teens serve as bailiffs, court clerks and jurors. The defendants are between the ages of 10 and 17 and have pleaded guilty.

"This is an opportunity for the youth in the community to get a second chance," said Anne Dubinsky, Teen Court coordinator. "If we can stop one youth from going down the wrong path, then that is what we want to do."

There are more than 80 Teen Court programs across Texas, including programs in Denton, Fort Worth, Dallas, Arlington and Grand Prairie.

In the Teen Court system, the defendants are never ordered to pay a fine. Instead, they are sentenced to do between six and 60 hours of community service for nonprofit organizations such as Christian Community Action, the Greater Lewisville YMCA, Habitat for Humanity and local humane societies. In addition to community service, the offenders are also sentenced to serve on the Teen Court jury. Depending on the offense, the teens can serve from one to four terms. One term is one night of cases.

Between 80 and 100 cases are heard in Lewisville Teen Court each year. In the first year, the teen court oversaw 36 cases with a 75 percent success rate. Last year, the court heard 91 cases with an 80 percent success rate, meaning the cases are dismissed. Youths in the other 20 percent may have failed to fulfill their requirements and had been remanded to municipal court.

Similar to adult trials

The Teen Court process is similar to the adult judicial process, said Judi Bertrand, the adult judge who oversees the Teen Court proceedings and is an alternate municipal judge for Lewisville.

"To have to get up there and testify makes them more nervous. This is better than just paying a fine, because they have to take responsibility."

On a typical Tuesday, the Teen Court prosecutors present about six cases after spending time with the defendants to learn about the circumstances surrounding the citations. Each trial runs about 20 to 30 minutes before the jury is sent out to decide the sentence. Most of the volunteers have spent numerous hours training, and Ms. Bertrand critiques their courtroom performance after each session.

Recently, a 15-year-old boy was on trial for stealing a $12 pair of cubic zirconia earrings at a mall while with a group of friends. He pleaded guilty, but he still testified in hopes of making his peers aware that he had already learned his lesson so that they might give him a lesser sentence.

"I didn't plan to steal anything, but when I saw them, I just grabbed them and walked out of the store," said the boy, who is not being identified because he is a minor. "This showed me that I can learn from what I have done. Instead of paying a fine, this has given me a chance to really think about what I did. It has given me a chance to correct myself."

After the jury deliberated for about 20 minutes, he was sentenced to 42 hours of community service and three jury terms. His parents also grounded him for four months.

The teen court process is a good learning experience, said the boy's mother. "I want this to teach him a lesson, and I think it is," she said. For some youths, Teen Court offers lessons about the legal system.

"I want to be a lawyer, so this is perfect practice for me," said Vynessa Hinojosa, 16, who is in her first year as a volunteer defense attorney. "I am getting to learn a lot about the system and how the process works, but I am also getting to help my peers."

Denton's program

In Denton, the Teen Court program also has been successful, said Roland Jones, coordinator of the Denton Teen Court and president of the Texas Teen Court Association.

The Denton program started in April 1995 and had 28 cases the first year. In 2001–02, the Denton Teen Court oversaw 613 cases. The Denton court has two models, one with an adult judge and another, a traffic court, with a teen judge. The Lewisville court has an adult judge.

Since the Denton program was initiated, 2,144 cases have been heard, and more than 14,600 hours of community service have been completed by those sentenced.

"We are able to use peer pressure because it shows these kids that even other kids don't always appreciate what they have done," Mr. Jones said. In fact, some say teen juries generally hand down tougher sentences than an adult court would.

"Research shows that the teen courts are more punitive than a regular municipal court," said Tory Caeti, assistant professor of criminal justice at the University of North Texas in Denton. "A lot of times the kids will hand out a lot more community service hours."

And that's exactly what some Lewisville teens said they liked about the program.

"This is a more comfortable setting than when you have an adult judge," said Peter Nguyen, 17, a juror who received 42 hours of community service for running a red light. "You feel comfortable because the others have been through the same thing. It is a really good experience."

Teen Court Never Loses Hope

by Amanda Alexander
(March 24, 2002, Midland Section, Copyright 2002 by
Aberdeen American News, reprinted with permission).

Each year about 100 youth in Brown County are sentenced by their peers for misdemeanor crimes like petty theft, disorderly conduct and underage drinking.

The maximum sentence is up to six nights of jury duty, two community service projects, 80 hours of community service, research papers, apologies and any other sanctions the peer jury deems appropriate.

Before a teen even gets in front of a peer sentencing jury, they have admitted their offense and agreed to accept whatever sentence is handed out.

And, as long as the teen successfully completes the sentence, the charge will not become part of his or her permanent record.

Sentences are meted out twice a month at Brown County Teen Court. That's when teens who have been specially trained to prosecute and defend peers who have gotten in trouble with the law gather in the third floor courtroom of the Brown County Courthouse to argue the merits of sentencing. It's been going on for about five years.

Experience: Melissa Madrazo, 17, is one of those teens.

Madrazo got in trouble for possession and consumption of alcohol in November of 2001. She was at a house party when the police showed up. Then she had to do what most teens dread: she had to call her mom to come and pick her up from the party.

"It was the first time I drank, and I got in trouble really fast," she said.

After serving her sentence—15 hours of community service, serving on two juries, one community connection (spending time with law enforcement on a particular topic) and completing a Northern Alcohol and Drug Referral and Information Center (NADRIC) class—she still attends teen court every other Thursday.

Even though Madrazo's first experience was as the defendant, she says it was so positive that she is now a teen court volunteer.

"It's a good program," Madrazo said. "It's fun, and you learn about other people's problems."

She added, "And it makes you think twice about what you do, definitely."

'Fun, yet serious': Emily Margolies, 15, is also a teen volunteer. While she likes prosecuting cases for stiff sentences, Margolies hasn't been in the sort of trouble with which teen court deals.

Margolies said she sees a lot of kids for possession and consumption of alcohol, and petty theft for things like pencils, notebooks and pop.

"It's fun, yet serious," Margolies said. "We're not there to make life miserable and get kids in trouble, we have a job to do."

The teens who serve as defenders meet with their clients before the hearing, much like a regular attorney would do. They go over the charges and discuss possible sentences.

The teens prosecuting also have time to put their case together before the hearing. Then they argue their case for a sentence in front of a six to 12 person jury. Area lawyers act as the judge.

Volunteers cannot talk about the specifics of the cases, and that can be hard, especially if you know the person, Margolies said.

Teen court is a 90-day diversion program for first-time offenders. The program diverts teens out of the juvenile court system and keeps their records clean. But that doesn't mean they get off easy. Sometimes their peers come up with harsh sentences.

For example, a teen who admits to underage drinking faces the minimum requirements of paying a $20 participation fee, serving on a jury for two nights, attending an eight-hour primary prevention class that costs $40 to $55, completing one community service project, attending a community connection and completing 20 hours of community service.

New trend: While teen court has been successful—97 percent of those receiving sentences completed them—a trend was beginning to develop.

"We noticed some were coming through at (age) 10 and 12 for petty theft and disorderly conduct," said Bonnie Siebrecht who coordinates the volunteers and program. "Then we would see them again at 15 and 16 for possession and consumption. We thought they deserved another chance."

So last fall, Brown County Teen Court added STOP, the second time offender program.

Brown County is very limited on diversion programs, Siebrecht said. Those diversion programs available are teen court, NADRIC and Hands Off, a program to stop shoplifting.

STOP is more intense, Siebrecht said. "They come before an advisory board of volunteers and are questioned for about a half hour. It's more one-on-one."

Those who are sentenced through STOP must also tour the juvenile detention center, among other sanctions. That could include further diversion programs like Hands Off, community service hours and projects, apologies, and improving or keeping good grades in school.

Transfer decision: But it's up to the Brown County deputy State's Attorney's office to determine if the teen can be transferred to the alternative court.

Each case is looked at individually, said Kim Dorsett, Brown County State's Attorney who handles juvenile cases.

"The first thing I look at is the seriousness of the charge," Dorsett said. "The policy is that felonies are not transferred to teen court, only misdemeanors."

On a drug charge, for example, Dorsett will look at how cooperative the teen was, the extent of that cooperation with law enforcement and how much of the drug showed up in a urine analysis, among other things.

"This is the prime opportunity to pick them up and put them on the right path," Dorsett said. "If you ignore it, it almost always escalates into something more serious."

"I'll admit I had reservations at first," said Judge Eugene Dobberpuhl, presiding Fifth Circuit judge. "But everything I've seen has been very effective, and the nicest part is that it allows a lot of young people to be a part of the judicial process and get a feeling for how our system really works."

If it weren't for people like Bonnie the program wouldn't happen, Dobberpuhl said. "We owe a great debt of gratitude to her. She volunteers her time for this, and does a great job of holding it together."

Individual choice: The option of teen court is up to each individual. "Very often you see families agree with the referral to teen court, but the teen doesn't accept the sentence," said Dorsett of the state's attorney's office. The teen then goes to regular juvenile court. "Then they are creating a juvenile record, whereas the crime may...(not be known)...if they successfully complete the teen court sentence."

Dorsett said that while a person's juvenile record is sealed, some employers and schools can make you disclose what's in your juvenile record, like if you're entering law school or want to be a police officer.

Said Siebrecht, "I just hope it opens their eyes and they think before they get into trouble."

———————

G. Domestic Violence Court

Another specialized court to have emerged in recent years is Domestic Violence Court, a court that combines both civil and criminal jurisdiction to deal with violence between intimates. The court considers criminal charges involving spousal battering and similar conduct occurring between unmarried individuals involved in an intimate relationship, and also may issue restraining orders and no-contact orders, attempting to prevent future acts of abuse. As with child abuse and neglect, a high percentage of domestic violence cases involve substance abuse on the part of one or both parties. As a result, it was perhaps natural that the principles and techniques of Drug Treatment Court would be adapted for application in this area. Unlike criminal courts generally, the Domestic Violence Court seeks not only to punish and hopefully rehabilitate the batterer, but also to provide support and needed services to the victim. The following newspaper accounts describe the functioning of the domestic violence court model, which has been increasingly adopted throughout the country.

Court Cracks Down on Domestic Violence

by Ray Rivera
(November 8, 1999, Final Section, pg. C1, Copyright 1999
by The Salt Lake Tribune, reprinted with permission).

Lucy Smith's ex-husband used to brag that he could talk his way out of anything, even charges of spousal abuse. Year after year, judges let him go with slaps on the wrist and orders to attend counseling—orders he simply ignored.

"He got to the point where he felt invincible, and he was," said Smith (not her real name). "The courts didn't run him. He ran the courts."

Even after the couple separated, he continued harassing her, showing up at her home in the middle of the night and tormenting her at work.

"He broke my nose twice, knocked out one of my front teeth," Smith said. "It was just bad, it was horrible."

And he remained free.

Then, in 1997, his charges were moved to a newly formed Domestic Violence Court started by 3rd District Judge Sheila McCleve. He was again ordered to counseling. But this time when he didn't obey the order, he was sentenced to 19 months in jail.

"I'll never forget what [McCleve] told him. She said: "Mark my word, do not ever come in my courtroom again. If I get one phone call from her saying you're bothering her, you will be back in prison,'" Smith said.

Tales of success abound from McCleve's specialty court, which handles all misdemeanor domestic-violence cases in Salt Lake City. Until now, however, there has been little empirical evidence on how the experimental program was working.

But new research by a victim's advocate with the Salt Lake City Police Department shows that Domestic Violence Court has produced 55 percent more convictions, and 80 percent of those people do not re-offend.

"What was happening before Domestic Violence Court and what is happening after was really quite dramatic," said Wes Galloway, who conducted the research.

Galloway and a volunteer assistant examined 300 cases pulled randomly from a pool of 3,500 offenders who had been placed on probation since 1997 when the court was founded. The sample included chronic and first-time offenders. He found that on average, eight of 10 people on probation did not re-offend.

And analyzing data from 1995 on, he found that misdemeanor domestic-violence filings have dropped significantly since the advent of the specialty court, while convictions have gone up. Filings averaged about 5,500 a year between 1995 and 1997. Last year, the number dropped by a thousand, and preliminary numbers for 1999 show a further decrease. In that same time span, convictions rose from about 65 to 70 a month to over than 100.

The research did not take into account such things as the offender's prior record. And Galloway did not track the number of first-time vs. repeat offenders in the sample. But scientific or not, his work offers the first statistical glimpse of the court's success.

"It gives us all quite a bit of satisfaction," said presiding 3rd District Judge Frank G. Noel, who expanded the court this year to include two more judges. "We hope it indicates that we are having a positive impact on people's lives."

Judges Robin Reese and Robert Hilder help with the crushing case load. They will rotate out in January and be replaced by two other judges yet to be named.

For McCleve, the research comes years ahead of the time that she expected to see positive results.

"Frankly, my hope when I started this was that we would have an impact on the second generation," said McCleve. "I didn't expect to have the adults that come in front of me change as much as I hoped to have some influence on their kids. So when I saw the numbers, I was pleasantly surprised."

McCleve hopes to expand the court's duties to include felony cases. Last year, domestic violence was the leading cause of Utah homicides.

The court's goal is to break what domestic-violence counselors refer to as the cycle of abuse. The cycle begins with tension and threats between a couple; erupts into slaps, kicks, choking or worse; then is followed by remorse, known as the "honeymoon" phase, in which the abuser may express guilt or shame and shower the victim with gifts and flowers.

Victims' advocates and abuse counselors have lauded the court's success from the start, saying the efficient processing of cases helps stop the cycle. The court also follows up on probation orders, forcing offenders to return to court at least three times to ensure they are continuing treatment.

That was how it helped Smith, by finally forcing her ex-husband to undergo counseling, and when he did not, by sending him to jail.

No longer afraid and no longer trapped in a violent relationship, the 33-year-old mother of two was able to put her own life in order, quitting drugs, finding a good job and starting college.

"It's even helped my kids," she said. "They realize there is a different way to be treated and that you can't accept that kind of behavior, no matter what."

Smith also credits advocate Galloway and the Salt Lake City Police Department's handling in recent years of domestic-violence cases.

"It surprises me how my life has turned around," she said. "I tried to leave him so many times but couldn't. Then when I got involved with the victim's advocate program and counseling, everything changed."

Our View: Boise Needs New Method to Stop Domestic Violence

(May 5, 2002, Local Section, pg. 8, Copyright 2002 by The Idaho Statesman, reprinted with permission).

At least three cases a day. Many days, more than twice that.

If you think domestic violence is someone else's problem, taking place in some other part of town, guess again.

"Imagine the outcry if we had three to 10 women battered along the Greenbelt, or battered downtown, or battered at the mall," Boise Police Chief Don Pierce said.

Day-in, day-out suffering—more than 1,000 cases a year of physical battery, at least that many cases of verbal abuse. And those numbers only start to make the case for a new court specifically to handle domestic violence cases.

Here's the painful clincher. It commonly takes months for a domestic violence case to be heard in a courtroom. What happens in the interim gets in the way of justice.

The victim's fears for safety become fears for the future. The terror that caused the victim to call 911 fades. The victim—who all too often has children, but no job or skills, and low self-esteem—starts to worry about finances.

"That's unfortunate, but that's kind of what we're faced with," said Angie Bevier, an officer in Boise police's domestic violence unit.

Meanwhile, the abuser's remorse fades. While advocates on one side encourage the victim to hold firm, the abuser is persuading the victim to forgive. In time, the remorse fades, and the attentiveness that comes with it disappears. Tension builds. It explodes in violence, often more severe than before.

Domestic violence is a different crime, partly because the lives of perpetrator and victim are intertwined. Because of that, it should be treated differently in the courts.

A domestic violence court would move cases in front of a judge more quickly. It would keep the victim working with the same judge and prosecutor; that means the victim doesn't have to repeat the story of abuse over and over, sometimes to the point of giving up.

It also puts the abuser into a system that offers treatment, when the abuser is most likely to take it. If someone is convicted of domestic abuse and is simply put behind bars, the chance of reoffense is higher. If the abuser gets treatment, it can change habits. It can put families back together.

The basic model for a domestic violence court is Drug Court, launched in 1999 by then-District Judge Dan Eismann. The idea behind Drug Court is to keep non-violent drug users out of prison and allow them to get their offenses purged from their records if they go through counseling and pass drug screenings.

Treatment is needed not just for the physical addiction at the heart of drug abuse, but for the behavioral cycle behind domestic violence.

"We can't just reprogram people like computers," said Eismann, now a state Supreme Court justice.

The challenge of domestic violence court, like Drug Court, is funding. Federal grants have paid for Drug Court since its inception, and by next year, the court will need a new funding source, Eismann said.

Money isn't the only obstacle. Some will question the need for a domestic violence court, and question whether Ada County will next need a shoplifting court.

Ada County needs a domestic violence court because the backlog of cases forces prosecutors to plead down cases—and forces victims through a long process that victimizes them again.

The system can do better. For neighborhoods, because domestic violence occurs all over the socioeconomic map. For children, who are present at more than half of the scenes of domestic violence Boise police investigate. And especially for victims.

————————

H. MENTAL HEALTH COURT

One of the most recent problem solving court models to have emerged is mental health court. The tightening of civil commitment standards and the policy of deinstitutionalization has led to thousands of people with mental illness living in the community. Many of these, released to communities ill-prepared to deal with their continued clinical, social, and housing needs, have become homeless. Many refuse to take needed medication in the community, and suffer a reemergence of their symptoms, often requiring re-hospitalization. Many get into trouble with the police, and are charged with minor offenses like trespassing, urinating in public, and petty theft. They are brought to jail, which typically has extremely limited mental health clinical resources. Subjected to the extreme stress of jail detention, they suffer further decompensation. Jail and the criminal court process is inappropriate for most of these individuals, whose problems are due more to their mental illness than to their criminality. As a result, mental health court has been developed to attempt to divert them from the criminal process to the treatment in the community that they need. The following newspaper account describes this important emerging problem solving court model.

Mental Health Courts Focus on Treatment; Criminals Often Overlooked in Traditional System are Sentenced to Hospital Care

by Richard A. Marini
(May 6, 2002, Metro Section, pg. 1C, Copyright 2002 by
San Antonio Express-News, reprinted with permission).

When Judge Ginger Lerner-Wren talks about her courtroom in the 17th Judicial Circuit in Broward County, Fla., she uses words that not many jurists would select. Words like "empathetic," "voluntary participation" and "helping court."

That's because Lerner-Wren presides over the nation's first mental health court. Established in 1997, the court's expressed purpose is to slow the revolving door of mentally ill patients who are repeatedly arrested and sent to prison when what they really need is treatment.

Or, as Lerner-Wren puts it, "if you're a criminal, you should be in prison. If you're sick, you should be in the hospital."

Since the Broward Court was established, mental health courts have sprung up across the country. There are now about 20 such courts in operation, according to the Judge David L. Bazelon Center for Mental Health Law in Washington, D.C., a nonprofit advocacy group. Another dozen or so have been proposed, including San Antonio and Austin.

According to the Justice Department, 16 percent of prison and jail inmates suffer some sort of mental illness. That's about 300,000 prisoners—more than four times the number of patients in mental hospitals.

The flood of mentally ill inmates began about 40 years ago when many huge, state-run mental hospitals—criticized for warehousing and, at times, abusing patients—were closed in a process that came to be known as deinstitutionalization. Smaller, community-based facilities were supposed to be opened to care for these just-released patients, but the money for these clinics never materialized. As a result, thousands upon thousands of the mentally ill, many suffering severe psychoses, were essentially left on their own, often to the streets, increasingly to jails and prisons.

The mentally ill are 64 percent more likely to be arrested, often for what Lerner-Wren calls "public acts of bizarreness."

"If you're a frat student (urinating) outside a party, the police may tell you to move along, but they're not going to arrest you," she explains. "But if you're delusional and talking to someone who's not there while you're doing it, they'll probably bring you in."

Once incarcerated, the mentally ill require resources the prison system is ill-equipped to provide.

"Treating someone with a mental illness requires separate settings and costly medications," explains Dr. John C. Sparks, medical director at the Bexar County Jail.

It also takes more time to treat someone in prison than it does on the outside, says Sparks. That's one reason why inmates with mental illnesses serve an average of 15 months longer for the same crime, compared to other prisoners.

Those who receive treatment are regarded as the lucky ones. Nationwide, only 41 percent of jail detainees and 60 percent of state and federal prison inmates who need mental health treatment receive it. Those who fall through the cracks are usually no better off, and often much worse, when they're finally released than when they first arrived. As a result, recidivism rates among these patients are high. Many return to prison.

Mental health courts, such as the one proposed for Bexar County, attempt to address these problems by diverting the mentally ill into treatment programs.

"If we get such a court here, there'd certainly be plenty of work to keep a judge busy," says Probate Court Judge Polly Jackson Spencer, who also oversees commitment hearings at the San Antonio State Hospital.

While each court operates differently, most have some sort of arrangement where incoming detainees can be referred into the system at any point in the arrest process—by the arresting officer, the defense attorney, even a family member.

While on the surface the mental health court hearing might resemble something Bobby Donnel or even Perry Mason would recognize, it's different from a typical trial.

Most of the time, the patient is involved voluntarily and can, at any time, ask to be transferred back to a traditional courtroom. And while a judge, defense attorney and prosecuting attorneys are usually present, there also may be social workers and mental health case workers on hand to evaluate patients and offer their expertise.

"We tend to come from a different perspective," explains Lerner-Wren, in whose courtroom patients are referred to not as defendants, but as "court participants." "We're looking to offer help, not simply legal adjudication."

Instead of sending defendants to jail, these courts "sentence" them to treatment. In some jurisdictions, patients who successfully complete treatment are released, their charges dismissed. In others, patients who are stabilized with drugs and other treatments, return to court to stand trial for their crimes.

Patients who fail to follow their prescribed treatment plan can be ordered to jail, much like a defendant who breaks parole.

Critics contend that, while mental health courts may sometimes serve a useful purpose, the mentally ill shouldn't have to be arrested before they receive treatment.

"Outreach programs and drop-in centers can catch those at-risk before they become entangled with the criminal justice system," says Tammy Seltzer, a staff attorney with the Bazelon Center. "That requires mental health teams going out and meeting these people where they are—under the bridges, in the parks—and building relationships so they'll accept the help that's offered.

Others criticize the courts because treating the mentally ill is expensive. In Riverside, Calif., for example, it costs $350 a day to keep a patient in a supervised environment, but only $70 a day to keep that person in jail, according to Judge Becky L. Dugan, who oversees one of the few mental health courts to adjudicate felony cases.

In comparison, it costs $650 a day to house a patient in a state mental hospital.

Still, the concept of mental health courts is so new that studies of their effectiveness are just now coming in.

An evaluation of the Seattle mental health court, for example, found that participation improves a defendant's chances of success in undergoing treatment, finding housing and developing other support systems. A similar review of the Kings County (Washington) court found that court participants spent fewer days in detention and were less likely to be re-arrested than those who chose not to participate.

Court proponents say there are other ways of measuring success, too.

"In the 16 months we've been running this court," says Dugan, "we've had 19 defendants earn their GEDs, six are attending college, 25 are working full-time jobs and many more are functioning well in the community, meaning they're not out there committing crimes.

"I feel a lot more productive as a judge working with these defendants than I do sentencing 19-year-olds to 25 years to life."

————————

I. A Hybrid Domestic Violence/ Mental Health Court

As these new problem solving court models proliferate, we are seeing the development of hybrid models—courts that bring together the techniques and approaches of two or more of these courts to deal with special populations with overlapping problems. An example, previously described, is juvenile dependency drug treatment court, which focuses on parents in child abuse and neglect cases who have substance abuse problems. The following newspaper account describes a court that combines the approaches of mental health court with those of domestic violence court to deal with domestic violence perpetrators suffering from serious mental illness.

Threat of Jail Helping Keep Mentally Ill on Medication: Domestic Violence Court Offering Program of Monitored Probation

by Tim Wyatt
(December 10, 2001, Metro Section, 2d ed., pg. 23A, Copyright 2001 by The Dallas Morning News, reprinted with permission).

Steve Muzyka spent last holiday season under the loading ramp of a Garland warehouse, depressed and suicidal over the failure of his second marriage.

The 37-year-old unemployed janitorial worker with an untreated mental illness said he hunkered down in his new home and tried to wait out the winter.

By spring, Mr. Muzyka ignored a court order to stay away from his estranged wife. He pinned her to the floor of her home and scrawled "Property of Steve Muzyka" across her chest with a felt-tip marker. While no physical harm was done, his fit of anger landed Mr. Muzyka in jail for six months.

He says it was the best thing to happen to him in years.

Two months into his sentence, Mr. Muzyka opted for two years of probation and monitoring under a new mental health program in domestic violence court rather than spend another 40 days in jail. The only catch: He had to stay on his medications.

"That's what inspired me to find the right mix of medications and stay with it," he said. "I feel like a normal human being again. My thoughts are clear."

Like many offenders in Dallas County's criminal justice system, trouble always had a way of finding Mr. Muzyka when he stopped taking medication for his bipolar disorder. On any given day, about 15 percent of the county's jail inmate population—almost 900 people—are known to have some kind of mental illness, according to jail psychiatric records.

Making a change

County Criminal Judge David Finn said that for the last two years, he has seen a steady increase of mentally ill defendants show up in his misdemeanor domestic violence court. After prompting from distraught family members who were terrified of loved ones who couldn't—or wouldn't—stay on stabilizing medications, he sought help and advice from Dallas mental health professionals and those who advocate alternatives to traditional court procedures or jail.

"The very next morning after I asked for suggestions, they were knocking on my door," Judge Finn said. "They jumped at the chance."

With no established mental health screening process available to the court, Judge Finn started his own. Defendants applying for probation were asked whether they had a history of mental illness. Case files were checked for any mention of psychiatric treatment. In some cases, psychiatric evaluations were ordered.

By late spring, the judge was able to offer a mental health docket to handle the counseling and referrals needed to keep probationers on medication with little or no risk to the public. Groups such as the Special Needs Offender Program pitched in with extra help for probationers eligible for housing assistance and referrals to indigent mental health care programs.

"By the time they hit our courtroom, families and defendants alike were despondent over their plight," Judge Finn said. "Now, we still hold offenders accountable for their actions, but we can also give them a sense of hope that things can get better if they'll stick with their prescribed regimens."

The judge said "quite a few" have failed the program by going back to medicating themselves with illegal drugs or alcohol. Still, he estimates that more than 80 offenders have completed the program.

Mr. Muzyka was in the first graduating class late this summer. Since then, another program allied with Judge Finn's court helped him move into his own apartment. Mr. Muzyka is still looking for a job but praises the program for giving him "a chance to change for the better."

During a session three weeks ago, Judge Finn asked several members whether they were making progress. When one young man shrugged, Judge Finn asked, "Tell me, would you still be on medication if the threat of jail wasn't hanging over you?"

"No," the man said.

"Well, you're honest," the judge said. "I'll give you that."

Another man's story

To give courtroom counseling sessions a sense of reality, Cliff Gay volunteers twice a month to share his own 20-year nightmare of refusing to accept and deal with his mental illness.

"My first episode, I spent a night in a padded cell strapped in a straitjacket, dodging snakes coming out of the drain," he told a group recently. "I thought the CIA and the FBI were after me, and I was taking orders from God through the radio."

As heads nod, Mr. Gay talks about his misdiagnosis more than 30 years ago as a paranoid schizophrenic. After 11 confused, chaotic years, Mr. Gay said, he learned from doctors that he was actually bipolar. From 1969 to 1992 he underwent four psychiatric hospitalizations, including two involuntary ones.

"Three of those hospitalizations were the direct result of going off my medication, which is why I'm so sold on preaching a medication regimen," he says.

Mr. Gay's last episode was almost 10 years ago. Since then, he says, he's stayed on his medications, begun to rebuild his life, and helped other mentally ill patients.

One of his current students is a 25-year-old mother of two. The woman's anger and self-hatred reached a boiling point last spring when, during a fight with her husband, her mother-in-law tried to intervene and was shoved to the floor.

The woman had abandoned medication for her bipolar disorder almost two years earlier and said she had become accustomed to self-medicating with alcohol.

Progress, and setbacks

The prospect of jail time—and the possible loss of her two young daughters—kept her compliant with a strict medication routine for the first month of counseling, the woman said. When she found a job this summer, she said, her confidence grew.

By the sixth session of counseling, she said, she realized she was getting stronger and feeling better. Her organizational skills returned, and she remembered important dates, met work deadlines, and "wasn't the person who was always late to work anymore."

Last week, Judge Finn received word from a family member that she had swapped her bipolar medications for marijuana after her husband was jailed for an unrelated offense.

"She started to go downhill from there," Judge Finn said.

The judge said that after she spent Thanksgiving weekend in the Dallas County Jail, he "brought her out of the holding cell and read her the riot act." He added another six months' probation to her assault conviction, ordered frequent random drug testing, and put her on electronic monitoring with a strict curfew.

It will be her last chance to serve the remainder of her probated sentence on the outside, he said.

"It just shows what an ongoing struggle this can be for people with mental illness," Judge Finn said. "They're never really out of the woods when personal trauma or added stress can drive them off their medication and start self-medicating again."

"I feel like a normal human being again," says Steve Muzyka, who is taking medication for bipolar disorder. He credits a program started in misdemeanor domestic violence court with motivating him to maintain his regimen. Now that his disorder has been diagnosed, Steve Muzyka is grateful for "a chance to change for the better."

J. REENTRY COURT

One of the most recently emerging of the problem solving court models is reentry court. It is designed to assist offenders released from prison to a form of judicially-supervised parole to effect a successful integration into the community. This model often uses the approach and techniques of drug treatment court, and seems especially useful for offenders about to be discharged from prison who have substance abuse problems. But as the following description, contained in an article by Judge Terry Saunders, the presiding justice at the Harlem Reentry Court, shows, this model can assist ex-offenders to deal with a wider variety of problems that, if left unresolved, could significantly interfere with their successful reintegration into the community. A reentry court model could likely be of considerable help even to those sentenced to short terms, such as Nando, the subject of the article at the beginning of this Part.

Staying Home: Effective Reintegration Strategies for Parolees
by Judge Terry Saunders
(Winter 2002, Vol. 41, No. 1; pg. 34, Copyright 2002
by Judges' Journal, reprinted with permission).

Like many urban communities these days, Harlem is a neighborhood grappling with the challenges of how to reintegrate ex-offenders upon their return from prison. Many of these parolees have been in prison for years, and their transition back into the community is fraught with potential problems. For someone who has a criminal record and has spent years away from family, friends, and other supports, simply finding a home or getting a job can be nearly insurmountable challenges.

Of course, many parolees have additional challenges: drug addiction, lack of education, family conflicts. Dealing with these challenges can mean the difference between building a law-abiding and productive life in the community or returning to a life of crime and, eventually, to prison.

In recent years, the parole system has been confronted with onerous caseloads. In Harlem, we're trying new ways to meet these challenges head-on. We are experimenting with new supervisory techniques to monitor parolees and assist their successful reintegration into the community. We call this experiment in problem solving justice the Harlem Reentry Court, which began operation in June 2001.

The Reentry Court, housed in the heart of the community, rigorously monitors parolees to ensure that they're complying with all the requirements of their prison discharge plan and provides them with the services—drug treatment, job training, family counseling—they need to succeed. Being located where parolees live, receive services, and work makes us a valuable resource that they and their families can utilize conveniently. Unlike traditional parole supervision offices in centralized downtown locations, the neighborhood setting provides a forum for addressing reentry on multiple fronts—as a dynamic that involves the individual and profoundly affects families and communities.

The Reentry Court relies on the strengths of the surrounding Harlem neighborhood by linking parolees to community-based organizations and local service providers. To my knowledge, there are very few parole programs that make these kinds of connections for not only parolees but family members as well.

A New Approach

The Reentry Court has dramatically changed my job. As an administrative law judge in the traditional parole system, I found my contact with parolees was limited to revocation hearings in which I made decisions about parolees who failed to meet the conditions of their parole or were charged with new crimes. I would see a parolee maybe once or twice at court appearances, talk to him and his lawyer for maybe ten or fifteen minutes, and conduct the hearing. During those ten years, I developed an extensive and intimate relationship with the negative aspects of parole.

I often heard parolees say, "I didn't get help on the outside. I needed a drug program but the parole officer didn't find one for me or help me to get into one," or "My parole officer didn't help me with getting a job."

Now, as the presiding judge of the Reentry Court, I no longer hear these complaints. I find we are having a greater impact on parolees' lives—we know more about them and their community, and that puts us in a better position to respond to problems before they lead to serious parole violations or to revocation. At the Reentry Court, we address parolees' priorities from the start. If a parolee needs job training, we immediately link the person with an appropriate program in the community. If they need transitional housing, we help them find it right away.

Following the model of a problem solving court, we monitor compliance by making parolees return frequently to court for drug tests and appearances before the bench. Like other problem solving courts, we use sanctions and rewards to encourage compliance. Sanctions include more restrictive curfews, more frequent court appearances, and electronic monitors (to check compliance with curfews). For continued drug use, we can place parolees in more intensive day treatment or residential drug treatment.

But we are working with the community members, churches, and businesses to develop an expanded rewards system that has the potential to make parolees' integration as successful as possible. Rewards for adherence to parole rules currently are tied to relaxation of sanctions.

How It Works

We began working with our first parolee in June 2001 and are now working with more than twenty parolees. Within a year, we expect our full caseload to number ninety-six clients.

Each parolee must complete three three-month phases, which are tailored to fit each parolee's needs. For example, our first parolee struggled to regain custody of his three-year-old son after release. When the man was arrested, his girlfriend had been placed in residential drug treatment and their child into foster care. During his two and a half years in prison, the parolee's mother continued to visit the child on his behalf. Nevertheless, while he was in prison, family court revoked his parental rights because of his conviction. Since his release, we have worked with him to demonstrate to family court that he is taking steps toward being a responsible and dedicated father. He currently attends parenting classes and drug treatment and holds transitional employment. He is doing everything we have asked of him, and in time we expect that he will be able to demonstrate to the court that he is ready to resume parental responsibility.

And that is just one story—there are so many others. Although we still are in the pilot phase, we learn every day and constantly try to improve operations. For example, our experience thus far has shown that housing is one of the most significant obstacles to successful reintegration. Housing provides the stability within the community that parolees need, especially right after release. When we accepted our first homeless parolees, we were under the gun to find them a place to live. Fortunately, Project Return, a local drug treatment program and parole contractor, was able to provide us with transitional housing. With its help, we now can place parolees in transitional living quarters immediately.

Immediate Response

By responding quickly to parolees' needs, the court significantly reduces the risks associated with release. We know that the immediate post-release period is a critical time during which parolees are vulnerable to returning to old haunts and activities. The Reentry Court tries to make things proceed as quickly and smoothly as possible.

Initially, the parole board sends us a list of potential parolees expected to return to the East Harlem area. We review the list and select clients who satisfy the following criteria: nonviolent, residents of East Harlem, and arrested for drug-related crimes (sales and/or possession). Parolees with serious felonies or severe mental illness are not eligible to enter the program.

The Queensboro Correctional Facility, a transitional prison for returning parolees operated by the state corrections department, is their last stop prior to release. During the parolees' time in Queens, approximately forty-five days—our clinical director and parole officers conduct comprehensive assessment interviews with them and their families. We assess their histories, goals, and particular needs, as well as any particular difficulties they are likely to face. We educate the inmates and their families about the Harlem Reentry Court and what will be expected of them. The Center for Employment Opportunities and North General Hospital, two of our partner agencies, also conduct pre-release orientations. These meetings are our chance to establish a connection with parolees and place ourselves in a strategic position to provide specific support immediately upon release.

Parolees report to me the same day of release. During this first visit, I acquaint them with our program and explain its terms and conditions. The requirements include meeting with me on a regular basis, attending outpatient drug treatment, keeping appointments with service providers, maintaining a clean record with the police, reporting to work on time, and adhering to curfew regulations.

Our relationship with the parolees' family members is crucial. They are at the front line, helping us help the returning members stay crime-free, so it is important that the families understand the program's guidelines and expectations. Family members also are encouraged to come to the court for the first visit to meet the parole staff, the clinical director, and myself. Our services are available to everyone involved, whether they need links to services for themselves or help with negotiating the bureaucracy of government agencies. One of our parolees was arrested some months before his girlfriend delivered their baby, and was incarcerated for two years. He met his daughter for the first time at the court after his release.

Teamwork

Teamwork is one of the hallmarks of the problem solving approach. The court's requirements mean our team, which includes program-dedicated parole officers, the clinical director, and various service providers, must work together to track the progress and ensure the successful reintegration of each of our parolees. Many of us are not used to being team players, but we have come to realize that coordinated strategies do a lot to make our work successful.

In the traditional parole system, independence is critical to an administrative law judge, especially when violations and possible revocations are being considered. That independent judicial role does not work in the Reentry Court. Everyone's roles intersect, and we require support from one another. The parole officers, clinical director, and I have worked hard to juggle and refine our roles so they benefit the team context. For example, in my previous job as administrative law judge, my only interaction with parole officers came at revocation hearings—I had no opportunity or authority to make suggestions about supervision issues.

In the team context, however, we share insights and information to enhance our effectiveness. We meet once a week to review the cases that will come before me the following Thursday and to troubleshoot problems with other cases. We are able to reach a consensus on most of our decisions because we are all committed to the same goal: Improving public safety by giving parolees the support and structure they need to become law-abiding citizens.

As we develop partnerships with service providers and draw outside resources into our network, we maintain the same structure of teamwork and collaboration. The Center for Employment Opportunities provides vocational training, job placement, and support; North General Hospital provides drug treatment and health care to parolees. Both community partners attend our meetings as requested and are available for consultation on decisions about and general understanding of parolees' needs. A good portion of the success of our project is the result of structured, solid community partnerships that have developed over time.

Measuring Success—An Evolving Model

On a weekly basis, parolees' progress can be difficult to measure because they experience a fair amount of ups and downs following release from prison. We base our success on whether parolees do what they are supposed to do—stay off drugs, make appointments on time, and avoid rearrest. In order to qualify as having been successfully reintegrated when leaving the program, parolees must provide evidence of all those things, as well as a solid job and paycheck. In addition, they must maintain an established residence, either their own household or with family members.

Soon, the Harlem Reentry Court will add female parolees to the program. This will require a period of adjustment, with the women bringing new and demanding challenges, histories of domestic violence, prostitution, and child abuse, for example. We already have a good head start on these issues, in that one of our community partners, Project Green Hope, is a drug program that provides residential treatment where mothers can live with their young children.

Another key to our program's success is that we have a manageable caseload that enables us to monitor parolees and conduct the necessary follow-up. Although the initial cost of paying close attention to parolees is not insignificant, the long-term benefits to reentry intervention are obvious. Nearly 55 percent of parolees return to prison before completing their parole term. Our goal is that the reentry court model will substantially improve on this figure and, in the process, eliminate costs associated with incarceration and community disrepair. But, beyond that, we think our approach will help build a safer and stronger neighborhood.

There have been no rearrests among our twenty-five parolees since the Reentry Court's opening. It is still early, but I am encouraged by this evidence of what we can do when we work together.

K. PROBLEM-SOLVING COURTS GENERALLY

The foregoing selections demonstrate well the exciting developments that have been emerging in recent years in the way the courts deal with a variety of social problems. The following selection provides a good summary of these developments, takes stock of where we are, and raises important issues for future consideration.

Problem-Solving Courts: A Brief Primer

by Greg Berman and John Feinblatt
(*Originally published in* Law and Policy, Vol. 23, No. 2, Copyright 2001 by Blackwell Publishing, reprinted with permission).

Introduction

The past decade has been a fertile one for court reform. All across the country, courts—in concert with both government and community partners—have been experimenting with new ways to deliver justice. This wave of innovation goes by many names and takes many forms. Domestic violence court in Massachusetts. Drug court in Florida. Mental health court in Washington. Community court in New York. Each of these specialized courts targets different kinds of concerns in different kinds of places. And yet they all share a basic organizing theme—a desire to make courts more problem-solving and to improve the kinds of results that courts achieve for victims, litigants, defendants and communities. "Problem-solving courts" are still very much a work in progress. As yet, there is no clearly articulated definition or philosophy that unites all of those who espouse or practice problem-solving justice. Viewed in the aggregate, however, it is possible to identify several common elements that distinguish problem-solving courts from the way that cases are typically handled in today's state courts. Problem-solving courts use their authority to forge new responses to chronic social, human and legal problems—including problems like family dysfunction, addiction, delinquency and domestic violence—that have proven resistant to conventional solutions. They seek to broaden the focus of legal proceedings, from simply adjudicating past facts and legal issues to changing the future behavior of litigants and ensuring the well-being of communities. And they attempt to fix broken systems, making courts (and their partners) more accountable and responsive to their primary customers—the citizens who use courts every day, either as victims, jurors, witnesses, litigants or defendants.

The proliferation of problem-solving courts raises some important questions. Why now? What forces have sparked judges and attorneys across the country to innovate? What results have problem-solving courts achieved? And what—if any—trade-offs have been made to accomplish these results?

This essay is an attempt to begin to answer these questions. It traces the history of problem-solving courts, outlines a basic set of problem-solving principles and poses a set of questions that are worthy of further study as problem-solving courts move from experiment to institutionalization.

The Rise of Problem-Solving Courts

Although Professor William Nelson of New York University Law School has argued that the roots of problem-solving courts may stretch back to the 18th century, the more immediate antecedent of this recent wave of judicial experimentation is the opening of the first "drug court" in Dade County, Florida in 1989. In an effort to address the problem of drug-fueled criminal recidivism, the Dade County court sentences addicted defendants to long-term, judicially-supervised drug treatment instead of incarceration. Participation in treatment is closely monitored by the drug court judge, who responds to progress or failure with a system of graduated rewards and sanctions, including short-term jail sentences. If a participant successfully completes treatment, the judge will reduce the charges or dismiss the case.

The results of the Dade County experiment have attracted national attention—and for good reason. A study by the National Institute of Justice revealed that Dade County drug court defendants had fewer re-arrests than comparable non-drug court defendants. Based on these kinds of results, drug courts have become an increasingly standard feature of the judicial landscape across the country. At last count, there were 500 drug courts nationwide, including one in operation or being planned in every state. An additional 281 are in the planning stages. In addition, several states, including New York and California, have begun to look at how some of the principles of drug courts might be institutionalized throughout a state court system.

Much of this activity (though by no means all) has been aided by federal funding decisions. In enacting the 1994 Crime Act, Congress authorized the Attorney General to make grants to establish drug courts across the country. (The office charged with administering these grants, the U.S. Department of Justice's Drug Courts Program Office, distributed $50 million in fiscal year 2000.)

This wave of judicial innovation has not been confined to drugs. In the years since the opening of the Dade County drug court, dozens of other specialized, problem-solving courts have been developed to test new approaches to difficult cases and to improve both case outcomes for parties and systemic outcomes for the community at large. One example is the Midtown Community Court, which was launched in New York City in 1993. The Midtown Court targets misdemeanor "quality-of-life" crimes (prostitution, shoplifting, low-level drug possession, etc.) committed in and around Times Square. Low-level offenders are sentenced to perform community restitution—sweeping the streets, painting over graffiti, cleaning local parks—in an effort to "pay back" the community they have harmed through their criminal behavior. The Court also mandates offenders to receive on-site social services, including health care, drug treatment and job training, in an effort to address the underlying problems that often lead to crime. At the same time, the Court has tested a variety of new mechanisms for engaging the local community in the criminal justice process, including advisory boards, community mediation, victim-offender impact panels and townhall meetings.

In Midtown's wake have come eleven replications. An additional two dozen community courts are in the works. This replication has taken place in jurisdictions big and small, rich and poor. And it has been driven by a variety of different players, including judges, prosecutors, community advocates and business leaders. As community courts have proliferated, so too have community court models. The next generation of community court innovators has not been content to simply replicate the Midtown Community Court. Rather, they have sought to push the model in new directions. This includes Portland, Oregon, which has created community courts throughout the city, in many instances holding court sessions at local community centers. It also includes Memphis, Tennessee, which is targeting problems related to neglected and abandoned property. As with drug courts, the U.S. Department of Justice has played a key role in community court replication, providing seed money to a number of jurisdictions and providing technical assistance and advice to dozens of others.

Similar stories can be told about the birth and expansion of domestic violence courts, mental health courts and others: an initial innovation seeks to address a recurring problem within the courts, attracts the attention of the press, elected officials and funders, and is quickly followed by a wave of replications.

Why now?

What's going on here? Why are judges, attorneys and court administrators all over the country experimenting with new ways of doing business? A number of social and historical forces have helped set the stage for problem-solving innovation. These include:

- Breakdowns among the kinds of social and community institutions (including families and churches) that have traditionally addressed problems like addiction, mental illness, quality-of-life crime and domestic violence.
- The struggles of other government efforts, whether legislative or executive, to address these problems. This includes the difficulties that probation and parole departments have faced in linking offenders to services and effectively monitoring their compliance.
- A surge in the nation's incarcerated population and the resulting prison overcrowding, which has forced many policymakers to re-think their approach to crime.
- Trends emphasizing the accountability of public institutions, along with technological innovations that have facilitated the documentation and analysis of court outcomes.
- Advances in the quality and availability of therapeutic interventions, which have given many within the criminal justice system greater confidence in using certain forms of treatment (particularly drug treatment) in an effort to solve defendants' underlying problems.
- Shifts in public policies and priorities—for example, the way the "broken windows" theory has altered perceptions of the importance of low-level crime or the way that the feminist movement has increased awareness about domestic violence.

But perhaps the most important forces that have contributed to the development of problem-solving courts are rising caseloads and increasing frustration—both among the public and among system players—with the standard approach to case processing and case outcomes in state courts.

In recent years, many state court systems have been inundated with growing caseloads. And in the eyes of many judges, attorneys and court administrators, much of this growth has been driven by the intersection of social, human and legal problems, including domestic violence, addiction and chronic low-level offending. From 1984 to 1997, for example, the number of domestic violence cases in state courts increased by seventy-seven percent. National research also suggests that as many as three out of every four defendants in major cities test positive for drugs at the time of arrest. Many jurisdictions have also experienced an explosion in quality-of-life crime. In New York City, for example, over the past decade the number of misdemeanor cases has increased by eighty-five percent.

The sheer volume of cases has placed enormous pressure on judges and attorneys to process cases as quickly as possible, with little regard to the problems of victims, communities or defendants. This has led many—victims, police officers, journalists and even judges and attorneys—to conclude that many front-line state courts are practicing "revolving door" justice. As New York State Chief Judge Judith S. Kaye has written:

> In many of today's cases, the traditional approach yields unsatisfying results. The addict arrested for drug dealing is adjudicated, does time, then goes right back to dealing on the street. The battered wife obtains a protective order, goes home and is beaten again. Every legal right of the litigants is protected, all procedures followed, yet we aren't making a dent in the underlying problem. Not good for the parties involved. Not good for the community. Not good for the courts.

Chief Judge Kaye is hardly alone in her analysis; a sense of growing frustration with 'business as usual' in the state courts can be felt among the general public, among judges and among attorneys.

Public. Public frustration gets expressed in many ways, most notably in declining confidence in the criminal justice system (and those who work within it) and increasing fear of crime (even as crime rates across the country fall). Michael Schrunk, the district attorney in Portland, Oregon, has said that his endorsement of problem-solving courts grows out of a concern about the gaps between communities and the justice system. According to Schrunk, "It's all well and good for us to read about the Microsoft trial or the O.J. Simpson trial, but that's a very, very small percentage of what goes on in the world of our constituents. I strongly believe we've got to work on public credibility, because a lot of citizens, quite frankly, they don't think judges are relevant."

Judges. Many state court judges have reported that the pressure of processing hundreds of cases each day has transformed their courtrooms into "plea bargain mills," which place the highest value on disposing of the maximum number of cases in the minimum amount of time. Additionally, they bemoan their lack of tools—both information and sentencing options—for responding to the complexities of drug addiction, mental illness and domestic violence cases. Chief Justice Kathleen Blatz of Minnesota neatly summarized the feelings of many judges: "Judges are very frustrated.... The innovation that we're seeing now is a result of judges processing cases like a vegetable factory. Instead of cans of peas, you've got cases. You just move 'em, move 'em, move 'em. One of my colleagues on the bench said, 'You know, I feel like I work for McJustice: we sure aren't good for you, but we are fast.'"

Attorneys. In recent years, many attorneys have begun to take a closer look at the roles they play and the outcomes they achieve. In addition to problem-solving courts, this examination has led some to advocate for new forms of lawyering, including calls for "therapeutic jurisprudence," "public safety lawyering," "client-centered counseling" and others. What all of these new approaches share is an understanding that lawyers need to employ new sets of tools—in many cases outside of the traditional adversarial model—to effectively represent the interests of their clients. According to Patrick McGrath, deputy district attorney in San Diego, California, "I think it's fair to say there's a sense of yearning out there [among attorneys]. If you grab a judge, a defense attorney and prosecutor and sat them down together and bought them a round of drinks...they'll all complain about the same thing: 'I have all of this education and what do I do? I work on an assembly line. I don't affect case outcomes.'" While the yearning for a new way of thinking about advocacy is far from universal—there are still, after all, plenty of practitioners of win-at-all-costs advocacy—the voices of reform are now plentiful and strong enough that they can no longer be easily dismissed.

Both internal and external critics of state courts have cited a number of examples to underline their concerns with the standard approach to case processing. For instance, they have pointed to low-level criminal cases, where many offenders walk away from court without receiving any conditions at all. Researchers found that prior to the opening of the Midtown Community Court in New York, more than forty percent of the misdemeanor cases in the downtown, centralized court received no court sanctions at all (e.g. sentences of "time served"). This means that four out of every ten offenders walked out of court without receiving either a meaningful punishment or any kind of help for their underlying problems. Outcomes in domestic violence cases are equally problematic. High probation violation rates are one sign that court mandates are not deterring continued violence. One study showed that thirty-four percent of batterers violated orders of protection. Nor is the problem of recidivism confined to domestic violence—it is estimated that over fifty percent of offenders convicted of drug possession will recidivate within two or three years.

In short, advocates of problem-solving justice have argued that state courts find it difficult to address the underlying problems of individual litigants, the social problems of communities or the structural and operational problems of a fractured justice system. As Ellen Schall of New York University's Wagner Graduate School of Public Service has noted, "I think we have to begin from the notion that the system from which the problem-solving courts have emerged was a failure on any count. It wasn't a legal success. It wasn't a social success. It wasn't working."

What is a Problem-Solving Court?

Problem-solving courts are a response to the frustrations engendered by overwhelmed state courts that struggle to address the problems that are fueling their rising caseloads. They are an attempt to achieve better outcomes while at the same time protecting individual rights. While drug courts, community courts, domestic violence courts, mental health courts and other problem-solving initiatives address different problems, they do share some common elements:

Case Outcomes. Problem-solving courts seek to achieve tangible outcomes for victims, for offenders and for society. These include reductions in recidivism, reduced stays in foster care for children, increased sobriety for addicts and healthier communities. As Chief Judge Kaye has written, "...outcomes— not just process and precedents—matter. Protecting the rights of an addicted mother is important. So is protecting her children and getting her off drugs."

System Change. In addition to re-examining individual case outcomes, problem-solving courts also seek to re-engineer how government systems respond to problems like addiction, mental illness and child neglect. This means promoting reform outside of the courthouse as well as within. For example, family treatment courts that handle cases of child neglect have encouraged local child welfare agencies to adopt new staffing patterns and to improve case management practices.

Judicial Authority. Problem-solving courts rely upon the active use of judicial authority to solve problems and to change the behavior of litigants. Instead of passing off cases—to other judges, to probation departments, to community-based treatment programs—judges at problem-solving courts stay involved with each case throughout the post-adjudication process. Drug court judges, for example, closely supervise the performance of offenders in drug treatment, requiring them to return to court frequently for urine testing and courtroom progress reports.

Collaboration. Problem-solving courts employ a collaborative approach, relying on both government and non-profit partners (criminal justice agencies, social service providers, community groups and others) to help achieve their goals. For example, many domestic violence courts have developed partnerships with batterers' programs and probation departments to help improve the monitoring of defendants.

Non-Traditional Roles. Some problem-solving courts have altered the dynamics of the courtroom, including, at times, certain features of the adversarial process. For example at many drug courts, judges and attorneys (on both sides of the aisle) work together to craft systems of sanctions and rewards for offenders in drug treatment. And by using the institution's authority and prestige to coordinate the work of other agencies, problem-solving courts may engage judges in unfamiliar roles as conveners and brokers.

The cumulative impact of these changes has been significant, and not just on the judges and lawyers who staff problem-solving courts. Problem-solving courts are still relatively new, but there are signs that they have begun to have a tangible impact on thousands of victims, defendants and community residents. This includes domestic violence victims who have been linked to safe shelter, residents of high-crime areas who no longer have to avoid local parks at night, formerly-addicted mothers who have been reunited with their children, and mentally-ill defendants who have received meaningful treatment for the first time.

Results

How much is known about the results of problem-solving courts? Rigorous, independent evaluations of their impacts are just starting to emerge, but the early results have been promising. As the most well-established brand of problem-solving court, drug courts have the longest track record. The evidence shows that drug courts have achieved solid results with regard to keeping offenders in treatment, reducing drug use and recidivism and saving jail and prison costs.

The most authoritative review of drug courts is a meta-analysis by Columbia University's National Center on Addiction and Substance Abuse (CASA) that looked at fifty-nine independent evaluations covering forty-eight drug courts throughout the country. Among other findings, this study revealed that drug court participants are far more likely to successfully complete mandated substance abuse treatment than comparable participants who seek help on a voluntary basis. One year treatment retention rates are sixty percent for drug courts, compared to ten to thirty percent among voluntary programs. In addition, the CASA analysis found that defendant drug use and recidivism are substantially reduced during the period of drug court participation. While less conclusive, there is also evidence to suggest that the benefits of drug court participation don't end when a defendant graduates from the program. According to the CASA study, drug court participants have lower post-program re-arrest rates as well. Of nine drug court evaluations that used a comparison group, eight found positive recidivism results.

In addition to these impacts on participants, the CASA meta-analysis found that drug courts generated significant cost savings. In general, incarceration is far more costly than either residential or outpatient treatment. As a result, drug courts save money even after accounting for administrative costs. A study of the Multnomah County, Oregon drug court found that over a two year period, the court had achieved $2.5 million in criminal justice cost savings, based on 440 participants. Additional savings outside the criminal justice system—reductions in victimization, theft, public assistance and medical claims—were estimated to be an additional $10 million.

The most detailed evaluation of a community court is the National Center for State Courts' recently-published assessment of the Midtown Community Court. The National Center's team of researchers found that the Court had helped reduce low-level crime in the neighborhood: prostitution arrests dropped sixty-three percent and illegal vending dropped twenty-four percent. The compliance rates for community service at Midtown were the highest in New York City—an improvement of fifty percent. Supervised offenders performing community service contributed more than $175,000 worth of labor to the local community each year.

Just as important, preliminary findings from a telephone survey of 500 area residents suggest that the Midtown experiment had made an impression in the court of public opinion. Sixty-four percent of the respondents said that they were willing to pay additional taxes for a community court. And according to evaluators, these results have been achieved without sacrificing efficiency. In fact, by keeping defendants and police officers in the neighborhood instead of transporting them to the downtown courthouse, the Midtown Court cut the time between arrest and arraignment in 1994 by forty-five percent.

Less is known about the impacts of domestic violence courts, family treatment courts, mental health courts, re-entry courts and other newer forms of problem-solving justice. Their self-reported results are, perhaps predictably, encouraging — improved services for victims of domestic violence, reductions in probation violations, and increased numbers of defendants receiving needed services. Whether these findings will withstand the rigors of independent evaluators remains to be seen. The days ahead will see the completion of several important evaluations of problem-solving courts, including a national, multi-site review of domestic violence courts by the Urban Institute.

Tensions

The preliminary results of problem-solving courts have earned these projects high marks from many corners, including elected officials, press and funders. They have also fueled the field's rapid expansion. Good initial results do not insulate problem-solving courts from scrutiny, however. After all, the problem-solving reform efforts of the last several years have taken place within a branch of government that is understandably cautious about innovation. Core judicial values — certainty, reliability, impartiality and fairness — have been safeguarded over many generations largely through a reliance on tradition and precedent. As a result, efforts to introduce new ways of doing justice are always subjected to careful scrutiny.

Problem-solving courts are no exception to this rule, nor should they be. Critics have questioned both their results and their ability to preserve the individual rights of defendants. While the academic literature on problem-solving courts is still emerging, it seems clear that there are a number of areas of potential tension between this new brand of jurisprudence and standard practice in state courts:

Coercion. What procedures exist to ensure that a defendant's consent to participate in a problem-solving court is fairly and freely given? Are problem-solving courts any more coercive than the current practice of plea bargaining that resolves the large majority of criminal cases in this country?

Zealous Advocacy. Is advocacy in a problem-solving court more or less zealous than in a traditional court? Does problem-solving demand new definitions of effective lawyering? How should attorneys measure their effectiveness — by the case or by the person? To what extent do problem-solving courts actually help attorneys—both prosecutors and defenders—realize their professional goals?

Structure. Do problem-solving courts give greater license to judges to make rulings based on their own idiosyncratic world views rather than the law? Or, with their predetermined schemes of graduated sanctions and rewards, do problem-solving courts actually limit the discretion of judges and provide more uniform justice than traditional courts?

Impartiality. As judges become better informed about specialized classes of cases, is their impartiality affected? As they solicit the wisdom of social scientists, researchers and clinicians, are they more likely to become engaged in ex parte communication?

Paternalism. Are problem-solving judges imposing treatment regimes on defendants without reference to the complexity of individuals' problems? Do problem-solving courts widen the net of governmental control? Or are they simply an effort by judges and attorneys to deal more constructively and humanely with the underlying problems of the people who come to court?

Separation of Powers. Do problem-solving courts inappropriately blur the lines between the branches of government? As judges become involved in activities like convening, brokering and organizing, are they infringing upon the territory of the executive branch? Are they, in effect, making policy? Or are judges simply taking advantage of the discretion they have traditionally been afforded over sentencing to craft more meaningful sanctions?

There are several important realities to keep in mind as one attempts to make sense of these tensions. The first is context. When weighing the merits of any reform effort, it's always important to ask the question: compared to what? Proponents of problem-solving courts have been adamant about not allowing critics to pick apart these new initiatives by comparing them to an idealized vision of justice that does not exist in real life. They point to the fact that the large majority of criminal, housing and family court cases today are handled in courts that Roscoe Pound and John Marshall would scarcely recognize. Judge Judy Harris Kluger, the administrative judge for New York City's criminal courts, has described standard practice in the state courts this way: "For a long time, my claim to fame was that I arraigned two hundred cases in one session. That's ridiculous. When I was arraigning cases, I'd be handed the papers, say the sentence is going to be five days, ten days, whatever, never even looking at the defendant." Under these circumstances, it is fair to question the extent to which many frontline state courts measure up to their own ideals of doing justice. While the excesses of today's "McJustice" courts do not justify any and all reform efforts, they do help explain why so many judges and attorneys have been attracted to new ways of doing business. And they do provide a valuable context for evaluating the merits of problem-solving courts.

In addition, any effort to separate the wheat from the chaff with problem-solving courts must take into account what might be called the "shoddy practice effect." Put simply, some of the concerns raised by critics of problem-solving courts are a response to the failings of individual judges, attorneys and courtrooms rather than an indictment of anything intrinsic to problem-solving courts. These issues include courts that have been created without any consultation with the local defense bar; courts that have failed to offer specialized training to the attorneys that work within them; courts in which defendants are not given a meaningful opportunity to raise factual and Fourth Amendment defenses; courts in which 'back-up' incarceration sentences for defendants who fail to comply are considerably longer than the sanctions that the defendant would have originally faced; and courts that have done little to ensure that social service interventions are effective and culturally appropriate.

While serious, these are all issues that might reasonably be resolved by better planning and the development and dissemination of best practices. In fact, there are already signs that problem-solving innovators in the field are beginning to adapt their models to address these issues. For example, problem-solving courts in Seattle and Portland have instituted structures that give defendants several weeks to test out treatment while their case is still pending. Defendants can use this period to decide whether to opt into or out of the program, while their defense attorneys can use the time to investigate the strength of the case against their client.

Fairness

Not all questions about problem-solving courts can be explained away by bad practice or the widespread problems of today's mill courts, however. The most pointed critiques have asked whether problem-solving courts' emphasis on improving case outcomes and protecting public order has come at the expense of the rights of defendants. Are problem-solving courts fair? Have they fundamentally altered the rights protections typically found in today's criminal courts? Courts have traditionally relied on zealous advocacy as a bulwark against these kinds of concerns, so the role of attorneys at problem-solving courts is an issue that merits special scrutiny.

Michael Smith of the University of Wisconsin Law School has been particularly vocal in articulating the importance of advocates to problem-solving courts: "One of the things that judges and courts are particularly useful at when they're not just milling people is fact-finding. But a fact-finding court is heavily reliant on advocates if its any good.... If we don't figure out a way to take advantage of that, then we're not going to have very good problem-solving courts. The courts will be no better than the social service clinics, which have failed to address these problems. So the adversary system and the presence of defense counsel are of enormous value in problem-solving."

The nature of advocacy in problem-solving courts is the subject of some debate. Some look at the "team approach" of drug courts, where all of the courtroom players work together to support defendant's participation in treatment, and declare that defense attorneys have abdicated their role as forceful advocates on behalf of their clients. Others argue that adversarialism is alive and well in problem-solving courts. They point to the fact that throughout the adjudication process—up until a defendant decides, by virtue of pleading to reduced charges, to enter treatment—prosecutors and defenders in problem-solving courts typically relate to one another as they always have: as adversaries. In addition to contesting the merits of each case, advocates in drug courts also argue about eligibility criteria, the length of treatment sentences and appropriate treatment modalities.

In general, what's different about problem-solving courts are the activities that take place after adjudication, as judges and attorneys become engaged in the ongoing monitoring of defendants instead of leaving this job to probation departments or community-based organizations (or, in all too many cases, to no one at all). (It is worth noting that some drug courts and community courts—and many domestic violence courts—depart from the standard problem-solving model, mandating defendants to pre-trial rather than post-disposition interventions. These courts may raise additional questions from those concerned with due process protections.) As John Goldkamp of Temple University has observed, "Generally, adversarial procedures are employed at the screening and admission stage and at the conclusion of drug court, when participants are terminated and face legal consequences or graduate. During the drug court process, however, formal adversarial rules generally do not apply." As Goldkamp's formulation makes plain, by and large, problem-solving courts seem to emphasize traditional due process protections during the adjudication phase of a case and the achievement of tangible, constructive outcomes post-adjudication. In doing so, problem-solving courts have sought to balance fairness and effectiveness, the protection of individual rights and the preservation of public order.

To what extent have problem-solving courts achieved this delicate balancing act? It varies from jurisdiction to jurisdiction. And it depends upon the perspective of the person asking the question. Conversations about the fairness of problem-solving courts often spark a Rashomon effect, with judges having one response, prosecutors another and defenders yet a third.

There is little doubt that the tensions between problem-solving courts and conventional state courts are felt particularly acutely by defenders. There is an almost palpable sense of ambivalence on the part of many defenders towards problem-solving courts. After all, defense attorneys have been arguing for years that courts should make more aggressive use of drug treatment, mental health counseling and other alternative sanctions. Problem-solving courts have begun to deliver on this expectation, but at the cost of greater state involvement in the lives of their clients. Are there any historical antecedents that might guide defenders as they wrestle with competing professional demands? What are their ethical obligations to their clients, given the changing judicial landscape? Is there a need for new standards of effective lawyering at problem-solving courts? These are issues that merit deeper investigation and additional scholarship.

Conclusion

Now is an important moment to begin to look at the questions raised by problem-solving courts. Problem-solving courts have achieved a kind of critical mass. They are no longer just a set of isolated experiments driven by entrepreneurial judges and administrators. According to John Goldkamp, "What we have now is not a bunch of little hobbies that judges have in isolated jurisdictions, but rather a paradigm shift that larger court systems are trying to come to grips with. They're at your doorstep. The question isn't: Gosh, are courts supposed to be doing this? It's: What are you going to do about it? How does it fit in? It's no longer a question of whether this should have been invented. They're here."

Problem-solving courts have begun to spark the interest of not just front-line practitioners, but the chief judges and administrators who make decisions about court policies and court operations. The signs are unmistakable. Problem-solving courts continue to multiply. California and New York are overhauling the way that their courts handle drug cases. And the Conference of Chief Justices and the Conference of State Court Administrators has passed a joint resolution that pledges to "encourage the broad integration, over the next decade, of the principles and methods employed in problem solving courts into the administration of justice."

Formal institutionalization of any new idea does not come easy, however. If problem-solving courts are to accomplish this goal—if they truly hope to infiltrate the mainstream of thinking about law and justice in this country—they must begin to preach to the unconverted. This means reaching out to the skeptics and the uninitiated within state courts—defenders concerned about due process protections, administrators worried about the allocation of limited resources, and prosecutors and judges who see nothing wrong with the way they've been doing their jobs for years. And it means reaching outside of the system as well—to law schools and bar associations and elected officials. In the process, advocates of problem-solving courts must tackle some of the policy and procedural concerns that have been outlined in this paper. And they must begin to think through the problems of going to scale, of how small-scale experiments can be translated into system-wide reform.

These are not insignificant challenges, to be sure. But given the tangible results that the first generation of problem-solving courts have achieved— reduced recidivism among drug-addicted offenders, reduced probation violation and dismissal rates in domestic violence cases, and improved public safety (and confidence in justice) in communities harmed by crime — they are challenges well worth pursuing.

———————

L. Therapeutic Jurisprudence in Courts of General Jurisdiction

The notion that judges function as therapeutic agents is not limited to the specialized courts thus far considered, but extends as well to judges functioning in courts of general jurisdiction. The new problem solving courts have served to raise the consciousness of many judges concerning their therapeutic role, and many former problem solving court judges, upon being transferred back to courts of general jurisdiction, have taken with them the tools and sensitivities they have acquired in those newer courts. Indeed, the proliferation of different problem solving courts, and the development of various "hybrid" models, suggests to us that the problem solving court movement may actually be a transitional stage in the creation of an overall judicial system attuned to problem solving, to therapeutic jurisprudence, and to judging with an ethic of care. The following selection is an essay by Judge William Schma, himself a former drug treatment court judge in Michigan who has resumed more general judicial duties. Judge Schma reflects upon his role as a drug treatment court judge and the lessons of that experience that he thinks apply to all judging.

Judging for the New Millennium
by Judge William G. Schma
(From *Judging for the New Millennium*, 37 CT. REV. 4
(Spring, 2000), Copyright 2000 by American Judges
Association, reprinted with permission).

Quickly complete this sentence: "The role of the law in society is _____." If you thought "to heal," close this journal and go to your next. You won't find much here you haven't thought about. Everyone else, read on to explore an emerging role for courts and judges in this new millennium.

The topic of this special issue of *Court Review* is "Therapeutic Jurisprudence," or "TJ" as it is commonly known. No single definition of TJ captures it fully.

One author offers the following definition as best capturing the essence of TJ: "the use of social science to study the extent to which a legal rule or practice promotes the psychological and physical well-being of the people it af-

87

fects." It is the study of the role of law as a healing agent, and it offers fresh insights into the role of law in society and those who practice it.

TJ can be thought of as a "lens" through which to view regulations and laws as well as the roles and behavior of legal actors—legislators, lawyers, judges, administrators. It may be used to identify the potential effects of proposed legal arrangements on therapeutic outcomes. It is useful to inform and shape policies and procedures in the law and the legal process. TJ posits that, when appropriate, the law apply an "ethic of care" to those affected.

TJ does not "trump" other considerations or override important societal values such as due process or the freedoms of speech and press. It suggests, rather, that mental and physical health aspects of law should be examined to inform us of potential success in achieving proposed goals. It proposes to consider possible negative psychological effects that a proposal may cause unwittingly. TJ doesn't necessarily dominate, but rather informs and in so doing provides insight and effective results. Such considerations enter into the mix to balance when considering a law, or a legal decision, or course of legal action.

It is important for judges to practice TJ because—like it or not—the law does have therapeutic and anti-therapeutic consequences. This is empirical fact. Consider the following situations; they are familiar to judges.

In busy dockets, it is common for judges to accept "no contest" or *nolo contendere* pleas in sex offense cases in lieu of a guilty plea. TJ will not dictate whether a judge should do this or not. It will, rather, ask the judge to consider the therapeutic effects that may follow as a consequence of such a plea. They may be considerable, because in the case of sex offenders a *nolo* plea may reinforce a process of denial that will frustrate the offender's rehabilitation. If the offender does not have to admit the crime to the judge, he or she may more easily deny it later to a probation officer or sex abuse counselor. Anti-therapeutic consequences such as frustration of rehabilitation and return to abusive behavior may result from the judge's acceptance of the plea. Ironically, this process would be started by the judge—the very person society most expects to promote the rule of law.

The same may be said of criminal cases involving an addiction to alcohol or other drugs. The biggest hurdle that an addict or alcoholic usually must overcome is denial. It is difficult to admit affliction with an uncontrollable disease, especially one to which our society has attached moral overtones. Nevertheless, those experienced with recovery know that this admission is critical. If, for whatever reason, a judge accepts a *nolo* plea in such a case and does not require the defendant to confront his or her addiction openly, the judge misses a critical "therapeutic moment." Moreover, as in the case with sex offenders, the judge may have set in motion a course of denial that will virtually guarantee the failure of subsequent rehabilitation efforts and the eventual return of the offender to the system.

Apology in tort law

med mal

Consider this final example: the role of apology in tort law. Practitioners familiar with medical malpractice cases know that many plaintiffs only want an apology from their health care provider for the adverse outcome they experienced. A lawsuit is the furthest action on their mind. And for negligent care providers, an apology for a regrettable mistake would be a therapeutic event. Unfortunately, some professional insurance practices prohibit an insured from having any contact with a patient who may file a claim. There is a good reason for this from the standpoint of the insured and the insurer: a non-privileged admission could end up in court as a *coup de grace*. The anti-therapeutic result, however, can be that the patient is deprived of what the patient may want most, and the health care provider cannot take necessary steps to cleanse his or her mind and return to productive work. Moreover, because the provider is forced by the law into a position of denial, the likelihood of reoccurrence increases.

TJ first identifies these anti-therapeutic elements that might otherwise go unexplored. Next, it asks whether an action could be taken to avoid them without "trumping" the established legal principles involved. It proposes such action and methods to evaluate it. TJ is, therefore, not merely a speculative exercise, but rather action-oriented. It seeks tangible results.

Permit me to describe some personal experience I have had in each of these areas to demonstrate how TJ applies. For more than five years I have refused to routinely accept *nolo* pleas in felony sexual abuse cases. Once my practice became known among local lawyers, no defendant has refused to go forward with a guilty plea. The attorneys prepare their clients for this in advance if they are in my court. (This suggests, of course, the significant role lawyers play to prepare clients for therapeutic or antitherapeutic court experiences, but that is a separate topic I leave for another day.) Moreover, since then I have never had a sexual abuser appear at sentence and deny to me that he or she committed the crime. Nor have I received a single letter from a family member denying that the defendant was capable of such an act. These were routine when I accepted *nolo* pleas. As a result, at sentencing, I can confront defendants much more effectively with the reality of their behavior and the wrongfulness of their conduct. This result is also more therapeutic for victims of such crimes.

Doesn't routinely accept nolo pleas

Beginning in 1992, I presided over a drug treatment court in my community. A drug court diverts certain non-violent, substance-abusing criminal defendants from the traditional adversarial criminal justice system into treatment and rehabilitation. Since then, more than 800 adult felony offenders addicted to alcohol or other drugs have been enrolled in this program. Fifty-five percent of women and 64% of men remain engaged in their recovery while they are in the program. The recidivism rate of participants is less than 15%. For graduates, it is less than 2%. This drug court and more than 400 others across the country apply TJ principles to criminal justice.

[margin note: "in good faith" conferences]

Recently in my court, I have experimented in medical malpractice cases with what I call "good faith conferences." As part of the settlement of two cases, one involving a death, a meeting was held between the interested parties, including the plaintiff or the family of the deceased and the physician-defendant. Attorneys were present at both conferences. One was held in my presence; the other occurred in the office of a neutral, experienced personal injury attorney. All participants agreed that anything said could not be used for any purpose. During these conferences, each side was permitted to speak about the feelings they had experienced because of the perceived malpractice and the lawsuit. The physicians explained why they had done what they had believed to have been medically appropriate in the circumstance, yet apologized to the family or plaintiff. Patients and their families expressed frustration and anger over everything from the physician's attitude to the care administered. The results have been mixed. However, the attorneys involved—all experienced in medical malpractice—and I agree that this method of dispute resolution meets significant litigant needs and is worth further refinement. But for the Therapeutic Jurisprudence movement, this project may never have occurred.

[margin note: Lincoln "be a peace-maker"]

These are not radical concepts; they are mainstream. They do give a fresh perspective on honored principles of the legal profession. Abraham Lincoln advised lawyers (and presumably judges): "Discourage litigation. Persuade your neighbor to compromise wherever you can....As a peace-maker, the lawyer has a superior opportunity of being a good man." Roscoe Pound spoke of sociological jurisprudence," arguing that law must look to the relationship between itself and the social effects it creates. Oliver Wendell Holmes said "the life of the law has not been logic: it has been experience," and he noted that the practical necessities of the times have always shaped the rules of law and the legal practices of a given age.

At a presentation to the annual meeting of the National Association for Court Management in 1996, the need to become "more therapeutic" in outcome was described as one of the top ten issues facing the courts in the future. In 1996, in a cover story in the American Bar Association Journal entitled, "The Lawyer Turns Peacemaker," the author noted public dissatisfaction with the justice system and argued for the need to apply a more therapeutic approach to litigation so that the parties' feelings of anger, resentment, or rejection could give way to a healing process.

[margin note: problem solving]

Recently, David Rottman and Pamela Casey, staff members of the National Center for State Courts and frequent authors on this topic, observed that courts are moving towards a "problem-solving" orientation to their responsibilities and forming problem-solving partnerships to address more effectively the complex social problems that have come to dominate their dockets in recent years. The Commission on Trial Court Performance Standards also raised the level of court consciousness on these matters through its Trial Court Performance Standards. Standard 3.5 is: "The trial court takes appropriate responsibility for the enforcement of its orders. No court should be unaware of or unresponsive to realities that cause its orders to be ignored." And Standard 4.5 states:

The trial court anticipates new conditions and emergent events and adjusts its operations as necessary. Effective trial courts are responsive to emergent public issues such as drug abuse, child and spousal abuse, AIDS, drunken driving, child support enforcement, crime and public safety, consumer rights, gender bias, and the more efficient use of fewer resources. A trial court that moves deliberately in response to emergent issues is a stabilizing force in society and acts consistently with its role of maintaining the rule of law.

There is already significant judicial leadership in this movement. Judith S. Kaye, Chief Judge of New York, wrote recently about the emergence of what she called "hands-on courts." She made these useful observations:

In these new courts, judges are active participants in a problem-solving process.... What's so different about this approach? First is the court's belief that we can and should play a role in trying to solve the problems that are fueling our caseloads. Second is the belief that outcomes—not just process and precedents—matter.

In a speech at the Holocaust Museum in 1997, Justice Richard J. Goldstone of the Constitutional Court in South Africa described this same role this way: "One thinks of justice in the context of deterrents, of retribution. But too infrequently is justice looked at as a form of healing." That healing role is at the heart of TJ, as noted by Michael D. Zimmerman, a member of the Utah Supreme Court and its former chief justice. He called for "involved judging" in which "judges and courts assume a stronger administrative, protective, or rehabilitative role toward those appearing before them, that they become more involved in what some have termed 'therapeutic jurisprudence.'" He recognized that this was a "new cultural reality" for most judges. Yet he pointed out that it will not go away, and, unless we craft our own response, it will be thrust upon us by society.

TJ acknowledges that the healing roots of the legal profession can be in tension with our highly developed adversarial system and with our emphasis on process. As David Wexler, cofounder with Bruce Winick of the school of TJ, has pointed out, the adversarial nature of our system has legitimate and crucial value for critical thinking. However, the legal system suffers from a *culture* of adversarial representation and relationships, in which argument rises to the level of a privileged status. This can obscure many important societal values that the legal system need not and should not ignore, such as outcome, social harmony, and the ethic of care. TJ is receiving attention precisely because it requires that we recognize such values, balance them with others, and make choices. Practitioners are discovering that TJ strikes a resonant chord in the legal system and community for beneficial and sensible outcomes of problems that come to light in legal trappings.

Judges must take the lead and assume appropriate responsibility for these issues. If we do not, as Justice Zimmerman observed, they may be resolved without us. More important, we will have failed in our responsibility as leaders. We will reap the resulting public disaffection with us and the system we supervise. We'll deserve it.

As Judge Schma's article demonstrates, a therapeutic jurisprudence and problem solving approach is by no means confined to specialized problem solving courts. All judges so inclined can introduce therapeutic jurisprudence and an ethic of care into their day to day work. In fact, Hawaii Judge Michael Town, who has been an international leader in this area, is of the view that problem solving courts have developed as a reflection of deep dissatisfaction with the judicial system as a whole and of the harmful—or "jurigenic"—effects of the ordinary judicial system. *See* Michael A. Town, *Court As Convener And Provider of Therapeutic Justice*, 67 Revista Juridica U.P.R 671 (1998). Judge Town thus sees the problem solving court movement, as we do, as transitional, hopefully a stepping stone to broad-based reform in the judicial profession as a whole.

And just as Judge Schma has returned to the "general bench" with a general therapeutic jurisprudence approach, Judge Town has brought such principles into play in work with felony trials in Honolulu.

Similarly, sensitive and creative judges can apply basic principles of therapeutic jurisprudence even in remote geographical areas and in jurisdictions with rather meager resources. For example, interested and innovative magistrates in the bush of Western Australia dealing with a large aboriginal community—and who are interested in the Therapeutic Jurisprudence approach to judging—have instituted important programs and are writing about their experiences. *See* Michael S. King, *Geraldton Alternative Sentencing Regime: Applying Therapeutic and Holistic Jurisprudence in the Bush*, 26 Crim. L. J. 260 (2002); Michael S. King & Stephen Wilson, *Magistrates as Innovators*, Brief (December, 2002). They have instituted creative sentencing schemes, and have incorporated aboriginal dispute resolution elements into their day-to-day work as magistrates.

The international cross-fertilization beginning to take place is an important and welcome development, and we hope this book will contribute to the enterprise.

Part I References

(The References below in bold type face appear either in entire text or excerpted form in Part II of the book)

Therapeutic Jurisprudence and the Courts Generally

Freiberg, Arie, *Problem-oriented Courts: Innovative Solutions to Intractable Problems?*, 11 J. Jud. Admin. 8 (2001).

King, Michael S., *Geraldton Alternative Sentencing Regime: Applying Therapeutic and Holistic Jurisprudence in the Bush*, 26 Crim. L. J. 260 (2002).

King, Michael S. & Wilson, Stephen, *Magistrates as Innovators*, 29 Brief 7 (2002) (published by The Law Society of Western Australia).

Symposium, *Problem-Solving Courts*, 29 Fordham Urb. L. J. 1755–2131 (2002).

Symposium, *Problem-Solving Courts*, 30 Fordham Urb. L. J. __ (Forthcoming, 2002).

Symposium, *Special Issue on Therapeutic* Jurisprudence, 37 Ct. Rev 1–68 (Spring, 2000).

Schma, William G., *Judging in the New Millennium*, 37 Ct. Rev. 4 (Spring, 2000).

Town, Michael A., *Court as Convener and Provider of Therapeutic Justice*, 67 Rev. Jur. U.P.R. 671 (1998).

Website for the International Network on Therapeutic Jurisprudence, at http://www.therapeuticjurisprudence.org.

Wexler, David B., *Robes and Rehabilitation: How Judges Can Help Offenders Make Good*, 38 Ct. Rev. 18 (Spring, 2001).

Winick, Bruce J., *Therapeutic Jurisprudence and Problem Solving Courts*, 30 Fordham Urb. L. J. __ (Forthcoming, 2002).

Drug Treatment Court

BELENKO, STEVEN, NEW YORK NATIONAL CENTER ON ADDICTION AND SUB-
STANCE ABUSE AT COLUMBIA UNIVERSITY, RESEARCH ON DRUG COURTS:
A CRITICAL REVIEW (2001).

Clark, Michael B., *Change Focused Drug Court: Examining the Critical Ingredients of Positive Behavior Change*, 3 NAT'L DRUG CT. INST. REV. 35
(Winter, 2001).

Donnellan, Eithne, Home News: New Drugs Court is Aiming to Rehabilitate — Minister says New Method of Dealing With Addicts May be Extended (Ireland), IRISH TIMES (Jan. 10, 2001).

Dorf, Michael C. & Sabel, Charles F., *Drug Treatment Courts and Emergent
Experimentalist Government*, 53 VAND. L. REV. 831 (2000).

Goldkamp, John S., *The Origin of the Treatment Drug Court in Miami*, in
THE EARLY DRUG COURTS: CASE STUDIES IN JUDICIAL INNOVATION, 19
(W. Clinton Terry, III ed., 1999).

Hoffman, Morris B., *The Drug Court Scandal*, 78 N. C. L. REV. 1437 (2000).

Hoffman, Morris B., *Therapeutic Jurisprudence, Neo-Rehabilitationism, and
Judicial Collectivism: The Least Dangerous Branch Becomes the Most Dangerous*, 29 FORDHAM URB. L. J. 2063 (2002).

Hora, Peggy F., *A Dozen Years of Drug Treatment Courts: Uncovering Our
Theoretical Foundation and the Construction of a Mainstream Paradigm*, 37
U. DEL. J. DRUG USE & MISUSE 1469 (2002).

Hora, Peggy F., Schma, William G. & Rosenthal, John T. A., *Therapeutic Jurisprudence and the Drug Treatment Court Movement: Revolutionizing
the Criminal Justice System's Response to Drug Abuse and Crime in America*, 74 NOTRE DAME L. REV. 439 (1999).

Martin, Yvonne, *Christchurch to Trial Drug Court for Teens (New Zealand)*,
THE CHRISTCHURCH PRESS (Jan. 10, 2002).

McKain, Bruce, Suitable Case for Treatment: Scotland's First Drug Court
Aims to Break the Cycle of Addiction and Crime (Glasgow, Scotland),
THE HERALD (Nov. 1, 2001).

NOLAN, JAMES L. JR., REINVENTING JUSTICE: THE AMERICAN DRUG COURT
MOVEMENT (2001).

Quinn, Mae C., *Whose Team Am I on Anyway? Musings of a Public Defender
About Drug Treatment Court Practice*, 26 N.Y.U. REV. L. & SOC. CHANGE 37
(2000–2001).

Reisig, Martin, *The Difficult Role of the Defense Lawyer in a Post-adjudication
Drug Treatment Court: Accommodating Therapeutic Jurisprudence and Due
Process*, 38 CRIM. L. BULL. 216 (2002).

Simmons, Pamela L., *Solving the Nation's Drug Problem: Drug Courts Signal a
Move Toward Therapeutic Jurisprudence*, 35 GONZ. L. REV. 237 (1999–2000).

Staples, John, Glasgow Launches Six-Month Pilot of American-Style Drug Courts (Scotland), THE SCOTSMAN (Nov. 9, 2001).
The Guardian (England), THE GUARDIAN (June 5, 2002).
Web site of the Australian Institute of Criminology, at http://www.aic.gov.au/research/drugs/context/courts.html (collecting information on Australia)
Web site for "Aboriginal Court Days" in South Australia, at http://www.courts.sa.gov.au/courts/drug_court/index.html.
Winick, Bruce J. & Wexler, David B., *Therapeutic Jurisprudence and Drug Treatment Courts: A Symbiotic Relationship*, in PRINCIPLES OF ADDICTION MEDICINE (Allan W. Graham, Terry K. Schultz, M. Mayo-Smith & B.B. Wilford eds. 3d ed., forthcoming, 2003).
Winick, Bruce J. & Wexler, David B., *Therapeutic Jurisprudence and Drug Courts: Therapeutic Jurisprudence Applied*, 18 TOURO L. REV. 479 (Spring, 2002).

Juvenile Court

Gilbert, Janet, Grimm, Richard & Parnham, John, *Applying Therapeutic Principles to a Family-Focused Juvenile Justice Model (Delinquency)*, 52 ALA. L. REV. 1153 (Summer, 2001).
Wexler, David B., *Just Some Juvenile Thinking About Delinquent Behavior: A Therapeutic Jurisprudence Approach to Relapse Prevention Planning and Youth Advisory Juries*, 69 UMKC L. REV. 93 (2000).

Juvenile Dependency Drug Court

Brown, Amy K., *Drug Courts Help Keep Families Together*, 28 FLA. B. NEWS 1 (Sept. 15, 2001).

Restorative Justice

BAZEMORE, GORDON & SCHIFF, MARA, EDS., RESTORATIVE COMMUNITY JUSTICE: REPAIRING HARM AND TRANSFORMING COMMUNITIES (2001).
Bazemore, Gordon & Umbreit, Mark, OFFICE OF JUVENILE JUSTICE AND DELINQUENCY PREVENTION, CONFERENCES, CIRCLES, BOARDS, AND MEDIATIONS: RESTORATIVE JUSTICE AND CITIZEN INVOLVEMENT IN THE RESPONSE TO YOUTH CRIME (1999).
BRAITHWAITE, JOHN, CRIME, SHAME AND REINTEGRATION (1989).

Braithwaite, John, *Restorative Justice and Therapeutic Jurisprudence*, 38 CRIM. L. BULL. 244 (2002).

Braithwaite, John, *Setting Standards for Restorative Justice*, __ BRITISH J. CRIM. __ (Forthcoming).

Johnny, Ronald Eagleye, *The Duckwater Shoshone Drug Court 1997–2000: Melding Traditional Dispute Resolution With Due Process*, 26 AM. INDIAN L. REV. 261 (2001).

Scheff, Thomas J., *Community Conferences: Shame and Anger in Therapeutic Jurisprudence*, 67 REV. JUR. U.P.R. 97 (1999).

Scheff, Thomas J., *Response to Comments*, 67 REV. JUR. U.P.R. 677 (1998).

STRANG, H. & BRAITHWAITE, JOHN EDS., RESTORATIVE JUSTICE AND CIVIL SOCIETY (2001).

VAN NESS, DANIEL W. & STRONG, KAREN HEETDERKS, RESTORING JUSTICE (2002).

Walgrave, Lode, ed., RESTORATIVE JUSTICE FOR JUVENILES: POTENTIALITIES, RISKS AND PROBLEMS FOR RESEARCH (1998).

Zion, James W. Jr., *Navajo Therapeutic Jurisprudence*, 18 TOURO L. REV. 563 (Spring, 2002).

Teen Court or Youth Court

Butts, Jeffery A. & Buck, Janeen, *The Sudden Popularity of Teen Courts*, 14 JUDGES J. 29 (Winter, 2002).

Shiff, Allison R. & Wexler, David B., *Teen Court: A Therapeutic Jurisprudence Perspective, in* LAW IN A THERAPEUTIC KEY: DEVELOPMENTS IN THERAPEUTIC JURISPRUDENCE 287 (David B. Wexler & Bruce J. Winick eds. 1996).

Weisz, Victoria & Lott, Roger C., *A Teen Court Evaluation with a Therapuetic Jurisprudence Perspective*, 20 BEHAV. SCI & L. 381 (2002).

Wexler, David B., *Just Some Juvenile Thinking About Delinquent Behavior: A Therapeutic Jurisprudence Approach to Relapse Prevention Planning and Youth Advisory Juries*, 69 UMKC L. REV. 93 (2000).

Domestic Violence Court

Fritzler, Randal B. & Simon, Leonore M.J., *Creating a Domestic Violence Court: Combat in the Trenches*, 37 CT. REV. 28 (Spring, 2000).

Fritzler, Randal B. & Simon, Leonore M.J., *The Development of a Specialized Domestic Violence Court in Vancouver, Washington Utilizing Innovative Judicial Paradigms.* 69 UMKC L. REV. 139 (2000).

Karan, Amy, Keilitz, Susan, & Denaro, Sharon, *Domestic Violence Courts: What are They and How Should We Manage Them?*, 50 Juv. & Fam. Ct. J. 75 (Spring, 1999).

Paradine, Kate, *The Importance of Understanding Love and Other Feelings in Survivors' Experiences of Domestic Violence*, 37 Ct. Rev. 40 (Spring, 2000).

Petrucci, Carrie J., *Respect as a Component in the Judge-Defendant Interaction in a Specialized Domestic Violence Court that Utilizes Therapeutic Jurisprudence*, 38 Crim. L. Bull. 263 (2002).

Tsai, Betsy, *The Trend Toward Specialized Domestic Violence Courts: Improvements on an Effective Innovation*, 68 Fordham L. Rev. 1285 (2000).

Winick, Bruce J., *Applying the Law Therapeutically in Domestic Violence Cases*, 69 UMKC L. Rev. 33 (2000).

Unified Family Court

Babb, Barbara A., *An Interdisciplinary Approach to Family Law Jurisprudence: Application of an Ecological and Therapeutic Perspective*, 72 Ind. L. J. 775 (1997).

Babb, Barbara A., *Fashioning an Interdisciplinary Framework for Court Reform in Family Law: A Blueprint to Construct a Unified Family Court*, 71 S. Cal. L. Rev. 469 (1998).

Babb, Barbara A. & Moran, Judith D., *Substance Abuse, Families, and Unified Family Courts: The Creation of a Caring Justice System*, 3 J. Health Care L. & Pol'y 1 (1999).

Brooks, Susan L. & Roberts, Dorothy E., *Social Justice and Family Court Reform*, 40 Fam. Ct. Rev. 453 (October, 2002).

Mental Health Court

Boothroyd, Roger A., McGaha, Annette, Petrila, John & Poythress, Norman G., *Preliminary Observations from an Evaluation of the Broward County Mental Health Court*, 37 Ct. Rev. 14 (Winter, 2001).

Fritzler, Randal B., *How One Misdemeanor Mental Health Court Incorporates Therapeutic Jurisprudence, Preventive Law, and Restorative Justice*, in Management and Administration of Correctional Health Care: Policy, Practice, Administration 14-1 (Jacqueline M. Moore, ed., 2003).

Goldkamp, John S. & Irons-Guynn, C., Office of Justice Programs, Bureau of Justice Assistance, U.S. Dep't of Justice, Emerging Judicial Strategies for the Mentally Ill in the Criminal Caseload: Men-

TAL HEALTH COURTS IN FT. LAUDERDALE, SEATTLE, SAN BERNARDINO, AND ANCHORAGE (2000).

Kondo, LeRoy L., *Advocacy of the Establishment of Mental Health Specialty Courts in the Provision of Therapeutic Justice for Mentally Ill Offenders*, 28 AM. J. CRIM. L. 255 (Summer, 2001).

Lurigio, Arthur J., Watson, Amy, Luchins, Daniel J. & Hanrahan, Patricia, *Therapeutic Jurisprudence in Action: Specialized Courts for the Mentally Ill*, 84 JUDICATURE 184 (2001).

Winick, Bruce J., *Outpatient Commitment: A Therapeutic Jurisprudence Analysis*, 9 PSYCHOL. PUB. POL & L. __ (Forthcoming, 2003).

Wolff, Nancy, *Courts as Therapeutic Agents: Thinking Past the Novelty of Mental Health Courts*, 30 J. AM. ACAD. PSYCHIATRY & L. 431 (2002).

Reentry Court

Ciappi, Silvio, Wexler, David, Agrait, Fernando & Traverso, Giovanni B., *Therapeutic Jurisprudence. Alcune Considerazioni su di Una Concezione Postliberale del Dirotto e Della Pena*, 6 RESSEGNA IT. DI CRIMINOLOGIA 1 (2001).

John Q. La Fond & Bruce J. Winick, *Sex Offender Reentry Courts: A Cost Effective Proposal for Managing Sex Offender Risk in the Community*, in SEXUAL AGGRESSION: UNDERSTANDING AND MANAGEMENT (Robert Prentky, Eric Janus & Michael Seto, eds, forthcoming, 2003).

Maruna, Shadd & LeBel, Thomas P., *Welcome Home?: Examining the "Reentry Court" Concept from a Strengths-based Perspective*, 4 WESTERN CRIM. REV. (2003), at http://wcr.sonoma.edu/v4n1/v4n1.htm.

PETERSILIA, JOAN, U.S. DEPT OF JUSTICE, NCJ 184253, WHEN PRISONERS RETURN TO COMMUNITIES: POLITICAL, ECONOMIC, AND SOCIAL CONSEQUENCES, SENTENCING & CORRECTIONS: ISSUES FOR THE 21ST CENTURY (Nov. 2000).

Saunders, Terry, *Staying Home: Effective Reintegration Strategies for Parolees*, 41 JUDGES J. 34 (Winter, 2002).

TRAVIS, JEREMY, U.S. DEP'T OF JUSTICE, BUT THEY ALL COME BACK: RETHINKING PRISONER REENTRY.

Problem Solving Courts Generally

Becker, Daniel J. & Corrigan, Maura D., *Moving Problem-Solving Courts into the Mainstream: A Report from the CCJ-COSCA Problem-Solving Courts Committee*, 40 CT. REV. 4 (Spring, 2002).

Carns, Teresa W., Hotchkin, Michael G. & Andrews, Elaine M., *Therapeutic Jurisprudence in Alaska's Courts*, 19 ALASKA L.REV. 1 (June, 2002).
Conference of Chief Justices & Conference of State Court Administrators, *Resolution in Support of Problem-Solving Courts*, 2 J. CENTER FOR FAMS., CHILD., CTS. 2 (2000) (CCJ RESOL. 22 & COSCA RESOL. 4).
Davis, Wendy N., Special Problems for Specialty Courts, 32 ABAJ __ (Feb. 2003).
Symposium, *Special Issue on Problem-Solving Courts*, MICH. BAR. J. (January 2003).
Rottman, David B. & Casey, Pam, *Therapeutic Jurisprudence in the Courts*, 18 BEHAV. SCI. & L. 445 (2000).
Rottman, David B. & Casey, Pam, *Therapeutic Jurisprudence and the Emergence of Problem-Solving Courts*, NAT'L. INST. JUST. J. 13 (Summer, 1999).
Simon, Leonore M. J., *Proactive Judges: Solving Problems and Transforming Communities*, in THE HANDBOOK OF PSYCHOLOGY IN LEGAL CONTEXTS (David Carson & Ray Bull, eds. 2d ed., forthcoming).
Website for the Center for Problem Solving Courts, at http://www.problemsolvingcourts.com/.
Website for The Center for Court Innovation, at http://www.courtinnovation.org/.
Winick, Bruce J., *Therapeutic Jurisprudence and Problem Solving Courts*, 30 FORDHAM URB. L. J. __ (Forthcoming, 2003).

Appellate Courts

Abrahamson, Shirley S., *The Appeal of Therapeutic Jurisprudence*, 24 SEATTLE U. L. REV. 223 (2000).
Anaya, S. James, *The United States Supreme Court and Indigenous Peoples: Still a Long Way to Go Toward a Therapeutic Role*, 24 SEATTLE U. L. REV. 229 (2000).
Arguelles, Luis Muniz, *Yelling, Not Telling: An Anti-therapeutic Approach Promoting Conflict*, 24 SEATTLE U. L. REV. 237 (2000).
Dauer, Edward A., *The Power of Myth: A Comment on Des Rosiers' Therapeutic Jurisprudence and Appellate Adjudication*, 24 SEATTLE U. L. REV. 297 (2000).
Des Rosiers, Nathalie, *From Telling to Listening: A Therapeutic Analysis of the Roles of Courts in Minority-Majority Conflicts*, 37 CT. REV. 54 (2000).
Des Rosiers, Nathalie, *From Quebec Veto to Quebec Secession: The Evolution of the Supreme Court of Canada on Quebec-Canada Disputes*, 13 CANADIAN J.L. & JURISPRUDENCE 171 (2000).
Des Rosiers, Nathalie, *The Mythical Power Of Myth? A Response to Professor Dauer*, 24 SEATTLE U. L. REV. 307 (2000).

Gothard, Sol, *Therapeutic Jurisprudence in the Appellate Arena—A Louisiana Jurist's Response*, 24 SEATTLE U. L. REV. 335 (2000).

Leben, Steve, *Thoughts on Some Potential Appellate and Trial Court Applications of Therapeutic Jurisprudence*, 24 SEATTLE U. L. REV. 467 (2000).

McGee, Linda M., *Therapeutic Jurisprudence and The Appellate Courts: Possibilities*, 24 SEATTLE U. L. REV. 477 (2000).

Ronner, Amy D. & Winick, Bruce J., *Silencing the Appellant's Voice: The Anti-Therapeutic Per Curiam Affirmance*, 24 SEATTLE U. L. REV. 499 (2000).

Stephani, A.J., *Therapeutic Jurisprudence in the Appellate Arena: Judicial Notice and the Potential of the Legislative Fact Remand*, 24 SEATTLE U. L. REV. 509 (2000).

Wexler, David B., *Lowering the Volume Through Legal Doctrine: A Promising Path for Therapeutic Jurisprudence Scholarship*, 3 FLA. COASTAL L. J. 123 (2002).

Wexler, David B., *Therapeutic Jurisprudence in the Appellate Arena*, 24 SEATTLE U. L. REV. 217 (2000).

International Developments in Therapeutic Jurisprudence

Allan, Alfred & Allan, Marietjie M., *The South African Truth and Reconciliation Commission as a Therapeutic Tool*, 18 BEHAV. SCI. & L. 459 (2000).

Birgden, Astrid & Vincent, Justice Frank, *Maximizing Therapeutic Effects in Treating Sexual Offenders in an Australian Correctional System*, 18 BEHAV. SCI. & L. 479 (2000).

Ciappi, Silvio, Wexler, David, Agrait, Fernando & Traverso, Giovanni B., *Therapeutic Jurisprudence. Alcune Considerazioni su di Una Concezione Postliberale del Dirotto e Della Pena*, 6 RESSEGNA IT. DI CRIMINOLOGIA 1 (2001).

Cunningham Launches Two Domestic Violence Courts, CANADA NEWSWIRE (Dec. 2, 1997).

Des Rosiers, Nathalie, *From Quebec Veto to Quebec Secession: the Evolution of the Supreme Court of Canada on Quebec-Canada Disputes*, 13 CANADIAN J.L. & JURISPRUDENCE 171 (2000).

Des Rosiers, Nathalie & Feldthusen, Bruce, *Legal Compensation for Sexual Violence: Therapeutic Concequences and Consequences for the Judicial System (Canada)*, 4 PSYCHOL. PUB. POL'Y & L. 433 (1998).

Donnellan, Eithne, *Home News: New Drugs Court is Aiming to Rehabilitate—Minister says New Method of Dealing With Addicts May be Extended* (Ireland), IRISH TIMES (Jan. 10, 2001).

Feldthusen, Bruce, *The Civil Action for Sexual Battery: Therapeutic Jurisprudence?*, 25 OTTAWA L. REV. 205 (1993).

Ferencz, Nicola & Mcguire, James, *Mental Health Review Tribunals in the UK: Applying a Therapeutic Jurisprudence Perspective* (England), 37 CT. REV. 48 (2000).

Freckelton, Ian, *Decision-Making About Involuntary Psychiatric Treatment: An Analysis of the Principles Behind Victorian Practice* (Victoria, Austl.), 5 PSYCHOL. PSYCHIATRY & L. 249 (1998).

Freiberg, Arie, *Australian Drug Courts*, 24 CRIM. L. J. 213 (2000).

Freiberg, Arie, *Policing-Prevention-Innovation-Beyond Enforcement*, Australian Drug Courts: A Progress Report, 2nd Australian Conference on Drug Strategy, Perth, W. Austl. (2002).

Freiberg, Arie, *Probation and Community Corrections: Making the Community Safer*, Specialized Courts and Sentencing, Australian Institute of Criminology and the Probation and Community Corrections Officers' Association, Perth, W. Austl. (2002).

Freiberg, Arie, *Problem-oriented Courts: Innovative Solutions to Intractable Problems?* 11 J. JUD. ADMIN. 8 (2001).

King, Michael S., *Geraldton Alternative Sentencing Regime: Applying Therapeutic and Holistic Jurisprudence in the Bush*, 26 CRIM. L. J. 260 (2002).

King, Michael & Wilson, Stephen, *Magistrates as Innovators* 29 BRIEF 7 (2002).

Levine, Murray, *The Family Group Conference in the New Zealand Children, Young Persons and Their Families Act of 1989*, 18 BEHAV. SCI. & L. 517 (2000).

Lippel, Katherine, *Therapeutic and Anti-Therapeutic Consequences of Workers Compensation* (Canada), 22 INT'L J. L. & PSYCHIATRY 521 (1999).

Martin, Yvonne, *Christchurch to Trial Drug Court for Teens* (New Zealand), THE CHRISTCHURCH PRESS (Jan. 10, 2002).

Martin, Yvonne, *Unease On Drug Court* (New Zealand), THE CHRISTCHURCH PRESS (Dec. 10, 2002).

McKain, Bruce, *Suitable Case for Treatment: Scotland's First Drug Court Aims to Break the Cycle of Addiction and Crime (Glasgow, Scotland)*, THE HERALD (Nov. 1, 2001).

Staples, John, *Glasgow Launches Six-Month Pilot of American-Style Drug Courts* (Scotland), THE SCOTSMAN (Nov. 9, 2001).

The Guardian (England), THE GUARDIAN (June 5, 2002).

Van Manen, Niels F., *The Secret of the Court in the Netherlands*, 24 SEATTLE U. L. REV. 569 (2000).

Video: THE JOURNEY (Magic Lantern Communications ltd) (relating to the Toronto Drug Treatment Court).

Website of the Australian Institute of Criminology, at http://www.aic.gov.au/research/drugs/context/courts.html (collecting information on Australia).

Website for "Aboriginal Court Days" in South Australia, at http://www.courts.sa.gov.au/courts/drug_court/index.html.

Website for New South Wales, at http://www.lawlink.nsw.gov.au (includes written opinions and judgments of the New South Wales Drug Treatment Court).

Website for New Zealand Drug Court, at http://www.stuff.co.nz/stuff/ 0,2106,2068940a11,00.htm.

Part II
From Description to Prescription:
Emerging Principles and Proposals

A. Therapeutic Jurisprudence as an Underlying Framework

In Part I, our goal was to present a rich and readable description of problem-solving courts and related approaches to what might be called "applied therapeutic jurisprudence" on the part of judges. Mostly, those courts and judicial approaches were developed by thoughtful, creative, and highly frustrated, judges and practitioners. Those judges and practitioners crafted practical, intuitive solutions to difficult social problems that ultimately presented themselves—in the form of real people—at the courthouse door.

At about the same time, across town in the academic arena, therapeutic jurisprudence began to develop as an interdisciplinary examination of the law's potential as a therapeutic agent. There is a clear symbiotic relationship between problem-solving courts and therapeutic jurisprudence. Simply put, problem-solving courts can serve as laboratories for therapeutic jurisprudence, insofar as therapeutic jurisprudence is especially interested in *which* legal arrangements lead to successful therapeutic outcomes, and *why*.

Accordingly, successful problem-solving courts can provide therapeutic jurisprudence with important food for thought in this regard, and developments in therapeutic jurisprudence can in turn be brought into problem-solving courts—and into courts in general—to improve the therapeutic functioning of the judiciary.

In the first selection of this part, which is in essence a "bridge" between Parts I and II, Winick and Wexler, working in the context of drug treatment courts, elucidate this symbiotic relationship. The essential task of therapeutic jurisprudence is to sensitize judges to the fact that they are therapeutic agents in the way they play their judicial roles and to develop some general principles that might improve judicial structure, function, and behavior in a manner that allows judges to be more effective therapeutic agents. Western Australia Stipendiary Magistrate Michael S. King recently put it well when he wrote: "For therapeutic jurisprudence to be validated in the context of problem solving courts, it needs to be shown that court processes themselves, as distinct from the rehabilitative programs ordered by the courts, are effective in promoting rehabilitation."

Part II, then, will focus on these court processes themselves, and will try to elucidate emerging "principles" of therapeutic jurisprudence that can be applied by problem solving courts and judges generally. At this exciting— but early—stage of development, these "principles" must, of course, be taken more as suggestions for ongoing discussion, dialogue, and investigation than as hard and fast rules to be set in stone. Although they can be seen as instrumental prescriptions for how judges can function in this regard, they are by no means algorithms that eliminate judicial discretion and practical judgment.

Before we begin, a word about style: In the interest of readability, we have generally eliminated footnotes and have supplied only "key" references. For full references and notes, the interested reader should consult the original article (cited at the beginning of each selection) from which the reading has been drawn.

Drug Treatment Court:
Therapeutic Jurisprudence Applied

By Bruce J. Winick & David B. Wexler
(Reprinted from *Drug Treatment Court: Therapeutic
Jurisprudence Applied*, 18 Touro L. Rev. 479 (Spring, 2002),
with permission from Bruce J. Winick and David B. Wexler).

Therapeutic jurisprudence is the study of law's impact on psychological well-being. It is an interdisciplinary approach to legal scholarship that has a law reform agenda. Therapeutic jurisprudence seeks to assess the therapeutic and anti-therapeutic consequences of law and how it is applied. It also seeks to affect legal change designed to increase the former and diminish the latter. It can be seen as a mental health approach to law that uses the tools of the behavioral sciences to assess law's therapeutic impact, and when consistent with other important legal values, to reshape law and legal processes in ways that can improve the psychological functioning and emotional well-being of those affected.

Therapeutic jurisprudence has been described as one of the major "vectors" of a growing movement in the law "towards a common goal of a more comprehensive, humane, and psychologically optimal way of handling legal matters." Besides therapeutic jurisprudence, these vectors include, among others, preventive law, restorative justice, facilitative mediation, holistic law, collaborative divorce, and specialized treatment courts. These specialized courts — "problem solving courts," as they are becoming known — include drug treatment court, domestic violence court, and mental health court.

Specialized treatment courts — including drug treatment courts — are related to therapeutic jurisprudence, but they are not identical with the concept. These courts can be seen as applications of therapeutic jurisprudence. They seek to solve a variety of individual problems, using principles of therapeutic jurisprudence in their work. In fact, the conference of chief justices and the conference of state court administrators recently approved a resolution supporting "problem solving courts" and their use of principles of therapeutic jurisprudence in performing their functions. These principles include ongoing judicial intervention, close monitoring of and immediate response to behavior, the integration of treatment services with judicial case processing, multi disciplinary involvement, and collaboration with community-based and government organizations.

Drug treatment court was pioneered in the late 1980's at the same time when therapeutic jurisprudence was being developed as an interdisciplinary approach to legal scholarship and law reform. Although drug treatment court developed independently, it can be seen as taking a therapeutic jurisprudence approach to the processing of drug cases inasmuch as its goal is the rehabilitation of the offender and it uses the legal process, and the role of the judge in particular, to accomplish this goal. Drug treatment court was a response to the recognition that processing non-violent offenders charged with the possession or use of drugs through the criminal courts and sentencing them to prison did not change their addictive behavior. Instead, it led to a revolving door effect in which such offenders resumed their drug abusing behavior after release from prison. The criminal court intervention thus failed to deal effectively with the underlying problem, and in this sense could be seen as antitherapeutic.

Instead of the traditional criminal justice approach, drug treatment court emphasized the rehabilitation of the offender and explicitly made the judge a member of the treatment team. Offenders accepting diversion to drug treatment court agree to remain drug-free, to participate in a prescribed course of drug treatment, to submit to periodic drug testing to monitor their compliance, and to report frequently to court for judicial supervision of their progress. Drug court judges receive special training in the nature and treatment of drug addiction, and through their supervision and monitoring of the offender's treatment progress, themselves function as therapeutic agents.

An important insight of therapeutic jurisprudence is that how judges and other legal actors play their roles has inevitable consequences for the mental health and psychological well-being of the people with whom they interact. Because drug treatment court judges consciously view themselves as therapeutic agents in their dealings with offenders, they can be seen as playing a therapeutic jurisprudence function. Moreover, principles of therapeutic jurisprudence can help the drug treatment court judge to play this function well.

Therapeutic jurisprudence has already produced a large body of interdisciplinary scholarship that analyzes principles of psychology and the behavioral sciences and attempts to show how they can be used in legal contexts to improve mental health. Recent scholarship has shown how judges in specialized problem solving courts can use principles of therapeutic jurisprudence in their work. Indeed, a recent symposium issue of Court Review, the publication of the American Judges Association, was devoted entirely to therapeutic jurisprudence and its application by the courts.

An understanding of the approach of therapeutic jurisprudence and of the psychological and social work principles it uses can thus improve the functioning of drug treatment court judges. Judge-defendant interactions are central to the functioning of drug treatment court. Judges therefore need to understand how to convey empathy, how to recognize and deal with denial, and how to apply principles of behavioral psychology and motivation theory. They need to understand the psychology of procedural justice, which teaches that people appearing in court experience greater satisfaction and comply more willingly with court orders when they are given a sense of voice and validation and treated with dignity and respect. They need to understand how to structure court practices in ways that maximize their therapeutic potential, even in such mundane matters as the ordering of cases in the courtroom to maximize the chances that defendants who are there awaiting their turn before the judge can experience vicarious learning. Offenders accepting diversion to drug treatment court are in effect entering into a type of behavioral contract with the court, and judges therefore should understand the psychology of such behavioral contracting and how it can be used to increase motivation, compliance, and effective performance.

Drug treatment court judges also need to understand how to deal with feelings of coercion on the part of the offender. A degree of legal coercion is undeniably present when a drug offender is arrested and must make the difficult choice of whether to face the consequences of trial and potential punishment in the criminal court or instead accept diversion and a course of treatment supervised by the drug treatment court. However, a body of literature on the psychology of choice suggests that if the defendant experiences this choice as coerced, his or her attitude, motivation, and chances for success in the treatment program may be undermined. On the other hand, experiencing the choice as voluntarily made and non-coerced can be more conducive to success. Judges therefore should not attempt to pressure offenders to accept diversion to drug treatment court, but should remind them that the choice is entirely up to them. A body of psychological work on what makes people feel coerced suggests how the drug court judge can increase the likelihood that offenders experience a sense of voluntary choice in their decision to accept drug treatment. To accomplish this, judges should always strive to treat offenders with dignity and respect, to inspire their trust and confidence that the judge has their best interests at heart, and to provide them a full opportunity to participate and to listen attentively to what they have to say. Judges treating drug court offenders in these ways can increase the likelihood that they will experience their choice to enter into treatment as voluntary and will internalize the treatment goal and act in ways that help to achieve it.

Although therapeutic jurisprudence can help drug treatment court judges to more effectively play their roles in the drug treatment process, it is important to recognize that therapeutic jurisprudence does not necessarily support all actions that may be regarded as pro-treatment. Nor does therapeutic jurisprudence require addiction to be characterized as a "disease." Even if viewed simply as a "problematic behavior", therapeutic jurisprudence principles could effectively apply in a diversion program agreed to by a person charged with criminal behavior who acknowledges having a problem. In addition, therapeutic jurisprudence does not take a position on whether increased or decreased criminalization or penalty for possession of drugs is warranted. Indeed, unless there are independent justifications for criminalization, therapeutic jurisprudence would not support continued criminalization solely to provide a stick-and-carrot approach to inducing criminal defendants to accept treatment in a drug treatment court diversion program.

Therapeutic jurisprudence would also encourage investigation and dialogue regarding the role of defense counsel in drug treatment court proceedings. Drug treatment court is often administered with a "team approach," under which the judge, prosecutor, and defense lawyer are seen as members of a team attempting to facilitate the rehabilitation of the offender. While this team approach might have therapeutic advantages, it might also have disadvantages, particularly if the offender comes to feel "sold out" by his own attorney. Therapeutic jurisprudence suggests that therapeutic goals not trump other important goals, and the due process right to effective counsel is one such goal. Moreover, respecting the role of counsel as advocate may even have considerable therapeutic merit.

In summary, then, therapeutic jurisprudence can contribute much to the functioning of drug treatment courts and the latter can provide rich and fascinating laboratories from which to generate and refine therapeutic jurisprudence approaches. But the two perspectives are merely "vectors" moving in a common direction, and are not identical concepts. * * *

B. Preliminary "Codifications" of Therapeutic Jurisprudence Principles

Therapeutic jurisprudence thus can be seen as providing instrumental prescriptions for judges functioning in the newly emerging problem-solving courts. Therapeutic jurisprudence principles can provide general guidelines for how these judges can play their roles, but are merely suggestive and must be adapted by the judge to the particular context presented.

Even when viewed as merely suggestive, however, there is often value in seeking to "codify" some of these emerging principles. This section of Part II accordingly collects some of the relevant documents and codifications.

The first is a joint resolution of the Conference of Chief Justices and the Conference of State Court Administrators, approved in the year 2000, supportive of problem-solving courts and calendars, and of the use by such courts of principles of therapeutic jurisprudence. The resolution lays out some of these principles—such as ongoing judicial supervision of cases—and is a giant step in endorsing problem-solving and therapeutic jurisprudence approaches as falling squarely within the realm of appropriate judicial conduct.

Drug treatment courts—the best known of the problem solving courts— have for some time operated according to "10 key components." Recently, the Florida legislature enacted a statute calling for drug courts to follow principles of therapeutic jurisprudence, and specifying the 10 key components. The Florida Statute is reprinted here.

Domestic violence courts developed through modifications made to the drug court model. Judge Randal B. Fritzler, who has been involved in creating a domestic violence court and a mental health court in Vancouver, Washington, worked with Dr. Leonore M. J. Simon, a criminal justice professor (now at East Tennessee State University) with training in both law and psychology, to draft pithy and practical principles for a domestic violence court, which we reprint from a therapeutic jurisprudence symposium in *Court Review*, the official journal of the American Judges Association, where those principles first appeared.

In essence, Fritzler and Simon proposed 10 key components for domestic violence courts. And, when he later began a mental health court, Judge Fritzler drafted 10 key components of a criminal mental health court, which we also reproduce.

Judge Fritzler was also instrumental in the formulation of a vision statement for the Clark County, Washington district courts—a vision statement embracing a therapeutic jurisprudence approach. The vision statement is especially significant because it is of general application, not restricted in its operation to specific problem solving courts. The statement, which we reprint, is rather general and inspirational. Yet, a judge following it should indeed find it a useful guide to behavior—and a selection by Wexler in a later portion of Part II K shows how the vision statement should lead to some concrete judicial "do's and don'ts."

Finally, we close this section by reprinting Maryland's Family Divisions' Standard 5.1, supporting a "therapeutic, holistic, ecological approach to family law decision making". This standard, which presents a new paradigm in family law adjudication, was drafted by Professor Barbara Babb (University of Baltimore School of Law) and by Attorney Jeffrey Kuhn, as part of a set of performance standards and measures now in use by Maryland's Family Divisions.

Conference of Chief Justices & Conference of State Court Administrators Resolution in Support of Problem-Solving Courts

(Conference of Chief Justices and Conference of State
Court Administrators Resolution CCJ/COSCA)
Adopted August 3rd, 2000

WHEREAS, the Conference of Chief Justices and the conference of State Court Administrators appointed a Joint Task Force to consider the policy and administrative implications of the courts and special calendars that utilize the principles of therapeutic jurisprudence and to advance strategies, policies and recommendations on the future of these courts; and

WHEREAS, these courts and special calendars have been referred to by various names, including problem-solving, accountability, behavioral justice, therapeutic, problem oriented, collaborative justice, outcome oriented and constructive intervention courts; and

WHEREAS, the findings of the Joint Task Force include the following:

- The public and other branches of government are looking to courts to address certain complex social issues and problems, such as recidivism, that they feel are not most effectively addressed by the traditional legal process;
- A set of procedures and processes are required to address these issues and problems that are distinct from traditional civil and criminal adjudication;
- A focus on remedies is required to address these issues and problems in addition to the determination of fact and issues of law;

- The unique nature of the procedures and processes encourages the establishment of dedicated court calendars;
- There has been a rapid proliferation of drug courts and calendars throughout most of the various states;
- There is now evidence of broad community and political support and increasing state and local government funding for these initiatives; *Funding)*
- There are principles and methods grounded in therapeutic jurisprudence, including integration of treatment services with judicial case processing, ongoing judicial intervention, close monitoring of and immediate response to behavior, multidisciplinary involvement, and collaboration with community-based and government organizations. These principles and methods are now being employed in these newly arising courts and calendars, and they advance the application of the trial court performance standards and the public trust and confidence initiative; and
- Well-functioning drug courts represent the best practice of these principles and methods;

NOW, THEREFORE, BE IT RESOLVED that the Conference of Chief Justices and the Conference of State Court Administrators hereby agree to:

Problem-Solving Courts

1) Call these new courts and calendars "Problem-Solving Courts," recognizing that courts have always been involved in attempting to resolve disputes and problems in society, but understanding that the collaborative nature of these new efforts deserves recognition.
2) Take steps, nationally and locally, to expand and better integrate the principles and methods of well-functioning drug courts into ongoing court operations.
3) Advance the careful study and evaluation of the principles and methods *Study + Evaluate* employed in problem-solving courts and their application to other significant issues facing state courts.
4) Encourage, where appropriate, the broad integration over the next decade of the principles and methods employed in the problem-solving courts into the administration of justice to improve court processes and outcomes while preserving the rule of law, enhancing judicial effectiveness, and meeting the needs and expectations of litigants, victims and the community.
5) Support national and local education and training on the principles and methods employed in problem-solving courts and on collaboration with other community and government agencies and organizations.
6) Advocate for the resources necessary to advance and apply the principles and methods of problem-solving courts in the general court systems of the various states.
7) Establish a National Agenda consistent with this resolution that includes the following actions:

a) Request that the CCJ/COSCA Government Affairs Committee work with the Department of Health and Human Services to direct treatment funds to the state courts.

b) Request that the National Center for State Courts initiate with other organizations and associations a collaborative process to develop principles and methods for other types of courts and calendars similar to the 10 key Drug Court Components, published by the Drug Courts Program Office, which define effective drug courts.

c) Encourage the National Center for State Courts Best Practices Institute to examine the principles and methods of these problem-solving courts.

d) Convene a national conference or regional conferences to educate the Conference of Chief Justices and Conference of State Court Administrators and, if appropriate, other policy leaders on the issues raised by the growing problem-solving court movement.

e) Continue a Task Force to oversee and advise on the implementation of this resolution, suggest action steps, and model the collaborative process by including other associations and interested groups.

Florida Statutes: Treatment-Based Drug Court Programs
§ 397.334, Fla. Stat. 2002

(1) It is the intent of the Legislature to implement treatment-based drug court programs in each judicial circuit in an effort to reduce crime and recidivism, abuse and neglect cases, and family dysfunction by breaking the cycle of addiction which is the most predominant cause of cases entering the justice system. The Legislature recognizes that the integration of judicial supervision, treatment, accountability, and sanctions greatly increases the effectiveness of substance abuse treatment. The Legislature also seeks to ensure that there is a coordinated, integrated, and multidisciplinary response to the substance abuse problem in this state, with special attention given to creating partnerships between the public and private sectors and to the coordinated, supported, and integrated delivery of multiple-system services for substance abusers, including a multiagency team approach to service delivery.

(2) Each judicial circuit shall establish a model of a treatment-based drug court program under which persons in the justice system assessed with a substance abuse problem will be processed in such a manner as to appropriately

address the severity of the identified substance abuse problem through treatment plans tailored to the individual needs of the participant. These treatment-based drug court program models may be established in the misdemeanor, felony, family, delinquency, and dependency divisions of the judicial circuits. It is the intent of the Legislature to encourage the Department of Corrections, the Department of Children and Family Services, the Department of Juvenile Justice, the Department of Health, the Department of Law Enforcement, and such other agencies, local governments, law enforcement agencies, and other interested public or private sources to support the creation and establishment of these problem-solving court programs. Participation in the treatment-based drug court programs does not divest any public or private agency of its responsibility for a child or adult, but allows these agencies to better meet their needs through shared responsibility and resources.

(3) The treatment-based drug court programs shall include therapeutic jurisprudence principles and adhere to the following 10 key components, recognized by the Drug Courts Program Office of the Office of Justice Programs of the United States Department of Justice and adopted by the Florida Supreme Court Treatment-Based Drug Court Steering Committee:

(a) Drug court programs integrate alcohol and other drug treatment services with justice system case processing.

(b) Using a nonadversarial approach, prosecution and defense counsel promote public safety while protecting participants' due process rights.

(c) Eligible participants are identified early and promptly placed in the drug court program.

(d) Drug court programs provide access to a continuum of alcohol, drug, and other related treatment and rehabilitation services.

(e) Abstinence is monitored by frequent testing for alcohol and other drugs.

(f) A coordinated strategy governs drug court program responses to participants' compliance.

(g) Ongoing judicial interaction with each drug court program participant is essential.

(h) Monitoring and evaluation measure the achievement of program goals and gauge program effectiveness.

(i) Continuing interdisciplinary education promotes effective drug court program planning, implementation, and operations.

(j) Forging partnerships among drug court programs, public agencies, and community-based organizations generates local support and enhances drug court program effectiveness.

(4) Treatment-based drug court programs may include pretrial intervention programs as provided in ss. 948.08, 948.16, and 985.306.

(5)(a) The Florida Association of Drug Court Program Professionals is created. The membership of the association may consist of drug court program practitioners who comprise the multidisciplinary drug court program team, including, but not limited to, judges, state attorneys, defense counsel, drug court program coordinators, probation officers, law enforcement officers, members of the academic community, and treatment professionals. Membership in the association shall be voluntary.(b) The association shall annually elect a chair whose duty is to solicit recommendations from members on issues relating to the expansion, operation, and institutionalization of drug court programs. The chair is responsible for providing the association's recommendations to the Supreme Court Treatment-Based Drug Court Steering Committee, and shall submit a report each year, on or before October 1, to the steering committee.

Principles of an Effective Domestic Violence Court
by Judge Randal B. Fritzler & Leonore M.J. Simon
(Excerpted from Creating a Domestic Violence Court: Combat in the Trenches, 37 CT. REV. 28, 31 (Spring, 2000), Copyright 2000 by American Judges Association, reprinted with permission).

Therapeutic jurisprudence (TJ) proposes that judges and lawyers be sensitive to the beneficial or harmful consequences that their actions and decisions have on the parties that come before them. In applying the TJ approach, the effectiveness of chosen practices depends upon the legal issues involved and the context in which these issues are presented. In essence, TJ is what good judges do anyway on a daily basis. The TJ approach forces all judges to reflect on and evaluate their effectiveness. As applied to domestic violence (DV), TJ suggests that some basic principles can achieve offender accountability and victim safety. They should be applied only where they do not violate other standards of good court performance.

1. When dealing with domestic violence, it is a mistake to try to force what one is doing into the drug court format. Drug courts ordinarily focus on nonviolent offenders whereas domestic violence cases deal with violent crimes against intimates. Although diversion and dismissal of charges may be appropriate after successful completion of a drug treatment program, the slate cannot be wiped clean in domestic violence cases. Rehabilitation of the domestic violence offender is desirable, but offender accountability and victim protection are paramount. Because of the seriousness of violent behavior and the repetitive nature of DV, a legal record needs to be maintained.

2. Judicial demeanor toward defendants and victims can increase compliance with court orders as well as have therapeutic effects. Judges can use their authority to make victims feel welcome in the court, to express empathy for their injuries, and to mobilize resources on their behalf. With offenders, judges can be respectful while insisting that offenders take responsibility

for their violence and acknowledge the court's authority over their behavior. Judicial recognition of offender success in treatment, compliance with court orders, and demonstrated alternatives to violence can give the offender a sense of self-efficacy and achievement.

3. One of the most important roles of a DV court is to confront the perpe- *Confront ther* trator's cognitive distortions. Distorted thinking includes minimizing/ *distorted* denying the violence and blaming the victim. Seize the opportunity provided *thinking* by the trauma of the arrest to intervene in the perpetrator's life while he is still receptive, and encourage voluntary mental health activities as well as alcohol evaluation and treatment. Be mindful that accepting a "no contest" plea and other compromises or plea bargains can serve to reinforce distorted thinking by allowing the offender to avoid full responsibility for his behavior. It also can be harmful by causing the victim and the offender to believe that the offender can escape responsibility for present and future acts with some degree of impunity. Instead, stress that domestic violence is a chosen behavior, and that contrary to what the perpetrator has believed in the past, it will not get him what he wants.

4. Involve the defendant in contracting with the court and assisting the *make a k* court in establishing the terms of no contact orders and terms of supervision *w/ D O* (i.e., distances, supervised visitation with children, how items of personal *w/ include the* property may be obtained). Including input from the offender in fashioning *in making* the order can increase compliance. It also lets the individuals know how seri- *in making* ously the court takes the "no contact" and protection orders. *terms*

5. We do not like the phrases "fast track" or "rocket docket" but are convinced that these cases need to be acted on immediately with continual court involvement, or the court loses judicial effectiveness. Continuances and other dilatory tactics need to be discouraged in every case.

6. Take advantage of the DV dockets to "red flag" children at risk. Appropriate referrals to child advocacy and child welfare agencies should be initiated.

7. Sentencing should be swift but not severe. Some jail time may get the *Sentencing: swift but not* offender's attention that there are consequences for his behavior, but it *severe* should be proportionate to his offense. Excessive fines should be avoided as *Fines: avoid excessive* they can rarely be collected and often take needed resources from the family.

8. Routine post-sentencing reviews should be calendered without cause and *Review* need to include DV treatment providers, victim advocates, and probation offi- cers to modify restrictions on the offender when there is substantial compli- ance as well as to impose graduated sanctions when there is non-compliance.

9. Within the framework of the American justice system, the DV TJ judge should also be an expert on the special evidentiary issues which arise repeat- *jury instructions* edly in the context of domestic violence cases. Using his or her familiarity with the law the judge may also apply these skills to draft custom jury in- structions that better frame the issues for jury consideration.

10. Coordinate DV cases with other cases occurring contemporaneously that may involve the perpetrator, victim or their family. The DV judge

should be particularly aware of related dissolution cases, other criminal matters, juvenile court cases, child abuse and neglect cases, and paternity proceedings. In issuing orders, especially those involving "no contact" or protection order provisions, be careful to avoid conflicting or incompatible orders.

---

10 Key Components of a
Criminal Mental Health Court
by Judge Randal B. Fritzler
(Copyright by Judge Randal B. Fritzler, reprinted with permission).

Mental health courts are a particularly fine example of a problem solving court. The mental health court provides essentially all of the benefits of the problem solving court approach including; a more rapid response, focus on the crime by a specialized staff and improved application of resources. Major commitment of new funds to achieve the benefits of a therapeutic court is not a necessity. This is really a process of reorganizing the manner in which the courts do business. Mental health courts, like other specialized courts may encounter resource and specific staffing problems, however, they can be overcome without a major influx of money. Partnering with the community and community involvement in the reorganization process ensures that the court is responsive to community needs, builds support and makes resources go further. The essence of a mental health court is a dedicated court team that works together to obtain positive outcomes for the court client. Risk management is a key best practice in the specialized court setting. Professor Bruce Winick has proposed that these courts may be structured in such a way as to allow them to function as instruments of risk management. Professor Winick suggests that in a dynamic risk management setting the specialized court can provide increased continuity, more effective monitoring and more flexible responses. These procedures can more effectively contain the risk of violence. This may involve a restructuring of the court itself.

Ten Key Components of the Criminal Mental Health Court
1.   *Therapeutic environment supported by a dedicated court team,* The court must create a team of individuals with the skills to manage the cases of mentally ill offenders. Examples of appropriate team members are; mental health treatment providers, substance abuse treatment providers, psychologists, case managers, specialized probation officers and specialized court staff. The court should create a therapeutic environment suitable for court customers who may have a wide variety of disabilities. Appearance in

court is traumatic for many people. The event may be confusing and even cause short-term memory loss in individuals. The court should take this into account and provide information to litigants in writing, as well as orally.

2.   *No Stigmatizing Labels,* The court should take steps to make sure that persons passing through the court shall not be branded or stigmatized. It is probably better practice not to label people by their medical diagnoses. The medical labels may reinforce stereotypes of people with disabilities and portray them is being powerless and dependent. Court records should not carry any unique designation or identification for those participating in the specialized court.

3.   *Diversion, stays and other deferred sentencing processes,* A mental health court may utilize a pre-plea diversion process, stays of prosecution or a post-plea deferred sentence process. Each of these approaches has a distinctive technical procedure and advocates that prefer one procedure over the other. It is not clear based upon our current experience and limited evaluation whether one of these procedures is superior. The process adopted by any mental health court may be dependent upon the local legal culture and the biases of local prosecution teams. It appears to be beneficial, however, to have a built in incentive such as avoiding conviction for criminal charges, to encourage clients to enter a specialized mental health court program. A pre-plea process seems to provide these benefit in the present context. However, additional comments on the criminal process pre-plea vs. post plea are in order. It is noted that the effect of avoiding conviction as an incentive to participate in the mental health court varies widely according to the individual and his or her circumstances. A few who are newcomers to the criminal justice system may have a high incentive to avoid having a conviction on their record. Others, however, that have many convictions and a long criminal history may not see a big advantage in avoiding one more misdemeanor conviction.

4.   *Least restrictive alternatives,* In fashioning remedies and imposing sentences the court should use the least restrictive means consistent with public safety, sound treatment considerations and the general welfare of the client. One of the purposes of the court is to get clients out of custody and into supportive programs that maximize therapeutic results.

5.   *Enhancement of basic treatment, the court as a clearing house,* The court should not promote any specific mode of treatment for mental illness but should act to promote, wherever possible, the welfare of the individuals who come before it. This involves the court being a neutral clearinghouse for local treatment options. Evidence exists that recidivist offenders often exhibit skills deficits in the areas of interpersonal problem solving, self management and social interaction. Basic mental health treatment should be enhanced, where appropriate with programs designed to

teach interpersonal problem-solving skills and other cognitive behavioral approaches. The court must also consider the availability of funding for any alternative sentences imposed. Since resources are always scarce the court should serve as an advocate for increasing resources for treatment and client support.

6.   *Interdependent decision making,* The court should support clients accepting responsibility for and affirmatively addressing their own mental health issues. A mental health court team should consider utilizing several models of supported decision-making for the clients of the court. This support may be in the form of assisted decision-making or some other interdependent decision-making process. The court process should allow clients to have reasonable participation and an opportunity to help determine the structure of their future. Involving the clients of the court in this way may improve compliance and help to address any issues of inferiority and powerlessness often faced by individuals appearing in court.

7.   *Technical rules do not apply after admission to mental health court,* Hearings involving pro-se litigants or any hearings involving direct participation by court clients should have technical rules suspended, including the rules of evidence, so that direct participation by those who are not attorneys is more viable and meaningful. The court should create an environment where attorneys may collaborate to create favorable outcomes. The court should also reduce combative approaches wherever consistent with the protection of individual rights. Client initiated court reviews of procedures, established by local court rules, may assist in honoring due process and other Constitutional principles.

8.   *Court Manual,* Each court will need to create a manual. The manual should include additional specific procedures to be adopted by local court rule and new forms or documents specifically for the mental health court operations. The court should also create a comprehensive statement of principles and a statement of rights for the clients of the court and make them available to all. User friendly explanatory material should be created and distributed to clients, providers and the general public.

9.   *Coordination of treatment,* As in the case of other courts utilizing therapeutic techniques, seize the opportunity provided by the trauma of the arrest to intervene in the perpetrator's life while he or she is still receptive. Voluntary mental health activities as well as substance abuse evaluation and treatment should be encouraged at the earliest opportunity. It should be noted that most of the criminal defendants served by the criminal Mental Health Court are "dually diagnosed." The term "dual diagnosis' in this context, means that they have significant substance abuse issues as well as mental health issues. This fact makes coordination of multiple treatment providers a key court responsibility. Coordination should acknowledge the fact that substance abuse treatment providers may be much

more comfortable with greater directness and varying degrees of coercion whereas other treatment modalities, by mental health providers, may not feel coercion is helpful. It is hoped, however, that the concept of mental health court clients taking responsibility for treatment decisions and taking responsibility for their own behavior will help to reverse a common stereotype of people with serious mental health problems as persons who are "out of control".

10.   *A meaningful review process with a unified perspective on part of the court team,* The court review process is essential. A meaningful review process depends on continued involvement by the mental health court team. Building a dedicated court team with a unified perspective is an absolute necessity. Having prosecutors, defense counsel, probation officers and treatment providers with a specialized caseload enhances efficiency, performance and outcomes. This team must continually reassess the clients' adjustment and response to changing conditions and life's challenges. This process is referred to as "dynamic risk management." The court rewards positive adjustment and sanctions willful non-compliance or behavior that endangers others. Judicial demeanor toward defendants and victims can also increase compliance with court orders as well as have therapeutic effects.

Postscript to the ten key components;
Risk Management and other tools
    The basic functions involved in dynamic risk management are not new to the American court system but the application and focus is revolutionary. Courts traditionally set conditions of release, establish bail, issue restraining orders and take other actions based on judges' predictions about the offender's future potential for abuse. An important question is: "How can police and courts more effectively and fairly make these predictions without violation of individual rights?" Additionally, judges must ask themselves, "What is reasonable under American constitutional restraints?" This author recognizes problems with the traditional "prediction model" for making these determinations. It may involve classifying people as dangerous based upon static considerations. This may result in stereotyping and classification based upon constitutionally impermissible criteria rather than upon evaluation of the individual in question. Additionally, the accuracy of these types of predictions whether made by clinicians or judges, has been seriously questioned. In fact, such predictions are often made based upon on unarticulated considerations and contaminated by the evaluator's own biases. The author's observations of trial court judges' practices would support this. Judges traditionally "shoot from the hip" in making decisions about release from custody and alternative sentences. To avoid such a haphazard approach, analysis of therapeutic models can aid judges in effectively assessing risk and ensuring

the safety of the public. By utilizing the court review process judges may engage in a process of continuing reassessment of the individual before the court. The judges can inquire into the individual defendant's response to therapeutic processes and compliance with court orders. In this way the court can assure placement of defendants in the least restrictive rehabilitative process that is consistent with public safety considerations. The court should be imaginative in developing viable alternatives to incarceration. This careful selection of alternatives enables the court to make better use of valuable system resources. In the new approach the court manages a dynamic interactive scheme, which involves both monitoring and guiding the individual through a therapeutic rehabilitative process. Feedback on dynamic factors may enhance the therapeutic effect often achieved through treatment, counseling and skill buildings sessions. Knowing that there are benefits to improved performance motivates the court client.

It is arguable that current law and predictive models increase the possibilities for violence and also exacerbate the revolving door syndrome. A mental health court with a regularly scheduled review process can monitor the dynamic nature of this phenomenon and make adjustments to a person's treatment, supervision and restrictions based upon dynamic factors that reflect increasing dangerousness. Dynamic factors are changing circumstances in the individual's life. Examples of dynamic factors include relationship problems, housing problems, employment termination, gambling, drug or alcohol use. Additionally the court monitors the client's schedule and factors—in missed appointments and problems such as failure to take medication. The criteria the court uses must be related to the court clients' propensity for criminal activity and the individual's past record.

It should also be noted that a common theme in criminal cases in the United States is the existence of substance abuse problems. In the past, the approach was generally to demand that substance abuse treatment proceed and be completed before addressing any other issues. Now using techniques under the heading of "dual diagnosis" and "co-occurring disorders" treatment programs the issues are more often addressed simultaneously. This emphasizes a need for courts to be "clearing houses" and resource coordinators to make sure that resources are being applied most efficiently and effectively and at appropriate times. The interactive procedures of dynamic risk management, court review, supervision and coordination of resources all fit together in new court review processes which utilize the judge in a new way to achieve favorable outcomes and meet the expectations of the community for their judicial system.

Positive reinforcement is almost always to be preferred over negative sanctions. Positive reinforcement is only limited by the imagination of the court and staff. Frankly, this can be a serious limitation. It is difficult to provide

appropriate positive reinforcement and incentives. That is why systemic incentives while limited, are so important. The pre-plea process is a significant
one. Mental health court staff always try to provide encouragement and
praise for good performance. A personal court calendar is provided to each
client. Special days and events are commemorated, just to let the client know
that the judge and court staff really care about them and that good behavior
and cooperation with the court is rewarded. The idea of love and support is
reinforced. Bad behavior is distinguished from the idea that someone is a
bad person. The court team always attempts to make clear that the entire
team is committed to the individual's success.

In addition to encouragement and rewards, intermediate sanctions are the
tools of the court. In this context, procedures such as alcohol and drug
detoxification programs (detox), etc. are not wholly punitive but applied to
address a specific transitory issue. Conceivably incarceration and/or involuntary commitment could be used but are so restrictive and costly that they are
reserved and imposed only as a last resort and when safety is an issue. Serious sanctions are employed only in the case of new felonies or an indication
that the integrity of the court would be threatened by allowing an individual
to remain out of custody. To provide a specific example incarceration was
used in Clark County mental health court in only two cases out of the first
forty-nine referred to the court.

When there is poor performance the court is much more likely to use some
of the following sanctions and tools in the place of jail or even partial confinement: (A.) A requirement of more frequent reporting (some are required to
report on a daily basis). (B.) Structure is increased and mandatory activities
are imposed or increased to fill up the individuals free time. These activities
sometimes reduce the client's choices or options. We stress that freedom of
choice comes with responsibility. (C.) There may be "house calls" by court staff
to check up on court clients. (D.) There may be increased drug and alcohol
screening. (E.) Telephone monitoring or electronic home confinement may be
used as a sanction. (F.) Active probation requiring the client to report to probation officer as well as to the bench may be necessary. (G.) Increased restitution payments or restorative justice projects may be required. (H.) Work crew
or alternative community service may be employed. (Note: we know that work
projects can enhance self-esteem and a feeling of accomplishment whether
these are part of regular employment or in the nature of "work crew.") In
mental health court, if the person can be employed, we prefer that the client
they seek gainful employment so that the person is rewarded with money as
well as satisfaction for a job well done. We note that our society equates money
with worth and we don't want to stress that aspect, yet it is understandable
that the idea of contributing by paying is good and adds to a person's self esteem.

Vision Statement for District Court
of Clark County, Washington

The judges of Clark County District Court envision that the Court may make a positive difference in people's lives by intervening before irreversible damage occurs to the person or the community.

Judges' Perception of their Role

We perceive ourselves as having the opportunity, as no where else in the criminal justice system, to save lives and make a positive difference in people's lives before it's too late.

We have the ability to craft individual solutions that are compatible with the high standard of justice. We make decisions in the context of people's lives and the need of the community not just in the context of crime or a civil dispute.

In our efforts to make a positive change in the lives of people who come before the court we will be guided by the principles of *Therapeutic Jurisprudence.*

Guiding Values

1. We have a strong belief in individual responsibility and accountability.
2. We also believe individuals are not condemned to a life of crime or despair by mental condition or substance abuse and that everyone can achieve a fulfilling and responsible life.
3. We believe that everyone, no matter whom, has something positive within their make up that can be built upon.
4. We understand our role and that it is interactive with the community services that are at our disposal such as treatment providers, emergency housing, education, and transportation.
5. We are committed to dealing with the root causes of community safety issues rather than simply using incarceration as a temporary solution.
6. We incorporate in our process checks and balances that protect people's options and constitutional rights.
7. We respect cultural, family, linguistic and educational backgrounds and take individual differences into account when clients appear before the court.
8. We strongly consider the person's life as a whole and his/her family and community context.
9. We are willing to step out of the traditional roles of an adversarial court system to facilitate a more positive, more effective outcome for the person who has committed a crime or wishes to resolve a dispute.

Maryland's Family Divisions Performance Standard 5.1: A Therapeutic, Holistic, Ecological Approach to Family Law Decision Making

by Barbara Babb & Jeff Kuhn
(Excerpted from *Performance Standards and Measures for Maryland's Family Divisions* (Oct. 2001), pp. 76–79, Copyright 2001 by Barbara Babb & Jeff Kuhn, reprinted with permission).

The approach of Maryland's Family Divisions to family law decision-making is therapeutic, holistic, and ecological in its perspective.

Commentary

A therapeutic approach to family law decision making involves resolving family legal disputes with the aim of improving the lives of families and children and maximizing the potential positive outcomes of court intervention.[1] The therapeutic potential of court intervention is enhanced by adopting an expanded concept of the family, or by acknowledging that neighborhoods, religious organizations, and other associations or institutions within which family members participate have the potential to influence the family's legal matters.[2] Accounting systematically for these competing influences on families' and children's lives by means of an ecological approach to family law decision making can help courts pursue strategies designed to establish and to strengthen connections among these influences and can enhance families' and children's functioning.[3] As Chief Judge Bell has commented, this is a "new paradigm" in family law adjudication. The need for this approach is clear, and the approach itself is sensible:

The adversarial process can be destructive for families. Family cases therefore require a different approach. That approach mandates that family cases be expedited to minimize the trauma of litigation and to ensure safety and support for all family members. Families are given every opportunity to make ultimate decisions themselves, through educational programs and alternative dispute resolution techniques. Finally, judges are trained to understand child development, the needs of the individual within the family, and the importance of family issues.

The courts also have begun to recognize that, because they function in many instances as a "trauma center," serving families in crisis, they are in a unique position to identify problems and connect those families with much-needed services. The goal of the family divisions and family service programs within the circuit courts is to provide an effective approach to the early resolution of family conflict.

Implementation Issues and Recommendations
    1. **Community Outreach.** The Family Divisions engage in a process of community outreach in order to promote the new paradigm. Involving the business community and cultivating resources available to the courts via partnerships with local business leaders complements and enhances the work of the court. For example, local businesses sponsor programs (such as an existing employment program in Baltimore County that links child support obligors with jobs) and provide volunteers for many court initiatives. In addition, linking with the business community provides the Family Divisions with models adaptable to the administration of the Family Divisions, such as information technology, consumer service delivery, and strategic planning. Publicizing partnerships with community service providers and the business community through the use of brochures, videotapes, and websites demonstrates the Family Division's commitment to the therapeutic, holistic, and ecological approach to family law adjudication.
    2. **Development of Problem-Solving Initiatives.** The Family Divisions have begun to develop problem-solving initiatives in the areas of substantive family law decision-making and court procedures. In addition, appropriate training programs for judges and court personnel educate these actors about the development of problem-solving processes consistent with their roles in family legal proceedings. These training programs, in turn, demonstrate the system's commitment to therapeutic justice.
    3. **Informing State and Local Executive and Legislative Branches.** State and local executives and legislators need to be informed about the new family law decision-making paradigm. Thus, Family Division personnel need to invite executives and legislators to meet with them periodically and to tour the Family Division facilities. In addition, state and local executives and legislators need to know about the existence of the Family Division Performance Standards and Measures, as well as the status of implementation and achievement of the standards. The Administrative Office of the Courts must continue to assess the level of assistance needed from the executive and legislative branches to ensure optimal Family Division functioning.

Tools of Measurement
    1. **Documentation of Community Outreach Initiatives.** The Administrative Office of the Courts, in cooperation with each Family Division, should work together to develop a plan for community outreach and should publish that plan in the Family Division Annual Report. The report should identify the major components of the plan and progress made toward its implementation. When appropriate, the plan should identify community or business entities that have pledged to work with or who are currently working with

the Family Divisions. In addition, key people in each Family Division should work with the Court Information Office to enhance publicity about community outreach efforts.

2. Documentation of Therapeutic Justice Education and Training Initiatives. Educational components on therapeutic justice are included within judicial and staff training programs. Thus, program agendas or workshop schedules should accurately reflect this topic. The Administrative Office of the Courts should coordinate with the Judicial Institute to ensure that Maryland's Family Division judges receive training appropriate to the mission and goals of the Family Division.

Notes

1. See generally Barbara A. Babb, Fashioning an Interdisciplinary Framework for Court Reform in Family Law: A Blueprint to Construct a Unified Family Court, 71 S. Cal. L. Rev. 469 (1998). See also Barbara A. Babb, An Interdisciplinary Approach to Family Law Jurisprudence: Application of an Ecological and Therapeutic Perspective 72 IND L. J. 775 (1997) [hereinafter Babb, An Interdisciplinary Approach to Family Law Jurisprudence].

2. See Babb, An Interdisciplinary Approach to Family Law Jurisprudence, supra note 58, at 786.

3. See id at 800–801.

C. Interpersonal Skills and the Psychology of Procedural Justice

This section examines the interpersonal skills that judges functioning in the problem-solving court arena should possess to play their roles well. Many of our insights about how judges should behave in these contexts, and, in particular, about how they should interact with clients (as defendants and parties are sometimes referred to by judges favoring a therapeutic jurisprudence approach) are drawn from the literature on the psychology of procedural justice. In all of their interactions with the individual, judges should be careful to apply procedures that fully respect the individual's participatory and dignitary interests. Therapeutic jurisprudence scholarship has frequently relied on principles derived from the psychology of procedural justice, suggesting that their application in a variety of contexts can achieve therapeutic benefits for the individuals involved. The literature on the psychology of procedural justice, based on empirical work in a variety of litigation and arbitration contexts, shows that if people are treated with dignity and respect at hearings, given a sense of "voice," the ability to tell their story, and "validation," the feeling that what they have said has been taken seriously by the judge or hearing officer, and generally treated in ways that they consider to be fair, they will experience greater satisfaction and comply more willingly with the ultimate outcome of the proceedings, even if adverse to them.

According individuals a full measure of procedural justice thus can help to increase compliance with and successful participation in a treatment or rehabilitative program. According individuals procedural justice also will diminish their perception of coercion in the judicial process, and increase the chances that they will experience the decision to enter into a treatment or rehabilitative program to have been voluntarily made. The resulting perception can itself help to increase the likelihood of genuine participation on the part of the individual, and can increase intrinsic motivation, program compliance, and treatment success. These utilitarian reasons for respecting the procedural rights of individuals coalesce with the historic commitment to fairness embodied in the concept of due process of law.

In our first selection, Judge Roger Warren, President of the National Center for State Courts, makes the interesting and important observation that procedural justice, of crucial importance to litigants, is also closely connected to public trust and confidence in the courts. The fairness of court processes may often be more important than case outcomes. For the benefit of litigants and for society as a whole, Judge Warren urges individual judges to introduce an "ethic of care" into court processes. While judges applying an ethic of care need to be sensitive to the emotional aspects of their interaction with the parties appearing in court, such as when to display sympathy or empathy, they should be careful not to abandon principal adjudicative values such as impartiality and independence. *See* Laura E. Little, *Adjudication and Emotion*, 3 Fla. Coastal L J. 205 (2002).

The next selection, by Michael D. Clark, a Michigan social worker and consultant to drug treatment courts, should put somewhat at ease those judges fearful of employing an ethic of care and of engaging clients in a change-oriented process. He notes that client factors themselves are most important in therapeutic efforts (accounting for 40% of change), and that specific therapeutic models and techniques only account for 15% of successful change. "Relationship" factors, however—the connection between client and the judge and treatment staff (e.g., whether those relations are characterized by empathy, acceptance, and encouragement)—account for a whopping 30% of the contribution to change. In addition, client "hope and expectancy" accounts for another 15% of successful change.

Thus, although the evidence seems clear that therapeutic endeavors can be successful, the lion's share of therapeutic work ought to be in encouraging active and meaningful client participation, in developing a strong relationship between client and the judge and change agent, and in fostering hope and expectancy of change. Clark's "good news" is that "therapeutic work is not just the domain of treatment professionals," and that "all professionals working with drug court participants, especially judges, lawyers, and probation officers may adopt and utilize techniques that most effectively induce positive behavior change."

The three final selections in this interpersonal skills and procedural justice section pick up on such judicial techniques for effectively inducing positive behavior change. Carrie Petrucci, a social work professor (California State University at Long Beach) who has worked in and carefully studied a domestic violence court, closely examines judge-defendant interactions at progress report hearings, and suggests that factors and behaviors that can be categorized under the concept of "respect" may be key components in defendant compliance and behavior change. Although Petrucci writes in the context of domestic violence court judges, what she has to say has broad application for all judges, and demonstrates the importance of judges acting in ways that respect the human dignity of those appearing before them.

The next two selections both relate to the process of civil commitment of the mentally ill. Once again, the implications are wide-ranging, rather than restricted to a particular setting, such as mental health law. But a focus on the civil commitment context is revealing for it brings into sharp relief the importance of fair process even in a setting where, given the serious mental disability of most respondents (patients), the outcome is very likely to be involuntary commitment.

Many observers might think that, with the eventual outcome not very much in doubt, procedural corners might be cut with impunity. But the procedural justice and therapeutic jurisprudence empirical work suggests quite the contrary.

A recent study by Cascardi and colleagues is very revealing. The study found that even seriously disturbed committed mental patients perceived differences in procedural fairness, such as the attentiveness of the judge, and whether the judge explained the procedures, gave the respondent an opportunity to speak, and explained the ultimate decision and the reasons for reaching that decision. Moreover, patients claimed that procedures that seemed fair and that reflected a sense of caring would have a favorable impact on their treatment in terms of their compliance, cooperativeness, their taking of medication, and their relationship with their treating doctors (Michele Cascardi, Alicia Hall & Norman G. Poythress, Procedural Justice in the Context of Civil Commitment: An Analogue Study, 18 Behav. Sci & L. 731 (2000)).

The selection by Winick applies the relevant procedural justice principles to suggest how the judge can conduct the civil commitment hearing so as to maximize its therapeutic value. Winick's recommendations—in terms of "do's" and "don'ts" for judges—should affect patient-respondent perceptions of fairness, ultimate adjustment to hospitalization, if ordered, and the efficacy of hospitalization and treatment.

Pennsylvania psychologist Charles Kennedy, in his research in civil commitment, rounds out the picture by concentrating not on the patient-respondent but on the reaction of the petitioner (usually a family member) to the judge and to the courtroom atmosphere. He found that petitioners, too, were highly sensitive to fair treatment, and that such treatment had an influence on the extent to which the petitioner seemed willing to care for the patient-respondent down the road (perhaps subsequent to hospitalization), and on the petitioner's future willingness to resort to the commitment process in case of a serious deterioration in the respondent's mental health. Thus, even in cases where the outcome of the hearing may be a foregone conclusion, judicial behavior may help pave the way for a favorable future.

Public Trust and Procedural Justice

by Judge Roger K. Warren
(Excerpted from *Public Trust and Procedural Justice*,
37 Ct. Rev 12, 14–16 (2000), Copyright 2000 by American
Judges Association, reprinted with permission).

How does the courtroom conduct of trial judges affect public trust in the court system?

In order to address these questions, one must first determine which sources of public dissatisfaction actually affect the overall level of public trust in the court system. The National Center's 1999 survey, as well as other research conducted by the National Center and other organizations, demonstrates that, among the various sources of public dissatisfaction, perceptions of the relative fairness of court dispute resolution processes are what ultimately determine the level of public trust. Although, for example, the public expresses great dissatisfaction with the high cost of access to the courts and the slow pace of litigation, it is not primarily those factors, but rather the fairness of court processes, that is associated with varying levels of public trust. This is especially true for minorities.

Importantly, it is the fairness of court processes, not the fairness of court outcomes or decisions, that are most important. Literature in the procedural justice field indicates that both litigants and the general public can—and do—distinguish between the fairness of the process, and the fairness, or even favorability, of the outcomes. In evaluating judicial performance, and in determining the level of trust in judicial authority, the fairness of the dispute resolution process is more important than even a favorable outcome. In the minds of litigants, the importance of a favorable outcome is consistently outweighed by the impact of an unfair process. In other words, a prevailing litigant might look back upon a recent court experience and say, "Yes, I won the case, but I don't know if it was worth it. It cost me too much, the judge wouldn't let me speak, I didn't understand what the judge was talking about, I was treated like dirt. I hope I never have to go through that again." On the other hand, an unsuccessful litigant can leave the courtroom saying, "I lost my case but I had my day in court, I was treated fairly, I can move on."

Not only do litigants and the public feel that fair processes are more important than favorable outcomes, but they also feel that courts do a somewhat better job in using fair procedures than in arriving at fair outcomes. The most recent public opinion survey conducted by the National Center in spring 2000 demonstrated * * * that 43% of litigants and 57% of the general public feel that court procedures are "always" or "usually" fair, whereas only 37% of litigants and 50% of the public feel that court outcomes were "always" or "usually" fair. Equally important, however, is that recent litigants are significantly less likely than the public generally to feel that either court procedures or court outcomes are fair. The percentage of recent litigants who feel that courts are fair is 13% to 14% lower than the comparable percentage of the general public.

These findings on the relationship between procedural justice and public trust are important for a number of reasons. First, most judges tend to focus on outcomes, not process, i.e., on the legal correctness of their rulings and decisions rather than on the fairness of their decision-making processes. Yet it is often the fairness of these decision-making processes, rather than the judicial decisions themselves, that are important to litigants and the general public, and it is this sense of fairness that forms the basis of judicial performance evaluation and determines the level of trust in judicial authority. As judges, we should pay more attention to the fairness of our decision-making processes.

Second, it is the fairness of our decision-making processes that makes our courts unique. The fundamental goals and values of the American court system are procedural, not substantive. It is *how* decisions are reached in our judicial system, rather than the decisions themselves, that distinguishes the work of American courts from the work of the other two branches of government and explains why the American judicial system is increasingly the envy of both developed and developing countries throughout the world. It is the values inherent in the Trial Court Performance Standards and in the concept of the rule of law that distinguish the decision-making processes of the judicial branch from those of the political branches. As former New York Governor Mario Cuomo said in his remarks at the National Conference on Public Trust and Confidence in the Justice System: "The judicial system is different from the political branches of our government and that difference makes all the difference to our strength and glory as a democracy."

Finally, procedural justice is a fundamental shared value—shared by litigants, the American public, and people around the world. It is the courts' commitment to procedural justice that can allow the courts to connect much more successfully with the communities that we serve.

But what is procedural justice? Procedural fairness can mean different things to different people. Among judges and lawyers, procedural justice is often defined as procedural due process, i.e., notice and opportunity to be heard before a neutral and detached magistrate. But what does fairness mean to litigants and the public? Something quite different. For litigants and the public, fairness appears to consist of four principal elements: (1) neutrality; (2) respect; (3) participation; and (4) trustworthiness.

The first element, "neutrality," is very familiar to judges. The notions of a "neutral" magistrate, an impartial decision maker, a judicial officer free of bias, interest, or improper motive, and committed to equality under the law, are central to the concepts of judicial independence and the rule of law.

Maybe Supreme Court Justice Anthony Kennedy puts it best when he refers to our law's "constitutional promise of neutrality."

The element of "respect" refers to whether the judicial officer is viewed as courteous and respectful, and the manner in which proceedings are conducted. The third element, "participation," refers to the extent to which the judicial officer allows the litigants an active voice in the decision-making process, whether litigants feel they have "been heard" and whether the judicial officer has good communication and "attentive listening" skills.

The fourth, and probably most important, element is "trustworthiness." Whether a judicial officer is trustworthy does not depend primarily on the officer's honesty or reliability. It is generally assumed that judges are honest. Rather, "trustworthiness" is based upon a perception of the judge's motives, i.e., whether the judge truly cares about the litigant (demonstrates "an ethic of care") and is seeking to do right by the litigant. Trustworthiness is not a measure of the judge's knowledge, skills, or abilities. It is a measure of the judge's character, not the judge's competence. The litigant usually does not feel qualified to evaluate the judge's competence, but often feels fully qualified, based upon the judge's reputation, demeanor, and behavior, to evaluate the judge's motives.

I noted earlier that the National Center's most recent survey found that litigants tend to be significantly less satisfied with the fairness of court procedures and outcomes than the general public. In the same survey, we questioned recent litigants regarding the four elements of procedural justice described above in order to determine the extent to which recent litigants feel that the courts demonstrate those qualities of fairness. The survey responses indicated that more litigants feel that courts are neutral and respectful than feel they are participative or trustworthy. * * * Respondents felt that the quality of trustworthiness was least often demonstrated by the courts.

How do these criteria—by which litigants evaluate judicial performance—compare with the criteria by which we as judges evaluate our own performance? An analysis of the criteria utilized by those states with court-sponsored judicial performance evaluation programs reveals that there are six basic criteria commonly used in such evaluations. * * * In comparing these criteria with the four elements of procedural fairness described above, several observations emerge.

First, knowledge of the law and the rules of legal procedure play a very limited role in evaluating judicial performance, both from the perspective of litigants as well as in court-sponsored evaluation programs. The criterion of substantive knowledge of law and legal procedure is but one of the six criteria. * * * Second, three of the four fairness qualities identified by litigants and the public (neutrality, respect, and participation) are also addressed by the performance criteria in court-sponsored evaluation programs.

Third, and most important, trustworthiness, one of the most critical elements of fairness to litigants and the general public, does not appear to be recognized at all in traditional judicial self-evaluation programs. Neither our current judicial self-evaluation processes, nor our current judicial education programs for that matter, appear to promote "an ethic of care" on the part of judges. The quality of trustworthiness is often most important to litigants, but least often demonstrated by the courts, and least often recognized in our own self-evaluation processes.

Recently, "problem-solving courts" (including drug courts, domestic violence courts, mental health courts, truancy courts, gun courts, etc.) have sought to introduce an "ethic of care" and principles of therapeutic jurisprudence into court processes. Focusing on the extent to which court practices promote the psychological or physical well-being of the people affected, these courts often try to address the social and psychological problems that underlie legal disputes. But they also seek to introduce an "ethic of care" into court processes and to generally refocus on the qualities of respect, participation, and trust-worthiness often cited by litigants and the general public.

What is the foreseeable impact on the level of public trust in the judiciary of initiatives like problem-solving courts, which refocus attention on these qualities of procedural fairness? In the National Center's most recent public opinion survey, we described some of the characteristics of problem-solving courts to respondents and asked whether, and how strongly, the respondents supported or opposed such courts. * * * Eighty-two percent of the respondents indicated support for such courts and 50% of the respondents indicated "strong" support. Efforts by the courts to improve the fairness of court processes in ways often identified by litigants and the general public appear to win strong public support. This finding supports the conclusion that improvement in the fairness of court processes would result in significantly higher levels of public trust.[1]

In addition, a less formal survey reported in *Court Review* indicated that judges who work in problem-solving courts report a higher level of litigant respect and gratitude than judges assigned to more traditional courtrooms. Ninety-two percent of judges working in drug treatment courts reported feeling respected by litigants, compared to 72% of judges serving in traditional family courts. Eighty-one percent of the drug court judges reported feeling that litigants were grateful for the help received from the court compared to 33% of the judges serving in traditional family court. The same survey also reported higher levels of judicial satisfaction among drug court judges. Ninety-one percent of drug court judges reported that their assignment had affected them in a positive way, compared with 64% of traditional family court judges. Moreover, it was the fact that litigants were grateful that appeared to result in the higher satisfaction levels of the drug court judges. The factor of litigant gratitude was the most common predictor of whether drug court judges felt positively affected by their assignment.

Conclusion

In order to improve public trust in the justice system, courts must improve their performance in key performance areas affecting fundamental goals and values: access, timeliness, fairness, equality, integrity, independence, and accountability. The area of court performance that most directly affects litigant and public evaluation of court performance—and levels of public trust—is the fairness of court processes.

As viewed by litigants and the general public, the fairness of court processes depends on the extent to which judicial officers are neutral and unbiased, respectful, allow those affected to participate meaningfully in the decision-making process, and, most importantly, are trustworthy. Trustworthiness depends, in the minds of litigants and the public, not on the competence of the judicial officer but on the judge's motives and character. Ultimately, as Justice Felix Frankfurter reminded us, the authority of the court is a moral one, rooted in fundamental shared values and the good character of its officers. And, ultimately, that authority rests on our ability as judges to live up to those values, to meet the reasonable expectations of litigants and the public, to put a human face on who we are, what we do, and how we do it, to show that we care about the people affected by our processes and decisions—in short, to demonstrate that we are worthy of the public's trust.

Notes

1. Greater procedural justice may also reduce recidivism. One study, for example, has shown that among men arrested for domestic violence those who felt that they were treated respectfully by the police went on to commit 40% fewer offenses. *See* Raymond Paternoster, Robert Brame, Ronet Bachman, & Lawrence Sherman, *Do Fair Procedures Matter? The Effect of Procedural Justice on Spousal Assault,* 31 Law & Soc. Rev. 163 (1997).

Key References

Chase, Deborah J. & Peggy F. Hora, *The Implication of Therapeutic Jurisprudence for Judicial Satisfaction,* 37 Ct. Rev. 12 (Spring, 2000).

Cuomo, Mario, *We Must Lead the Charge,* 36 Ct. Rev. 14 (Fall, 1999)

Rottman, David B., *On Public Trust and Confidence: Does Experience with the Courts Promote or Diminish it?* 35 Ct. Rev. 14 (Winter, 1998).

Tyler, Tom R., *Citizen Discontent with Legal Procedures: A Social Service Perspective on Civil Procedure Reform,* 45 Am. J. Comp. L. 887 (1997).

A Change-Focused Approach for Judges
by Michael D. Clark, MSW, CSW
(Excerpted from *Change Focused Drug Court: Examining
the Critical Ingredients of Positive Behavior Change*, 3(2)
NAT'L DRUG CT. REV. 35 (Winter, 2001), Copyright 2001 by
National Drug Court Institute (NDCI), reprinted with permission).

* * *

The American Psychological Association (APA) supported a research initiative that assembled the world's leading outcome researchers to review forty years of psychotherapy outcomes and detail the subsequent implications for direct practice. The initial findings of this research indicate that treatment *is* effective in helping human problems. The authors of this study, Mark Hubble, Barry Duncan, and Scott Miller observe effective catalysts of positive behavior change: "Study after study, meta-analysis, and scholarly reviews have legitimized psychologically-based or informed interventions. Regarding at least its general efficacy, few believe that therapy needs to be put to the test any longer."

Clinical outcome authors and researchers, Ted Asay and Michael Lambert, commenting on previous studies report, "These reviews leave little doubt. Therapy is effective. Treated patients fare much better than the untreated." These studies parallel research regarding the efficacy of treatment delivered by drug courts. Steven Belenko, reporting on drug court outcomes for the National Center on Addiction and Substance Abuse, found that there is a reduction in drug use and criminal activity while participants are in drug court programs.

* * *

Common Factors
Having concluded that treatment is effective, the APA's study made a second finding that is at least equally significant: None of the numerous treatment models studied has proven to be reliably better than any other. Barry Duncan and Scott Miller report: "Despite the fortunes spent on weekend workshops selling the latest fashion, the competition among the more than 200 therapeutic schools amounts to little more than the competition among aspirin, Advil, and Tylenol. All of them relieve pain and work better than no treatment at all. None stands head and shoulders above the rest." This conclusion has been repeatedly upheld in subsequent studies.

If no theory or model can claim that it is better than the others, then what accounts for the overall efficacy of treatment? Researchers, including Michael Lambert and Mark Hubble, sifted through four decades of outcome data to postulate that the beneficial effects of treatment largely result from processes shared by the various models and their recommended techniques. Simply put, similarities, rather than differences, in the various models seem to be responsible for change. Each of the varied treatment models aids change by accessing certain common factors that, when present, have curative powers. Lambert concluded from extensive research data that there were four of these common factors:

- Client factors—the client's preexisting assets and challenges;
- Relationship factors—the connection between client and staff;
- Hope and expectancy—the client's expectation that therapeutic work will lead to positive change; and
- Model/technique—staff procedures, techniques, and beliefs.

These factors that raise the effectiveness of treatment are transtheoretical—that is, all of the various treatment theories and approaches recognize their importance to some degree. Without intentionally focusing on them, all therapies seem to be more effective when they promote these common factors in their own unique ways.

Hubble, Duncan, and Miller speak to this important research finding:

> In 1992, Brigham Young University's Michael Lambert proposed four therapeutic factors...as the principal elements accounting for improvement in clients. Although not derived from strict statistical analysis, he wrote that they embody what empirical studies suggest about psychotherapy outcome. Lambert added that the research base for this interpretation for the factors was extensive; spanned decades; dealt with a large number of adult disorders and a variety of research designs, including naturalistic observations, epidemiological studies, comparative clinical trials, and experimental analogues.

Hubble, Duncan, and Miller also drew upon Lambert's earlier work that rated some factors as more influential in changing behavior than others and ascribed a weighting scale to them. Lambert then ranked and prioritized the common factors according to their amount of influence on positive behavior change.

* * *

Client Factors

According to Lambert, client factors—not what offenders and their families receive from staff, but what they possess as they enter the doors of our drug courts and agencies—are the largest contributor to behavior change (forty percent). Client factors are both internal (optimism, skills, interests, social proclivities, aspirations, past successes) and external (a helpful uncle, employment, membership in a faith community). Client factors also include fortuitous events that are controlled by neither the drug court staff nor the program participant: an abusing boyfriend moving out and away from the family, a chance school or employment experience instilling renewed interest, a lesson "hitting home" as, for example, when a close friend or peer is seriously harmed by illicit drug use.

The difficulties of encouraging referrals to participate in treatment are two-fold: first, staff must build trust and find effective methods to encourage those in treatment to participate. Second, staff must be persuaded to break the 'norm' of dictating behavior, and allow participants increased choice and autonomy.

Many treatment programs are not individualized (regardless of their claims), nor do they offer true choices in programming. Furthermore, staff often resists client input. The views and opinions of probationers may be markedly different from those of staff. Consequently, staff may be resistant to seeking and integrating input from participants about "what works" in their own treatment. Staff should recognize that acknowledging and accepting the beliefs and positions of a participant is not the same as agreeing with or acquiescing to them.

Such an approach affirms the participant's role in his or her treatment. Indeed, the common-factors research confirmed just this point: that it is the drug court defendant and his or her family, not the staff or providers, who make treatment work. This finding does not conclude that program structure or staff efforts are useless. It does suggest, however, that the instruction in interventions and treatment models offered by universities and training institutes may be more effective if coupled with a focus on the input of those actually in treatment.

Duncan and Miller summarize this research by noting the real 'engine' of change is the client, thus implying that our time might be better utilized by finding more ways to employ the client in the process of change. Ironically, what it takes to realize difficult behavior change in the real world is not always fostered or modeled during staff-client interactions. Change rests with a participant's full participation, energy and commitment. However, if staff assumes a role where their ideas and expertise consistently trump those of the client, the participant is relegated to a passive role. If client's experiences and know-how are subjugated to the wisdom and methods of the professional, then the term drug court "participant" could well be in danger of becoming an incongruous or contradictory term.

Many research endeavors examine the process of engagement and work with voluntary clients. This context is not always comparable to the mandated nature of drug court efforts. Drug court clients are generally conceived of as "involuntary," where withdrawal from substance use is a non-negotiable mandate. While keeping our directives in focus, it is important to consider we have more latitude in allowing greater participant input, both in how one might strive for sobriety and how one might sustain it.

Therapeutic Relationship Factors

Relationship factors, or therapeutic alliance, make up about thirty percent of the contribution to change. *Alliance* means the extent that the counselor and client can collaborate. Conditions that engender an alliance include reciprocal understanding, mutual affirmation, emotional attachment and respect. *Relationship* means the strength of the alliance that develops between the program participant and staff. Relationship factors include perceived empathy, acceptance, warmth, and self-expression.

Perceived Empathy

Communication studies consistently report that verbal communication is prone to error; the listener does not always receive the complete message. Parts of the intended message are either inadequately articulated by the speaker or incorrectly understood by the listener. A dialogue between two people resembles listening to a cell phone that crackles with static from weak reception: even if one listens closely, much of the transmission will be garbled or missing.

Perceived empathy involves a drug court participant's belief that they are listened to and understood. Relationships develop as staff becomes committed to understanding their clients and make consistent efforts toward "filling in the gaps" of communication. An important technique for improving communication is "reflective listening," in which the staff member constantly checks the accuracy of what he or she believes the client has said. This author believes that most staff members, regardless of whether they have previously been trained in reflective listening, seldom, if ever use this technique. The technique is simple to understand but difficult to use consistently and correctly.

Evidence shows that "accurate empathy" is a condition of behavior change. William Miller and Stephen Rollnick state: "Accurate empathy involves skillful reflective listening that clarifies and amplifies the client's own experiencing and meaning, without imposing the therapist's own material. Accurate empathy has been found to promote therapeutic change in general and recovery from addictive behaviors in particular." Compliance can occur without the program participant feeling understood, but real change cannot.

Perceived empathy is a term that corrects a previous bias in research. Most outcome studies measured empathy and the strength of the staff-client alliance through counselor reports. But in fact, the drug court participant's assessment of the alliance matters more. Experts on the therapeutic relationship and authors of the 1999 book "*How Clients Make Therapy Work: The Process of Active Self-healing,*" Karen Tallman and Arthur Bohart, report "[f]indings abound that the client's perceptions of the relationship or alliance, more so than the counselor's, correlate more highly with therapeutic outcome." Further research completed at the University of Quebec by Canadian psychologist Alexandra Bachelor found that the client's perception of the alliance is a stronger predictor of outcome than the counselor's view.

The tendency to privilege staff evaluations over clients' perceptions occurs frequently in justice work. For example, while providing onsite technical assistance to an established juvenile drug court, the author experienced a chance encounter with a group of juvenile probationers who were milling outside the court building awaiting their weekly progress review hearings. The author began an impromptu conversation, inquiring as to their personal evaluations of their drug court program. Their responses were both forthcoming and enthusiastic. Encouraged, the author brought this information to the next staff meeting, only to find that the program staff members immediately dismissed this important information because of its source.

Acceptance

Acceptance relates to the extent that any treatment program fits into the participant's and family's worldview and beliefs. Kazdin (1980) found that the client's ability to accept a particular procedure is a major determinant of its use and ultimate success.

More recent studies found a greater acceptance of treatment and better compliance with interventions when rationales were congruent with clients' perceptions of themselves, the target problems, and the clients' ideas for changing their lives.

An acid test for any drug court program lies in the answer to the question, "To what extent are interventions predetermined?" That is, are participants turned into passive recipients of prepackaged programming, or is programming flexible enough that it may be customized to the individual? Progressive drug court programs make an effort to include clients and promote their participation. In workshops on strength-based programming, many staff is surprised to learn that they have more leeway to alter and adapt programming than they first believed. The results of this effort can be remarkable. As solution-focused therapy expert John Murphy notes, "The notion of acceptability reflects good common sense: people tend to do what makes sense to them and what they believe will work. It is hardly profound to suggest that the best way to determine what is appealing and feasible for people is "to ask *them*" (Emphasis added). In this "asking" profound differences in efficacy are realized. Solution-focused therapists Ben Furman and Tapani Ahola report that the counselor-client relationship is developed and the alliance strengthened as clients and their families are allowed to have a say in defining the problem[s], setting goals, and deciding what methods or tasks will be used to reach those goals.

Drug court team members have extenuating circumstances to consider when allowing client participation at this advanced level. In the mandated arena of drug court programs, abstinence from drugs and alcohol is a primary goal that is non-negotiable—the goal remains in force whether the participant agrees or not. However, the drug court can still seek the client's thoughts and possible ideas for his or her ideas to achieve that goal. Drug courts should be analogous to a job hunter who wanders a community career fair looking for the most interesting and profitable "fit" with prospective employers. Programs should allow choices to be made across a "smorgasbord" of treatment options, allowing the referral to choose the option that is most relevant to them. Being allowed to choose (or collaboratively design) a treatment option that makes sense to the participant—aligned with the participant's age, gender, culture, way of thinking/life experiences—will increase the participant's motivation to participate. John Murphy is clear as to this effort, "[t]he therapeutic alliance is enhanced by... [t]ailoring therapeutic tasks and suggestions to the client instead of requiring the client to conform to the therapist's chosen model and beliefs." A previous justice article on strength-based practice argues that programs need to stay close to the probationer's and family's definition of the problem (and their own unique methods), as they are the ones who will be asked to make the necessary changes. Researchers who have studied the influence of hope and expectations on counseling outcomes, C.R. Snyder, Scott Michael, and Jennifer Cheavens echo this idea, arguing that staff must listen closely to program participants. If staff do not, they may establish therapeutic goals "that are more for the helper than for the helped."

Warmth/Self-Expression

These two conditions for building relationships are intertwined. Extending warmth (attention, concern, and interest) occurs in tandem with allowing a drug court client's self-expression. All staff must understand and embrace a long-held credo from the counseling field: Listening is curative. As Karen Tallman and Arthur Bohart report, "Research strongly suggests that what clients find helpful in therapy has little to do with the techniques that therapists find so important. The most helpful factor [is] having a time and a place to focus on themselves and talk." Others have found that giving traumatized individuals a chance to "tell their story" and engage in "account making" is a pathway to healing. A rather obscure but interesting earlier study showed that paying juvenile delinquents to talk into a tape recorder about their problems and experiences led to meaningful improvements in their behavior, including fewer arrests.

Staff would be wise to critically examine their methods in building alliances with participants, both programmatically and individually. Duncan and Miller state emphatically, "Clients' favorable ratings of the alliance are the best predictors of success—more predictive than diagnosis, approach, counselor or any other variable."

Hope and Expectancy

The next contributor to change (fifteen percent) is hope and expectancy; that is, the referral's hope and expectancy that change will occur as a result of entering drug court programming. This author believes that in practice, staff may encourage hope and expectancy by (1) conveying an attitude of hope without minimizing the problems and pain that accompany the offender's situation; (2) turning the focus of treatment toward the present and future instead of the past; and (3) instilling a sense of empowerment and possibility to counteract the demoralization and passive resignation often found in drug court participants who have persistent problems.

Conveying an Attitude of Hope
Without Minimizing the Problem

Instilling hope has more complexity than simple encouragement. Participants need to believe that taking part in drug court programming will improve their situation. Therefore, during the orientation phase of programming, many successful drug court programs provide convincing testimonials of success and program efficacy. Researchers on the condition of hope, Snyder, Michael, and Cheavens, indicate that the new client must sense that the assigned staff member, working in that particular setting, has helped others reach their goals.

Troubled participants and their families often feel "stuck" in problem states. This feeling can be based partly on negative attitudes that allow no escape from problems (i.e., "I can't change," "You don't understand—I have to hang out with my using friends"). Strength-based work may instill hope while also acknowledging problems and pain. One strength-based strategy encourages staff to allow the participant's problem to coexist with the emerging solution. In many instances within remedial drug court work (and throughout the helping professions), there is a mindset to conquer, eliminate, or "kill" the problem. Oftentimes it is helpful and much more expedient to allow the problem to remain, to coexist with an emerging solution or healthy behavior that is being developed.

Bill O'Hanlon, a strength-based author and therapist, describes a helpful metaphor that originated in an old vaudeville routine: Two ingratiating waiters approaching the narrow kitchen door repeatedly defer to the other. "After you," one offers. "No, please, after you," the other replies. Finally, at the same moment, they both decide to act and turn into the door simultaneously, only to wedge their shoulders in the small opening. O'Hanlon advises adult staff to consider the idea of "creating a second door" and allowing conflicting feelings and conditions to coexist. A client could feel scared and hopeless about his ability to begin abstinence from drugs and yet marshal the confidence to avoid using "just for today." A painfully shy young woman may simultaneously fear the crowded gathering and yet find the courage to join it. Trying to convince the shy client that there's "no need to be shy," or that there's "nothing to be afraid of," is an uphill climb with dubious results. The conflicting dichotomies of continuing drug use or movements toward sobriety, hesitancy or action, fear or confidence may exist as "both/and" rather than being framed as an "either/or" choice. Staff need not eliminate the negative to instill the positive.

This is not just a meaningless play on words. There is a popular slogan among practitioners of strength-based approaches: "The person is not the problem; the problem is the problem." Strength-based practice takes that idea a step further to assert that the problem is actually the person's *relationship* to the problem.

Becoming Future-Focused

Focusing on past failures usually results in demoralization and resignation. Hope is future-focused. When any drug court staff member keeps remedial efforts focused on the future, positive outcomes are enhanced. The "problem" is generally found in the present and its roots in the past. The "solution," however, is generally started in the present with efforts aimed at the future.

European therapists Ben Furman and Tapani Ahola, authors of the book, *Solution Talk: Hosting Therapeutic Conversations*, report that the single most useful thing remedial staff could do in the time they spend with troubled drug court clients is to get them to look ahead and describe what is happening when the problem is envisioned as "solved," or is not considered to be as bad. These therapists, using strength-based strategies, believe that if goals are to be immediately helpful and meaningful to the program participant and family, they must first be conceived and constructed through visions of a "problem-free future." It is through this forward looking, "harnessing" of the future, that goals for present actions (first steps) become known.

An important way to "harness" the future is by employing "miracle," or outcome questions: "What if you go to sleep tonight and a miracle happens and the problems that brought you into this drug court are solved?" "Because you are asleep, you don't know the miracle happened. When you wake up tomorrow, what would you notice as you go about your day that tells you a miracle has happened and things are different?" "What else?" "Imagine, for a moment, that we are now six months or more in the future, after we have worked together and the problems that brought you to our drug court have been solved. What will be different in your life, six months from now, that will tell you the problem is solved?" "What else?"

The miracle question is the hallmark of the solution-focused therapy model. A "miracle" in this context is simply the present or future without the problem. By this treatment method, the counselor orients the drug court participant and family toward their desired outcome by helping them construct a different future. Helping a participant and family establish goals needs to be preceded by an understanding of what they want to happen. If therapists find no past successes to build on, they may help the family form a different future by imagining a "miracle." As many justice workers have experienced, it often is difficult to stop a family from engaging in "problem talk" and to start searching for solutions. If a program participant and family are prompted to imagine a positive future, they may begin to view their present difficulties as transitory. The miracle question is used to identify the client's goals to reach program completion or other successful criteria.

The miracle question is followed by other questions that shape the evolving description into small, specific behavioral goals: "What will be the smallest sign that this (outcome) is happening?" "When you are no longer (using drugs, breaking the law, etc.), what will you be doing instead?" "What will be the first sign this is happening?" "What do you know about (yourself, your family, your past) that tells you this could happen for you?"

Empowerment and Possibility

Drug court programs encourage hope and expectancy when they help clients establish goals and act to realize them. All programs will list large (macro) outcomes or final goals to reach graduation and program completion. Similarly, most remedial plans are established for large issues and longstanding presenting complaints. These plans usually list large problem behaviors to be resolved by a specified date set many months into the future. The problem is that these goals are too big for day-to-day work. Instead, efficacious goal setting should "think small." Goals should be shaped into small steps. According to the "one-week rule" of strength-based practice, a worker and a drug court participant should never mutually establish any goal that cannot be reached in the next seven days. Some staff go further and employ a "48-hour rule" to make a goal seem more obtainable and to begin behavior change. Short time frames propel "first steps" and put into motion small incremental movements to change. "What can you do after you get home today? By tomorrow afternoon?"

Snyder, Michael, and Cheavens found that a large portion of client improvement, studies suggesting as much as 56% to 71% of total client change, can occur in the early stages of treatment. Interestingly, this improvement happens before clients learn the methods or strategies for change that programs stand ready to teach. How could change begin to occur before program direction, teaching, and support may be delivered? These motivational researchers posit:

> As Ilardi and Craighead (1994) pointed out, clients have usually not even learned the supposedly "active" mechanism for change by the time improvement occurs in these early stages of treatment. Rather, the rapid response of clients must be a product of the common factors—especially hope. On this point, several researchers and authors have highlighted the pivotal role that hope plays in early and subsequent improvement in psychotherapy...

Ilardi and Craighead note that the instillation of hope and expectancy of change is not simply a precondition for change; it is change.

Model and Technique

Another small contributor to change may be found in model and technique (fifteen percent): staff procedures, techniques, and beliefs, broadly defined as our therapeutic structure and healing rituals. It is humbling to consider that a majority of what practitioners have been taught—the various models of interventions and their suggested techniques—might well constitute one of the smallest contributions to change. Furthermore, programs and techniques are deemed helpful only to the extent that they promote the other common factors.

Nevertheless, the strategies and methods that staff provides to drug court participants are helpful, yet for reasons that are contrary to popular beliefs. Tallman and Bohart explain:

> Clients utilize and tailor what each approach provides to address their problems. Even *if* different techniques have different specific effects, clients take these effects, individualize them to their specific purposes, and use them....In short, what turns out to be most important is how each client uses the device or method, more than the device or method itself. Clients then are the "magicians" with the special healing powers. [Staff] set the stage and serves as assistants who provide the conditions under which this magic can operate. They do not provide the magic, although they may provide means for mobilizing, channeling, and focusing the client's magic. (Emphasis in original)

It appears that, rather than mediating change directly, techniques used by staff simply activate the natural healing propensity of participants. Therefore, it is important to use techniques and develop requirements that facilitate a participant's progress.

* * *

All drug court team members can become *change-focused*.

Duncan and Miller list several interesting research findings regarding drug court team members in direct service roles:

- Andrew Christensen and Neil Jacobson, in their evaluation of counselor effectiveness with clients, found no differences between professionals and paraprofessionals or between more and less experienced therapists.
- Hans Strupp and Suzanne Hadley found that experienced therapists were no more helpful than a group of untrained college professors.
- Jacobson (1995) determined that novice graduate students were more effective at couples' therapy than trained professionals.

It may be surprising to learn that there is little or no difference in effectiveness regardless of training and experience. It is not the author's intent to impugn credentials or expertise. Rather, these findings convey that these novices or paraprofessionals were able to match treatment effectiveness by somehow integrating the common factors where the trained professionals may have lost sight of what was truly effective.

Indeed, the findings offer important support to drug court staff. Knowledge of the four common factors penetrates the mystique surrounding "therapy" and illuminates what is truly "therapeutic": positive behavior change. By applying strength-based techniques in their work, more staff members (across multiple disciplines) may begin to build the all-important alliance with clients and work to enhance the factors of change with drug court referrals and their families. Because of the complexity found in many presenting problems, professional therapy and therapeutic treatment will always be needed as adjunct services to specialty courts. The "good news" of this common factors research is that therapeutic work is not just the domain of treatment professionals. All professionals working with drug court participants, especially judges, lawyers and probation agents may adopt and utilize techniques that most effectively induce positive behavior change.

Key References

Duncan, B. L. and S. D. Miller, The Heroic Client: During Client-Directed, Outcome-Informed Therapy (2000) (San Francisco: Jossey-Bass).

Furman, B. & T. Ahola, Solution Talk: Hosting Therapeutic Conversations (1992) (New York: W. W. Norton).

Hubble, M. A., Duncan, B. L., & Miller, S. D. The Heart and Soul of Change: What Works in Therapy (1999) (Washington, D.C.: American Psychological Association).

Lambert, M. J., Psychotherapy Outcome Research: Implications for Integration and Eclectic Therapists, in Hardbook of Psychotherapy Integration (J. C. Norcross and M. R. Goldfried, eds., 1992) (New York: Basic Books).

Snyder, C. R., Mitchell, S., and J. Cheavens, Hope as a Psychotherapeutic Foundation of Common Factors, Placebos, and Expectancies, in The Heart and Soul of Change: What Works in Therapy (M. A. Hubble, B. L. Duncan, and D. D. Miller, eds, 1999) (Washington, D.C.: American Psychological Association).

Tallman, K. and S. C. Bohart, The Client as a Common Factor: Clients as Self-healers, in The Heart and Soul of Charge: What Works in Therapy (M. A. Hubble, B. L. Duncan, and S. D. Miller, eds., 1999). (Washington, D.C.: American Psychological Association).

The Judge-Defendant Interaction:
Toward a Shared Respect Process
by Carrie J. Petrucci, Ph.D.

Prior to conducting research in the courts, my sole experience with (real and not TV) judges and courts sprang from having testified a handful of times as a child protective services worker and a program director for a community corrections agency. In the former, I ended up before juvenile judges to testify on behalf of foster youth on my caseload who had been arrested, trying to get them one more chance. In the latter, my purpose was often the opposite. I appeared in court when the probationer was out of compliance. Despite the cross-purposes for my testimony, I was left with three common ambivalent impressions of court procedure: a mystifying process, multi-tasking and seemingly distracted judges, and being interrupted while I testified because I talked too fast for the court recorder to keep up with me.

It was armed with these impressions that I began an in-depth study of a domestic violence court in 1999. The impetus for my study was a desire to know more about this thing called "specialized courts," in this case, specialized domestic violence courts. Having worked with adults on probation for several years, I questioned how important the court process might be to the offenders themselves. Based on well over a thousand intake interviews with probationers, my general impression of *their perception* of court was close to mine—they seemed confused by it, seldom understood what was said by the judge, and often didn't know the court outcome. Or they sometimes took an opposite tact—they blamed the court, specifically the judge or the attorney, for their current situation. Could these "specialized courts" be that different from this? And if they were different, could the process itself have an impact on subsequent offender behavior?

This court room is also where I discovered therapeutic jurisprudence. The judge introduced me to the concept. I was fortunate to see it in practice, and I followed up with my own exploration of the topic. A caveat or limitation to this work is that because I studied only one setting, it is impossible to disentangle three things: what is this judge's approach, from what is specific to a domestic violence court, from what can be attributed to therapeutic jurisprudence. Nonetheless, this work contributes a foundation from which to begin future multi-site studies.

What follows is based on my observations, one day a week for 6 months, and 29 open-ended interviews with professionals involved in the court, including the judge, law enforcement, public defenders, district attorneys, translators, court reporters, the court clerk, bailiffs, and treatment professionals as well as defendants who had successfully completed their 52 weeks of domestic violence counseling, community service, fines and restitution, and jail time. The primary focus of my observations was the progress report hearings, which were the judicial monitoring hearings that occurred on a post-conviction basis after defendants had served any required jail time. Defendants appeared for 7–10 progress report hearings during their year-long court-ordered batterer's treatment counseling. I observed well over 300 of these. These progress report hearings occurred in open court at the beginning of each day and were the first calendared item. Anywhere from a few to 20 defendants might appear on one day. These hearings could take as long as half an hour to process all defendants for that day. Defendants were called up one at a time, and could hear and see all that was said between the judge and those offenders that had hearings before them.

What did I find? My analysis identified a series of components or techniques observed in the domestic violence court that fell into four main categories (see FIGURE 1). I organized these key techniques starting from the smallest, most specific unit (the judge-defendant interaction) to increasingly general components indicative of the larger process (the general court process, legal procedures, and legal rules). Recall that all this information derived from my open-ended interviews with the various professionals as well as defendants involved with the court and so this component structure is a consequence of what those interviewed saw as important.[1] This essay focuses on the group of techniques within the judge-defendant interaction. I hypothesize how these components can be brought together in what I refer to as a "shared respect process". (In research, we "hypothesize" until we have ample evidence to "know" something, which often takes so long that by the time researchers say they "know" something, practitioners have already accepted it as "common knowledge". Thus the reputation that social science research confirms the obvious. In this case however, empirical research of therapeutic jurisprudence within the specialized court process is in its nascent stages, so stating these findings as "hypotheses" seems more appropriate.) Space does not permit discussion of all eight categories of techniques within the judge-defendant interaction. However, the first five (judicial and defendant demeanor, defendant perceptions of judge, judicial role and approach, and specific content of hearings) are included here to illustrate their nature as observed in this court. It is also hoped that with further discussion and study, these components can contribute to a "best practices" approach to therapeutic jurisprudence and specialized courts.

I also found that this shared respect process fits in with current social science theories and research. Notable among these is Sarah Lawrence-Lightfoot's qualitative study published in her book, *Respect: An Exploration*, in which she observed six traditionally hierarchical relationships among helping professionals. Out of her work, she identifies six key aspects of respect: attention, empowerment, healing, dialogue, curiosity, and self-respect. A significant point that she makes that is mirrored in my research is that respect is a "dynamic interaction" rather than a static concept and that "respect generates respect." In my own observations of the court, these two notions were evident in the judge's demeanor, what he said, and what he did and how defendants then responded. Other work in respect has taken this process-approach.[2] Central to Lawrence-Lightfoot's work and mine is that a *relationship* between a judge and defendant can and does emerge, and second, that this relationship can indeed have impact. Therapeutic jurisprudence posits this quite clearly in its emphasis on legal actors and therapeutic consequences. This emphasis on a relationship also has distinct practice implications; most importantly, it supports the notion of a one judge-one defendant approach and explains how it may be more effective. A detailed discussion of this respect process is available in my previously published work already noted. The remainder of this essay will describe five of the techniques observed in judge-defendant interaction in the court.

Techniques in a Shared Respect Process

Judicial Demeanor
Important in any interaction but not easily captured except through observation was the demeanor between the judge and the defendant as the progress reports occurred. The following factors emerged.

How the Judge Spoke to Defendants
The judge spoke slowly and clearly to defendants during their appearances. He spoke loud enough to be heard by all those present in court. He also spoke at a pace at which what he was saying could be understood. He referred to defendants by name (for example, Mr. Smith or Ms. Jones), rather than using the word "defendant" or referring to defendants by a case number. The judge also took particular care in pronouncing names carefully and to the best of his ability.

The judge's tone of voice when he spoke to defendants conveyed concern for the defendant as a person, without pity, disdain, or obvious condescension. The judge appeared to believe what he was saying. He often referred to the defendant as "sir" or "ma'am" and always as "Mr." or "Ms." rather than on a first-name basis. He gave defendants his full attention during the hearing. He regularly asked if defendants had any questions. At the same time, he didn't allow defendants to "get away" with excuses or inconsistent information.

Body-language of the Judge
The judge's attention always appeared to be focused on what was currently happening in the court. He maintained eye-contact with those to whom he was speaking, whether it was a defendant or an attorney, only oc-

casionally looking down to refer to the case file. He sat up, attentive to the court proceedings, eyes focused toward whomever he was speaking.

Listening

Out of necessity, the judge moved through progress reports quickly, however, he did not rush defendants during the hearings. He did expect defendants to be ready immediately upon being called, and he wasted no time calling up the next defendant upon finishing with the current one. However, defendants were given the opportunity to speak, during which the judge listened. The judge seldom interrupted them, and he appeared to be listening attentively to what defendants were saying and responded appropriately.

Defendant Demeanor

Also important is the defendant's demeanor during progress report hearings. Variation existed across defendants, but in most cases, the following can be said about how defendants appeared in court.

How Defendants Spoke to the Judge

Most defendants spoke for themselves during progress report hearings. The public defender (who represented the majority of defendants) was present during the hearings, as was the district attorney. However, the defendant was expected to answer the judge directly (or through the services of a court translator).

The defendant's tone of voice varied from indiscernible due to one-word answers, to speaking loud enough to sound genuine about what he was saying. As defendants answered the judge's questions, their tone indicated that at least for the moment, they seemed to believe what they were saying. At the very least, the tone of voice indicated an interest and attention in what the judge was saying. At the most, it suggested the defendant's commitment to what was being said. Many defendants appeared nervous, talking softly or quickly, but their comfort level seemed to increase if the progress report continued for any length of time.

Body-language of the Defendant

Defendant's came into the forward section of the court and stood either behind or to the right of the table for the attorneys. Most defendants stood up straight, looking directly at the judge. They often put their hands in their front pocket, or crossed them hand-to-wrist. Many defendants exhibited some discomfort with what to do with their hands. Their dress seemed to match their professions—many appeared in dark colored jeans, and cotton shirts. Most defendants appeared well groomed, with pressed clothes and hair worn neatly. Shirts were usually tucked in, or as fashion dictated, sometimes worn out. Whatever defendants were wearing, most seemed to have taken efforts to appear neatly dressed.

Listening

Defendants also appeared to be listening to what the judge was saying, based on how they faced the judge, as well as their responses to the judge.

The Judicial Role and Approach

Consistency

Perhaps the most prominent feature of the judge's approach was the consistency with which he dealt with defendants. Repeatedly stating the rules to all defendants in the open forum of the progress report hearings allowed defendants to observe for themselves this consistent treatment across defendants. The judge said that he wanted defendants waiting to appear to see that they were treated with consistency and fairness. The judge's same approach was therefore easily observed and was commented on by defendants and legal professionals who worked closely with the judge.

Multiple, Non-Traditional Role

By his own admission and through the observation of others in the court, the judge took on multiple non-traditional roles and seemed comfortable with this. He saw these multiple dimensions to include authority-figure, problem-solver, motivator, and monitor. These roles were instrumental to achieving his most important goal for defendants: keeping them on the right track and giving immediate consequences for failure or success.

Genuine, Caring, Consistent, and Firm

The judge described his method in the courtroom as the use of two seemingly opposing aspects that worked together; what he referred to as "constructive intimidation" and a caring attitude. Central to this was a zero tolerance for domestic violence. The judge exhibited a concern for defendants through a caring attitude, largely exhibited by taking an interest in the defendant as an individual and through a concern for the defendant's family. A genuine and caring approach was also evidenced by the judge taking on a problem-solving role. For example, defendants were often juggling custody or visitation requirements. The judge might assist a defendant in figuring out how to carry out a visit with his children without violating any court orders. If the defendant was not doing well in the counseling, the judge used "constructive intimidation" by immediately bringing the defendant's problematic progress to his attention. The judge's response might range from a warning to remanding a defendant to jail, depending on the severity of the defendant's actions.

Defendant's Perceptions of the Judge

Respect for Authority of the Judge

Defendants' perceptions of the judge were stated in mostly positive terms. It is notable that all the defendants interviewed knew the judge by name.

One defendant described the judge as a "good" judge, "straight when he had to be", but also having a "heart". Another defendant described the judge as being "keen" and appreciated that the judge was "on it". "You can't play. They're hip to it." This defendant recognized that the judge did not allow defendants to get away with trying to outwit the judge or make excuses. The judge's familiarity with domestic violence cases was evidenced in another defendant's statement that "he sees this all the time, so he knows how to deal with you." At the same time, however, the judge was generally perceived as "a pretty fair guy," "going by what the law says." Defendants sought to present themselves well in front of the judge and perceived the judge as genuine and fair.

Being Updated on their Progress

Defendants saw the court appearances as something "you have to do" and seemed comfortable with it. Being provided with updated information on their progress was viewed as helpful because then defendants knew whether they were in compliance or not. Several defendants said they appreciated it when the judge said how well they were doing. They also appreciated it when the judge told them what they were doing wrong, so they could correct it.

Awareness of Flexibility of the Court

Defendants were aware that the judge was willing to schedule court appearances on the defendant's day off, or at a time of day that did not conflict with the defendant's work schedule.

Familiarity with Consequences

Consequences meted out by the judge were familiar to defendants. It was well known that the judge would issue a bench warrant if a defendant did not attend counseling, or that certain things written in the progress report by batterer's treatment counselors could lead to going back to jail. Defendants also recalled being put in jail themselves by the judge, usually for not going to the counseling, or failing to appear in court.

The Specific Content of
Progress Report Hearings

Statement Types

Transcripts from all progress reports on 3 different days were content-analyzed. Observations indicated that progress report hearings usually lasted a few minutes if all was well and slightly longer if the defendant's progress was problematic. The nature of the dialogue between the judge and the defendant in the progress report hearings involved a series of statement types by the judge and the defendant. These "statement types" were constructed by the researcher based on a listing of the general purpose of each sentence or idea spoken during the progress report. What follows are the statement types for the judge and the defendant and an example when helpful.

The judge's statements to defendants were comprised of a combination of the following: naming and greeting (good morning, Mr. Smith); instructing (please bring your progress report next time); informing defendants of their status (you have completed your community service); asking questions (how are you liking the counseling?); explaining (you need to attend both counseling and NA each week); negotiating (can you enroll in a counseling program by next Friday?); ordering (return on June 7th at 8:30am); giving positive comments (your attendance is good at the counseling program); cautioning (watch your absences); warning (if you do not attend counseling, I will remand you to jail); responding to questions asked by the defendant, and thanking the defendant.

Defendant statement types included: naming and greeting (good morning, Judge); responding or answering to the judge's questions, asking questions (Can I switch programs?), negotiating (Can I pay part of my fine next week?), and thanking the judge.

In one of the examples of a progress report hearing, more interactions between the defendant and the judge occurred when the defendant was not doing well. The judge took time to attempt to head off a violation before it occurred. The judge also spent more time informing the defendant of the issues and then explaining what needed to happen in order for the defendant to avoid a violation. While the judge did most of the talking, he also checked in with the defendant for responses throughout the exchange.

Conclusion

Therapeutic jurisprudence suggests that *how* legal actors interact with defendants may indeed influence therapeutic or anti-therapeutic outcomes. This study suggests a shared respect process as a mechanism that may provide a link between what is experienced in court and subsequent offender behavior. This detailed illustration of aspects of what a judge says and how he or she says it, and equally important, how a defendant receives that information and responds to it, is intended to contribute to ongoing dialog and research in therapeutic jurisprudence and specialized courts.

Notes

1. My efforts to meet with agencies working with victims/survivors of domestic violence were unsuccessful, and so their perceptions are not included in this analysis. This is another notable limitation of this research.

2. For a complete discussion, see Petrucci (2002). Respect As a Component

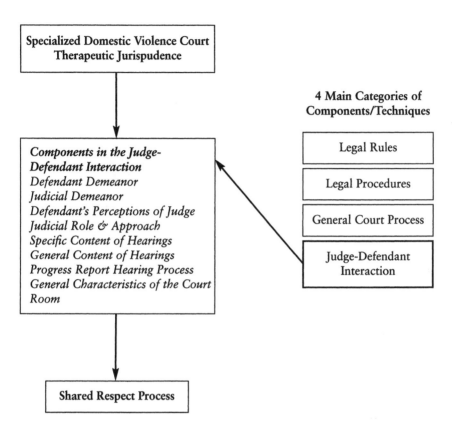

Figure 1. Main Components in a Domestic Violence Court and Components that Produce the Respect Process.

in The Judge-Defendant Interaction in a Specialized Domestic Violence Court That Utilizes Therapeutic Jurisprudence. *Criminal Law Bulletin 38*, 2, 263–295.

References

Lawrence-Lightfoot, S., Respect: An Exploration (2000).

Petrucci, Carrie, *Respect as a Component in the Judge-Defendant Interaction in a Specialized Domestic Violence Court That Utilizes Therapeutic Turisprudence*. 38 *Crim. L. Bul.* 263 (2002).

The Therapeutic Value of the
Civil Commitment Hearing

Excerpted and adapted by Bruce J. Winick
(Excerpted and adapted from Therapeutic
Jurisprudence and the Civil Commitment Hearing
10 J. CONTEMP. ISSUES 57–60 (1999)).

Judges in civil commitment hearings need to be sensitive to the therapeutic potential of the roles they play so that their conduct can enhance the therapeutic potential of the commitment hearing. Judges need education in the psychology of procedural justice and in the psychological value of choice and disadvantages of coercion. Judges play an important symbolic role. The literature on the psychology of procedural justice demonstrates that people place a high value on how they are treated by legal authorities. They value the affirmation of their legal status as competent citizens and human beings entitled to be treated with dignity and respect. Judges who conduct commitment hearings in ways that seem to assume that the person is an incompetent subject of paternalism and that deny him or her respect frustrate the dignitary value of the hearing. In furthering the dignitary goal, patients should be permitted to dress appropriately for the hearing, rather than being required to appear in hospital garb, as sometimes occurs. Through his or her actions, the judge should affirm the patient's dignity and humanity. How the judge conducts the proceeding can convey to the patient that it is a process designed for his or her welfare and that he or she is valued and will be treated with fairness and dignity.

Both the judge and the expert witness can play an important role in providing the patient with a sense of "information control." The patient, facing the uncertainties of a hospital commitment that he or she is objecting to, will predictably experience a high degree of stress and anxiety at the hearing. The judge and clinical experts, by reassuring the patient and demonstrating concern for his or her welfare, can help to relieve at least some of that stress. By carefully and understandably conveying information to the patient about the hearing process and what will occur at the hospital if commitment is ordered, the judge can diffuse much of the stress that the commitment process itself might produce.

The patient should not be treated as invisible at the hearing. Rather, the judge and expert witnesses should address the patient and attempt to communicate in his or her language rather than in professional jargon. If the expert witness recommends commitment, the reasons why this would be beneficial should be explained in ways that are designed to be convincing to the patient. Moreover, a sense of optimism should be conveyed to the patient. The patient should be told that although he or she suffers from a mental illness, such illness is very likely to respond to hospital treatment within a reasonably brief period. The benefits of psychotropic medication and other forms of treatment should be explained to the patient in ways that are calculated to persuade the patient as to their value. The judge should listen attentively to the patient and convey the impression that what he or she has to say is important and will be given full consideration. According voice and validation in this way can considerably enhance the patient's feeling of participation and can inspire trust in the judge. Too often, the judge conveys the impression that what the patient has to say will not be considered and that the results of the hearing are a foregone conclusion. Such an impression can inspire distrust by the patient in the judge and the belief that he or she is not being treated fairly and in good faith. In addition to paying close attention to the patient's testimony, the judge should ask questions of the expert witness in a way that demonstrates that the judge will make an independent decision, rather than merely "rubber stamping" the witness's recommendation.

At appropriate points in the proceedings, recesses should be taken to give the attorney and client an opportunity to consider whether, in light of the testimony, the client might wish to explore the possibility of a negotiated voluntary admission in order to avoid what might appear to be the inevitable and more restrictive and stigmatizing involuntary commitment. Indeed, judges can suggest to the patient's lawyer that if commitment seems to the attorney to be the likely outcome, counsel should consider the possibility of explaining to the client the legal and other advantages of accepting voluntary admission and recommend this option to him or her. A client's choice of voluntary admission at this point, as long as the client perceives it as voluntary, may increase the potential that hospital treatment will be efficacious.

If a negotiated settlement in favor of voluntary admission is not possible, and if the judge concludes that commitment is warranted, the judge may consider giving the patient a final opportunity to accept voluntary admission in view of the judgment that the judge feels compelled to make as a result of the testimony. If this final opportunity is not accepted, the judge should seek to explain the commitment decision to the patient, addressing the patient directly, and offering to answer any questions that the patient may have.

Whenever possible, the treating clinician should not be permitted to also function as the expert witness testifying in favor of the patient's commitment. Such testimony may give the patient the impression that the clinician is an enemy, a perception that can seriously undermine the clinician's treatment role.

One final therapeutic jurisprudence consideration worth noting is the impact that restructuring the civil commitment hearing in the way suggested could have on the lawyers, judges, and clinicians who work in the commitment process. Participating in a sham process that distorts the roles that they are supposed to play may in the long run pose negative psychological consequences for these professionals. In contrast, playing their assigned roles in ways that can help to improve the psychological functioning of their clients/patients and increase the likelihood that their hospitalization and treatment will be more effective can bring personal and professional satisfaction that can increase the professionals' own mental health.

Judicial Behavior and the Civil Commitment Petitioner

by Charles J. Kennedy, M.Div., Ph.D.

For over 30 years, the involuntary civil commitment hearing has served as the means of assessing the appropriateness of initiating and continuing an individual's involuntary psychiatric hospitalization. Full consideration of the individual's rights was one of the goals recognized through the introduction of this judicial procedure. It replaced the previous medical model—a model that relied upon the psychiatrist's opinion of need-for-treatment as the sole criterion for involuntary admissions. The emphasis of mental health law and individual rights developed with the recognition that involuntary confinement and treatment without established cause was a denial of constitutionally protected freedom.

Since its inception, very little research has investigated the impact that the involuntary commitment hearing has created. This article describes a study that applies the insight and approach set forth by the tenets of therapeutic jurisprudence (Wexler, 1990; Wexler & Winick, 1996; Winick, 2001) to the area of procedural justice and the civil involuntary commitment. As a model, therapeutic jurisprudence is intended to raise scholars' and legal policy makers' consciousness in regard to the manner in which law functions. The question was raised as to whether effective legal procedures might have undesirable psychological consequences. It was suggested that legal practice could have the effect of serving as a social force and, in certain cases, work against the very principles that it attempts to uphold. To avoid this unintended outcome, therapeutic jurisprudence endeavors to raise consciousness and calls for empirical analysis of this interaction.

When civil rights advocates stepped forward and legalized the procedure required for the involuntary hospitalization of individuals with a mental illness, important decision making powers were removed from the medical profession and assumed by the courts. Whereas once the psychiatrist operated independently of outside influence, standards were introduced that are now reviewed by third party legal representatives. Questions have been raised as to whether the legal profession was prepared for this partnership with the mental health professional, the individual with a mental illness, and the family.

One of the few empirical studies in this area was conducted by Cascardi, Poythress, and Hall, (2000). This study investigated the patient's awareness within the setting of a simulated civil commitment hearing. Within this study, patients who had been actually committed to involuntary treatment were exposed to videotapes of mock commitment hearings in order to explore their responsiveness to procedural justice manipulations. Results suggested that patients are indeed positively influenced by such procedural justice characteristics. This present article will report on a study that investigated, not the patient involved in the civil commitment hearing but an equally pertinent character, the caregiver who serves in a supportive role to the patient and is often responsible for the future support and well being of the individual's life.

This present study utilized a social justice survey instrument adapted to a mental health context. Whereas previous research has explored reactions of the patients, the present study examined caregiver's responses to the civil commitment hearing. Responses of 226 participants who had recently petitioned for an involuntary psychiatric admission on behalf of their relative or friend were investigated. Hypotheses were tested that involved an understanding of the characteristics that affect evaluations and assessments of satisfaction with the hearing itself as well as an inquiry into the expressed willingness of the caregiver to continue support of the mentally ill hospitalized patient and to again invoke the commitment process, if it should prove necessary. Results supported the hypotheses. These findings suggest that the experience of the social interactions between the judge and the participants exceeds that of the outcome in contributing to the individual's satisfaction with the experience and their willingness to continue patient support.

Family/Caregiver's Role in the Life of the Patient

Due to the major changes that took place in the mental health field, families of individuals with mental illness were thrust into a position of caregiving that they were ill prepared to assume. Beginning in the 1960s, state psychiatric hospitals began reducing the population of those in their care as treatment was transferred to the newly federally mandated community mental health centers. As part of the civil rights movement, this transformation represented recognition of the legal protection of constitutionally guaranteed rights of individuals with mental illness. The person could no longer be involuntarily hospitalized without evidence of serious impairment involving a life or death situation. Unfortunately, local mental health facilities could not always offer the individual adequate support and treatment. Most commonly, that support became the responsibility of a relative or friend (Marsh and Johnson, 1997).

Thus, today, in the majority of cases, an individual with a mental illness is dependent upon the family or close friend to maintain basic life supporting care (Lefley, 1996). In the case of an emergency, where the individual might display dangerous behavior or, in some states demonstrate "grave disability" due to a mental illness, a petition can be signed and the person will be admitted on an emergency basis to a psychiatric hospital. A hearing that is held within a specified brief period of time follows. The purpose of the hearing is to review the legitimacy of the admission and decide on the need for continued care. In a majority of jurisdictions, the petitioner must testify as to observations of the individual's behavior in order to "make a case" that the individual has met criteria for psychiatric admission. The decision to continue hospitalization is made by the mental health review officer, representing the court, after reviewing testimony from this petitioner as well as the attending psychiatrist. The decision to continue hospitalization or release the individual is ultimately in the hands of the court.

From a spectator's point of view, one might be inclined to think that the winner of this dispute would emerge the most satisfied and supportive of those involved. In the case of the involuntary commitment, it is known that in the majority of cases the judge will find the patient in need of continued care and extend the commitment. This finding has been explained as a function of the weight that the judge places upon the professional opinion of the psychiatrist (Turkheimer and Parry, 1992; Costello, 1996). In this regard, the judge is aware that the psychiatrist would not request a hearing if there was not professional concern over the clinical need for extended commitment. The psychiatrist would simply discharge the individual or offer the option of transfer to a voluntary status.

Without investigating this assumption, it could be assumed that the caregiver would be satisfied by virtue of the positive outcome, i.e., continued hospitalization. Tyler (1992) suggests, however, that there may be other factors at work other than the outcome that influence the manner in which an individual arrives at a sense of satisfaction. In concert with the research that has been conducted in the area of social justice, this present investigation points to the outcome of the dispute as only partially contributing to the evaluation of satisfaction with the hearing. Results suggest that, while the participants did not ignore the outcome of the involuntary commitment hearing, it was but one factor contributing to a person's evaluation of the experience. A considerably stronger association of satisfaction with the hearing experience was found with the procedural characteristics; that is, individuals placed more importance on factors such as participation in the process, dignities extended, and trust in the judge's genuine concern than on the judge's decision. Additionally, it was observed that a significant relationship existed between the caregiver's satisfaction with the hearing and a willingness to pledge continuing support and to again use the civil commitment process, if necessary.

Results of this study revealed that the participants weighed the quality of personal interactions during the court hearing more heavily than the outcome itself—even when the outcome was unfavorable. Questions posed that elicited characteristics of personal interaction in this study included: Would caregivers find satisfaction solely achieving their aim of hospitalization of the individual? Would families look at alternate factors in evaluating the experience? Additionally, would there be factors other than the outcome associated with the individual's willingness to continue support of the individual? A strong association was found between the person's level of satisfaction and a willingness to continue support and to again invoke civil commitment, if needed. This relationship was found independent of the outcome, as hypothesized. These characteristics of personal interaction involved basic transactions of fair play and fair consideration.

Indeed, the present findings of a strong relationship between satisfaction with the hearing experience and procedural factors point to procedural justice serving as an important therapeutic tool. Implied also in this reasoning, and supported by the present findings, is the suggestion that a satisfying assessment of this judicial experience leads to continuing support of the patient. Thibaut and Walker (1975) originally suggested that dispute resolution would best be facilitated by just procedures, procedures that ensured some personal control by the participants. This insight was further extended by research that outlined social factors involved in the assessment of a dispute resolution. Tyler and Lind (1988) have shown significant relationships between social factors at play and an assessment of satisfaction with specific judicial encounters. Tyler (1992) subsequently proposed that procedural justice applied at the civil commitment hearing would have therapeutic advantages for patients, and Winick (1999) suggested a restructuring of the civil commitment hearing in order to achieve these therapeutic advantages. Cascardi, Poythress and Hall (2000) provided a measure of empirical verification for Tyler's (1992) therapeutic jurisprudence hypothesis. This present study both supported and extended this understanding to the area of mental health and specifically to the encounter of the petitioner within the commitment hearing. This study lends strong support to the analysis of therapeutic jurisprudence that the law serves more than a perfunctory ceremony or means of bringing order to a confusing situation. In this present context, empirical research has resulted in an analysis of legal protocol utilizing insight from behavioral science. The results suggested that psychological attributes exist within the civil involuntary commitment process that are strongly associated with an evaluation of a therapeutic experience.

Importance of the Judge's Role: Implications

Controversy regarding the judge/attorney's role in the mental health context has resulted in a confusing array of potential legal approaches. How does the judge actually view his or her role in the hearing procedures? Does he or she believe fully in, and behave consistently with, due process or does their behavior reflect actions conducted "on behalf of" the patient? If outcome is only partially responsible for the person's positive experience, will preconceived judicial attitudes interfere with therapeutic aspects of the experience? As has been demonstrated, caregivers are not passive participants. An ongoing evaluation of the judge's behavior has a strong relationship with how the petitioners perceive the fairness of the hearing, as well as the individual's willingness to continue support.

As can be readily understood, the outcome of the involuntary commitment hearing cannot be controlled. Outcome is a decision based both on the facts of the case and evidence considered by the mental health review officer. Even though, in the majority of cases, the outcome conforms to the result the petitioner set out to achieve, i.e., continued hospitalization. In truth, the facts explain that the procedures of the hearing are more strongly associated with a sense of petitioner satisfaction than with outcome. In concert with the literature of therapeutic jurisprudence, the present study supports the notion that legal procedures involve far more than attention to the civil rights of the individuals involved or even control of the hospitalization. The tenets of therapeutic jurisprudence suggest that there are factors present in the commitment hearing that affect people psychologically unrelated to the outcome of the hearing. Factors, such as those hypothesized, suggest such an alternate explanation to individual's attitudes. In other words, the commitment process itself seems to have therapeutic implications.

This present investigation suggested that inclusion of the petitioner in all appropriate aspects of the hearing will be associated with an increase in satisfaction with the hearing experience and continued support of the patient. The strong relationship revealed between satisfaction and support as well as that between procedures and satisfaction point towards consideration of the involuntary hearing as something other than simply a legal transaction. Implications are clear. The involuntary commitment hearing should be regarded not only as a legal procedure that protects the rights of the individual, but also as a treatment intervention. Caregivers who come forward to petition the court on behalf of their loved-one should not be regarded as passive bystanders. They are indeed significantly influenced by the conduct of the court, and their future support of the patient and their willingness to again invoke the court's processes when necessary may well be affected by this experience.

The results of this study suggested that the judge should not only be proficient with the law, but should also strive to develop the social-justice skills described—skills that are not always intuitive. The present investigation identifies the judge as the key participant in this experience, strongly influencing the person's satisfaction with the hearing. With the realization that participants are continuously alert and attentive to the behavior and attitudes of legal counsel, judges and attorneys can begin to examine their conduct and approach. It is the judge who sets and maintains the tone of the interchange among all parties present. This study suggested that the petitioner will focus less upon the outcome than upon the more elusive attributes of procedural justice—attributes present such as the judge's perceived motivation. The present study revealed that the participants in the civil commitment hearing asked themselves the following questions: Was there a level playing field? Did the judge attempt to be fair? Was one person favored over the other? Additionally, these findings suggested that the petitioner will focus upon perceptions of standing within the group and it was discovered that they were keenly attuned to the responses of these questions: Was I treated with respect and politeness? Was I offered full consideration of my rights? Was I given full opportunity to explain myself? Finally, this study suggested that the petitioner would respond to concerns over the impact of his/her testimony and whether it was felt that it made a difference in the final outcome: Was it felt that the judge was thorough and had all the information that was needed to arrive at a good decision?

The findings of the present investigation suggested that a person's sense of judicial-satisfaction point to basic human values of fair play and fair treatment. It was also learned that anticipated future support of the patient is associated with satisfaction of the hearing experience. These findings can serve as clear directives to both the legal and mental health professions that evidence points to their behavior as central to the ultimate outcome of the hearing, i.e., the welfare of the family and the patients themselves. With the knowledge that a sense of procedural fairness influences the petitioner, professionals should strive to conduct themselves in a respectful and non-biased manner. For reasons suggested by this present study, it seems paramount that both disciplines join together in an endeavor to work towards a system that enhances therapeutic outcomes.

References

Cascardi, M., Poythress, N.G., & Hall, A. (2000). Procedural justice in the context of civil commitment: An analogue study. *Behavioral Sciences and Law, 18*, 731–740.

Costello, J. C. (1996). "Why would I need a lawyer?" Legal counsel and advocacy for people with mental disabilities. In B. D. Sales & D. W. Shuman (Eds.), *Law, mental health, and mental disorder*, New York: Harcourt, Brace. pp. 15–39.

Lefley, H. P. (1996). *Family caregiving in mental illness*. Thousand Oaks, CA: Sage Publications.

Marsh, D. T., & Johnson, D. L. (1997). The family experience of mental illness: implications for intervention. *Professional Psychology: Research and Practice, 28*, (3), 229–237.

Thibaut, J. W., & Walker, L. (1975). *Procedural justice: A psychological analysis*. Hillsdale, NJ: Erlbaum.

Turkheimer, E., & Parry, C.D.H, (1992). Why the gap? Practice and policy in civil commitment hearings. *American Psychologist, 47*, No. 5, 646–655.

Tyler, T. R. (1992). The Psychological consequences of judicial procedures: Implications for civil commitment hearings. *Southern Methodist University Law Review, 46*, pp. 433–445.

Wexler, D. B. (1990). *Therapeutic jurisprudence: The law as a therapeutic agent.* Durham NC: Carolina Academic Press.

Wexler, D. B., & Winick, B. J. (1996). *Law in a Therapeutic Key: Developments in Therapeutic Jurisprudence.* Carolina Academic Press, Durham, NC

Winick, B. J., Therapeutic Jurisprudence and the Civil Commitment Hearing, 10 Journal of Contemp. Legal. Issues, 10, 37–60 (1999).

Winick, B. J., (2001). The Civil Commitment Hearing: Applying the Law Therapeutically. In L.E. Frost & R.J. Bonnie (Eds.) *The Evolution of Mental Health Law.* American Psychological Association, Washington, DC

D. COUNTERING DENIAL AND MINIMIZATION

In the criminal process, judges may help pave the way to positive behavior change by encouraging an offender to be forthcoming about past behavior and problems. Accordingly, this section deals with the judicial role in countering offender denial and minimization. As is well known, the overwhelming majority of criminal cases are disposed of through pleas of guilty or *nolo contendere* rather than trial. The focus of this section is on the plea process, and it consists of two selections.

The first, by Wexler, is on sex offenders and the plea process, and suggests ways in which judges might engage sex offenders in a colloquy that will promote disclosure. Such a course of action is likely to steer the offender toward a rehabilitative path and, at the same time, is likely to be highly therapeutic for the victim. The second selection, by Stephanos Bibas, a law professor at the University of Iowa with prior experience as a federal prosecutor, deals with the anti-therapeutic consequences of *nolo contendere* (no contest) and so-called *Alford* pleas (where a defendant is allowed to plead guilty but, at the same time, proclaim his innocence). Bibas opposes the availability of these pleas on various grounds, including the negative effects on rehabilitation that they may produce. He also details how guilty pleas might be taken so as to maximize their therapeutic yield.

Sex Offenders and the Plea Process
by David B. Wexler
(Excerpted from *Therapeutic Jurisprudence and the Criminal Courts*, 35 WM. & MARY L. REV. 279, 284–291 (1993), Copyright 1993 by David B. Wexler, reprinted with permission)

One of the most striking features of sex offenders, particularly child molesters, is their heavy "denial and minimization" of their behavior. Clinicians have studied and classified these "cognitive distortions," which are evidenced by statements such as "nothing happened," "something happened but it wasn't my idea," or "something happened and it was my idea but it wasn't sexual." Moreover, mental health professionals believe that "the key issues....of offender denial, motivation to change and cooperation in the

165

process of treatment...are all aspects of the offender's functioning which are just as amenable to analysis and modification as the sex offending behavior itself." In fact, manuals exist for the treatment of child molesters which cover such matters as "cognitive restructuring." One approach to cognitive restructuring uses the technique of role-reversal: "the therapist role-plays being a child molester who uses the various...cognitive distortions, [and] the patients are asked to take the role of a probation officer, a policeman, a family member or anyone who might interact with a child molester, and attempt to confront the beliefs role-played by the therapist." The role-reversal process is used to lead the offenders to "rethink their own cognitions."

A therapeutic jurisprudence approach to the sex offense area might ask whether the law, including the rules, procedures, and roles of lawyers and judges, operates therapeutically or antitherapeutically upon sex offenders. For example, does the law in this area promote cognitive restructuring? Or does it instead promote cognitive distortion, and thus perhaps contribute to psychological dysfunction and criminality? It may well be, as one British psychologist has observed, that "many aspects of the justice system are inadvertently geared towards fostering offender denial." In that connection, the therapeutic jurisprudence approach applied to sex offenders produces the following suggestions.

Sex offenders usually are extremely unwilling to admit guilt, even when the state's evidence is impressive, and therefore, they often seek to plead "no contest," or nolo contendere. A nolo plea permits the sex offender to accept the consequences of a conviction without going to trial and without admitting guilt. Indeed, some offenders will seek to enter a so-called Alford plea which permits the defendant to plead guilty while at the same time protesting his innocence.

Courts may and often do accept such pleas, although generally they have no obligation to do so. The acceptance of *nolo* and *Alford* pleas from sex offenders, however, may reinforce cognitive distortions and denial. This frame of mind may lead the offenders to reject offers of treatment directed at decreasing their deviant sexual arousal and increasing their nondeviant sexual arousal and social/sexual skills. Alternatively, the mindset may undermine the potential success of such treatment even if the offender is persuaded or required to participate in it.

Moreover, judicial willingness to accept *nolo* and *Alford* pleas may make it easy, perhaps too easy, for defense attorneys to arrange plea bargains acceptable to their clients. If judges were reluctant to accept pleas in sex offender cases unaccompanied by an admission of guilt, defense lawyers would need to coax more actively those clients who lack plausible defenses to admit guilt and accept the bargain. Professor Alschuler's written remarks in a somewhat different context are relevant:

It may often be a lawyer's duty to emphasize in harsh terms
the force of the prosecution's evidence: "What about this fact? Is
it going to go away? How the hell would you vote if you were a
juror in your case?" It may sometimes be a lawyer's duty to say
bluntly, "I cannot possibly beat this case. You are going to spend a
long time in jail, and the only question is how long."

Thus, if jurisdictions refused to recognize *nolo* and *Alford* pleas, or if judges
were reluctant to accept them in sex offender cases, the law would induce defense lawyers to engage their clients in an exercise of "cognitive restructuring," including role-reversal. For example, the defense attorney may ask the
sex offender how he would vote as a juror in the case. In therapeutic jurisprudence terms, the result would be a revised legal arrangement that
would restructure the role of the defense lawyer in a way that would promote therapeutic values.

The therapeutic potential of the role of the judge also could be enhanced
in guilty plea cases if the court engaged in detailed questioning of the defendant about the factual basis of the plea. Specifically, the judge could address,
on the record, some of the matters typically subject to cognitive distortion
by sex offenders. In his classic study of guilty pleas, Donald Newman describes one metropolitan court's procedure that may be particularly pertinent for our purposes: a post-plea-of-guilty hearing in which, "[a]fter receiving...a guilty plea from a defendant...the court requires the defendant to
take the stand, under oath, and state that he did commit the crime and exactly how he committed it." Judges could buttress the effect of pleas with full
admissions of guilt by means of a judicial sentencing policy particularly un-
sympathetic to sex offenders who stand trial and offer a defense that the jury
rejected and that the judge independently found perjurious.

A plea procedure that encourages a sex offender to make a detailed admission of guilt should work, therefore, against denial and cognitive distortion
and toward cognitive restructuring. Moreover, should the offender vacillate
and deny his guilt when in a correctional institution or community treatment
program, an "adequate record with which to confront the person" may induce
him again to accept responsibility and perhaps "to participate in institutional
therapy programs" or to participate more meaningfully in such programs.[1]

This new therapeutic jurisprudence approach to sex offenders and the plea
process is, of course, merely suggestive. Ultimately, the question whether cognitive distortions are impacted by judicial behavior in accepting a guilty plea is
an empirical one. If therapeutic jurisprudence has an influence on criminal
law scholarship, part of that influence will be in encouraging empirical studies.

Many of the matters seem readily testable. For instance, there are existing
methods of measuring cognitive distortions of pedophiles. Moreover, legal
anthropologist Susan Philips of the University of Arizona has observed

change of plea hearings and has concluded that judges do indeed have different styles of ascertaining the factual basis of a plea:

> Some judges described the events that led to the defendant being charged, or had either the prosecution or defense lawyer describe them, and then asked the defendant if he agreed with the description. Other judges tried to get the defendant himself to describe those events. The latter strategy...requires more involvement from the defendant and a more confessional mode of admission and met with more resistance from defendants.

Philips categorizes the judges as either "Procedure Oriented" or "Record Oriented." The Procedure Oriented judges emphasize the personal involvement of the defendant, while the Record Oriented judges minimize that involvement and view their role as making a neat record invulnerable to collateral or appellate attack. From wide-ranging interviews with the judges in her study, Philips concludes that the Procedure Oriented judges are politically liberal and the Record Oriented judges are politically conservative. The irony is that, if the therapeutic jurisprudence speculation holds true upon empirical examination, the liberal judges may be performing a greater crime control function than their conservative counterparts.

In any event, it would be feasible to undertake a post-plea study to determine whether defendants in sex cases who, presumably through a process of random assignment, appear and plead before Procedure Oriented judges retain fewer cognitive distortions than those who plead before Record Oriented judges. Alternatively, one might study the issue of cognitive distortion through a more indirect, policy-oriented approach. That is, one might investigate whether sex case defendants pleading before Procedure Oriented judges are more willing than the control group defendants to participate in therapy sessions which are later offered to them. If the results of such studies are promising, a further therapeutic jurisprudence undertaking could develop "model" colloquies for establishing the factual basis of pleas to various sex offenses and other offenses, and eventually subject those colloquies to empirical study.

We know, especially from therapists' reports, that denial, minimization, and cognitive distortions are particularly pronounced among sex offenders and child molesters. What we do not yet seem to know is whether sex offenders are unique in their harboring of strong cognitive distortions, or whether other types of offenders—or perhaps offenders in general—are as prone to cognitive distortions.

Reports exist from clinicians who treat sex offenders, but reports do not exist on the extent to which offenders such as carjackers cognitively distort, claiming that "I didn't do it," "I did it but it wasn't my idea," or "I did it, and it was my idea, but I was only kidding around." If rehabilitation reclaims a legitimate role in the criminal justice system, the potential role of the judge in cognitive restructuring for purposes of corrections and rehabilitation may become important well beyond the area of sex offenders.

Several current issues in the general law of sentencing also may appear somewhat different if looked at through the therapeutic jurisprudence "lens." For example, would rehabilitation be advanced if sentencing courts, or sentencing guidelines, formulated sentences based upon such factors as a defendant's "acceptance of responsibility," or a defendant's "obstruction of justice" for committing perjury during his or her trial?

Notes

1. A final factor which may be relevant to "cognitive restructuring through law" relates to the type of plea bargain offered a sex offender. An offender might be charged with the actual crime the state believes he committed, and might receive a sentence concession for an "on-the-nose" plea to that charge. Alternatively, he may be charged with the actual crime, but be allowed to plead to a reduced charge. "Charge" bargaining, rather than "sentence" bargaining, is particularly prevalent in jurisdictions in which mandatory sentencing has shifted discretion from the courts (in sentencing) to the prosecution (in charging). Albert W. Alschuler, Sentencing Reform and Prosecutorial Power: A Critique of Recent Proposals for "Fixed" and "Presumptive" Sentencing, 126 U.Pa.L.Rev. 550 (1978). An interesting and generally unasked question regarding the wisdom of alternative sentencing and bargaining schemes is whether "charge" bargaining feeds into cognitive distortion more so than does "sentence" bargaining.

Key References

Newman, Donald J., Conviction: The Determination of Guilt or Innocence Without Trial (1966).

North Carolina v. Alford, 400 U.S. 25 (1970).

Philips, Susan U., Ideology in the Language of Judges: How Judges Practice Law, Politics, and Courtroom Control (1998).

Using Plea Procedures to Combat Denial and Minimization

by Stephanos Bibas[1]

Criminal defendants are often loath to admit guilt to others or even to themselves. They are ashamed of their actions, fearing the censure of family, friends, and the public. And they feel guilty, leading them to deny guilt even to themselves. Thus, guilty defendants are often reluctant to plead guilty, even when faced with overwhelming evidence of guilt. To gain the benefits of guilty pleas without admitting guilt, defendants in most states may enter *Al-*

ford or nolo contendere pleas. These pleas are quite common in sex offense cases but are also used in crimes against children or the elderly, heinous murders, domestic assaults, drug crimes, and other cases. Defense lawyers and many judges and prosecutors like these pleas because they are efficient: they clear dockets and move cases along without the ordeal of trials.

This efficiency, however, comes at a steep price. The defendants who most want to use these pleas are the ones in deepest denial. They may deny that they committed the acts, that they were aware of the acts, or that their acts were wrong or harmful. For example, a child molester might say "It wasn't sexual, and anyway there's nothing wrong with having sex with children." These denials manifest deeper cognitive denials and distortions, which impede treatment.

Admitting one's wrong is the first step toward moving past it. In Alcoholics Anonymous and other twelve-step programs, one must admit that one has a problem in order to conquer it. This admission shatters one's illusions of goodness; the recognition that one has fallen is a prerequisite for standing up again. Admissions also provide essential details to therapists. Therapists use these details to examine cognitive distortions, detect warning signs, foster empathy for victims, and frame therapeutic responses. And, if offenders later deny or minimize their behavior, therapists can keep them honest by confronting them with the details of their earlier admissions. Admissions are so central to therapy that most sex-offender-treatment programs refuse to admit offenders who deny any sexual conduct. In short, denial obstructs treatment, which in turn greatly increases the risk of recidivism.

The solution to this denial is not to be supportive and passive; this type of therapy usually fails. Instead, therapists must confront offenders with the facts and force them to see their actions. Firm challenges can be very effective in breaking down denials. By challenging offenders' excuses and rationalizations, therapists can trigger feelings of guilt and use this guilt to spur change.[2]

Ideally, of course, offenders would acknowledge their own guilt and confront their responsibility without prompting. Sometimes, however, harsher goads are necessary. Even external pressures, such as the threat of imprisonment, can be effective inducements. Outside challenges and pressures can shatter offenders' illusions and start them on the journey of coming to grips with their actions.

Confessions and denials have these effects not only in therapy, but also in the legal system. Confessions in open court, even if induced by the fear of punishment, can begin to crack the dam of denial. In contrast, repeated, unchallenged denials to lawyers and judges only exacerbate the denial reflex and impede future treatment.[3] Offenders continue to say things like "I never said I was guilty" or "I have not committed a crime." The result is that offenders who enter *Alford* or nolo contendere pleas remain in denial and resist successful treatment, making them much more likely to reoffend. In short, the act of confessing, as well as the legal system's labels and ascriptions of blame, influence offenders' thoughts and treatment processes.

Of course, most defendants do not plead guilty because they are contrite. They plead guilty and feign repentance to earn sentence reductions. This may be the most we can hope for from many defendants. But even feigned or induced repentance may teach some offenders lessons. The act of confessing during a guilty-plea allocution underscores the victim's injury, the law violated, and the community's condemnation. Indeed, feigned repentance may lead to true repentance. Many people find confessing hard. (Some defendants may confess cavalierly. This is least true, however, of the defendants in deepest denial who insist on *Alford* and nolo pleas precisely to avoid admissions.) Confessing requires admitting one's shameful acts, dropping the shield of excuses, and taking responsibility. This is why defense lawyers must work with many defendants for a long time before they are willing to plead guilty. Even insincere admissions of guilt involve lowering denial mechanisms, opening the path to reform, and bringing closure to victims and the community. Plea bargains, on this view, induce guilty defendants to confess and start on the road to repentance.

Some guilty defendants cannot or will not admit guilt. For these recalcitrant guilty defendants, as well as for innocent defendants, we have jury trials. Jury trials are more than just truth-seeking mechanisms; they are morality plays. Trials reinforce the community's moral norms, pronounce judgment, vindicate victims, and exonerate or brand defendants. Trials engage wrongdoers in examining their own acts, as well as justifying the community's moral code and its responses. The parade of live witnesses and the solemn pronouncement of guilt may perhaps break through denial and drive home the wrongfulness of crimes. Trials teach and reinforce the community's sense of right and wrong, and they are cathartic for victims and the community.

If trials serve these purposes, then *Alford* and nolo contendere pleas are cop-outs. Regular guilty pleas and trial convictions send unambiguous messages of guilt, bringing closure. In contrast, *Alford* and nolo contendere pleas are patently ambiguous. These pleas of guilty-but-not-guilty muddy the criminal law's moral message. These pleas show that the law does not care enough about crime to insist upon clear, candid resolutions. They exalt swift, efficient case disposition over proclaiming clear moral messages and vindicating victims. Plea bargains may already do this covertly, but *Alford* and nolo contendere pleas do it shamelessly. The message is that questions of justice do not matter enough to resolve.

Some authors favor *Alford* and nolo contendere pleas as tools to promote defendants' autonomy and protect their privacy and dignity. These values, however, come at a high price. Offenders have abused their autonomy and privacy, forfeiting their right to live autonomously and privately outside prison walls. They have exalted their dignity at the expense of victims and need to acknowledge guilt and accept responsibility for their wrongdoing. Full-fledged jury trials and guilty-plea allocutions drive home this acceptance of responsibility to offenders, victims, and the community. Quick *Al-*

ford and nolo contendere pleas short-circuit the process. These pleas are most attractive to those who deny guilt to others and perhaps themselves. But these are precisely the offenders who need help to break down their illusions, excuses, and pride. If they cannot remember the past, they are doomed to repeat it.

These pleas also hurt others. Victims very much want apologies, but *Alford* and nolo contendere pleas generally mean that offenders refuse to admit guilt and apologize. So, when victims learn of impending *Alford* and nolo pleas, they often try to block them. If offenders are able to enter these pleas, victims go without vindication. They lose their day in court, their chance to vent their sorrows, without even an admission of wrongdoing, let alone an apology. And non-lawyers often interpret these pleas as meaning that courts are buying offenders' denials. Rape and molestation victims, for example, can suffer more harm when courts appear to accept offenders' denials. Judicial acceptance of *Alford* and nolo pleas in these cases seems to suggest that the victims are liars.[4]

Lawyers often view the legal system's labels and ascriptions of blame as mere words, but lay people are not so cynical. What offenders say in court matters to their and others' perceptions of their guilt. One judge told me that he used to allow nolo contendere pleas. What he found was that a defendant would remain silent in court. Then, upon reporting to a probation officer for a pre-sentence interview, he would deny guilt. He would also tell his family that he had not done the crime but his lawyer had made him plead guilty. Family members would write angry letters to the judge, complaining about what a travesty of justice it was to convict an innocent man. They would say, for example, that the rape victim was a tramp who consented to sex. At sentencing, the defendant and his family would continue to deny guilt and, at least implicitly, blame the victim. Victims would be visibly frustrated when making statements at sentencing, feeling that they had to justify themselves instead of being able to heal. After sentencing, these convicted defendants would continue to deny guilt, impeding therapy or treatment. Then, this judge stopped permitting most nolo contendere pleas. Defense lawyers, knowing that they could not slide by with nolo pleas, confronted clients and brought them to admit guilt; almost none insisted on going to trial. They did not renege on these admissions after leaving court. Defendants evidently stopped denying guilt to themselves and their families, as the complaining letters from families stopped. Defendants and families no longer denied guilt at sentencing. Victims took satisfaction in feeling vindicated and were able to express healthy outrage at sentencing instead of frustration. To this judge, the victims appeared to be healing better. And the judge, having heard a detailed plea colloquy, was much better able to confront defendants with the details and wrongfulness of their acts.

What can the legal system do to combat these problems of *Alford* and nolo contendere pleas? The simplest solution is for legislatures to abolish them.

These pleas may well be constitutional but nonetheless unwise. Short of that, judges retain discretion to reject these pleas, as the judge described above does. These pleas may be needed in exceptional cases, such as where defendants were truly too intoxicated to remember anything and victims would find testifying traumatic. But such cases are extremely rare; lawyers and judges report that intoxication is much more often a fig leaf than a cause of true memory loss.[5] And several judges who routinely refuse these pleas have told me that defendants rarely go to trial as a result. Most defendants, faced with the choice between trial and guilty plea, eventually come around and allocute to their guilt.

Judges can take other steps to further repentance, contrition, apology, and catharsis. For example, at guilty-plea hearings, defendants can fully and honestly admit guilt and express remorse. If they do so and commit to reform in front of judges and loved ones, compliance theory suggests that they are more likely to reform. Often, however, they make bare-bones or grudging admissions of crimes, mixed with excuses, evasions, and blaming others. The federal Sentencing Guidelines are vague about when guilty pleas earn sentence reductions for acceptance of responsibility. In practice, many federal judges automatically give defendants full acceptance-of-responsibility credit for any guilty plea, no matter how grudging the admissions and remorse. This approach rewards all pleas that clear the judge's docket, instead of treating some pleas as better than others. But it makes little sense to speed up plea procedures in the name of efficiency if those procedures undercut the aims of having criminal law in the first place. Judges should focus less on efficiency and more on moral education, reform, catharsis, and healing.

A corollary of this argument is that judges need to observe defendants' demeanors at plea hearings before imposing sentence. Judges must observe how contrite defendants are and what lessons they need to learn, so they can make punishments fit crimes and criminals. This observation conflicts with the common federal practice of farming out guilty pleas to magistrate judges. Because district judges must impose sentences, they should hear guilty pleas themselves. Once judges make clear that they care about contrition, defense lawyers will encourage their clients to be contrite. Of course some defendants will feign contrition, but even this effort may lead to real contrition and satisfy victims and the community.

Also, judges could do more than just recite lists of rights at plea hearings and sentencing-guidelines formulae at sentencing. They could insist on more detailed allocutions and use more overtly moralistic language, driving home the wrongfulness of crimes. They (or prosecutors) could notify victims of hearings and allow them to speak at pleas or sentencing, venting their grief. This opportunity would heal victims and leave them more satisfied that courts had listened to them.

I have suggested that judges should put less emphasis on efficient case processing and more on repentance, education, reform, catharsis, and healing. The same is true of other actors in the criminal justice system. Prosecutors, for example, often try to maximize the number of convictions. Instead of focusing solely on the quantity of dispositions, they should also strive to consider their quality. Victims can help to counteract prosecutors' assembly-line mentality, reminding the repeat players of their unique suffering. This outsider perspective is an important justification for victims' bills of rights.

Defense lawyers should also shift their attitudes towards plea procedures. Currently, some (though not all) defense lawyers avoid friction by allowing clients to enter *Alford* or nolo pleas instead of pressing them to confront the evidence. So, some commentators argue, these pleas are good because they avoid straining the attorney-client relationship. This path of least resistance is a vice rather than a virtue, however. Some friction between lawyer and client can be productive. Defense lawyers can be more than hired guns. They should educate and transform their clients' misperceptions and short-term desires. Psychological blocks, such as denial mechanisms, prevent clients from seeing their long-term interests. Lawyers can see that substance abuse, mental illness, psychological denial, or simple short-sightedness impedes their clients' rationality. They can persuade clients to face up to patterns of behavior that, if left untreated, will lead to more crime and punishment. They can confront their clients with the truth, shattering their denials and beginning the process of reform. As Albert Alschuler has noted, defense lawyers can engage in cognitive restructuring by confronting their clients with the incriminating evidence:

> It may often be a lawyer's duty to emphasize in harsh terms the force of the prosecution's evidence: "What about this fact? Is it going to go away? How the hell would you vote if you were a juror in your case?" It may sometimes be a lawyer's duty to say bluntly, "I cannot possibly beat this case. You are going to spend a long time in jail, and the only question is how long."[6]

By making clients see the evidence through jurors' eyes, defense lawyers can shatter illusions and open their clients' eyes. When defense lawyers know that judges will not allow *Alford* or nolo pleas, they are more likely to engage their clients in facing the truth.

Conversely, where judges permit them, defense counsel are free to suggest *Alford* and nolo pleas without first challenging denials. The psychological literature indicates that those defense lawyers who do not challenge their clients' denials enough exacerbate denial mechanisms.[7] Clients interpret this failure to challenge as confirmation and become even more resistant to the challenges of therapy. Instead of repenting and making amends, guilty offenders may pity themselves and keep using collateral attacks to protest their innocence. *Alford* and nolo contendere pleas are more likely to exacerbate this denial.

The moral of the story is that *Alford* and nolo contendere pleas purchase efficient, swift resolutions at too high a price. The psychological literature, as well as anecdotal evidence, suggests that these pleas reinforce psychological denials. Admissions of guilt, however, are essential first steps on the road to reform, apology, and healing. Criminal justice is not just about swift, efficient convictions; it is also about educating and healing along the way. One hopes that judges and lawyers will see the importance of these goals and be much less willing to allow pleas that undercut them.

Notes

1. Associate Professor, University of Iowa College of Law (bibas@philo.org), former Assistant U.S. Attorney, U.S. Attorney's Office for the Southern District of New York. (c) 2002 by Stephanos Bibas; all rights reserved. This chapter draws upon research done for a more extensive forthcoming article on the same subject, entitled *Harmonizing Substantive Criminal Law Values and Criminal Procedure: The Case of Alford and Nolo Contendere Pleas*, 88 Cornell L. Rev. (forthcoming September 2003). Readers interested in more detail should consult that article.

2. Gad Czudner & Ruth Mueller, *The Role of Guilt and Its Implication in the Treatment of Criminals*, 31 Int'l J. Offender Therapy & Comp. Criminology 71, 73–74 (1987).

3. W.L. Marshall, *Treatment Effects on Denial and Minimization in Incarcerated Sex Offenders*, 32 Behavioral Research Therapy 561, 562 (No. 5 1994) ("This tendency to resist challenges is all too frequently exacerbated by the fact that their [*sic*] defense lawyer has, perhaps unintentionally, encouraged them [*sic*] to present an exculpatory view of the offense.... This encouragement by lawyers[,] and a failure to challenge by professionals, are seen by the offender as confirmation of his claims and this, of course, makes him all the more resistant to challenges. Repeated disclosures followed by supportive challenges are, therefore, necessary.").

4. William O'Donohue & Elizabeth Letourneau, *A Brief Group Treatment for the Modification of Denial in Child Sexual Abusers: Outcome and Follow-Up*, 17 Child Abuse & Neglect 299, 299–300 (1993) ("[C]ontinued denial can cause further harm to the abused child in that implicitly or explicitly, the child is being characterized as a liar and perhaps not believed by some.").

5. One might argue for another exception for minor traffic offenses, where insurers ask their insureds to enter no-contest pleas so that their pleas will not estop later civil litigation over the accident. Because the offense charged is a traffic violation or misdemeanor, and because a civil case will ultimately resolve the issue, it may be less necessary to insist upon a clear resolution in the criminal case.

6. Albert W. Alschuler, The Defense Attorney's Role in Plea Bargaining, *84 Yale L.J. 1179, 1309 (1975).*

7. *See supra* note 4.

———————

E. FACILITATING MOTIVATION TO CHANGE

It seems almost tautologically true that defendants are more likely to recognize problem behavior, to regard themselves as "clients," and to participate in rehabilitative efforts, if they are motivated to change. And although, as we have seen, "client factors" carry enormous weight in the change process, courts can play an important part in helping clients to identify the strengths they possess that will facilitate their successful rehabilitation, in marshalling offender motivation and, relatedly, in enhancing the offender's sense of voluntary participation. The next two subsections of the book pursue these general themes.

1. Creating Therapeutic Opportunity Out of Crisis

In this subsection we include two short selections. The first, by Judge Peggy Hora (Alameda County, California), Judge William Schma (Kalamazoo, Michigan), and attorney John Rosenthal, underscore the importance of "timing" in the overall enterprise. The conventional wisdom, at least in the addiction area, is that the addicted person is most likely to be receptive to intervention efforts when he or she is in crisis—such as precipitated by arrest and incarceration. Drug treatment courts—especially of the diversion variety—seek to capitalize on this receptivity by offering treatment at a very early stage.

The next selection, by Michael Clark, relates to ascertaining and encouraging change. Apparently, the crisis of arrest often, in and of itself, precipitates some positive attitudinal or behavioral changes. These positive changes are highly important, but are often overlooked by professionals, and Clark gives us suggestions about ascertaining the changes and building on them. Within the context of an existing psychological literature on what is known as "stages of change," arrest and court involvement can be seen as presenting a teachable moment or therapeutic opportunity. These stages of change— pre-contemplation, contemplation, preparation, action, and maintenance— call for differing approaches by treatment professionals and others who seek to motivate the individual to undertake change. Australian forensic psycho-

177

logist Astrid Birgden has creatively applied this work in her discussion of how criminal defense attorneys can engage in motivational interviewing with clients who seem resistant to change (Astrid Birgden, *Dealing with the Resistant Criminal Client: A Psychologically-Minded Strategy For More Effective Legal Counseling*, 38 Crim. L. Bull. 225 (2002)). Although these insights from the motivational interviewing and stages of change literature have not as yet been adapted for judicial application, we mention Birgden's article in the hope that this will encourage the development of work in that area.

The Importance of Timing

by Judge Peggy F. Hora, Judge William G. Schma & John Rosenthal
(Excerpted from *Therapeutic Jurisprudence and the Drug
Treatment Court Movement: Revolutionizing the Criminal
Justice Systems Response to Drug Abuse and Crime in*
America, 74 Notre Dame L. Rev. 439, 473–474 (1999),
Copyright 1999 by Judge Peggy Hora, Judge William Schma
& John Rosenthal, reprinted with permission).

As compared to traditional court structure, DTCs recognize that immediacy is a key component of the treatment process. To reinforce this effect, the structure of a DTC places the offender quickly before a single judge and DTC team because an arrest "creates an immediate crisis [for the substance abuser] and can force substance abusing behavior into the open, making denial difficult." In a DTC—through regular court appearances before the same judge, rigorous case management, and treatment—addicts are forced to confront their denial of substance abuse, accept their addiction problem, and embrace the recovery process. "In a drug [treatment] court, the treatment experience begins in the courtroom."

The DTC structure of a single unified drug court supports and enhances the effectiveness of the procedures which the court utilizes to engage the offender in her own treatment. In recognizing and addressing the compulsive behavior of the drug-addicted defendant, DTCs use procedures designed specifically to interrupt the offender's addictive behavior. "The court process actually becomes part of the treatment," and DTC procedures reflect that therapeutic ideal. DTC procedures try to ensure that the court does not miss the "critical window of opportunity for intervening and introducing the value of... [drug] treatment [into the defendant's life]."

In contrast to the traditional court system, which may or may not adjudicate a drug offender's case for months after the original arrest, DTCs place the defendant into the program immediately. In some instances, the defendant may find herself inside DTC within two days of her release from jail after the original arrest. The first DTC appearance by the defendant happens quickly and "[t]reatment...begin[s] as soon as possible following the first drug court appearance, even the same day." In Miami, the DTC "transports the defendant by van directly from the court to the treatment program to begin treatment." The Oakland F.I.R.S.T programs require that defendants granted diversion "go directly to the Probation department (a five-minute walk) for an immediate Diversion orientation session." In Hayward, California, treatment providers attend every DTC session and enroll new DTC participants on the spot. All of these DTC procedures are calculated to take advantage of the fact that a "drug addict is most vulnerable to successful intervention when he or she is in crisis (i.e., immediately after initial arrest and incarceration)."

Ascertaining and Encouraging Change

by Michael D. Clark, MSW, CSW
(Excerpted from *Influencing Positive Behavior Change: Increasing the Therapeutic Approach of Juvenile Courts*, 65 FED. PROBATION 18 (2001), Copyright 2002 by Michael D. Clark, reprinted with permission).

Viewing drug court participants through a change-focused lens, listening and remaining alert to how they are changing, will help staff recognize the participants' resources and the strengths that are enabling and supporting their progress. Staff may utilize two lines of inquiry to help identify this change. First, questions could be asked about "pretreatment change": "After serious trouble has occurred, many people notice good changes have already started before they start in our drug court. What changes have you noticed in your situation? How is this different from before? How did you get these changes to happen?"

Numerous studies from the counseling field have found that a majority of clients make significant changes in their problem patterns in the time between scheduling their initial appointment and actually entering treatment. Just experiencing some type of start or initiation of change can begin positive movement. Single-subject research has recorded similar responses from youth and families newly assigned to the author's juvenile probation caseload. The important point is that client and family rarely report these changes spontaneously. Staff must ask questions about these changes or they remain hidden. Many believe that if problems are ignored, they seem to move underground, where they grow and fester and return even stronger. However, when solutions are ignored, they simply fade away unnoticed and, more importantly, remain unused.

The second (and ongoing) line of inquiry identifies change that occurs between appointments or program sessions. When change is found, drug court staff need to investigate and amplify: "How did you do this?" "How did you know that would work?" "How did you manage to take this important step to turn things around?" "What does this say about you?" "What would you need to do to keep this going (do this again)?" When sitting down with a participant during a scheduled report time, many staff will check on issues by using a preformed mental list of questions. These questions become routine: "Were there any violations of program rules this week?" "Have all urine drops been 'clean'?" "Are you in compliance with all program requirements?" "Have you missed any school/work this past week?" "Have you made all treatment sessions since our last meeting?" These questions are important, but they do not represent a full line of inquiry. When inquiries become routine, they narrow the investigation and bypass many other instances of change. Open-ended questions that search for positive changes should be asked as well.

Finally, becoming change-focused summons drug court teams to be students of motivation and behavior change. Drug court teams would be wise to consider how the Motivational Interviewing model integrates two theories of motivation and self-change. The first involves value/expectancy theory, where the participant attempts to answer the initial questions, "Should I do this?" "Is this me?" Or more specifically, "*Why* should I do this?" Motivational Interviewing model developers William R. Miller and Stephen Rollnick believe "why" is an important issue that must be resolved, and participants usually wrestle with this at the initial or earliest stage of treatment.

Participants will then move to grapple with a second important issue — self-efficacy theory. Here, participants attempt to answer the questions, "Now that I've decided I should do this...can I?" "Do I have the skills?" "Is this too hard for me?" Regarding self-efficacy issues, researchers Snyder, Michael, and Cheavens call for interventions to raise self-efficacy by employing two efforts. First, inducing "personal-efficacy thinking" (e.g., "I can do it") and then setting mutual, concrete, and obtainable goals to enhance "pathways thinking" (e.g., "Here's how I do it").

Instilling self-efficacy is critical. Motivation experts Miller and Rollnick caution that programs can bombard incoming participants with prescriptive advice on "how to" change, while the participant is still deciding whether to change, and fording the commitment to change. Miller and Rollnick believe that giving prescriptive advice too early can steal focus from these early value decisions and can actually impede motivation.

The author has advised drug court staff to focus program retreats on these two theories for revising their programs and practices. Drug court teams can easily spend a morning examining the motivational issues embedded in the participant dilemma "why should I change" and then spend the afternoon examining the two self-efficacy issues of "can I do this" (personal-efficacy thinking) and "how do I do this" (pathways thinking). Meeting these two conditions helps turn the wheel of behavior change.

2. Sparking Motivation and Reducing Perceived Coercion

The next selection, by Winick, follows a similar theme of how the courts and the system can encourage offender change. Winick's context is considerably more general than the crisis situation. Rather, Winick discusses the overall area of how judges can spark motivation for change, and the relationship to motivation of the individual's perception of whether his or her decision to accept rehabilitation has been coerced or made voluntarily. Winick argues that how choices and rehabilitative options are presented in court—the very way judges address defendants and frame the available alternatives—may set the stage for enthusiastic participation and, ultimately, successful completion of a treatment program. Winick also addresses one of the most controversial questions raised by the new problem solving courts, namely whether they are coercive. Although some problem solving court judges have embraced the concept of courts applying a benign coercion, Winick suggests that these courts need not be regarded as coercive. They are not coercive in a legal sense, he argues, and if they apply the techniques he suggests and those discussed generally in this book, they should not give rise to the perception of coercion on the part of those who opt to participate in them. Although problem-solving courts undeniably function within a coercive context, judges need to understand how to act so as to avoid provoking feelings of coercion. Providing a healthy measure of procedural justice can have the opposite effect, enabling clients to understand their choices as having been made voluntarily, a feeling that can pave the way for successful rehabilitation.

The Judge's Role in Encouraging Motivation for Change

by Bruce J. Winick
(Excerpted and adapted from *Therapeutic Jurisprudence and Problem Solving Courts*, 30 FORDHAM URB. L. J. _ (Forthcoming, 2002), reprinted with permission from Bruce J. Winick).

* * *

Attempting to facilitate the individual's acceptance of responsibility for his or her wrongdoing and to motivate the individual to accept help for an underlying problem that may contribute to it requires a high degree of psychological sensitivity on the part of the problem solving court judge.

It is important for problem solving court judges to avoid paternalism in these judge-offender interactions. The judge may be fully aware that the individual suffers from an emotional or psychological problem that produces repetitive criminality and that could respond effectively to available rehabilitative programs. A paternalistic attitude, however, is not likely to help in facilitating the individual's recognition of these realities.

Paternalism is often experienced as offensive by its recipients. It may produce resentment, and as a result, may backfire, producing a psychological reactance to the advice offered that might be counter-productive. Many offenders will be in denial about their underlying problems, and paternalism is unlikely to succeed in allowing them to deal with such denial. Instead, it may produce anxiety and other psychological distress that will make it harder for them to do so.

Problem solving court judges thus should respect the autonomy of the individuals they are seeking to help, allowing them to make decisions for themselves about whether to accept treatment, rather than mandating treatment participation. An individual charged with a drug offense, for example, should be reminded that he or she is free to deal with the charges in criminal court, and accept a sentence to prison if found guilty. Drug treatment court is an alternative option, but is not one the defendant is required to elect. The choice, the judge should remind the offender, is up to him or her. And the individual should not elect drug treatment court unless he or she is prepared to admit the existence of a problem and express a willingness to deal with it. This approach can be empowering to such individuals, who often feel powerless and helpless.

The role of the problem solving court judge in discussing rehabilitation with the offender should be seen as one of persuasion rather than of coercion. Judges should be aware of the psychological value of choice. Self-determination is an essential aspect of psychological health, and people who make their own choices, if perceived by them as non-coerced, function more effectively and with greater satisfaction. People who feel coerced, by contrast, may respond with a negative psychological reactance, and may experience various other psychological difficulties. In appropriate circumstances, the judge, of course, should communicate to the individual the judge's own views concerning the individual's best interests, but should cede choice to the individual. To succeed, treatment or rehabilitation will require a degree of intrinsic motivation on the part of the individual. If he or she participates in the program as a result of extrinsic motivation only, internalization of program goals and genuine attitudinal and behavioral change will be less likely.

The individual should be afforded choice not only in deciding whether to elect to participate in problem solving court, but also in the design of the rehabilitative plan, when feasible. There typically may be many options available in fashioning such a plan, including variations in rehabilitative techniques and service providers. The problem solving court judge can lay the options out for the individual, who then can exercise choice. The individual's choice concerning the various issues that arise in the design of the treatment plan can be empowering, and can influence the likelihood of success.

Some problem solving court judges describe what they do as benevolent coercion, and extol the virtues of judicial coercion as an essential ingredient in the rehabilitative enterprise. While many individuals in drug treatment court or other problem solving courts who agree to participate in a course of treatment or rehabilitation will benefit from the structure that the treatment program provides and from the supervision and compliance monitoring that the court will enforce through sanctions for non-compliance, I suggest that it is neither appropriate nor desirable to regard this as coercion. An individual deciding whether to accept diversion to drug treatment or some other problem solving court, or to plead guilty and accept treatment in a problem solving court program as a condition of probation, is making a choice that is legally a voluntary one as long as he or she is not subjected to duress, force, fraud, or a form of improper inducement. People making such choices may be functioning within a coercive context. They face hard choices, none of which may be agreeable. But they find themselves in such difficult situations as a result of their own actions. They were arrested, for example, because they possessed drugs or committed some other crime, not as a vehicle for forcing them into treatment. They are free to plead not guilty and face trial, or plead guilty and receive an appropriate sentence. Extending them the additional option of accepting a rehabilitative alternative does not make the choice they then will face a coercive one.

An analogy to plea bargaining is appropriate. Although offenders offered plea deals may experience the choice they are required to make as coercive, as long as the offer made by the prosecutor was not illegal, unauthorized, unethical, or otherwise inappropriate, the courts have held that it does not constitute legal coercion. If the decision faced by an individual charged with crime about whether to accept a guilty plea is not coerced, then the decision whether to accept diversion to a problem solving court or to plead guilty and accept treatment through the auspices of such a court as a condition for probation also would not constitute coercion in a legal sense. Plea bargaining is an example in which individuals face hard choices, but where, absent an offer that is improper, illegal, or unethical, the choice will not be considered to be coercive.

Another example is presented by parole from prison. An individual may be released prior to the expiration of his or her prison term on parole, provided that he or she accepts certain conditions of parole. These may include, for example, an undertaking that the individual not use alcoholic beverages or associate with other individuals who have a criminal record. Unless the conditions of parole are improper or illegal, we would consider the individual's choice to accept these conditions as voluntary rather than coerced. Even though the individual's desire for release from prison might be so powerful that he may feel that he has no real choice other than to accept the conditions of parole, it would be absurd for the law to invalidate his choice on grounds of coercion. As long as the conditions of parole are not unlawful, improper, or unreasonable, parole accords the individual an opportunity that he may find more desirable than serving the remainder of his sentence in prison.

Opportunities for diversion from the criminal process are essentially similar. An individual charged with crime who must decide between facing his charges and accepting diversion into a rehabilitative program may be facing a hard choice. However, it is a fair and reasonable one, and is not one that the law will invalidate on grounds of coercion.

The line between coercion and choice can be a narrow one. Moreover, the concept of legal coercion does not necessarily coincide with the psychological perception of coercion. In helping individuals considering whether to opt for a problem solving court rehabilitative alternative to criminal court, judges, attorneys, and other court personnel should avoid coercion and negative forms of pressure, instead relying on persuasion or inducement. Once the individual chooses in favor of such a treatment option, of course, his or her future actions are constrained, but they are constrained as a result of a choice voluntarily entered into. Thus, the individual, as a condition for accepting drug treatment court, may agree to attend a drug treatment program, to remain drug-free, and to submit to periodic drug testing. The individual knows that if he or she fails to comply, the court can apply sanctions, typically graduated sanctions agreed to in advance by the individual. Moreover, the individual knows that repeated non-compliance can result in expulsion from the program and return to criminal court or a violation of probation if the individual had pled guilty. While in a manner of speaking, these potential sanctions may pressure the individual to comply and even induce his or her compliance, there is no need to regard this as coercion. It is not legal coercion, and if properly applied, may not even be experienced by the individual as psychologically coercive.

In this connection, problem solving court judges must understand what makes people feel coerced and makes them feel that they have acted voluntarily. They should be aware of the implications of recent research conducted on coercion by the MacArthur Research Network on mental health and the law. This research examined the causes and correlates of what makes people feel coerced. Conducted in the context of mental patients facing involuntary hospitalization, this research concluded that even though subjected to legal compulsion through involuntary civil commitment, patients felt non-coerced when treated with dignity and respect by people who they perceived as acting with genuine benevolence and as according them a sense of voice, the ability to have their say, and validation, the impression that what they said was taken seriously. This research also shows that the degree of perceived coercion is strongly dependent on the kinds of pressures the individual was subjected to. Negative pressures, such as threats and force, tend to make individuals feel coerced, whereas positive pressures, such as persuasion and inducement, do not. Even though such people are being subjected to the legal compulsion of civil commitment, if treated in these ways, they tend to feel un-coerced.

Problem solving court judges should apply the lessons of the MacArthur research on coercion, treating the individuals they face with dignity and respect and according them voice and validation in the interactions they have with them. They should avoid negative pressures and threats, relying instead on positive pressures like persuasion and inducement. If they do so, it is more likely that they will experience the treatment they have consented to as voluntary rather than coerced, and as a result, will experience the psychological benefits of choice and avoid the negative psychological effects of coercion. People resent being treated as incompetent subjects of paternalism and suffer a diminished sense of self-esteem and self-efficacy when not permitted to make decisions for themselves. To the extent that the individual experiences his or her decision to participate in a problem solving court treatment or rehabilitative program to be voluntary, this can have significant positive effects on treatment outcome.

Problem solving court judges therefore should avoid paternalism and respect the individual's autonomy. They should encourage the individual to accept needed treatment or rehabilitation, urging him or her in this direction. They should use techniques of persuasion or inducement. But they should avoid a heavy-handed approach, strong negative pressure, and coercion.

If handled properly by the problem solving court judge, conversations about the need for treatment or rehabilitation can be an opportunity for empowering the individual in ways that can have positive psychological value. They can build self-esteem and self-efficacy, without which they may not feel they can succeed in what might be a long and difficult path to rehabilitation. These conversations can facilitate the individual's sense that he or she has made a voluntary choice in favor of treatment, which can increase the individual's commitment to achieving the treatment goal and set in motion a variety of psychological mechanisms that can help to bring it about.

Persuasion, not coercion, thus should be the hallmark of judge-offender interactions in problem solving court contexts. Involvement in the judicial process itself can provide an important motivating force that may prompt the individual to reexamine past patterns and to seek to undergo change. The process of attempting to persuade the individual in this direction often will occur in conversations with the individual's own defense attorney. At times, however, the judge will participate in the persuasion process through conversations with the individual occurring in open court. When such occasions present themselves, judges functioning in the problem solving court context should remember that judicial conversations that are perceived by the individual as coercive may be counterproductive, and that there is an important difference between coercion and persuasion.

When the context calls for the judge to attempt to persuade the individual to accept treatment or rehabilitation, the problem solving court judge's ability to be an effective persuader will be augmented if he or she understands the social psychology of persuasion. This body of psychological research identifies three elements of the persuasion process as critical—source, message, and receiver. The likelihood of persuasion is significantly influenced by both the content of the message and the way it is delivered.

Persuasion theory has postulated an elaboration likelihood model, under which certain persuasive elements are seen as being influenced by the extent to which the receiver of information is actively involved in the processing of the information presented. Under this theory, the potential for successful persuasion is maximized when the individuals receiving the information have a high likelihood of elaboration, i.e., when they engage in issue-relevant thinking about the content of the message itself. It is more likely that people will be persuaded if the message has personal relevance to them and they have prior knowledge about the issue.

Individuals facing criminal charges will wish to minimize the risk of imprisonment, and will value strategies that can achieve this result. They should be presented with information concerning the rehabilitative alternatives to criminal court that drug treatment court or other problem solving courts present, and the positive consequences for them of successfully completing the program, including in many cases, the dismissal of charges. They should then be left free to engage in instrumental thinking concerning the value of electing these rehabilitative alternatives. They should be given the opportunity to ask questions about their options, and be given the freedom to engage in their own processing of the information and to reach their own decision. They should be encouraged fully to discuss their options with counsel, and should be given a reasonable opportunity to do so and to think it over. This form of persuasion, known as "central route persuasion," can be more effective than pressuring the individual to make the decision and can allow him or her to internalize the rehabilitative goal and increase the intrinsic motivation needed to accomplish it.

The likelihood elaboration model of persuasion is similar to the technique of motivational interviewing that has been developed for use by clinicians in helping to motivate people to deal with problems of addiction and alcoholism. Problem solving court judges thus also should master the techniques of motivational interviewing. Although treatment staff and the individual's own attorney will be primarily involved in conducting such motivational interviews, occasions will arise in which problem solving court judges will engage in such interviewing themselves or will have the opportunity to reinforce the motivational effects of such interviewing conducted by treatment staff or the defense attorney.

Five basic principles underlie this technique. First, the interviewer needs to express empathy. This involves understanding the individual's feelings and perspectives without judging, criticizing or blaming. Second, the interviewer, in a non-confrontational way, should seek to develop discrepancies between the individual's present behavior and important personal goals. Applying this approach, the judge should attempt to elicit the individual's underlying goals and objectives and, through interviewing techniques, including open-ended questioning, reflective listening, the provision of frequent statements of affirmation and support, and the elicitation of self-motivational statements, should attempt to enable the individual to recognize the existence of a problem. For example, if the individual wishes to obtain or keep a particular job, the judge can ask questions designed to probe the relationship between his drinking or substance abuse and poor performance in previous employment that may have resulted in dismissal. Only when people perceive the discrepancy between how they are behaving and the achievement of their personal goals will motivation for change be created.

Third, the interviewer should avoid arguing with the individual, which can be counter-productive and create defensiveness. Fourth, when resistance is encountered, the interviewer should attempt to roll with the resistance, rather than becoming confrontational. This requires listening with empathy and providing feedback to what the individual is saying by introducing new information, thereby allowing the individual to remain in control, to make his own decisions, and to create solutions to his problems.

Fifth, it is important for the interviewer to foster self-efficacy in the individual. Unless the individual feels that he or she can reach the goal, overcome barriers and obstacles to its achievement, and succeed in effectuating change, change will not be attempted.

Problem solving court judges, court officials and treatment professionals working with them, and lawyers counseling clients about their options to enter into problem solving court rehabilitative programs should learn the techniques of motivational interviewing and apply them in their conversations with offenders concerning their problems and the desirability of them dealing with them through rehabilitation. These techniques of motivational interviewing have recently been adapted for application by criminal defense lawyers dealing with clients who have recurring problems and are in denial about their problems and resistant to change, and to lawyers representing clients in mental health court, as well as mental health professionals and mental health court judges dealing with them. These techniques can be particularly effective when the individual finds himself in a situation when change is being contemplated. The individual's arrest and the need to face criminal charges can present the pressures needed to create such a teachable moment or therapeutic opportunity in which the individual is ready to contemplate change, to accept responsibility for wrongdoing, and to consider making a genuine commitment to rehabilitation. The use of motivational interviewing and related psychological strategies for sparking and maintaining motivation to accept needed treatment can substantially increase the potential that problem solving courts may have to help the individual solve his or her problem.

Key References

Carroll, Kathleen M., et al., *Motivational Interviewing to Enhance Treatment Initiation in Substance Abuses: An Effectiveness Study*, 10 AMERICAN J. OF ADDICTIONS 335 (2001).

MILLER, R.D. & ROLLNICK, S., MOTIVATIONAL INTERVIEWING: PREPARING PEOPLE TO CHANGE ADDICTIVE BEHAVIOR (1991); *see also* 2d ed. 2002.

MORRISEY, J. & MONAHAN, J., EDS., COERCION IN MENTAL HEALTH SERVICE (Forthcoming).

F. Enhancing the Development of Problem-Solving Skills

Rehabilitation efforts can be enhanced, as we have seen throughout this discussion, if an offender has input into his or her disposition. The following selection is written in the context of juvenile delinquency cases but, again, is applicable in many other contexts, such as substance abuse and criminal law generally. The selection suggests that courts can play a rehabilitative role by encouraging clients, such as those who may be released on probation, to think through their high-risk situations (e.g., weekends at a particular disco, hanging out with a particular friend) and, with professional assistance, to propose a relapse prevention or safety plan to avoid such high-risk situations. In essence, a would-be probationer would be suggesting some of the conditions for a proposed probationary disposition. In this excerpt, Wexler applies cognitive/behavioral research on rehabilitation to the judicial setting, and suggests that judges can promote the development of problem-solving skills and, at the same time, effectively manage the risk of future criminality.

Problem Solving and Relapse Prevention in Juvenile Court
by David B. Wexler
(From *Just Some Juvenile Thinking About Delinquent Behavior: A Therapeutic Jurisprudence Approach to Relapse Prevention Planning and Youth Advisory Juries*, 69 UMKC L. Rev. 93-105 (2000), Copyright 2000 by David B. Wexler, reprinted with permission).

I. Introduction

This chapter proposes the importation of problem-solving skills development into the juvenile justice system, and proposes the exploration of the use of Youth Advisory Juries (YAJs) as a structural device for enhancing the development of those skills. It draws upon, extends, and integrates two strands of prior therapeutic jurisprudence work: (1) the use of relapse prevention planning principles in a criminal law context, and (2) the structure and functioning of teen court. The integration of these strands is facilitated because each is illustrative of the type of cognitive/behavioral problem-solving approach to rehabilitation that has recently been recognized as having real promise, especially in empirical studies involving juvenile delinquency.

II. The Cognitive/Behavioral Approach and Relapse Prevention Planning

After approximately two decades of subscribing to a dispiriting "nothing works" rehabilitative philosophy, a chorus of correctional researchers is finally beginning to sing a reasonably optimistic tune, at least about certain rehabilitative approaches. In an edited collection entitled What Works: Reducing Reoffending, British psychologist-editor James McGuire brings together descriptions and evaluations of the most promising programs. These are programs of the "cognitive-behavioral" variety: "treatments that have a more concrete behavioral or skills-oriented character," such as the widely used "Reasoning and Rehabilitation" training package.

These cognitive skills programs flow from the finding that "for many persistent offenders, a central problem that is linked to their offending behavior is their lack of, or failure to apply, a number of problem-solving skills." These include "the ability to identify when they have a problem, to think of alternative courses of action, to plan the steps toward solution of a problem, to anticipate consequences and to consider the effects of their actions upon others."

One approach to help offenders better consider the impact of their actions on others—to increase their empathy—is through a "perspective-taking" exercise where they are asked to consider the crime from the victim's viewpoint, even to reenact the crime, playing the role of the victim. Moreover, to increase offender self-control, successful programs help offenders develop internal self-management systems "designed to interrupt the seemingly inexorable chain of events that lead to an offense."

The self-management systems ask offenders to identify the chain of events culminating in criminal behavior, and then has them develop "(a) strategies that help the offender avoid high-risk situations, and (b) strategies that minimize the likelihood that high-risk situations, once encountered, will lead to relapse."

These relapse prevention principles are already employed in many correctional contexts. In Vermont institutions, for example, the Cognitive Self Change program teaches offenders "to observe their own thinking, to recognize the consequences of that thinking, and to learn specific skills for controlling that thinking." Then, each offender in the program must: (1) identify the patterns of thinking that have led him or her to perform acts of crime and violence in the past and that pose a risk of such behaviors in the future; (2) learn specific skills for intervening in and controlling these patterns of thinking; and (3) summarize these patterns and interventions in the form of a plan for controlling their high-risk thinking in the community. This becomes his or her "relapse prevention plan."

Once released, Vermont offenders apply their relapse prevention plans and meet to evaluate their efforts at managing their thinking and their behavior. According to the McGuire What Works anthology, a similar program is available—but to probationers rather than to prisoners—in South Wales. There, probation officers, who have themselves received four or five days of specialized in-service training, instruct probationers in the successful Reasoning and Rehabilitation ("R & R")-type STOP (Straight Thinking on Probation) Program, which courts often order probationers to attend.

In other publications, I have explored how these promising rehabilitative principles might be brought into the criminal/correctional system. Here, however, my focus will be on the juvenile justice system. Probation officers and social workers in judicial, community, and institutional settings should receive training (of four to five days) in teaching R & R sessions.

Such sessions—which seem to range from twenty-one to thirty-five 2-hour classes—should be available to youths in a wide variety of settings, institutional and community, pre- and post-adjudication. In appropriate cases, attendance at such programs could be made a condition of probation. A more subtle therapeutic jurisprudence inquiry, however, is how the legal system itself might facilitate rehabilitation through the process of offender reasoning.

The Vermont Cognitive Self-Change program offers an obvious starting point. There, institutionalized offenders participate in an R & R program, eventually prepare a relapse prevention plan, and seek to adhere to that plan when they return to the community.

It is but a short stretch to suggest the following: Juvenile parole, correctional, or "aftercare" authorities—the counterparts to adult parole boards—could themselves become acquainted with the principles of relapse prevention and cognitive self change.[1] They could, in addressing a juvenile's readiness for release to aftercare, ask the juvenile, with the assistance of a treatment team member from social services, to prepare and submit a relapse prevention and aftercare plan. The plan should address the juvenile's proposed adjustment to the community as well as methods for avoiding or coping with high-risk situations. At a conditional release eligibility hearing, the hearing board could question the juvenile about the plan, could raise and discuss its own concerns about high-risk situations and behaviors, and could hear from the juvenile how he or she plans to avoid or confront such situations.

With that input, the authority could decide whether to release the juvenile on aftercare and, if so, whether to accept the submitted relapse prevention plan or a revised one based upon concerns expressed at the hearing. Note that conditional release conditions derived from the dialogue at the hearing would basically be conditions suggested by the juvenile to cope with anticipated high-risk situations. By tailoring those conditions specifically to the juvenile's situation, and by giving the juvenile "voice" in framing the conditions, we should expect the juvenile not to regard the conditions as particularly unjust, and, relatedly, we should expect the process to increase the likelihood that the juvenile will in fact comply with the release conditions.

If juvenile aftercare authorities begin to gear their hearings and release decisions more explicitly toward relapse prevention principles, they will, by such action, motivate institutionalized juveniles to follow suit. Indeed, we should then expect juveniles to gravitate toward institutional treatment programs conducted along Reasoning and Rehabilitation lines, even if participation in such programs were not to be technically required.

Under the just-described scenario, a juvenile parole board or juvenile correctional authority makes the release or conditional release decision. If, however, the juvenile court by statute retains jurisdiction, it will be able, at required periodic review hearings or at hearings initiated by the institution, to order changes in the juvenile's placement or treatment plan. In essence, then, the juvenile court, under different terminology, may be able to shape a disposition substantially akin to conditional release or a so-called "intermediate" sanction, such as attending a day-reporting center, which falls somewhere "between" institutionalization and conditional release.

In authorizing a less restrictive placement, a court can tap into the relapse prevention planning principles in the same way that a parole board might; it can expect juvenile involvement in formulating and defending the liberalized placement. Indeed, juvenile judges having the authorization and the inclination to coordinate this reintegrative placement process are in a prime position to function as "reentry courts."

Of course, the involvement of the judicial branch in promoting relapse prevention planning principles can, in the juvenile justice system, easily be accomplished in the ordering of probation. The juvenile court, during the dispositional phase of a delinquency proceeding, will decide whether to order institutionalization or whether to release a juvenile on probation. If a good R & R program is in place, if and when a juvenile court orders probation, it may specify as a condition of release that a given juvenile participate in—or continue in—such a program. But juvenile courts can do even more. They can induce juveniles to engage in relapse prevention planning and cognitive self change in the first place—even before probation is ordered.

For example, juvenile courts could easily become acquainted with the rudimentary principles of relapse prevention and cognitive self change. Then, in a situation of probation eligibility and a reasonable likelihood of probation being awarded, a court should encourage the development of appropriate problem-solving skills by requiring the juvenile, with the assistance of counsel and probation/social service staff, to prepare and submit a relapse prevention plan as the basis of a possible probationary disposition.[2] The plan should address methods—and relevant release conditions—for avoiding (e.g., remaining home on weekend nights) or coping with (e.g., making an excuse to avoid partying at Joe's place) high-risk situations.

Were juvenile courts to take this approach to the granting of probation, counsel would expectedly adapt and, in the process, would further the rehabilitative aims of juvenile cognitive self change. Besides helping the juvenile prepare a relapse prevention plan, competent counsel will prepare the juvenile for the dispositional hearing, and should discuss with the juvenile the anticipated concerns of the court.

With proper preparation, the juvenile should be able to specify how the proposed plan addresses those concerns or how it might be modified to do so. The dispositional hearing could then serve as a forum for ventilating the court's concerns regarding appropriateness and compliance, and could lead to the crafting of additional risk-reducing probation conditions suggested by the give-and-take dialogue between the court and the juvenile.

While counsel can of course participate in that dialogue, it is important that the juvenile play a pivotal role in preparing, defending, and suggesting modifications in the plan. It is, after all, the juvenile, not counsel, who is engaged in cognitive self change and compliance. By involving the juvenile centrally, the court can insure that counsel and client have engaged in a therapeutically appropriate division of labor, and that counsel has not preempted the process.

Note that this overall suggested legal process is itself relapse prevention planning in living color. The process, moreover, taps nicely into psychological principles for promoting compliance. For example, by responding to the court's concerns and defending the plan, the juvenile will be anchoring himself or herself in the position that the proposed plan is workable—and in this respect different from the situation that landed him or her in court in the first place. This process—of defending one's proposed course of action when presented with "mild counterarguments"—has been linked to increased treatment compliance. Indeed, the recommended procedure as a whole squares very well with principles for promoting compliance.

Relapse prevention planning principles are, by their very nature, highly suitable for use in the juvenile justice system. This essay has underscored their use in aftercare[3] and probation. Other potential uses abound; relapse prevention plans may, for example, be helpful in making decisions about the appropriateness of diversion and in the judicial task of deciding whether or not to transfer a case—and an individual—to adult criminal court.

Later, I will return to a discussion of these promising principles, and will explore how they might, in certain contexts, be even more effectively employed with the procedural creation of Youth Advisory Juries. To reach that point, however, we must first look, if only briefly, at the procedural mechanism from which the proposal of the Youth Advisory Jury flows—the Teen Court programs now flourishing in many communities.

III. Teen Court Programs

While the juvenile court is regarded as an alternative to adult criminal proceedings, the teen court is itself a juvenile court diversion program. Typically, the teen court alternative is offered to first-time misdemeanor defendants, often charged with traffic offenses, assault, possession of alcohol, theft, disorderly conduct, and the like. Typically, too, the program requires the teen defendant to admit his wrongdoing, so that that teen court is in essence a dispositional decision-making body. The juvenile and his or her parents consent to the diversion from juvenile court.

Presided over by an adult judge (e.g., an actual judge or an attorney volunteering for such service), the dispositional decision-making body is a teen jury, composed of both volunteers from local intermediate and high schools and of former teen defendants. Requiring former teen defendants to serve at least once on a teen jury is an important feature of teen court programs. In essence, service on the jury is a type of reintegration ceremony, indicating to the former defendant that he or she is capable of participating responsibly in society. Sometimes, a teen defendant is ordered to serve several times as a juror, and some become volunteer jurors when no longer required to serve.

Apart from ordering a teen defendant to serve as a future juror, the dispositional jury may order the defendant to make restitution, to engage in community service, to write essays (the danger of drinking and driving; how to avoid negative peer pressure), to apologize to victims, and to attend traffic survival school, drug and alcohol counseling, or workshops on self-esteem or conflict mediation. Incarcerative sentencing is not an option.

If a defendant successfully completes the sentence, he or she is not formerly charged in juvenile court. On the other hand, failure to complete the sentence can result in the resumption of juvenile court proceedings.

Different jurisdictions have different models of teen juries. One model is the so-called "trial model," so called even though it does not resolve disputed facts. Under that model, a teen prosecutor and defense counsel present the dispositional case to the teen jury. Under a competing model, the "peer jury model" (sometimes called a "grand jury" model), teen attorneys are not involved, and the teen panel members question the defendant directly.

Philosophically, teen courts are highly consistent with the "balanced approach mission" and the restorative justice model, trying to tie together offender, victim, and community components in resolving the dispute. By demanding an admission of offender wrongdoing for eligibility into the progam, teen court paves the way for offender "accountability," which is based on "offenders understanding the harm caused by their actions, accepting responsibility for the harm caused, and making amends."

Teen courts, then, marshall peer pressure so that it might operate positively. The goal is rehabilitative with respect to teen defendants and former teen defendants serving as jurors, and preventive—an "inoculation" if you will—for the volunteer jurors and other participants, many of whom may themselves be at risk for delinquent behavior during this turbulent stage of life.

Although the results must be read cautiously, preliminary findings indicate that teen court may indeed function as a promising therapeutic tool. Even so, the difficulty, in policy terms, is that the program is generally limited to minor offenses and to first-time offenders. Efforts to expand teen court "jurisdiction" are likely to encounter serious problems either in offering diversion in felony-type cases, or, on the other hand, in allowing teen jurors to impose incarcerative dispositions.

In an earlier article on the teen court concept, Allison Shiff and I, intrigued by the workings of teen court, suggested that we "explore the possibility of increasing teen involvement—and extensive victim participation—in ordinary juvenile court." We recognized, of course, that "teens could not be the principal participants or decision-makers in such courts," but noted that "that does not prevent the use of teens (including former defendants participating as part of a sentence) as 'advisory juries' on adjudication or disposition, or as legal assistants to attorneys representing the state, the defense, or victims."

In the next section, I indeed take the step of proposing the exploration of Youth Advisory Juries in the juvenile court disposition stage—and perhaps elsewhere in the juvenile justice system, such as in the making of aftercare decisions. Moreover, the proposal ties the functioning of Youth Advisory Juries to the previously discussed literature on the promising cognitive/behavioral rehabilitative programs, particularly relapse prevention planning and empathy-development through "perspective-taking."

IV. Youth Advisory Juries as Problem-Solving Courts

One of the most important criminological research findings of recent years is that, by and large, offenders do not specialize. In fact, most of them commit crimes impulsively and opportunistically, without stopping to think of alternatives and consequences. In essence, the typical offender simply displays rather low self-control, which manifests itself in the commission of a variety of crimes as well as in other high-risk behaviors—careless driving, drug-taking, and so on. One reason for the success of the problem-solving, skill-development, cognitive self change rehabilitative programs may well be that cognitive/behavioral programs indeed encourage offenders to stop, think, plan ahead, consider alternatives and consequences—that they in essence teach self-control.

In fact, current cognitive/behavioral training materials recognize the need for developing problem-solving skills over a broad domain of both non-criminogenic and criminogenic situations, including matters such as susceptibility to peer pressure and the like. It is probably safe to say that the more exposure offenders—especially "generalists"—receive in grappling with real-life problem situations, including risky situations encountered by other offenders, the more they will be able to hone their general problem-solving skills, and the more likely they will be to lead law-abiding lives.

If the recommendations made earlier were to be adopted, high quality problem-solving training would become widely available in the juvenile justice system. Moreover, courts and aftercare releasing authorities would encourage the development of such skills by requiring the submission of relapse prevention plans for probation or aftercare consideration. A condition of conditional release—probation or aftercare—could include the completion of a problem-solving course and, taking a page from teen court, subsequent service on a Youth Advisory Jury (YAJ). YAJ service could involve youths commenting on the adequacy of relapse prevention plans submitted by other juveniles seeking probationary or aftercare dispositions.

What I envision is a 6–8 member Youth Advisory Jury (YAJ) composed of a mix of both conditionally released juveniles and volunteers (who may also receive some problem-solving training), sitting in select juvenile court dispositional hearings (and perhaps also in aftercare eligibility hearings). When the juvenile seeking conditional release presents his or her plan, the members of the YAJ, operating a bit like the "peer jury" teen court model, could ask questions and could make comments: "Do you usually get in trouble when you're with Joe? Why? Do you feel you need to show off in front of him? Who else do you show off in front of? What can you do about that in the future?" I doubt that an actual group decision need be reached, and many different models could be experimented with, including ones that do and ones that do not deliberate before jurors ask questions and make comments and suggestions.

A YAJ with some problem-solving experience is likely to ask some good questions. The jurors may become fairly savvy about patterns of offending behavior, a topic central to the problem-solving R & R type course designed by James McGuire: "Does most of your offending behavior occur in the same place? At similar times of the day or week? In the presence of the same person or persons?" These inquiries may spark responses, modifications in the juvenile's proposed relapse prevention plan, and may result in appropriate conditions of release: "I will not go out on Friday nights," or "I will not go to the disco on weekends," or "I will attend the workshop on 'resisting peer pressure.'"

The discussion sparked by the YAJ may indeed be helpful to the judge or aftercare authority. And the knowledge on the part of the juvenile that he or she will be questioned by a savvy group of peers—all of whom have had some problem-solving training and some of whom have themselves previously prepared and defended relapse prevention plans—should be a powerful motivator in his or her preparation of a good, defensible, relapse prevention plan.

On the other hand, the fact that the YAJ will be questioning and commenting only, and not rendering a group decision, should also mean that this process will not threaten the court's actual or perceived authority as the dispositional decision maker. The judge will, however, need to be skillful at integrating valuable juror comments in the release decision and of tactfully dealing with rejected ones. "I think Vanessa's point that these problems and fights usually occur when you hang around after school is a good one, and I'm glad, Robert, that you've decided to change your relapse prevention plan to say you will go home from school right away unless you have basketball practice; I'm accordingly going to make that an additional condition of your probation." "I understand Andy's concern about the violent movies Fred sees, and I'd like to suggest Fred think about this, but I don't feel comfortable actually being a censor here." "Some of these ideas are very good, especially about not going to discos, but I think John's situation requires a residential response. If he does well there, I hope the juvenile parole board will think about this disco scene when he is released on aftercare, and I'm going to put a note to that effect in his file."[4]

The crucial point, however, is not only that this process may well be useful to the court and to Robert, Fred, and John, but that it is also likely to be extremely beneficial for Vanessa and Andy, YAJ members who themselves may have been previously adjudicated delinquent. At the least, it should serve a preventive function for YAJ volunteer members who have not had problems with the law.

While most release conditions will relate very directly to public safety and relapse prevention, some other conditions may relate to an offender's accountability and need to make amends to the victim. These matters are terribly important to victims and to their psychological well-being. They are also important to the offender and to his or her development of empathy. To the extent an offender learns better to understand the consequences of his or her actions on another, this too renders the offender less likely to re-offend (and, in that sense, also relates to public safety and to relapse prevention).

To enhance victim voice and to develop offender empathy, courts, at disposition hearings, should accept victim impact statements and testimony. Moreover, a subsequent dialogue should be permitted between the YAJ members and the juvenile regarding restitution, apologies, and related matters. Again, in addition to promoting fairness, this process should help the YAJ members develop a heightened sense of empathy for crime victims.

Indeed, by asking them not only to listen to a victim's story (which is like attending a victim impact panel) but also to discuss the appropriate apology and restitution response, YAJ members are actually engaging in a type of "perspective-taking" through law, putting themselves, if only briefly, in what they imagine to be the victim's situation.[5] This empathy training for YAJ members should be a valuable rehabilitative/preventive endeavor. Once again, of course, a court should treat juror comments/suggestions with respect, but there is no need to regard YAJ restitution/apology remarks as anything but advisory, and the authority of the juvenile judge is accordingly unaffected.

V. Conclusion

This essay proposes that the juvenile justice system share in the enthusiasm that delinquent behavior may indeed be interrupted—that some interventions may indeed work. I have suggested that cognitive/behavioral problem-solving programs be introduced into the system, and that courts and aftercare authorities should encourage juveniles to participate in the programs. Finally, I have suggested the creation of Youth Advisory Juries as a procedural device to help courts, aftercare authorities, juvenile offenders, and, indeed, as a rehabilitative/preventive tool for the YAJ members themselves.

Many questions remain, especially regarding the YAJ. How many jurors? What balance between volunteers and former defendants? Should they deliberate before commenting? There are legal questions, too: What about confidentiality? Public access to the hearings? And strategic questions: Is there enough space? How much extra time will this take? Can we hear another case while one YAJ deliberates?

This essay is designed to put both the broad issues and the technical ones on the table. And the recommendations relating to problem-solving and to YAJs are, of course, separable. A jurisdiction could introduce problem-solving programs without also creating YAJs. But given the apparent success of teen court programs—and, at the same time, the real limitations for extending teen court jurisdiction—the creation of YAJs should be given serious consideration. Perhaps the best place to start would be a jurisdiction with a very successful teen court, where confidentiality or closed hearings are not legal mandates,[6] and where there is, as there are in several states, statutory provision for jury trial, so that the courtrooms are presumably already physically equipped to accommodate YAJs. A few experimental programs should be established to gain experience and to iron out the kinks. We need constantly to experiment, to evaluate, and to rethink matters if we wish to contribute meaningfully to the literature on "what works."

Notes

1. Perhaps a tailored, streamlined course of half-day or so could be devised specifically for judges, far more abbreviated than the four-to-five day "teacher training" course designed for professional probation officers. Judges should be sympathetic to the material and the approach, for it is anything but a farfetched psychobabble therapy; instead, it comports fully with judicial common sense, and is related to the questions a court would ordinarily worry about: Can this juvenile be released without undue risk? On what conditions? What confidence do I have that the juvenile will comply with those conditions?

2. Of course, participating in—or continuing in—an R & R-type problem-solving course can be one of those conditions. At times, a disposition decision might even be deferred to enable a juvenile to complete a course and to design a proposed relapse prevention plan.

3. Aftercare itself is ordinarily an executive branch function. Some juvenile court judges have indirectly asserted aftercare-like authority by granting a juvenile a "pass" from an institution, sometimes authorizing the pass for a considerable period of time, so long as the juvenile abides by certain conditions. Interview with Judge Francisco R. Agrait, in San Juan, Puerto Rico (October 1, 1999). If and when judges exercise that authority, they could of course encourage or require relapse prevention plans. Moreover, juvenile courts often have explicit statutory authority to review a juvenile's treatment plan and placement, to modify a disposition, or even to terminate juvenile court jurisdiction. Both in theory and in practice, such judicial authority in many ways overlaps with the administrative aftercare or parole function.

4. Of course, under a model where the juvenile court judge retains jurisdiction, holds review hearings, and decides matters of release and restrictiveness of placement, the judge could put such a notation in the case file for later judicial consideration.

5. Serving as a legal assistant to the prosecution (or to a separate victim's attorney), and working with the victim in preparing a victim impact statement and accompanying court testimony, would be another route to "empathy training through law."

6. Of course, even where confidentiality and closed hearings are provided for, a juvenile and his or her parents could presumably consent to the presence of others (including a YAJ) in the courtroom.

Key References
McGuire, James (ed.), What Works: Reducing Reoffending (1995).

G. Risk Management

"Risk management" is at center stage in the next selection, where Winick urges judges in domestic violence court to regard themselves, in part, as risk managers. Winick notes the existence of some new risk assessment instruments, and explores how they may be employed not only to predict future risk but, also, to motivate a defendant to change some "dynamic" risk factors (such as substance abuse) so as to maximize continued liberty and, at the same time, to take a substantial step in the rehabilitative direction. The domestic violence area is ripe for the approach suggested by Winick but, once again, the general risk management perspective and principles he commends can be applied to many other legal settings—for example in reentry court generally, in sex offender reentry court, and in applications of drug treatment court and mental health court to populations presenting a risk of danger to the community. In fact, in Judge Fritzler's discussion of effective principles and practices for a criminal mental health court, printed earlier , risk management principles are specifically applied to the mental health court context.

Domestic Violence Court Judges as Risk Managers
by Bruce J. Winick
(Excerpted from *Applying the Law Therapeutically In Domestic Violence Cases*, 69 UMKC L. Rev..33, 45–60 (2000), Copyright 2000 by Bruce J. Winick, reprinted with permission).

Because domestic violence typically is characterized by a repetitive pattern of abuse and threats of abuse, a significant police and judicial task in this area is the prevention of future violence. In a variety of contexts, police responding to domestic violence incidents and courts dealing with decisions about the issuance of civil restraining orders or the setting of conditions for defendants electing diversion, bail, or probation are faced with the need to make predictions about the offender's future potential for abuse. How can police and courts most effectively make these predictions?

Three basic approaches can be said to exist by which police and judges can attempt to assess the risk of future violence. The first approach, the one traditionally used by police and judges and probably still used by most, involves an intuitive judgment made by the police officer or judge based upon whatever knowledge may be available about the individual in question.

This approach is problematic for a number of reasons. First, the information available about the individual is likely to be seriously incomplete. Information may simply not be available at the time the prediction judgment must be made. In addition, the police officer or judge may be unaware of many of the various factors that are relevant to predicting violence. Second, given the lack of training available to police officers and judges in the prediction of violence and the absence of any systematic collection of information about the individual, predictions may reflect the police officer's or judge's own preconceptions and biases, which may include conscious or unconscious racism, classism, and other types of prejudice that are legally and morally improper. Yet these biases will remain unstated and hence will evade detection and correction. Third, police officers and judges making predictions about future violence are likely to receive considerable highly negative feedback concerning their false negative predictions, i.e., when they predicted that the individual would not be violent but were wrong and violence occurred. However, they are likely to receive far less negative feedback when they have predicted that the individual will be dangerous, in large part because the intervention that their prediction will likely produce, such as arrest, the setting of high bail, a denial of diversion or probation, or a lengthier sentence, itself will reduce the individual's future opportunities for violence. This differential in feedback is likely to bias decision-making in the direction of producing predictions that the individual will be violent in cases in which the decision-maker remains uncertain about the risks presented. For all of these reasons, predictions of violence by police officers and judges based largely upon intuitive judgment produce unacceptably high risks of inaccuracy.

Two other basic approaches exist by which predictions about future violence can be made—a prediction model and a risk assessment model. Predicting future dangerousness is an important task not only in the area of domestic violence, but also in a variety of other legal contexts. Predictions about future recidivism, for example, are an essential part of two recent statutory approaches for dealing with sex offenders. When a sex offender registers pursuant to a sex offender community registration and notification law, in jurisdictions that use three tiers of risk with differing notification consequences, the prosecutor must determine into which tier of risk a particular offender should be placed. This determination is based largely on an assessment by the prosecutor of the risk of future recidivism presented by the offender. Similarly, under sexually violent predator statutes, a form of civil commitment applied to dangerous sex offenders at the expiration of their prison terms, the determination as to whether a sex offender should be subjected to civil commitment is based largely on an assessment of the likelihood of the individual's reoffending.

A similar assessment of the risk of future dangerous behavior arises in other legal areas. It occurs in civil commitment of those with mental illness predicted to be dangerous. It occurs in the determination of whether a criminal defendant convicted of a capital crime should receive the death penalty, or whether a convicted defendant should receive probation rather than a term of imprisonment, and of whether sentenced offenders should be released on parole before the expiration of their prison terms. It also occurs in decision making about whether a defendant charged with crime should be subjected to preventive detention pending trial.

In domestic violence contexts, police and court officials make various assessments of the risk of repeated domestic violence in responding to domestic violence incidents or to requests for restraining orders and in determining bail and conditions of probation, diversion, and punishment for offenders.

In all of these contexts, the risk of future dangerousness must be ascertained. In many of these contexts, (but less frequently in the area of domestic violence), the law has traditionally made use of clinical prediction models through which judges and other officials have relied upon the testimony of psychiatrists and psychologists functioning as expert clinical evaluators. Such a clinical prediction model is designed to determine the probability of the occurrence of a specified event within a future time period. Determinations of future violence made using a prediction model can be seen as dichotomous—the individual is determined to be either dangerous or not—and static—involving a one-time prediction based upon factors existing at the time the prediction is made.

The prediction model traditionally involved judicial processes that relied almost exclusively on the recommendations of clinical evaluators after an examination of the individual in question. In the past 30 years, however, serious questions have been raised about the accuracy of clinical prediction. Monahan's review of the literature on clinical prediction of dangerousness in the civil commitment process, for example, suggested that clinical predictions of future violent behavior were accurate only one out of three times. Although recent evidence suggests that clinical predictions may be more accurate than this, the most accurate predictions that studies seem to show still are no more accurate than about 1 out of 2, and there is persistent concern about the accuracy of predictions based exclusively on clinical evaluation.

Second, as with predictions based upon intuitive judgments, clinical predictions are problematic for a number of reasons. First, they often are based on the observations and experiences of clinicians that have not been scientifically tested and validated. A clinician's observations may be idiosyncratic, and the theories used to support predictions of violence may be invalid. Clinical predictions rely upon unsystematic methods of data gathering and synthesis that often vary widely from clinician to clinician. Second, as with predictions based upon intuitive judgments, clinical evaluations may be contaminated by the evaluator's own biases and the heuristics that he or she relies on. Moreover, like police officers and judges making intuitive judgments about the risk of violence, clinical evaluators often use unstated criteria that may mask the use of improper considerations. Third, as with police officers and judges asked to predict future violence, clinical evaluators assigned this task experience differential feedback concerning the results of their efforts that itself can have biasing effects. False negative predictions will often receive publicity when an individual predicted not to be violent commits a violent act, and will impair the credibility of the clinical evaluator. By contrast, false positive predictions of violence will evade public attention, with the result that the clinical evaluator's reputation will remain unimpaired. As a consequence, the accuracy of clinical predictions has consistently been poor, and the errors made consistently involve false-positive predictions of dangerousness. Clinical predictions of future violence thus suffer from some of the same difficulties that make reliance upon the intuitive judgment of police and judges unacceptable. A third alternative approach has been emerging, however. This approach, involving the use of statistical or actuarial methods of assessing risk, has received much recent attention. Actuarial approaches have long been used in various criminal justice contexts, such as the prediction in parole release decision making of the potential that an offender might recidivate. They also have recently been used in making predictions about the potential for violence presented by persons suffering from mental disorder. In addition, these actuarial approaches are now being used in the prediction of the likelihood of recidivism on the part of sex offenders. Such an actuarial approach is reflected in two instruments now being used in predicting risk in domestic violence cases—the SARA Guide (Spousal Abuse Risk Assessment) and the Mosaic-20.

Actuarial approaches have several advantages over approaches relying upon either intuitive judgments or clinical predictions. In contrast to these two approaches, actuarial methods explicitly identify the criteria used and how each should be weighted. Moreover, the criteria used are empirically derived, based upon research concerning the degree to which potential risk factors correlate with future violence. Although some of the actuarial forms now in use may still be in a relatively primitive state and may not yet be ready for clinical application in violence prediction, it can be predicted that future social science research on risk variables will produce refinement that will make these instruments more useful and accurate. Research on these actuarial tools is advancing rapidly, and it can be anticipated that future actuarial techniques will continue to improve, will be empirically validated to an increased extent, and will be more rigorous, involving the mathematical combination of variables to produce the prediction.

Moreover, future refinements will enable better use of actuarial methods in combination with the consideration of case specific information, thereby further enhancing accuracy. This has been termed the "anamnestic approach," which calls for identification of factors that characterize an individual's prior display of violent behavior. Clinicians or other evaluators who seek to supplement risk assessment tools with such anamnestic approaches will peruse archival information concerning the individual and interview the individual and others who know him in an effort to construct the individual's past history of violence, and thereby seek to discover repetitive themes that cut across his prior violent occurrences. Using risk assessment tools together with the added information gleaned from the anamnestic approach can help the evaluator to identify individual or situational factors that, within the context of the individual's history, seem conducive to a prediction of future violence. The combination of these approaches thus can remedy one of the significant problems associated with actuarial risk assessment — its inability to consider case specific information. The use of such a combined approach in the domestic violence area, in which non-clinical evaluators use the SARA Guide in addition to case-specific information, has recently been empirically validated for "structured professional judgment" in domestic violence cases.

Another shortcoming of the actuarial approach is the practical problem of getting judges and police officers to use it. While many police officers and judges may be unfamiliar with these instruments, training in their proper use will increasingly occur. Such training also will tend to produce greater accuracy.

It can thus be predicted that increased use will be made of actuarial approaches to assessing risk as a means of supplementing either intuitive judgments or clinical predictions concerning future violence, and that accuracy will be increased as a result. The accuracy of both intuitive judgment and clinical prediction models can be enhanced when evaluators are aware of risk factors that have been validated actuarially. Both intuitive and clinical judgment can be improved if actuarial information concerning risk is used to anchor and structure police, judicial, and clinical discretion.

Recent scholarly thinking about the prediction of violence, building upon these actuarial models, but moving beyond them, has begun to reject the prediction model in favor of what has been termed the "risk assessment" or "risk management" model. A paradigm shift has occurred in which the focus has moved from dangerousness to risk. This emergent reconceptualization is characterized by a shift away from the legal concept of dangerousness and in the direction of the decision making concept of risk; greater acceptance of the notion that prediction issues should be viewed as being on a continuum, rather than as dichotomous; the trend away from "a focus on one-time predictions about dangerousness" made for the court to "ongoing day-to-day decisions about the management and treatment" of those presenting the risk of violence; and increased recognition of the need for "balancing the seriousness of possible outcomes with the probabilities of their occurrence based on specific risk factors." Unlike prediction models based on intuitive judgment or clinical assessment, which are essentially static, measuring risk at a particular date based on information then in existence, the risk management model is dynamic, considering information concerning the individual as it may develop over time in light of the individual's ongoing behavior and response to treatment and other interventions. While prediction models are designed to assess dangerousness through predicting the probability of the event's occurring, the risk management model attempts to reduce the risk of such behavior. Managing and reducing risk through treatment and rehabilitation, and protective interventions becomes the focus. The use of actuarial techniques can increase accuracy through the use of stated criteria that are empirically validated, thereby minimizing the biases that often characterize predictions based on intuitive judgments and clinical assessment. In addition, the risk management approach should lead to greater accuracy inasmuch as it considers more data points and is continuously open to reevaluation of the degree of risk as it changes over time. Prediction models based on either intuitive or clinical judgment, in contrast, do not allow new information to be taken into account. The risk management model thus has several distinct advantages. It can be more useful to legal decision makers. It is likely to be more accurate. Furthermore, it involves an interactive component that is calculated to reduce the extent of risk.

In addition, the risk management model is supported by principles of therapeutic jurisprudence. By involving a dynamic process that factors in new information about individuals as it unfolds, the risk management model provides a feedback loop to individuals that can help them shape their behavior to produce a reduction in the level of risk presented. By contrast, with the use of a prediction model, individuals have little incentive to effect change in ways that will reduce the degree of risk they present. Inasmuch as the prediction model is static, producing predictions of risk that are frozen in time and will not change, nothing the individual may do after the determination will succeed in altering the evaluation that initially was made. The risk management model, on the other hand, provides individuals with an incentive to alter their behavior to minimize or avoid the interferences with their liberty that are justified as a result of the determination that they are dangerous. The risk management model can thus be seen to function as a method of behavior management that harnesses principles of psychology to reduce risk. Police and judicial practices in the area of domestic violence should be restructured to reflect a risk management approach.

Risk assessment tools like the SARA Guide should be used at the point of the initial incident report and thereafter to assess and reassess risk as it may change over time. Armed with this information, police and judicial officials can make more informed decisions about the processing of domestic violence cases, deciding when and how to intervene with greater accuracy and effectiveness. These risk assessment tools may not be perfect, but their use by police and judges to supplement and sometimes replace other modes of violence prediction can increase the accuracy of the risk assessment process. Moreover, combining risk assessment tools with case specific information can further increase accuracy. These techniques will increase in sophistication, utility, and accuracy in the future as they seem to have generated enormous interest in the scholarly community.

These approaches should be used in domestic violence cases because they will allow decisions to be based upon greater information, and more effective use of this information. Whether a restraining order or an order requiring an alleged batterer to vacate the marital home should be issued and what conditions should be attached to such an order, for example, may turn upon the extent of risk presented. Whether an alleged batterer should be arrested similarly may turn upon the extent of the risk he presents. The amount of bail that should be set for an arrested batterer and the conditions that might be attached to release on bail also may depend upon a consideration of risk. Whether an offender should be given diversion or placed on probation rather than incarcerated may similarly depend upon the extent of risk presented.

The literature has begun to identify a number of risk factors that correlate with future abusing behavior. Some of these are the same factors used in assessing dangerousness in other areas with other risk assessment instruments such as the revised Hare Psychopathy Check List (HPCL), the Violence Risk Assessment Guide (VRAG) and the Sex Offender Risk Appraisal Guide (SORAG). Others are more unique to domestic violence cases, such as the occurrence of prior acts of domestic violence or violations of protective or restraining orders, the existence of marital estrangement, a child custody dispute, attitudes that support or condone spousal assault, obsessive-possessiveness, or acute perceptions of betrayal, the seriousness of past acts of abuse, and whether the violence occurred in the presence of children or the individual is a non-biological parent of children residing in the household. The age of the alleged batterer and the existence of a prior criminal record also are risk factors that are correlated with future acts of abuse, as is alcoholism or substance abuse. In some jurisdictions, risk factors are used in addition to those set forth in the SARA Guide. Most of these are static risk factors. Some, however, like ongoing alcohol or substance abuse, extreme denial or minimization, attitudes that support or condone spousal assault, or attendance at treatment programs, are dynamic risk factors. Other dynamic risk factors that research has found to be correlated with future domestic violence include acute perceptions of betrayal, an obsessive attachment to the victim, explicit or implicit threats to the victim, stalking behavior, destruction of the victim's property, possession of or access to a weapon, a material change in circumstances such as job loss, and whether the individual is the non-biological parent of children residing in the household or takes personal risks such as public exposure or job related risks.

Care should be exercised in the selection of risk factors to avoid the potential that they can function as surrogates for racism, classism, or other improper considerations. Prior arrests, for example, may be visited disproportionately upon minority groups as a result of the discrimination that often continues to permeate the criminal justice system. When risk factors may be proxies for race or other inappropriate considerations, those using actuarial instruments that use such factors should apply an extra measure of scrutiny in an effort to ascertain, for example, whether a previous arrest seemed valid or instead seemed to be the product of racism, in which case, reliance upon the risk factor in question should be reduced or eliminated.

The Miami, Florida police and judicial response to domestic violence is moving in the direction of the risk management approach suggested here. Both the Miami-Dade Domestic Violence Court and the City of Miami Rapid Enforcement and Containment Tracking (REACT) program utilize risk assessment tools in their processing of domestic violence cases. The Police REACT program, for example, uses a form containing six major categories of risk. Police officers, shelter staff, and injunction court intake specialists all receive training concerning these categories of risk and how to assess the degree of danger presented. Based on information provided by the victim and others, these personnel reach a determination of the degree of risk presented in a particular case. When risk is assessed as high, the Police REACT program responds as rapidly as possible to effect an arrest.

Similarly, the Miami-Dade Domestic Violence Court uses risk assessment tools that include the SARA factors and others. The rehabilitative program mandated for all offenders who accept diversion or are placed on probation and which may be required for those who violate a civil restraining order involves a 26 session program of education, counseling, and rehabilitation for the offender. The Miami-Dade court is planning to change this one-size-fits-all twenty-six session program into differing ones calibrated to the risk presented by the offender. Those rated in a low risk category could participate in a sixteen-session program; those in a medium risk category could be placed in a more intensive twenty-six-session program; and those in a high-risk category could be placed in a still more rigorous forty-two-session program. The extent of monitoring and supervision by the court will presumably vary with each risk category.

This differential approach based upon the extent of risk presented can be seen as the application of a risk management model in this area. The court, in effect, functions as a case manager or risk manager, varying interventions and the extent of monitoring and the restrictiveness of conditions imposed based upon the degree of risk presented. The concept of case management is already being applied in domestic violence court, usually to refer to the administrative role of the intake unit of the court. In many domestic violence courts, the probation department plays a monitoring role to insure compliance with court orders, including attendance at treatment programs and compliance with restraining orders. This coordinated monitoring function helps to hold the batterer accountable and to insure that court orders are obeyed. By increasing compliance with both restraining orders and participation in treatment, this coordinated monitoring functions to reduce the risk of future violence. What is suggested here is that the domestic violence court itself can be conceptualized as a risk manager, applying case management and risk management approaches to reduce the risk of violence. This is parallel to the role of the modern hospital practicing disease management and other forms of case management to teach patients how to manage their own illnesses, to encourage preventive approaches by patients, to increase the likelihood that patients receive appropriate medical interventions, and to decrease the risk of medical malpractice.

Having the domestic violence court play such a risk management role can have the salutary effect not only of minimizing the risk of future domestic violence, but of enhancing the therapeutic opportunity these programs may provide for offenders. To the extent that differential responses are based upon dynamic risk factors such as alcohol or substance abuse, program participation, and the other dynamic risk factors identified above, the offender will receive feedback that will provide an incentive for him to modify his behavior in order to reduce the extent or restrictiveness of the conditions imposed by the court. For this approach to be an effective motivator for change on the part of the offender, the offender must be made to appreciate the relationship between his abusive behavior in regard to these dynamic risk factors and the court's response.

General criminal courts would be far less able to apply this approach in domestic violence cases than would specialized domestic violence courts. Jurisdictions therefore should adopt the domestic violence court approach and should structure such courts in ways that allow them to play this important risk management function. There is need for more social science research on risk factors that correlate with repeated acts of abuse, and the development and validation of more effective risk assessment instruments in this area. At present, risk assessment instruments are far from perfect, but it can be anticipated that they will continue to evolve and improve and will become extremely helpful tools for police and court officials to use in domestic violence decision making. I do not suggest the use of actuarial instruments in the adjudication of guilt. When a defendant charged with domestic violence pleads not guilty, he is entitled to a full and fair trial in accordance with the mandates of due process. The determination of guilt requires the judge or jury to decide whether the prosecution's evidence supports a finding of guilt beyond a reasonable doubt that the individual committed the past act or acts with which he is charged. Predictions about the potential for future violence are irrelevant to this determination, and would be inadmissible at the criminal trial. Moreover, when there are contested issues of historic fact presented at a motion for a civil restraining order, predictions about future violence are likewise irrelevant and would be inadmissible. Such predictions are relevant, however, when the court has decided to issue a restraining order and needs to decide what conditions to impose upon the individual who will be restrained, in the determination of whether conditions should be imposed upon a criminal defendant's release upon bail, and in determining whether to allow diversion, and if so, in setting the conditions for such diversion. Moreover, assessment of the risk of future violence also is relevant when a criminal defendant has pled guilty and the judge must determine whether to sentence him to a term of probation, and if so, what conditions should be attached to probation. Such an assessment of risk also is relevant when the judge must determine what to do and a defendant has violated a restraining order or a condition of diversion or probation. This use of risk assessment tools in assisting courts in the making of these determinations would not infringe the presumption of innocence or otherwise violate the defendant's due process rights.

Courts need to develop a wide range of response options that can be calibrated to the extent of risk presented, and to use risk factors more in decision making about appropriate interventions, monitoring, supervision, and protective strategies. Risk assessment should be regarded as an on-going process rather than as a one-time event, thereby affording offenders an opportunity to earn less onerous restrictions or requirements when warranted, and thus providing a meaningful incentive that can motivate behavior in line with program goals. In these ways, the domestic violence court can function not only as an adjudicator of cases, but as an effective manager of risk, reducing violence and facilitating rehabilitation.

A criminal court processing domestic violence cases resolves issues in a piecemeal fashion. It tends to view a particular case or issue to be adjudicated like a still photograph, rather than seeing the incident or event that requires adjudication as being part of a larger, dynamic process. A domestic violence court applying the risk management approach proposed here, by contrast, can see the larger picture. It can understand and deal more effectively with the on-going dynamic that exists between the batterer and the victim. Rather than looking at what might only be a small piece of the puzzle, it can see the broader context and adjust its responsiveness to on-going events in ways that can more effectively use resources and appropriately timed interventions to ameliorate the problem. Domestic violence is a process, not an event, and as a result should be treated by our institutions with a risk management strategy tailored to the situation, with responses calibrated to events as they develop over time. A criminal court is capable only of individual responses to isolated events, but a domestic violence court applying a risk management strategy can develop an individualized, appropriately resourced and timed rehabilitative and risk-reduction plan that is flexible, capable of changing over time in response to changing circumstances, and hence more effective.

Key References
Heilbrun, Kirk, *Prediction Versus Management Models Relevant to Risk Assessment: The Importance of Legal Decision-Making Context*, 21 Law & Hum. Behav. 347 (1997).
Johnson, Janet A. et al., *Death by Intimacy: Risk Factors for Domestic Violence*, 20 Pace L. Rev. 262 (2000).
Kropp, P. Randall & Hart, Stephen, *The Spousal Assault Risk Assessment (SARA) Guide: Reliability and Validity in Adult Male Offenders*, 24 Law & Hum. Behav. 101 (2000).

H. Enhancing Compliance

When an offender agrees to a rehabilitation plan that will likely reduce risk, the court's concern will shift in part to questions of compliance. How judges can enhance compliance is given full coverage in this selection by Wexler, which reviews in considerable detail the psychological literature on compliance with healthcare advice and then applies those principles in the context of the conditional release of insanity acquittees. It should come as no surprise that the compliance principles are highly consistent with Clark's point, made earlier, regarding active client involvement and participation.

Of course, as is typical for the readings in Part II, the relevant therapeutic jurisprudence principles transcend the legal context in which they are illustrated. The principles for enhancing compliance, for example, can find a fit, to a greater or lesser degree, in many legal contexts besides the conditional release of insanity acquittees. Other contexts include reentry courts, probation and parole, outpatient commitment, domestic violence protective orders, and family safety plans.

Health Care Compliance Principles and the Judiciary
by David B. Wexler
(From *Health Care Compliance Principles and the Insanity Acquittee Conditional Release Process*, 27 Crim. L. Bull. 18 (1991), Copyright 1991 by David B. Wexler, reprinted with permission).

The medical profession has long known that patients often fail to comply with prescribed treatment regimens. Increasingly, the health care compliance problem has attracted the attention of psychologists interested in understanding, predicting, and improving patient compliance. Now, Donald Meichenbaum and Dennis Turk have marshalled the literature and have published a book entitled *Facilitating Treatment Adherence: A Practitioner's Guidebook*. The book presents a set of principles designed to help the medical profession increase patient treatment adherence.

The book does not deal with the legal system at all. And although it discusses the research on compliance and noncompliance by mental health outpatients (particularly those diagnosed as having schizophrenia, bipolar disorder, and alcoholism), it cannot be classified as a book specializing in mental patient compliance. Nonetheless, the Meichenbaum and Turk principles have the potential of making a substantial contribution to the field of mental health law The purpose of the present chapter is to demonstrate how health care compliance principles might be used by the judiciary and the legal system to increase the medication and treatment compliance of a very worrisome group—conditionally released insanity acquittees.

More specifically, the chapter will suggest how, consistent with psychological principles of health care compliance, insanity acquittee conditional release hearings might be restructured, and how the judicial role in such hearings might be altered, so as to enhance the probability of adherence by the patients eventually granted conditional release. As such, the topic falls squarely within the research agenda of therapeutic jurisprudence.

Before turning to the health care compliance principles, we had best review briefly the law and practice regarding insanity acquittee conditional release. It is that body of law that will ultimately be scrutinized for its ability to accommodate and exploit the Meichenbaum and Turk principles.

The Legal Landscape

Commitment

In a distinct minority of jurisdictions, insanity acquittees are committable only through the generic civil commitment procedure. As such, the duration of their confinement and the mechanisms for their securing institutional passes and conditional and unconditional releases are no different from those governing civilly committed mental patients who have not had contact with the criminal justice system. For that group, trial visits, conditional release, and even ultimate release are usually within the unilateral discretion of the hospital authorities, unscrutinized by the courts.

Far more common, however, especially since the *Hinckley* verdict, are "special" commitment systems governing the commitment, duration of confinement, and release (conditional or otherwise) of insanity acquittees. Some jurisdictions regard an insanity acquittal as sufficient grounds for *automatic* commitment; others require a fresh judicial inquiry into the acquittee's *present* mental condition and likely future dangerousness. Once committed, the acquittee might constitutionally face a potentially indefinite confinement period. A number of jurisdictions, however, limit the confinement of the acquittee to the maximum sentence that could have been imposed had a conviction, rather than an insanity acquittal, followed the criminal trial. In those jurisdictions, at the expiration of the "hypothetical maximum criminal sentence," the insanity acquittee would have to be released or, if warranted by the acquittee's current mental condition and predicted dangerousness, civilly committed under the applicable generic civil commitment code.

Even more pertinent for purposes of the present chapter are the provisions governing release, particularly conditional release and shorter-term institutional leaves, variously referred to as passes, trial visits, and furloughs. The states invariably allow the acquittee and his or her attorney to file, at specified intervals, a petition for release and a request for a judicial hearing. Typically, the acquittee will bear the burden of persuasion at the release hearing.

Further, whenever the superintendent believes the acquittee is ready for conditional or unconditional release, a hospital-initiated petition for release may be filed. In progressive jurisdictions, a period of conditional release will usually precede an application for outright release. Indeed, under a "graduated release" model, even conditional release is typically preceded by passes or trial visits. Under modem statutes, particularly those passed post-*Hinckley*, even short-term hospital absences ordinarily require court approval, especially if the acquittee is to enter the community unaccompanied by public officials.

When a superintendent files a petition for an acquittee's conditional release, some jurisdictions require a court hearing on the matter, while others permit such a hearing on the court's own motion and require a hearing only if the prosecuting attorney objects to the proposed conditional release. In any event, a study of the District of Columbia practice concludes that "although holding a court hearing is optional, some form of hearing occurs in virtually all cases, to make a record, test the opinion of the Hospital and wisdom of its recommendation, and to assure protection for the public." That same study concludes that, in the "vast majority of cases," the court will concur with the hospital's recommendation. When a conditional release is granted, the court will order the acquittee to comply with certain conditions. Under the federal statute, for example, the court shall

> (A) order that he be conditionally discharged under a prescribed regimen of medical, psychiatric, or psychological care or treatment that has been prepared for him, that has been certified to the court as appropriate by the director of the facility in which he is committed, and that has been found by the court to be appropriate, and
>
> (B) order, as an explicit condition of release, that he comply with the prescribed regimen of medical, psychiatric, or psychological care or treatment.

Typical conditions that have been imposed by courts relate to taking medication (perhaps in the presence of another), to living in a particular household, to keeping weekly outpatient therapy appointments, and to attending Alcoholics Anonymous meetings. Failure to comply with the conditions can, of course, lead to revocation and rehospitalization, typically triggered by a due process hearing.

Jurisdictional Matters

When courts are charged with making conditional release decisions, a jurisdictional issue also arises. Typically, the criminal court—which becomes the committing court when a defendant is acquitted by insanity—has jurisdiction over conditional release matters. Under some schemes, however, jurisdiction is vested in the probate court of the county in which the hospital is located. These jurisdictional niceties are skirted in a state like Oregon, where release and conditional release decisions of committed insanity acquittees reside in an administrative body known as the Psychiatric Security Review Board.

Administrative Model

Oregon's highly regarded Psychiatric Security Review Board is composed of five members (a psychiatrist, psychologist, lawyer, parole expert, and a member of the public). By majority vote, the Board elects a chair and conducts other business. Much of its business consists of making insanity acquittee conditional release decisions. The Board holds hearings, retires to deliberate, makes findings, and, within 45 days of the conclusion of a hearing, issues written notice of its derision.

The administrative model of the Psychiatric Security Review Board is the chief competitor to the traditional model, which vests insanity acquittee release decisions in the hands of the judiciary. Later, the discussion returns to this issue and, indeed, to virtually all the legal material presented in this section. Now, however, it is time to turn to the psychological principles of health care compliance.

Health Care Compliance Principles

This section will set forth those health care compliance principles discussed by Meichenbaum and Turk that have potential relevance to the insanity acquittee conditional release process. In the current section, the principles will be discussed without reference to the legal system. Integrating the psychology and the law is the task of the ensuing sections.

As noted earlier, Meichenbaum and Turk deal in part with mental patients, but their volume covers the full gamut of health care patients and professionals. The principles they propound have apparent general applicability to both physical and mental health compliance. This section will assume the accuracy and efficacy of the principles, which were derived from an extensive review of the research and clinical literature. Further research is obviously needed, but that is typically the case. From a therapeutic jurisprudence perspective, it should be highly instructive to regard those principles as tentatively true, and to examine how the legal system might be reshaped to accommodate them.

Adherence Process

One of the most important reasons for nonadherence is the failure of the health care professional (HCP) to instruct the patient adequately about the treatment regimen. Indeed, although physicians seem not to commonly acknowledge it, "the behavior of the HCP plays a critical role in the adherence process." Nonadherence is promoted when the HCP is distant, looks and acts busy, reads case notes during the interview, uses jargon, asks patients questions calling for "yes or no" answers, cuts off the patient, does not permit patients to tell their stories in their own words, fails to state the exact treatment regimen or states it in unclear or technical terms, adopts a moralizing, high power stance, fails to sit at the same keel as the patient, keeps a desk between the HCP and the patient, and terminates the interview abruptly. By contrast, Meichenbaum and Turk advise HCPs to introduce themselves, to avoid unexplained jargon, and to elicit patient suggestions and preferences.

The patient's active involvement in negotiating and designing the treatment program is of tremendous importance to adherence and favorable outcome. Even giving a patient a choice over some of the more minor details—such as the form of medication and the scheduling of injections—can have salutary effects.

To promote patient adherence, the HCP should linguistically cast the treatment program in a manner that capitalizes on the patient's involvement and agreement. For example, directive terminology such as "What you are to do is..." should be replaced by a softer, more bilateral statement, such as "So what you have agreed to try is..." Adherence will be further nurtured if the HCP has high prestige and is perceived to be competent, attentive, practical, and to be motivated by the best interests of the client.

In questioning a patient, the compliance literature also suggests the HCP needs to achieve a delicate balance with respect to the nature of self-disclosure requested of patients. Thus, "seeking high self-disclosure or asking patients about material that they would not usually share with other family members or friends" seems detrimental to adherence. In contrast, a moderate (rather than low) level of self-disclosure, focusing both on personal strengths and weaknesses, seems to increase perceived self-efficacy and the patient's adherence. A particularly profitable avenue of HCP questioning relates to the patient's past compliance efforts: "What kinds of things in the past have you tried that were unsuccessful? How is what you have agreed to do now different?"

Relatedly, it is profitable for the HCP to raise mild counterarguments about the patient's prospective compliance. When the HCP indicates to the patient certain obstacles and drawbacks to compliance, the patient will have an opportunity to minimize and counter the HCP's arguments, thus "fostering the patient's sense of control, commitment, and degree of hope." A patient presented with mild counterarguments to compliance who nonetheless announces to a prestigious HCP his or her intention to comply will be "anchored" to the compliance decision by anticipated disapproval from the HCP and by anticipated self-disapproval.

Involving significant others—such as family members—in the treatment process is also likely to enhance patient adherence. Family members aware of the treatment regimen can encourage, remind, and prod the patient, and can help the HCP assess patient compliance. One suggested technique for involving significant others is for the HCP to bring in family members and to have the patient personally explain to them the nature of the illness and the proposed treatment

So long as the patient is agreeable to the involvement of certain family members, their presence and participation is likely to be beneficial. Greater patient adherence has been found, for example, among patients accompanied to evaluations by family members than among those patients who attended those evaluations alone.

When an HCP has a patient explain her medical problem and agreed upon course of treatment to family members, the active patient participation provides an opportunity to "assess her comprehension, to elicit a public commitment, and to strengthen her adherence-related attitudes."

One reason why the presence of significant others enhances patient compliance is that "public commitment leads to greater adherence than does private commitment." In addition to the motivational power of anticipated self-disapproval and the anticipated social disapproval of the HCP, discussed above, a patient who has previously made a commitment to significant others will be anchored to compliance by their anticipated disapproval as well. Thus, Meichenbaum and Turk note that "insofar as patients can be encouraged to inform one or more people (in addition to the HCP) of their intentions to follow the treatment regimen, there is an increased likelihood of adherence."

Behavioral Contracting

When negotiating a course of treatment with a patient, HCPs can profit from the behavior modification literature regarding "behavioral contracting." Such "behavioral" or "contingency" contracting "capitalizes on the patient-HCP relationship by actively involving the patient in the therapeutic decision-making process and by providing additional incentives (rewards) for achievement of treatment objectives."

The relevant literature seems to suggest that behavioral contracting works best when the contract is individually tailored to the particular needs and desires of a given patient, when it defines the target behavior expected of the patient with specificity, when it spells out the positive and aversive consequences that will attach, respectively, to compliance and to noncompliance, when significant others (rather than the HCP alone) deliver the consequences, when the contracts include the "specific dates for contract initiation, termination, and renewal," when the patient's commitment is solicited in both oral and written form, and when the contract is "signed by at least two parties as well as other interested and relevant" ones.

Unfortunately, despite evidence of short-term benefits flowing from behavioral contracting in the health area, the longterm benefits have yet to be established. There is evidence that health-related behavioral changes "are maintained only for the duration of the contract, and after its termination or when the treatment contract is withdrawn the patient may stop performing health-related behaviors (e.g., pill taking, diet, exercise)."

Some principles may be invoked to lessen the chances of disappointing post-termination results. For example, during the contract period itself, "the greater the continuity of care whereby patients can see the same HCP upon repeated visits, the greater the likelihood of adherence." The HCP should not abruptly terminate treatment but should instead gradually wean the patient from the process. While doing so, the HCP should help the patient make "self attributions" about successful behavioral changes. It is best that patients attribute beneficial changes to themselves rather than to external events or persons.

HCPs and Compliance

Interestingly, although Meichenbaum and Turk devote much of their volume to patient nonadherence to HCP recommendations, they close with a discussion of why HCPs themselves might not adhere to the recommendations set forth in the book: Patients *should* take their advice or simply suffer the consequences of noncompliance; the principles simply will not work with their particular patient populations; the recommended procedures are too complicated and numerous; there is simply no time in day-to-day practice to implement the procedures; the system does not support frills like adherence counseling; and, finally, they cannot make use of the principles because most HCPs are not mental health professionals and accordingly have not been trained in psychological techniques of adherence.

Meichenbaum and Turk provide powerful counterarguments to the anticipated HCP reluctance to implement the recommended health care compliance principles. Thus, although the procedures many seem a bit complicated initially, they will soon require less attention and will in the longrun improve the quality of service. At the early stages, the HCP can use checklists as memory prompts. Finally, with regard to clinical skill, the authors note that "no great amount of specialized training" is ordinarily required to use the recommended enhancement techniques.

Applying the Health Care Compliance Principles in the Insanity Acquittee Conditional Release Process

To varying degrees, health care compliance principles can be invoked in a variety of legal contexts—such as insanity acquittee conditional release, parole, probation, and outpatient civil commitment. The only example to be considered here, the insanity acquittee conditional release process, is the legal mechanism most suitable for incorporating the health care compliance principles. In fact, to maximize the potential application of the health care compliance principles, the insanity acquittee conditional release process will itself be discussed in a somewhat limited legal and geographical context.

From a legal perspective, only *hospital-initiated* conditional release petitions are examined, and not conditional release claims triggered by patients over the objection of the hospital. As a practical matter, hospital-initiated petitions are the most viable ones—the ones that typically lead to conditional release rather than to continued hospitalization.

Geographically, for reasons of efficiency, security, and transportation, the recommended principles will be easiest to implement if the hospital, the criminal court where the insanity acquittal occurred, and the acquittee's home community all fall within the same general area. In that case, the inconvenience to the hospital, to the community facility, and to the patient and patient's family will not be great even if a series of conditional release hearings is held.

The Courts' Role in Adherence

With the above limitations and caveats in mind, let us turn our attention to the means by which a court versed in the health care compliance principles might exploit those principles to increase the adherence behavior of a patient proposed by the hospital for conditional release status. Such hospital-initiated cases are likely to lead to conditional release (whether the prosecutor supports or opposes the hospital's recommendation), and in this relatively low stress context the court might rather comfortably see its role as facilitating as well as predicting compliance.

It is important to recognize, however, that courts might sometimes increase eventual patient adherence not by simply deferring to the hospital's conditional release recommendation but by truly scrutinizing hospital-initiated conditional release petitions for their conformity to the health care compliance principles. To the extent that HCPs may themselves fail to comply with the recommended procedures for facilitating treatment adherence, as, Meichenbaum and Turk worry they often will, courts can encourage HCP compliance by denying (or deferring action on) hospital petitions that demonstrate insufficient use of the fundamentals of treatment adherence.

The use of some of the fundamentals will be easier for courts to monitor and oversee than will others. Courts may not have much control over the give-and-take of doctor-patient office dialogue, for example, but they can—through the actions of denial and deferral—encourage the hospital, patient, and community facility to negotiate, prepare, sign, and submit with the judicial petition a rather specific behavioral contract setting forth the terms and conditions of the proposed conditional release.

The Conditional Release Hearing

Once the behavioral contract is "signed by at least two parties [the patient and the hospital] as well as the other interested and relevant parties [the community facility and perhaps family members]," the court can use the contracts as the basis of a judicial conditional release hearing, and can view the hearing as somewhat akin to (but far less routinized than) the framework of a Federal Rule of Criminal Procedure 11 hearing held to approve a previously negotiated plea agreement. Rule 11 hearings require a dialogue with the defendant in open court to assure that the defendant understands and agrees to the plea. Similarly, the conditional release hearing can actively involve the acquittee—to test the patient's understanding of the treatment regimen and to insure that the patient agrees with it and had input into its design.

The court can structure and shape the conditional release hearing so as to invoke a number of other important health care compliance principles—principles that may or may not have been used by the HCP when negotiating the plan with the patient. For example, the hearing will serve as a forum for the patient to make a "public commitment" to comply with the treatment regimen. That way, the commitment will be made not only to the HCP, but also to a high-status judicial official and to any significant others—such as family members—whose presence at the hearing has been approved by the patient.

A conditional release hearing can also provide an excellent opportunity for the court to seek from the patient the appropriate level of self-disclosure, particularly regarding past unsuccessful compliance efforts and the extent to which the current treatment plan differs from any earlier, unsuccessful ones. The hearing is also an ideal forum for presenting the patient with "mild counterarguments" to compliance, enabling the patient to counter those arguments and accordingly to become "anchored" to the compliance decision.

Where the hospital-initiated conditional release petition is unopposed by the prosecution, the judge might personally elicit the patient self-disclosure and might personally express concern in the form of "mild counterarguments." Where the hospital's petition is opposed by the prosecution, those matters will naturally fall to the prosecuting attorney.[1]

As a result of matters ventilated at the hearing, the behavioral contract may be somewhat revised before it is finally approved by the court. When the agreement is finally approved, however, the patient's commitment will have been solicited both orally and in writing,[2] and the other important behavioral contracting principles (e.g., individually tailored, specific regarding expected patient behavior and positive and aversive consequences, involvement of significant others, specification of termination or renewal dates) will have been attended to as well.[3]

In terms of court approval of the conditional release, the statutes—especially the federal one—convey the flavor of a court ordering a passive acquittee to be "conditionally discharged under a prescribed regimen of...

treatment that has been prepared for him," and ordering "as an explicit condition of release, that he comply with the prescribed regimen." Despite the unfortunate linguistic flavor of the statutes, a court is free to follow the more therapeutic course and to conceptualize and frame the conditional release as an agreement ("So what you have agreed to try is...") rather than as an order ("What you are to do is...").

A Model of Judicial Behavior

Indeed, to the extent that the court is in some sense shaping or approving the release conditions, the court is itself an HCP, and the judge should therefore attend to the HCP behavioral factors thought to enhance patient adherence. For instance, the judge can make sure to introduce himself or herself to the patient, can be attentive, can avoid using legal or medical jargon, can allow the patient to tell his or her story without undue interruption, can make sure the patient understands the precise treatment regimen, and can even sit at the same level and at the same conference table as the patient—perhaps in a mental health facility conference room rather than in a courtroom.

The suggested model of judicial behavior is remarkably similar to the model employed in some jurisdictions by judges presiding at civil commitment hearings. In the civil commitment context, that model has been criticized as appearing "confusingly like a treatment conference...." The criticism is well taken in a context, like civil commitment, where the state is seeking to deprive an individual of liberty and where the model might lead us to relax our due process guard. In the insanity acquittee context, however, the acquittee has already lost his or her liberty, and following the hearing on the hospital-initiated conditional release petition, the acquittee is likely to regain a taste of liberty. In that context, it seems somewhat less crucial to maintain traditional judicial formalities. In any event, there is of course no inherent conflict between maintaining judicial decorum and treating an insanity acquittee respectfully; nor is there an inherent conflict between being competent, expert, and of high prestige and nonetheless being motivated by the acquittee's best interest.

Initial Patient Reentry Transitions

In order to enable the insanity acquittee to reenter the community gradually, and to allow the relevant authorities to keep close tabs on the patient's adjustment, it is probably best that the acquittee first return to the community not under conditional release, but under the authority of very brief passes or furloughs. In fact, such leaves, which by statute increasingly require court approval, should perhaps be used, much more than they currently are, as a partial substitute for conditional release.

For example, after laying the conditional release groundwork by according an acquittee a series of brief furloughs, a court might be inclined to grant the acquittee conditional release status. Instead of granting a full-blown conditional release, however, the court might grant the acquittee a longer, time-limited furlough. The furlough could be issued according to a behavioral contract obliging the acquittee to follow an agreed-upon therapeutic program, and compliance could be rewarded by renewal of the furlough. In all other respects, the agreements and hearings could follow the suggestions given above for the conditional release process.

By using a series of furloughs as a precursor to conditional release, the court may be able to tap some additional health care compliance principles. Furlough termination and renewal dates can be noted with great precision, and the acquittee can have some input into the appropriate duration — and renewal date hearing — of each furlough. Significant others can be nominated by the patient to monitor compliance and to appear and testify at follow-up (renewal) hearings. The follow-up hearings will provide a type of "continuity of care," especially if the same judge is able to oversee the acquittee's community adjustment. The fade-out from furlough to full-fledged conditional release can be gradual, giving the court an opportunity to help the patient make "self-attributions" about the patient's continual progress. Further monitoring, follow-up, and fading-out can and should of course occur during the period of conditional release proper.

If the health care compliance techniques are brought by the judiciary into the insanity acquittee furlough and conditional release process in the manner described above, the therapeutic value of that process may be enhanced without treading upon values of justice. Of course, the law in some jurisdictions will make it easier than in others for the judiciary to import the health care compliance principles. Accordingly, the next section briefly assesses the ability of various legal schemes to accommodate the compliance principles.

The Law and the Health Care
Compliance Principles

Certain legal schemes stand out as frustrating the application of the health care compliance principles to the insanity acquittee conditional release process. For instance, those states that process insanity acquittees through the civil commitment system typically leave release, conditional release, and furlough matters to the hospital itself; the courts accordingly play no role in such matters and therefore lack leverage to urge the adoption of appropriate adherence techniques. Almost as bad—in terms of lack of leverage—are special insanity acquittee commitment laws that nonetheless *mandate* the court to order release in the absence of objection from the prosecution. And even worse are legal systems where insanity acquittees fall under special commitment laws but where those laws are read as not even authorizing conditional release.

The Courts' Active Involvement

Laws favorable to the use of principles expressed here are those requiring court approval even of furloughs, and those authorizing or even requiring conditional release hearings. Jurisdictionally, it is probably best if release matters are heard in the original commitment court, rather than in the probate court of the county where the hospital is located. Such a resolution, although not taking advantage of any specialized knowledge that probate courts located in the vicinity of the hospital might develop, spreads the judicial work load more equitably, appears not to lead to harsher treatment of insanity acquittees, and will make more feasible the holding of follow-up hearings at which the most important witnesses should be the patient, the community treatment facility staff, and the patient's family. Of course, as a practical matter, such hearings will be easiest to conduct when, as noted earlier, the committing court, hospital, and the patient's home community are all located in the same area.

Recommended Period of Control

Because of the behavioral contracting data suggesting diminished treatment adherence after the expiration of the contract period, the period a releasee can be held on conditional release ought not to be too short. On the other hand, the *indefinite* control over an insanity acquittee is probably not necessary, and may be countertherapeutic if its prospect leads defendants not to assert the insanity defense in the first place. State control over an acquittee for the period of the "hypothetical maximum criminal sentence" should be sufficient, especially since persons acquitted by insanity of very serious crimes will be under state control for a long-term, and perhaps for a lifetime.

Administrative Model

Curiously, Oregon's administrative model—the Psychiatric Security Review Board—does not fare very well when scrutinized from the perspective of the compliance principles. The Board may perform exceptionally well in terms of monitoring and in terms of other important areas beyond the scope of the present chapter. The model seems to fall short, however, in terms of its potential for inducing compliance through the hearing process itself.

The Board, composed of five members, might have some difficulty departing sufficiently from formality to play the HCP role described earlier. Further, following the hearing, the Board is expected to deliberate in closed session and, by majority vote, to reach a decision and later issue its findings and order. Such a model does not comport ideally with the model developed earlier in the chapter: a single judge holding a hearing to review a previously negotiated agreement, questioning the patient about the agreement, putting the final touches on it, extracting from the patient a public commitment to comply, setting a follow-up hearing at which the same judge will preside, and, in the presence of the patient, entering an order approving the patient's temporary release according to the terms and conditions set out in the agreement. Given the attractiveness of the PSRB in other respects, a worthwhile future project would be to consider ways in which the PSRB could be modified to better incorporate health care compliance principles.

Conclusion

This exercise in therapeutic jurisprudence demonstrates which legal structures square best with importing health care compliance principles into the insanity acquittee conditional release process and, even more, demonstrates how courts can restructure the process and the hearings to facilitate treatment adherence. In their text, Meichenbaum and Turk express the fear that, for a variety of reasons, HCPs themselves will not comply with the recommendations. In this chapter, the issue of HCP noncompliance has been partly finessed, for courts can exert compliance leverage over a hospital seeking to conditionally discharge an insanity acquittee. Only one major issue seems to remain: Will *courts* comply?

Courts may resist for reasons similar to those given by HCPs: Patients should adhere or else suffer the consequences; the principles will not work on a population of insanity acquittees; the procedures are too complicated and numerous; there is no time in day-to-day courtroom practice to implement the procedures; the system does not support frills like adherence-enhancing strategies; and, finally, courts cannot make use of the principles because judges are not mental health professionals and accordingly have not been trained in psychological techniques of adherence.

The responses given by Meichenbaum and Turk to the HCPs are similar to those that can be given to the courts: the procedures may seem complicated at first, but, after a hearing or two, should require less attention; in the long run the modification in procedures should improve patient adherence and thus better serve society; manuals and checklists can be used to introduce courts to the procedures and principles; and, finally, no particularly specialized training is necessary to implement the procedures.

Just as "the behavior of the HCP plays a critical role in the adherence process," it is probable that, like it or not, the behavior of courts plays a critical role in the adherence behavior of conditionally released insanity acquittees. Ultimately, of course, the issue is an empirical one. Ideally, the judicial role in influencing patient compliance is a matter that should receive careful empirical examination.

Notes

1. A familiarity with the compliance literature and with the legal reality should serve to keep the prosecutor's behavior within the bounds of restrained advocacy. True, if the prosecution is very forceful, the hospital's conditional release petition may be denied. Typically, however, the courts will follow the hospital's conditional release recommendation despite the prosecutor's objec-

tion. If conditional release is, in any event, likely, and if high, as opposed to moderate, patient self-disclosure lessens the prospects of adherence, a prosecutor who seeks anything more than moderate patient self-disclosure runs the risk of contributing to the conditionally released patient's noncompliance.

2. Presumably, in cases where the hospital itself petitions for the patient's conditional release, the patient will be cooperative, have insight into his need to adhere to treatment conditions, and have had input into the shaping of the conditions. Under those circumstances, the patient should identify with the plan to a sufficient degree so that psychological "reactance" (reacting against the proposed conditions) will be avoided. *See* S. Brehm & J. Brehm, *Psychological Reactance: A Theory of Freedom and Control* (1981).

3. The agreement may require the acquittee to live in a particular place, attend an outpatient clinic on a weekly basis, and take prescribed medication—perhaps in the presence of others. Positive reinforcers of a "bonus" variety can be dispensd by family members so as to capitalize on the "immediacy effects" that flow from promptly reinforcing appropriate patient behaviors. Under the principle of "response cost," the patient might even agree to part with items of his own—items that can be earned back from family members by engaging in appropriate behavior. Patient lawyers can play an important role in negotiating such "side agreements" with family members and in working with the hospital to present a forceful petition for conditional release.

Key References

Meichenbaum, Donald & Dennis Turk, Facilitating Treatment Adherence: A Practitioner's Guidebook (1987).

I. Behavioral Contracting

Many of the compliance principles are captured by the psychological power of behavioral contracting. Behavioral contracting is explicitly used in many drug treatment court programs, and is in essence employed when an individual opts for treatment, rather than routine criminal court processing, in other settings, such as domestic violence court or mental health court.

Behavioral contracting or contingency management has a rich literature that can be useful to judges offering offenders a rehabilitative route. We accordingly include a short selection, by Winick, which provides an orientation to the area, together with references for those interested in deeper exploration of the topic.

How Judges Can Use Behavioral Contracting
by Bruce J. Winick
(Excerpted from *Therapeutic Jurisprudence and Problem Solving Courts*, 30 FORDHAM URB. L.J. __ (Forthcoming, 2002), reprinted with permission by Bruce J Winick).

A behavioral psychology technique known as behavioral contracting or contingency management may be helpful in insuring the individual's compliance with a treatment or rehabilitative program. An explicit, formal contract is entered into between the parties in which specific goals are set forth. Motivation to achieve the goal is facilitated through contract terms providing for a combination of agreed-upon rewards or positive reinforcers for success or aversive conditioners for failure. This technique is frequently used in clinical practice, and the combination of positive reinforcement to encourage compliance and aversive conditioning to decrease or extinguish non-compliant behavior can be quite effective. The behavioral contract provides not only rewards and penalties for the achievement and non-achievement of a long-term goal, but also on the occurrence or non-occurrence of intermediate goals. Partial rewards or sanctions can be provided periodically as intermediate goals are either achieved or missed, measured at intervals that occur frequently, thereby facilitating the progressive shaping of the individual's behavior. Tailoring the rewards and punishments to the individual's incentive preferences and involving the individual in the process of selecting the goals and reinforcers, when practicable, can significantly increase motivation to comply. Such sub-goals will best maintain self-motivation and provide inducements to action, and guideposts for performance, and their attainment will produce the self-satisfaction that sustains effort.

The behavioral contract makes explicit the expectations of all involved. Target behaviors are objectified, measurable, and well understood by all parties. The setting of explicit goals is itself a significant factor in their achievement. The behavioral contract is a successful method of ensuring compliance in part because of the goal-setting effect, which posits that the mere setting of a goal produces positive expectancies for its achievement that themselves help to bring about success. Goals serve to structure and guide the individual's performance, providing direction and focusing interest, attention, and personal involvement. The behavioral contract also engages other mechanisms of psychology that help to achieve effective performance, including intrinsic motivation, cognitive dissonance, and the psychological value of choice.

Such behavioral contracts are explicitly used in many drug court treatment programs. Whether or not formally negotiated and executed, individuals agreeing to participate in treatment or rehabilitation in a variety of problem solving court contexts are in effect engaging in behavioral contracting with the courts. Offenders agreeing to participate in reentry court and to submit to supervision by the reentry court judge also are engaging in behavioral contracting. Perpetrators of domestic violence who agree to enter a batterer's intervention program as a condition of bail, diversion, or probation are in effect engaging in behavioral contracting with the domestic violence court. People with mental illness in mental health court who agree to accept treatment in the community as a condition for diversion from the criminal court similarly are engaging in behavioral contracting with the mental health court. These contracts should be explicitly negotiated, written, and agreed to by both the court and the individual in a formal and public way.

Judges in these problem solving courts should understand the psychology of behavioral contracting and how it can be used to increase motivation, commitment, compliance, and effective performance. Behavioral contracting also increases the satisfaction of people involved in problem solving court programs. Moreover, the process through which the behavioral contract is negotiated and entered into can itself provide an important opportunity for minimizing feelings of coercion that might undermine compliance and successful performance.

Rather than rushing through the process in which the individual is asked to make an election in favor of drug treatment court or another problem solving court rehabilitative program, the court process should regard the individual's decision and the behavioral contract that he or she is in effect entering into as a significant opportunity for reducing feelings of coercion and inspiring the perception of voluntary choice. According individuals a sense of voice and validation, treating them with dignity and respect, and conveying to them that the court is acting in good faith and in their best interest will diminish the perception of coercion and increase the perception of voluntary choice. Individuals opting for a rehabilitative program should be reminded that the choice is entirely up to them, and should be given the opportunity, when practicable, to participate in the negotiation of the behavioral contract and the selection of the reinforcers and sanctions that will be used and the conditions under which they will be applied. This participation and involvement should occur in ways that respect their need for voice and validation. If handled properly, the negotiation of and entry into the behavioral contract can constitute an important opportunity to engage intrinsic motivation and commitment, and to establish a mechanism that will help to assure compliance in ways that the individual will regard as fair.

By requiring an individual accepting drug treatment court to agree to periodic drug testing and reporting to court, the drug treatment court is monitoring compliance with the behavioral contract. When the drug test shows the individual to be drug-free, the drug treatment court judge praises the individual, often in the presence of a roomful of attorneys, court personnel, and other drug treatment court participants. Such praise is an important form of positive reinforcement that rewards the individual for compliant behavior, helps to shape future behavior, and builds much needed self-esteem and self-efficacy. When drug treatment court participants observe the "graduation" of a fellow participant in court, a ceremony occurring at the successful completion of the program at which the individual typically receives a "diploma," often presented by the arresting officer, praise by the judge, and general applause, they themselves receive a form of vicarious reinforcement.

When the individual's drug test is positive for drugs, the judge applies an agreed-upon sanction and aversive conditioner designed to deter future non-compliant behavior. Future incidents of non-compliance are subjected to graduated sanctions that were agreed to in advance by the individual, as well as verbal disapproval, occurring in the presence of others. The individual reports to the court every ten to fourteen days, thereby enabling the court to receive frequent feedback from the treatment team and information concerning whether the individual has remained drug-free, enabling close monitoring and supervision of the treatment process.

The periodic delivery of positive reinforcement or sanctions contingent upon whether the individual has met intermediate goals helps to maintain the individual's commitment and motivation during the one and one-half to two year period that drug treatment court typically requires. In this way, what the drug treatment court does can be seen as an application of behavioral contracting or contingency management, a technique which, if properly applied, can substantially increase the likelihood of treatment success. Other courts should adapt this approach, and all judges in these courts should receive training in its application.

Key References

Winick, Bruce J., *Harnessing the Power of the Bet: Wagering with the Government as a Mechanism for Social and Individual Change*, 45 U. MIAMI L. REV. 737 (1991).

J. Working with Offender-Victim Emotions

When judges act sensitively to encourage offender reform and rehabilitation, they also need to recognize that, in many contexts, victims as well as offenders will be "clients." What courts do and how judges speak and behave will inevitably have a powerful therapeutic—or antitherapeutic—impact on the victims.

In a prior selection, Professor Bibas, a former prosecutor, noted the importance of the victim perspective in his discussion of the guilty plea process (Part II D). This section is devoted to "working with offender-victim emotions." It consists of an article by sociologist Thomas Scheff (University of California at Santa Barbara), set in the restorative justice context of observed Australian community conferences. Although such conferences are typically held as an alternative to court proceedings, the lessons about offender and victim emotions and shame, and how a mediator can best work to help both parties heal, are very apt for judges working in criminal and juvenile courts.

Working with Shame and Anger in Community Conferencing
by Thomas J. Scheff
(From *Community Conferences: Shame and Anger in Therapeutic Jurisprudence*, 67 REV. JUR. U.P.R. 97-119 (1999), Copyright 1999 by Thomas J. Scheff, reprinted with permission).

I. Introduction
In Western societies, crime occupies an undue proportion of our time, attention, and resources. We are moving toward a siege state, with alarmed homes, cars, and prisons. We continue to pass more laws and build more prisons, while our schools are underfunded. Yet we seem not to have made much progress: Crime remains at the top of the list when the public is polled about the problems that concern them most. Crime is clearly the primary form of conflict on our public agenda.

In recent years, an alternative approach to law, a worldwide movement, has been building momentum. This movement has two vectors, restorative justice and therapeutic jurisprudence (RTJ). RTJ has the potential to resolve many kinds of conflict and reduce inequities in the legal system. Compared to the traditional legal model of justice, courts, judges, lawyers and prisons, restorative justice and therapeutic jurisprudence are quite similar. The difference between the two is mostly conceptual. As a frame within which to criticize and modify legal justice, therapeutic jurisprudence offers a strikingly different model, the mode of therapy as it is used in medical and psychological treatment. Although close inspection reveals that the therapeutic model is quite diverse, and therefore somewhat ambiguous, it does offer a framework to contrast with the legal model. Although restorative justice is the larger movement of the two, it suffers from the lack of such a model. Without a model, restorative justice offers piecemeal changes to correct the present legal system, one step at a time. Perhaps a welding together of the two models into one, RTJ, would make the movement more effective.

II. Community Conferences: The Australian-New Zealand Model

One form of RTJ relevant to crime control is victim-offender mediation, which is in use around the world. This essay focuses on a new form of victim-offender mediation that could decrease crime and violence: community conferencing (also called family group conferencing).

Community conferences divert the offender away from the court into an alternative system that utilizes a meeting between victim, offender, and other interested parties to reach a settlement of the case. Since 1989, when a conferencing law was passed in New Zealand, more than half of all juvenile offenders in that country have been dealt with in this way, rather than through the courts. In Australia, conferences are being used for both juvenile and adult crimes. And last year, this format was introduced in Philadelphia, in the United States and in London, England.

The community conference is the most developed form of victim-offender mediation. In 1996 my co-investigator, Suzanne Retzinger, and I served as consultants for a comparative study of crime control being conducted in Australia, the United States, and England. We attended nine conferences in three Australian cities (Adelaide, Canberra, and Campbelltown), viewed videotapes about community conferences, and consulted with police officers, facilitators, and researchers. We came away from this experience with a strong impression of the potential of community conferences for reshaping all modern systems of justice.

Because it deals directly with emotions, the community conference corrects a particular deficiency of the court/prison system: its failure to attend to the victim's needs. Although conferencing is not appropriate for every offender, its use in selected cases could have a powerful effect on our crime crisis.

The format of community conferences involves a facilitator, the victim and his or her supporters, and the offender and his or her supporters. In the conferences in Australia, the facilitator is usually a police sergeant, but in some jurisdictions, social workers, mediators, or others are used. Unlike most mediation, this format always involves representatives of the larger community participating directly in the outcome. The groups can range from only the offender and the victim and their parents or other supporters to as many as 30 or more participants.

The involvement of representatives of the community avoids the "white room" effect. In most mediations, only those persons directly in conflict are present. The absence of other interested parties isolates the proceedings from the outside world and often, therefore, precludes effectiveness. In contrast, community conferences closely resemble the form that justice takes in most traditional societies, in which small communities handle their own crimes rather than delivering the offenders into the hands of legal and correctional professionals.

Offenders who participate in community conferences are selected by the police or the court according to the type of crime and whether or not there are questions of fact to be decided. If there are significant questions of fact, the offender goes to court; if not—that is, if the offender has confessed to the crime—he or she may be diverted to a conference. In Australia, sex crimes must go to court, * * * but many other serious crimes are conferenced.

A well-known case in New Zealand involved armed robbery of a convenience store by two juveniles. Both offenders were required to make restitution and do community service. However, the victim, an elderly woman, was so taken with one of the juveniles that she hired him to work for her. The other offender was required to return to Australia to live with his mother (a punishment he apparently perceived as cruel and unusual). The successful outcome of this case was the result of direct communication between offenders and victim, rather than of a procedure for ascertaining facts, which is the function of the courts.

III. Why Mediation?

It is widely recognized that the court/prison route is both expensive and not very effective in controlling crime. Evidence is now available that victim-offender mediation is not only cheaper than court and prison, but also more effective in decreasing recidivism. One of the great advantages of mediation is that in the confrontation between offender and victim, the offender who confesses his or her crime, is likely to recognize its consequences for the victim, and therefore is able to accept responsibility for his actions. For the most part, the court/prison system encourages offenders to deny their responsibility, which may be one reason for the high rate of recidivism.

Conferencing also may be relevant to the problem of youth gangs, since its extended format allows for bringing together gang members with the families and officials of a neighborhood or community. Such a meeting might lead to discussion, and even resolution, of more fundamental problems than just the particular offense that led to the conference. At the very least, some of the conflict in values between the gang and the community could be aired. Such a meeting might be as educational for the community as for the gang.

The conference procedure promises both to reduce the cost of crime control and to make it more effective. To the extent that police forces become involved, conferences could also transform officers' attitudes toward their job and toward offenders, since face-to-face meetings allow them to see both offenders and victims as human beings. In Australia, all of the groups participating in the conference process were highly satisfied, but it was the police who expressed the highest degree of satisfaction. And because representatives of the community participate directly, conferences also might be a significant step toward rebuilding community in our cities.

Admittedly, mediation is not useful for truth-finding. For crimes in which significant facts are in dispute, there is still no substitute for a court trial. Courts of law are truth machines: the adversarial system and the rules of evidence are necessary for cases in which facts are disputed. The court system is the best mechanism we have for dealing with such conflict. However, if the facts are not disputed—that is, if there is a confession or a plea bargain—then the cumbersome and expensive court machinery is unnecessary. A large majority of criminal cases are settled without trial (either by confession or by plea bargain). The array of highly paid professional personnel—judges, attorneys, court reporters, bailiffs, etc.—need not be involved in the majority of cases.

This is not to say courts and prisons are not necessary, even in these cases. Their very existence leads to many confessions and plea bargains, because many, if not most, offenders confess or plea-bargain in order to avoid trial and imprisonment. The existing court system serves many necessary functions; but it need no longer be the first line of defense against crime. The first line could be the conferencing-mediation system I describe here.

The conference format typically involves four steps. First, the offender describes his or her offense in detail. Next, the facilitator asks the offender to describe the consequences of the offense, how it affected him, and how it affected the victim and others. Thirdly, the victim and the victim's supporters tell how the crime affected them. This step is often highly emotional, with visible tears and/or anger. The last part of the conference entails working out a settlement that is acceptable to both victim and offender.

This last step, the working out of the settlement, is an informal version of court procedures. But the first three steps all involve crucial emotional elements—the exchange of feelings and developments in the relationships between the participants. These processes are virtually absent in the court/prison system. When this emotional part of the conference is managed successfully, the new procedure has a powerful advantage over the one that takes place in the courtroom.

The most important strength of mediation is that it allows direct communication between the offenders and their victims. With direct communication arises the possibility of community involvement in the disposition of the case. Direct communication also allows for the possibility of negotiation, understanding, confession, reconciliation, and forgiveness—that is, symbolic reparation. Because direct communication between offender and victim is ruled out by the court system, so is the possibility of symbolic reparation. Since symbolic reparation is much less well understood than the material aspects of reparation, most of what follows is concerned with spelling out how it works.

IV. Material and Symbolic Processes in Crime Control

A. Material Reparation

Material and symbolic reparation occur side by side in community conferences. Material reparation leads to the actual settlement: the undertakings agreed upon by the participants to compensate the victim and society for the offender's crimes. These reparations almost always consist of restitution or compensation for damage done, as well as some form of community service. The process of arriving at a settlement is verbal, highly visible, and largely unambiguous; it provides the ostensible purpose for the meeting.

Underlying the process of reaching a settlement, however, is the much less visible and more ambiguous process of symbolic reparation. This process involves social rituals of respect, courtesy, apology, and forgiveness, which seem to operate somewhat independently of the verbal agreements that are reached. Symbolic reparation depends on the emotional dynamics of the meeting and on the state of the bonds between the participants. The emotion of shame and the negotiation of shame dynamics, in particular, are of critical importance to this process.

B. The Core Sequence

For symbolic reparation to occur, two steps seem to be necessary. First, the offender must clearly express genuine shame and remorse over her actions. In response, the victim can then take a first step toward forgiving the offender. I call these two steps the core sequence. It is the core sequence that generates repair and restoration of the bond that was severed by the offender's crime. The repair of this bond symbolizes a more extensive restoration that is to take place between the offender and the other participants, the police, and the community. When the offender accepts responsibility for her actions, then the stage is set for his reacceptance into the community: she need not become a habitual offender. Even though the emotional exchange that constitutes the core sequence may be brief—even a few seconds—it is the key to reconciliation, victim satisfaction, and decreasing recidivism.

The core sequence, as crucial as it is in itself, also affects the material settlement. Emotional conciliation typically leads directly to a settlement that satisfies the participants—one that is neither too punitive nor too lenient but seems more or less inevitable. Such a settlement is a creative response to the situation, and develops naturally out of it. Without the core sequence, the path toward settlement is impeded; whatever settlement is reached does not decrease the tension level in the room but instead leaves the participants with a feeling of arbitrariness and dissatisfaction. Thus, it is crucially important to give symbolic reparation as much importance as the material settlement. Unless this is done, conferences may turn out, in the long run, to be only marginally better than traditional court practices. Symbolic reparation is the vital element that differentiates conferences from all other forms of crime control.

C. Community Conferences Observed

In our study of crime control, my co-investigator and I were impressed by the power of the conference format. We consider it to be a justice machine, as contrasted with the court, which is a fact-finding and punishing machine. In a conference—independent of the development of a material settlement—the movement seems to be toward justice and reconciliation. Nevertheless, in eight of the nine cases we observed, we had the feeling of difficulty, tension, and arbitrariness in reaching an agreement. The vital component of symbolic reparation, the core sequence, occurred only once during the formal part of the nine conferences we observed. But in three cases, the core sequence seemed to occur immediately after the formal meeting was over.

The exception in which the core sequence occurred during the formal meeting was a case in Adelaide. It involved a large and powerful juvenile who had stolen from one of his fellow residents in a halfway house. This offender stonewalled through most of the formal proceedings, giving minimal responses and showing the other participants the top of his head (his chin resting on his chest) and the soles of his shoes. But when it came time for his apology, he surprised everyone present by looking directly at the victim and making a heartfelt statement that went far beyond the formal requirements. His action drained away the tension in the room, so that the settlement that was reached seemed satisfying and inevitable.

In three of the cases, the vital movement from shame and remorse to forgiveness may have occurred immediately after the formal end of the conference. In two of these cases, we observed the victims in what appeared to be normal conversation with the offenders while they waited to sign forms. In the third case, the facilitator, who escorted the participants out of the building, reported that the victim had patted one of the offenders on the shoulder after he had made a tearful apology to her. These three instances suggest that it might be advantageous to build in a delay after the formal end of the conference, such as the signing of a written agreement. This would allow the participants to complete their unfinished business of symbolic reparation.

V. Reintegrative Shame

Some community conferences work better than others. How can the difference between an effective and an ineffective conference be explained? The emphasis here is on a new idea: the emotion of shame. This emotion, which is usually hidden, is a strategic part of the conference process (and of all forms of mediation); if managed properly, it can be the key to a successful conference.

One framework for understanding the role of shame in community conferences can be found in Braithwaite's concept of reintegrative shaming: that is, enough shaming to bring home the seriousness of the offense, but not so much as to humiliate and harden. There was a time in England when thieves were punished by branding their foreheads with the letter F (for felon). This punishment actually led to an increase in crime: since the branded felons were excluded from ordinary life, they had no alternative but to become professional thieves and highwaymen. The symbolic branding of the offender is one of the key pitfalls not only of the court/prison system, but also of the community conference: too much shame can be just as destructive as too little.

With juveniles, the problem of too little shame in the conference seldom arises. Even before the first words are spoken, the typical offender is deeply ashamed. If asked to nominate friends for participating in the conference, the young offender will usually recoil: he or she doesn't want friends to know. But with adults, the issue of too little shame comes up frequently. In the widespread problem of "drink-driving" (as it is known in Australia), the typical offender doesn't feel guilty of any offense. He was simply stopped at a police barricade and found to have too high a level of blood alcohol. Another difficulty in many of these cases is the absence of a victim, and therefore of high levels of emotion. In the drink-driving conference I observed in Canberra, the offender and his family denied feeling any guilt at all. Even the facilitator, a police sergeant, seemed to agree that a real man could hold a six-pack of Australian beer. In these types of cases, creative means of overcoming denial and lack of emotion are sorely needed. But in any and all cases, the effective management of shame dynamics may be the key to a successful outcome.

For conferences to be maximally effective, two separate movements of shame should occur. First, all shame must be removed from the victim. The humiliation of degradation, betrayal, and violation that has been inflicted on the victim must be relieved. This step is a key element in the victim's future well-being; it is the shame component—the victim's feeling that if only he or she had acted differently, the crime wouldn't have occurred or would have been less painful—that leads to the most intense and protracted suffering. The usual handling of crimes through courts and imprisonment does very little to relieve the victim of his or her suffering. Perhaps this is the main reason that many victims and much of the voting public want to visit excessive punishment on offenders, to make them suffer as their victims have.

The removal of shame from the victim is accomplished by the second move: making sure that all of the shame connected with the crime is accepted by the offender. By acknowledging his or her complete responsibility for the crime, the offender not only takes the first step toward rehabilitation, but also eases the suffering of the victim. For the shaming of the offender to be reintegrative, however, the facilitator must take care that it not be excessive, as already indicated. Humiliating the offender in the conference makes it almost impossible for him both to accept responsibility and to help remove shame from the victim. By recognizing and encouraging the core sequence of emotions, as described below, an effective facilitator can direct the offender toward rehabilitation and help relieve the victim's suffering.

VI. Hidden Shame

It is difficult to discuss shame dynamics as a major factor in conferences because of the repression and suppression of shame in Western societies. In certain Asian and other non-Western societies, shame covers a wide variety of feelings, including embarrassment, modesty, and shyness, as well as more intense and negative feelings such as inadequacy, rejection, and humiliation. But in Western societies, shame has been restricted to only the intensely negative feelings. For that reason, in Western societies shame leads an underground life.

The idea of hidden shame has been popularized by John Bradshaw. Bradshaw has been effective because he comes out of the tradition of Alcoholics Anonymous (A.A.), the one institution in our society that recognizes shame. Shame is an integral part of many of the exercises required by A.A., such as the listing and acknowledgment of shameful actions by the participants.

In earlier publications, Retzinger and I have argued that shame is subject to disguise and hiding in modern societies. A key finding in our work is that one can feel shame about shame, and shame about that, and so on, without end. This idea that one can be ashamed of being ashamed leads to the concept of continuous loops of shame, which may be the explanation of how repression works. In the case of crime, this kind of stigmatizing shame by self and/or others leads to the exclusion of offenders from the community.

In order to manage shame beneficially, it is necessary to recover the positive, reconciliatory uses of normal shame from the maws of repression and silence, and to relearn its value as a powerful emotion for forming community. As sociologist/psychoanalyst Helen Lynd notes, "The very fact that shame is an isolating experience also means that if one can find ways of sharing and communicating it [,] this communication can bring about particular closeness with other." The idea expressed in this passage is crucially significant for community conferences: If the offender can come to the point of "sharing and communicating" his shame instead of hiding or denying it, the damage to the bond between the offender and the other participants may be repaired.

The nature of the formal apology in community conferences provides a good example of the crucial part that acknowledging shame plays in the drama of conflict and reconciliation. Formal apologies are an important step in all forms of victim-offender mediation. The chance that a conference will produce healing and repair is significantly linked to the quality of the apology—that is, its genuineness.

But what is a genuine apology? One formulation is that not only must one say that one is sorry, but one must feel sorry. What are the emotions involved in feeling sorry? As the word sorry itself indicates, one of the emotions is sorrow or grief; a genuine apology involves sadness. But the most important emotion in a genuine apology is probably shame: the offender must be ashamed of what he did, and this shame must be visible to the person receiving the apology. It is this shame—along with other emotions, such as grief—that allows a preliminary bond to be formed between offender and victim, because the offender's visible expression of emotion allows the victim to see the offender as a human being.

Another reason that recovering the full breadth of the shame concept is important for the conference process is that shame often spreads among all of the participants. The offender will be ashamed because she stands publicly accused of wrongdoing. The offender's supporters will be ashamed because of their relationship to her. The victim will be ashamed in the sense of feeling betrayed, violated, and/or impotent. The victim's supporters, insofar as they identify with her, will share this kind of shame. If all this shame is disguised and denied, it inhibits the participants from repairing the bonds between them, and therefore interferes with symbolic reparation.

It is therefore an issue of great importance for the operation of conferences to distinguish between pathological and normal shame. Braithwaite has proposed that effective crime control requires normal (reintegrative) rather than pathological (spiraling) shame. By paying close attention to the particular way shame is manifested, it is possible to distinguish, moment by moment, between the two forms of shame as they occur in the conference.

According to Retzinger, manifestations of normal shame, although unpleasant, are brief, sometimes lasting only a few seconds. Shame, anger, and other related emotions that persist continuously for many minutes are pathological. Shame is a highly reflexive emotion, one which can give rise to long-lasting feedback loops: as already mentioned, one can be ashamed of being ashamed, and so on, around the loop, resulting in withdrawal or depression. Or one may be angry that one is ashamed, and ashamed that one is angry, and so on around that loop. Furthermore, shame-anger loops can occur between, as well as within, participants. Indignation can be contagious, resulting in mutual and counter-indignation. Both individual and social emotional loops can last indefinitely. Continuous, relentless emotions (such as continuing embarrassment, indignation, resentment, and hatred) are always spirals.

Shame plays a crucial role in normal cooperative relationships as well as in conflict. Shame and embarrassment are normal signals of a threat to any social bond. If the other person is too close in some way, one feels invaded or exposed. If the other is too far, one feels invisible or rejected. Cues to shame and embarrassment (such as blushing, stammering, speaking too softly, looking away, and so on) allow one to know where one stands in a relationship. Similarly, pride signals a secure bond. Shame is the emotional cognate of a threatened or damaged bond, just as threatened bonds are the source of shame. Normal shame is thus an essential building block of relationships and of community.

If, as Goffman and others have argued, normal shame and embarrassment are an almost continuous part of all human contact, we can see why the visible expression of shame by the offender looms so large in symbolic reparation. When we see signs of shame and embarrassment in others, we are able to recognize them as human beings like ourselves, no matter the language, cultural setting, or context. The central role of shame in human contact has long been recognized in the scientific-humanist tradition, as expressed by Darwin, Nietzsche, Sartre, and many others. To understand the way that successful conferences run on normal, reintegrative shame, we first need to overcome our view of shame as a disgraceful emotion to be denied and hidden from self and other.

VII. Paths to Symbolic Reparation: Reframing Indignation and Eliciting Painful Emotions

In order for the offender to clearly express genuine shame and remorse, the trigger for symbolic reparation, he needs to be in a state of "perfect defenselessness." At the critical moment, the offender needs to place himself completely at the mercy of the victim, uncovering his repressed emotions. The victim also has a role to play, being aware of the offender's feelings. Since, in modern societies, states of perfect defenselessness and keen awareness are unusual even in private, much less in a public gathering, this is a task of some magnitude. How can the offender and victim be encouraged to overcome the effects of repression in the presence of the participants, whose own emotions are highly repressed?

The principal paths seem to be:

1. reframing displays of aggressive emotions such as anger and moral indignation against the offender, and/or
2. eliciting a vivid expression of the painful emotions caused by the crime from at least one of the participants, usually a victim or a supporter of the victim.

These two paths to symbolic reparation are related; as described below, reframing aggressive emotions can lead to vivid expressions of painful ones.

VIII. Moral Indignation

The aggressive emotion that predominated at the conferences I observed was moral indignation by the victim, the victim's supporters, and—when he or she was present—the arresting officer. I understand moral indignation to be a particular manifestation of shame and anger. The victim, especially, is likely to feel the shame of helplessness, impotence, betrayal, and/or violation in response to the offense against him or her. However, this shame is usually not acknowledged—by the victim or others—but masked by the more visible emotion of anger. Repetitive and relentless anger at the offender is an effective defense against feeling shame. It is unacknowledged shame that drives repetitive episodes of moral indignation. If this shame can be acknowledged (along with other hidden emotions such as grief and fear), anger and moral indignation directed toward the offender will be relatively short-lived and constructive.

The shame component, the main emotional freight carried by indignation, is hidden even in the dictionary definitions of the word indignation, which emphasize only anger. To find the shame component, one has to go to the root word, indignity, which means a humiliating insult to one's self-respect.

How is one to detect moral indignation? One study hinted at the key indicators when it described "helpless anger" (shame-anger) in one subject, Rhoda, direct toward her aunt, Editha: "She [Rhoda] is so choked with emotion at the unreasonableness of Editha's behavior that she cannot begin to describe it accurately." This study describes the indicators of helpless anger, using terminology such as "helpless exasperation" and "sarcastic exasperation." Rhoda's language implies that Editha's "violation of normal standards is so gross to the point of straining our verbal resources."

This description of "helpless anger," and especially "exasperation," comes close to what I saw as moral indignation in the conferences. The helplessly angry person feels unable to describe the enormity of the other's trespass, not because she is particularly unable, but because the trespass feels so overwhelming that it would defy description by anyone. The feeling that an emotion is so unmanageable is a clue to the repression of the occluded emotions that are driving the conscious one.

Furthermore, the use of "sarcastic" points toward a second dimension of indignation. The subject seems to feel that the enormity of the trespass is so glaring that her audience should (but doesn't) feel as strongly about it as she does. The sarcasm is directed not only at the offender, but also at the audience that is not as riled about the offense as it should be.

Protracted indignation thus interferes with a feeling of mutual identification (a secure bond) not only between the victim and the offender, but also between the victim and the rest of the participants. To the extent that indignation, a shame-anger loop, pervades a conference, it isolates the participants from one another.

This analysis suggests a central point about the management of indignation: if it is to be discharged, the expression of anger should be reframed so that the underlying emotions (shame, grief, fear) can surface and be discharged. Unless shame is acknowledged, expressions of indignation are likely to continue without relief. The detection and reframing of moral indignation is thus a crucial component of effective conferences, requiring skill and sensitivity on the facilitator's part.

The crucial point about moral indignation is that when it is repetitive and out of control, it is a defensive movement. It involves two steps: denial of one's own shame, followed by projection of blame onto the offender (I am not dishonorable in any way, whereas the offender is entirely dishonorable). For the participants to identify with the offender, they must see themselves as alike rather than unalike (there but for the grace of God go I). Moral indignation interferes with the identification between participants that is necessary if the conference is to generate symbolic reparation. Thus, uncontrolled, repetitive moral indignation is the most important impediment to symbolic reparation and reintegration. On the other hand, to the extent that it is rechanneled, moral indignation can be instrumental in triggering the core sequence of reparation.

Shame-rage spirals can take forms other than moral indignation. Forms such as self-righteous rage or narcissistic rage are not often seen in conferences. These other forms are likely to be more intense than indignation, and more likely to lead to verbal or physical assault. Compared to these other forms, the unacknowledged shame in moral indignation is close to the surface, and more easily accessed by skillful questioning.

IX. Two Types of Moral Indignation: Self-Righteous Indignation and Moral Superiority

In the cases I witnessed, moral indignation appeared in two forms: self-righteous indignation, the more flagrant form, and moral superiority, the more covert form.

A. Self-righteous Indignation

This was expressed most frequently and relentlessly by the victims, but also in some cases by the victims' supporters and even the offenders' supporters, especially the offenders' parents. This emotion was conveyed not only by what was said, but more strongly by how it was said, and in what context.

For example, the two victims in a fraud case in Canberra bombarded the offender with demands for material reparation (one demanded the return of the money, the other that the offender help protect the victim's reputation). Their manner as well as their words conveyed their self-righteousness, their feelings of betrayal by the offender, their distrust of him, and their feelings of helplessness and anger. The repetition of their demands, especially—in spite of the responses by the offender, the crying of the offender's wife, and the attempts by the facilitator and the investigating officer to intervene—clearly signaled the victims' intense indignation. The repetition of a request, when it disregards the other's responses, is at best challenging and in many cases actually insulting. Such repetition is disrespectful and rejecting: it implies that the indignant person is not listening to the offender, that the offender is not listening to the indignant person, or, more potently, that the offender is lying.

Self-righteous indignation was also expressed frequently and intensely in a break-in and theft case in Campbelltown. In this case, not only the victim, but also the parents of the offenders expressed indignation. In the case of the victim, her flagrant indignation took the form of incredulity; she was incredulous not so much that the crime could have been perpetrated against her, but that the offenders were capable of such a deed. As for the parents, they could hardly believe that their children could be involved, that is, that the conference involved them (the parents). Similarly, the parents in a Canberra shoplifting case also expressed incredulity that their son could be a thief, but indirectly; most of their comments seemed geared to distance them from the offender (their son), because they saw themselves as hardly the kind of people to be spending time in a police station. Incredulity, hardly being able to believe what has happened, is a highly visible sign of self-righteous indignation.

B. Moral Superiority and Overt Threats

A second, more covert form of moral indignation is moral superiority. It occurs frequently in the form of lecturing to the offender, particularly by police. The arresting officer in the cases we saw in Adelaide always gave some form of moral instruction to the offender. This tactic signals the moral superiority of the instructor to the offender, and therefore threatens the bond of mutual identification between them. In one case, in Campbelltown, even the facilitator joined the chorus; he gave the offenders a lengthy lecture on the nature of conscience.

The lecture usually contained a threat as well, which also disrupted rather than forged the social bond. A threat implies that the offender is not responsible but needs an external goad to behave. When there is mutual identification, threat is unnecessary. In Adelaide, the arresting officer always threatened the offenders with court. In the break-in and theft case we observed there, the arresting officer was at first highly respectful toward the offender, and solicitous of his rights. But later in the conference, perhaps because she felt the offender had not sufficiently expressed shame and remorse, she became very emotional, lecturing the offender on how "stupid" and "silly" it was to break the law, and on the certainty of strong punishment. At this point her outburst showed self-righteous indignation as well as feelings of moral superiority.

In the same conference, the victim of the break-in expressed moral indignation and perhaps a sense of violation by her repetitive description of each of her material losses and of the loss of the keys and locks for her house. The discussion of finding the stolen key and of the problem and cost of changing the locks went on at some length. Along with her account of the material losses, this discussion absorbed a significant proportion of the conference time.

In this instance, and in several other cases, a skilled facilitator might have been able to interrupt the display of indignation by interpreting it in terms of a sense of betrayal, helplessness, loss, and violation. In the Canberra fraud case, however, it would have taken a great deal of skill and self-confidence on the part of the facilitator to be able to stem the torrent. Although it may be necessary to allow a preliminary outburst of indignation at the offender, it is important that the facilitator be trained to detect repetitive waves of indignation, and that he or she be skillful enough to reframe them. To be able to manage most of their cases successfully, facilitators need to be trained not only in procedures, but also in detecting and reframing covert emotions.

X. The Hidden Shame in Indignation

In a case of school vandalism, the moral indignation of one of the victims was so indirect as to be difficult to detect and manage unless the facilitator was highly skillful. It is worth looking at this instance in some detail, since it illustrates the way in which the shame that underlies indignation can be hidden not only from others but from oneself. The victim, Fred Johnson (a pseudonym), was a middle-aged teacher at the school that was vandalized. The vandalism consisted of defamatory statements about the teachers spray-painted on the walls of the school. Johnson was the principal victim, since he was the subject of three insults, each of the other teachers having been the subject of only one. To make clear the nature of these insults, it is necessary to quote the actual defamations:

> Johnson is an old folgie [fogey?].
> Mr. Johnson sucks dick with Mr. Smith [another teacher].
> Mr. Johnson is a bald-headed cocksucker.

The author(s) of these particular defamations was unknown. The offender admitted to spray-painting only one statement, intimating a homosexual relationship between two students. Under repeated questioning, the offender maintained that he had no knowledge of who had spray-painted the graffiti about the teachers.

From the beginning of the conference, the pattern of Mr. Johnson's behavior suggested unacknowledged shame. When she introduced him, the facilitator was puzzled by his presence, since she had understood that he was to attend only if the principal couldn't be there to represent the school. Mr. Johnson explained that he had decided to attend along with the principal because he wanted to comment also.

When his turn to speak as a victim came, Mr. Johnson first denied injury to himself. He explained that having taught as long as he had, "this kind of slander was water off a duck's back." He further denied injury by explaining, somewhat defiantly, that contrary to what students think, teachers stick together; one of his fellow teachers had phoned him about the defamations so that he wouldn't be surprised by them. Like his presence at the conference, these comments were somewhat gratuitous; they seemed unnecessary, and they were carefully addressed to the air rather than to any particular person.

Having denied injury, Mr. Johnson then launched into an indirect verbal assault on the offender. He stated that when he counsels students, he tells them that such slander is cowardly. Johnson was insulting the offender but only indirectly, since he was calling him a coward only by implication. He repeated this insinuation three more times, saying that students who resort to such actions are cowards, underhanded, and have no guts. When it was her turn, the offender's mother felt called on to refute the charge of cowardice by saying that her son couldn't be a coward because he played rugby!

Mr. Johnson's words and manner suggest a shame-rage spiral. He seems to have been humiliated by the defamations, but he could not acknowledge this feeling even to himself. A statement such as "I was upset and offended by the graffiti" would have been a step toward the acknowledgment of shame. Instead, rather than express his shame and anger, he denied injury and attacked his putative attacker with an indirect verbal assault on the offender.

The basic problem with indignation, which is a kind of impotent anger (a shame-anger loop), is that if it is repeated enough it can damage the potential bond between the victim and the offender. The torrent of criticism and disrespect from the victim or other indignant participant almost surely gives rise to defensiveness in the offender; this is the very opposite of what is needed for symbolic reparation, namely, that the offender open himself to be able to express true remorse. Moreover, since the offender usually displays his "cool" from the beginning, his behavior unfortunately triggers defensive anger in the participants, and therefore sets up a vicious circle. This cycle of insult and counter-insult is counterproductive; it is the basis for destructive and unending conflict.

Perhaps the basic job of the facilitator is to ask questions that cut through the defensive stance of the participants. In this way a successful conference maintains a balance between anger toward and respect for the offender, between shaming and reintegration. Patient, respectful questioning by the facilitator could have helped Mr. Johnson acknowledge some of his feelings of being ridiculed and insulted, and thereby might have eased the attack on the offender.

Another way of helping an offender to acknowledge her responsibility would be to enlarge upon the formula used in Canberra when separating the offense from the offender. For example, if the air is thick with indignation, after condemning the offense, the offender's supporters might be asked to name some of the offender's good traits. The facilitator could then summarize their positive comments to bring the distinction between the bad offense and the good offender into high relief. This tactic would need to be handled with some skill and discretion to avoid antagonizing the victim's camp.

Such initial support might make it possible for the offender to remain emotionally open in the face of moral indignation. Perhaps if a space of this kind were created initially for the offender, she would become less defensive whatever the participants' emotional responses.

XI. Encouraging the Expression of Painful Emotions

A complement to the reframing of moral indignation is the tactic of encouraging the expression of painful emotions. This idea was developed by Terry O'Connell, a police sergeant whose work in a predominately Aborigine community was instrumental in bringing conferencing to Australia. The offender may express genuine shame and remorse, even if she has defended herself against moral indignation, under certain conditions. If the victim or supporters of the victim clearly express painful emotions (such as grief) that were caused by the offender's crime, the offender may be caught off guard and identify with that pain, to the point that her defenses are breached. Under these conditions, she will then show the shame and remorse that are necessary to generate the beginning of forgiveness in the victim. In a case already mentioned above, the victim was highly indignant during the whole formal conference. Yet, afterward, when the offender offered her a tearful apology, she patted him on the shoulder, indicating identification and a step toward forgiveness. This entire episode took less than a minute, yet it was probably the most important event in the entire conference.

O'Connell gives emotionality pride of place in the conference process. The chief focus of the facilitator in organizing and presiding should be setting the conditions that will allow painful emotions to be felt, expressed, and shared by the victim, the offender, and other participants. However, it is important to realize that the kinds of emotions that O'Connell is referring to are primarily the painful emotions, such as grief and shame, and not the aggressive ones, such as rage and anger. The goal of the facilitator is to encourage the former and rechannel the latter. As already indicated, if aggressive emotions are interrupted and reframed, they may give rise to the expression of the painful emotions that are needed to trigger the core sequence.

The skills needed to facilitate a conference successfully involve detecting and negotiating emotional and relational states, a far cry from the traditional concerns in police recruitment and training. In fact, these skills are unusual in our Western society as a whole. Even in the training of psychotherapists and mediators, behavioral and cognitive skills are emphasized, to the detriment of emotional and relational skills. To the extent that police officers and other facilitators develop the understanding and skill needed for managing conferences, to that extent will they also begin to transform prevailing police attitudes and the relationship between law enforcement and the community.

This transformation and the building and empowering of the community are the three great goals of the conferencing movement. Therefore, the use of conferences and the training of facilitators for them could represent a powerful force for reducing crime and changing our society.

Key References

BRADSHAW, JOHN, HEALING THE SHAME THAT BINDS YOU (1988).

BRAITHWAITE, JOHN, CRIME, SHAME, AND REINTEGRATION (1989).

Braithwaite, John, & Mugford, Stephen, *Conditions of Successful Reintegration Ceremonies*, 34 BRIT. J. CRIMINOLOGY 139 (1994).

K. ENCOURAGING AND
MAINTAINING DESISTANCE

Judges can play a useful role at early stages by instilling hope and encouraging offender change, and can play a very important role later on, in helping maintain law-abiding behavior. Accordingly, in this selection, Wexler draws heavily on the important new "desistance" work of Cambridge University criminologist Shadd Maruna. In this excerpt, Wexler illustrates the importance of judicial praise and suggests that the kind of graduation ceremonies typically held in drug treatment courts likely have real therapeutic value, and are accordingly not merely "ceremonial" in nature. These rehabilitative court sessions can be used in many judicial settings, such as the termination or early termination of probation.

Robes and Rehabilitation
By David B. Wexler
(Excerpted from *Robes and Rehabilitation: How Judges Can Help Offenders Make Good*, 38 CT. REV. 18, 20–23 (Spring, 2001), Copyright 2001 American Judges Association, reprinted with permission).

* * *

Who decides to change course, and *how* and *why*, seem to be questions locked away in what Shadd Maruna calls the "black box" of the "what works" literature. Maruna's book, *Making Good: How Ex-Convicts Reform and Rebuild Their Lives*, published in 2001 by the American Psychological Association is * * * a meaty work chock full of therapeutic jurisprudential implications. In the remainder of this essay, I would like to explore how Maruna's findings might be relevant to judges—how, with these insights, judges might help offenders "make good."

Briefly, in his "Liverpool Desistance Study," Maruna interviewed both "persistent" offenders and those who, after a steady diet of criminal behavior, eventually become "desisters." His objective was to use a "narrative" approach—consistent with the notion of "narrative therapy"—to see how the two offender types described and made sense of their lives.

Maruna's principal contribution, of course, relates to "desisters." These ex-convicts need to develop a "coherent, prosocial identity," and need an expla-

249

nation for "how their checkered past could have led to their new, reformed identities." Presumably, these explanatory narratives are not merely a *result* of desistance behavior, but should also be understood as "factors that help to *sustain* desistance."

Maruna notes that there is much drifting and zigzagging in and out of criminal activity. Accordingly, desistance is best seen as a "maintenance process," rather than as a specific event.

Generally, a desister's narrative establishes that the narrator's "real self" is basically good; that the narrator became a victim of society who turned to crime and drugs to cope with a bleak environment; that the narrator then became trapped in a vicious cycle of repeated criminal activity and imprisonment; that someone in conventional society believed in and recognized the potential of the narrator, thereby allowing him or her to make good.

But "reformation is not something that is visible or objective in the sense it can be 'proven.'" It is a construct that is interactional in nature: desisting persons must in some way accept conventional society and conventional society must in turn accept them. Thus, their conversion "may remain suspect to significant others, and most importantly to themselves."

Accordingly, the desisting interviewees in Maruna's study "seemed almost obsessed with establishing the authenticity of their reform." During the interviews, many provided supporting documents—letters from college teachers and from parole officers, copies of offense records showing the date of last conviction. Others urged the investigator to speak with family members, girlfriends, or to the manager or receptionist of a drug treatment clinic.

Not surprisingly, "while the testimony of any conventional other will do, the best certification of reform involves a public or official endorsement from media outlets, community leaders, and members of the social control establishment." In his final chapter, Maruna undertakes an exercise that is essentially a therapeutic jurisprudential one: he speaks of instituting and institutionalizing redemption rituals. These include graduation ceremonies upon successful completion of correctional programs, reentry courts "empowered not only to reimprison each felon but also to officially recognize their efforts toward reform," and "rebiographing" clean ex-offenders through officially recognized record expungement procedures.

How Courts Can Help

Two judicially related proposals mentioned by Maruna—graduation ceremonies and reentry courts—are matters of considerable current interest.

In drug treatment courts, for example, applause is common, and, in some courts, even judicial hugs are by no means a rare occurrence. In Judge Judy Mitchell-Davis's Chicago courtroom, "upon successful completion of a drug court sentence, the offenders invite their friends and family to a graduation ceremony in the courthouse." Some of the graduates make speeches, and all receive a "diploma" from the court. In some such courts, "participants have asked that their arresting officer be present at their graduation."

These lessons from drug treatment courts can be extended, of course, to other specialized treatment courts and to ordinary juvenile and criminal cases. Judicial praise, family and friend attendance, and graduation ceremonies can all occur, for example, at the successful completion of—or early termination of—a period of probation imposed in a "routine" criminal case.

Such a ceremony would acknowledge a former offender's progress and, taking a page from Maruna, may, at the same time, itself *contribute* to the maintenance of desisting behavior. The strong suggestion that these ceremonies are themselves therapeutic, and are therefore not merely "ceremonial," might readily justify their widespread use. Relatedly, if they seem themselves to contribute to reduced recidivism, that crucially important societal benefit could easily justify their time-consuming nature.

Besides graduation ceremonies, Maruna endorses the notion of reentry courts "empowered not only to reimprison each felon but also to officially recognize their efforts toward reform." The apparent success of drug treatment courts, based on a team approach and ongoing judge-defendant interaction, has led to proposals for importing the model to the prisoner reentry process.

Reentry courts could tap many principles of therapeutic jurisprudence, and could serve a very important function. The problem, however, is that, at least in the United States, "in most jurisdictions, the authority for reentry issues is not within the judicial branch."

Nonetheless, the function Maruna would like to see served—official recognition of efforts toward reform—can be performed by courts in at least some contexts. For example, unlike adult criminal courts, juvenile courts do typically retain a post-dispositional review authority, and such courts can in effect serve a major reentry function.

The main lesson, of course, is that review hearings—for juveniles, for probationers, for conditionally released insanity acquittees—need not only be meaningful if one is to be "violated" and there is a real threat of revocation. Such hearings can and should also be meaningful—and not just routine and perfunctory—when all is going *well*. In many legal settings, courts have the discretion to set review hearings at intervals shorter than those mandated by law. Judges should consider taking such action even when they are not especially worried about an offender's compliance, for such a hearing could indeed recognize and applaud an offender's efforts and itself contribute to the maintenance of desistance.

Recall that desistance is best thought of as a "maintenance process." And recall that desisters—especially at the early stages of desistance—desperately need outside validation to convince *themselves* of their conversion.

The judge, of course, is the perfect prestigious person to confer public and official validation on the offender and the offender's reform efforts. Ideally, at a deferred sentencing hearing or at an "all is going well" review hearing, the judge also can comment favorably upon the sorts of matters that Maruna found to be so important to desisting offenders: impressive meeting attendance logs, for example, and letters from or the occasional live testimony of members of conventional society: college teacher, probation or parole officer, mother, girlfriend, manager and receptionist at the drug clinic, and the like.

When all goes well, of course, it is relatively easy for the judge to constitute the respected member of conventional society willing to "believe in" the defendant and to see the defendant's "real me"—the diamond in the rough. But all does not always go well. Review hearings will often be rather "mixed," and sometimes they will require revocation. Sentencing hearings will not invariably lead to probationary dispositions. Often, judicial discretion regarding disposition will be severely circumscribed.

Even in these far from favorable situations, the court can play a highly important—albeit a more long-range—role in potential offender reform. Consider the "vision statement" of the District Court of Clark County, Washington. That vision specifically embraces the use of principles of therapeutic jurisprudence to "make a positive change in the lives of people who come before the court."

Some of the vision statement's "guiding values" relate remarkably well to Maruna's findings regarding desister narratives. One guiding value, for example, is that "individuals are not condemned to a life of crime or despair by mental condition or substance abuse and that everyone can achieve a fulfilling and responsible life." Another is the belief that "everyone, no matter whom, has something positive within their make up that can be built upon."

A judge committed to this vision will not regard these guiding values as mere fluff. Such a judge, for example, is unlikely to tell a woman that she is simply "no good as a mother." And, even when imposing a severe sentence, such a judge is not going to say, "You are a menace and a danger to society. Society should be protected from the likes of you."

Instead, especially in light of Maruna's findings, a judge committed to the vision statement should search for and comment on whatever favorable features might eventually be woven together by the offender to constitute the "real me" or the "diamond in the rough." Sometimes, such a favorable feature might mitigate the sentence. If the judge takes the pains to emphasize it as a real quality—not simply as a mechanical mitigating factor—it may eventually constitute a meaningful component of the offender's self-identity. Such a judge might say something like this:

> You and your friends were involved in some pretty serious business here, and I am going to impose a sentence that reflects just how serious it is. I want to add one thing, however. There's been some testimony here about how you showed some real con-

cern for the victim. I'm going to take that into consideration in your case. You know, according to some of the letters that were submitted, it looks like that sensitive nature is something you displayed way back in grade school. Nowadays, it seems to peek out only now and then. But if I could peel away a few layers, I'll bet I could get a glimpse of a pretty caring person way down there. In any case, under the law in this state, I'm able to reduce your sentence by a year for what you did when that caring quality came peeking out last March.

Sometimes, a search for and discovery of a favorable feature or quality may not influence the disposition at all, but it may nonetheless plant a helpful seed, like this:

> I don't really know what went wrong here. I do know you committed a robbery and someone was hurt. And I know that it is only right that I impose a sentence of such-and-such. What I don't understand is why this all happened. You are obviously very intelligent and were always a good student. Your former wife says that, until a few years ago, you were a very good, caring, and responsible father. You obviously have a real talent for woodworking, but it's been years since you spent time on a real woodworking project. Beneath all this, I see a good person who has gotten on the wrong path. I hope you'll think about this and change that path. With your intelligence, personality, and talent, I think you can do it if you decide you really want to.

Conclusion

Even if the sentence imposed is unaffected, following this process is likely to be worth the judicial effort. Maruna notes that both narrative development and desistance each constitute ongoing processes. In rewriting the narratives of their lives, desisting offenders often look to instances in their pasts when their "real" selves shone and when respected members of conventional society recognized their talents and good qualities.

Thus, even in instances where desistance seems not to have occurred, judges can use principles of therapeutic jurisprudence in the hope that their judicial behavior may constitute the building blocks of eventual reform and rehabilitation. This sort of judging may therefore have both short-term and long-term benefits. Ultimately, the benefits may be for offenders, and, in turn, for society as a whole.

And lets not forget the benefits to the judges, whose sense of professional satisfaction may soar. Who would not feel immense satisfaction receiving letters, as Chicago drug treatment court Judge Judy Mitchell-Davis (dubbed "Judge Judy" by defendants) often does, like this one?:

Judge Judy, I just want to thank you for being the loving and caring woman that you are. You've really helped make a positive change in my life. I believe I'm going to make it. It feels so amazing to control my own thoughts and feelings. I feel so good about myself for the first time.

Key References

Maruna, Shadd, Making Good: How Ex-Inmates Reform and Rebuild Their Lives (2001).

L. BUILDING STRENGTHS

Many of the kinds of problems that will be presented in problem-solving courts will respond effectively to available treatment, but only if the individual perceives that he or she has a problem and is motivated to deal with it. Michael Clark has noted, in the article a portion of which is excerpted in Section C, that treatment programs in general are effective, but that factors related to the individual's own strengths may be more important in treatment efficacy than the particular form of treatment used. In these situations, the problem-solving court judge cannot simply order the individual to recognize the existence of the problem and to obtain treatment. People must come to these realizations for themselves. Problem solving court judges must understand that, although they can assist people to solve their problems, they cannot solve them for them. The individual must confront and solve his or her own problem, and assume the primary responsibility for doing so. The judge can help the individual to realize this, and together with treatment staff, can help the individual to identify and build upon his or her own strengths and use them effectively in the collaborative effort of solving the problem.

In the previous selection, Wexler makes use of Shadd Maruna's important work on desistance. In this selection, Maruna speaks for himself when he and State University of New York at Albany criminologist Thomas P. LeBel focus on recognizing and building offender strengths. This "strength-based" model, which also is discussed in the article by Michael Clark, is more positive in nature than the mere management of risk or avoidance of future criminality. Maruna and LeBel explain the strength-based approach—an approach that can be profitably used by the judiciary—and apply it in the interesting context of a proposed "reentry" court.

Welcome Home?: Examining the "Reentry Court" Concept from a Strengths-Based Perspective
by Shadd Maruna and Thomas P. LeBel
(Reprinted from 4 WESTERN CRIM. REV. (Forthcoming, 2003), at http://wcr.sonoma.edu/v4n1/v4n1.htm, with permission from Shadd Maruna and Thomas LeBel, and the Western Criminology Review).

In the book *After Prison — What?* Maud Booth writes, "When one thinks that this prejudice and marking of discharged prisoners robs them of any chance of gaining a living, and in many instances forces them back against their will into a dishonest career, one can realize how truly tragic the situation is" (119). That was written in 1903. According to Verne McArthur, in his book *Coming Out Cold: Community Reentry from a State Reformatory*, "The released offender confronts a situation at release that virtually ensures his failure" (1). That was written in 1974.

Unfortunately, the conditions faced by ex-convicts today have not improved much and may have even deteriorated since these conclusions were reached. Fast forwarding to the present, Jeremy Travis and Joan Petersilia (2001:301) write, "Prisoners moving through the high-volume, poorly designed assembly line (of corrections)…are less well prepared individually for their return to the community and are returning to communities that are not well prepared to accept them." Additionally, there has been a radical change in the scale of the reentry problem over the last 100 years. Nearly 600,000 individuals will be released from US prisons this year (that is over 1,600 per day) compared to 170,000 in 1980 and only a few thousand at the turn of the century when Booth was writing.

In addition, largely due to new "tough on crime" approaches in paroling practice, re-entering society has been made a more difficult and precarious transition than ever before. Of the 459,000 US parolees who were discharged from community supervision in 2000, 42% were returned to incarceration—11% with a new sentence and 31% in some other way (Bureau of Justice Statistics 2001). In a recent study of 272,111 prisoners released in 15 states in 1994, 67.5% were rearrested within three years as compared to an estimated 62.5% in a similar study of 1983 releases (Langan & Levin 2002). Because of the enormous growth of the prison population since the early 1980s, this small change translates into huge numbers. In 1980, 27,177 paroled ex-convicts were returned to state prisons. In 1999, this number was 197,606. As a percentage of all admissions to state prisons, parole violators more than doubled from 17% in 1980 to 35% in 1999. In California, a staggering 67% of prison admissions were parole failures (Hughes, Wilson, & Beck 2001). These figures indicate that the reentry problem is not only a product of the 1990's incarceration boom, but is actually a leading *cause* of the boom as well. It is no wonder then that former Attorney General, Janet Reno (2000:1) referred to ex-convict reentry as "one of the most pressing problems we face as a nation."

As such, the broad, new proposals for revamping reentry policy through a "jurisprudential lens" (Travis & Petersilia 2001:291) that have emerged in recent years (e.g., Office of Justice Programs 1999; Travis 2000) could not be more welcome or better timed. Before leaving office, the Clinton Administration developed a series of relatively large-scale initiatives intended to address the reentry crisis through a scattering of experimental, pilot programs. The Clinton Administration's reentry proposals (OJP 2001) were never fully implemented, but the Bush Administration has developed its own reentry project (OJP 2002), which borrows much of the content of its predecessor plan.

Among the most significant of the new proposals[1] is the "reentry court" experiment, based on the drug court model, which would cast judges as "reentry managers" (Travis 2000:8). Whereas, the role of the judiciary typically ends after sentencing, the reentry court model would move the court system into a "sentence management" role, overseeing the convicted person's eventual return to the community.

A reentry court is a court that manages the return to the community of individuals being released from prison, using the authority of the court to apply graduated sanctions and positive reinforcement and to marshal resources to support the prisoner's reintegration, much as drug courts do, to promote positive behavior by the returning prisoner (OJP 1999:2).

The concept of the reentry court is very much still under development, and the pilot sites in California, Colorado, Delaware, Florida, Iowa, Kentucky, New York, Ohio, and West Virginia all differ significantly in their emphases and approaches. Still, the underlying premises are largely borrowed from drug treatment courts and other problem-solving courts. According to the Office of Justice Programs (1999:7–9), these core elements include:

- *Assessment and strategic reentry planning* involving the ex-offender, the judiciary and other key "partners"—this sometimes involves the development of a "contract" or treatment plan.
- *Regular status assessment meetings* involving both the ex-offender and his circle of supporters or representatives from his family and community.
- *Coordination of multiple support services* including substance abuse treatment, job training programs, faith institutions, and housing services.
- *Accountability to community* through the involvement of citizen advisory boards, crime victims' organizations and neighborhood groups.
- *Graduated and parsimonious sanctions* for violations of the conditions of release that can be swiftly, predictably, and universally applied.
- *Rewards for success* especially by negotiating early release from parole after established goals are achieved, or by conducting graduation ceremonies similar to those used in drug courts.

The working assumption is that "offenders respond positively to the fact that a judge is taking an interest in their success." In addition, "The frequent appearances before the court with the offer of assistance, coupled with the knowledge of predictable and parsimonious consequences for failure, assist the offender in taking the steps necessary to get his life back on track" (OJP 1999:6). With the explicit intention of reducing recidivism and assisting ex-offenders, reentry courts clearly have the potential to embody the principles of therapeutic jurisprudence (Wexler 2001) in the same way that drug treatment courts often do (see Hora, Schma & Rosenthal 1999). Reentry court advocates also hope that these courts will achieve the level of popular and political support that drug courts have enjoyed.

As with any transplantation of a model from one context to the next, however, one must be cautious about applying the drug court model to the reentry process. After all, the success of the drug court movement in many ways might be attributable to features unique to addiction recovery or to the population of clients participating in the programs (i.e. non-violent, drug-involved offenders). Pioneering drug court judge, Hon. Richard Gebelein (2000) makes a case to this effect in trying to explain the popularity of drug courts in an era in which there is allegedly little support for the rehabilitative ideal. Gebelein argues that drug courts have succeeded because, unlike previous failed rehabilitative efforts, the drug court movement has been able to provide a clear narrative of what is causing the criminal behavior of the drug court clients and what they need to get better. Drug court's "advantage over 'plain old' rehabilitation," Gebelein (2000:3) suggests, is "the focus on one problem (addiction) that is causally related to crime committed by one group of offenders (addicts)." He argues that the narrative that addiction is a disease, and as such, needs to be treated by professionals, is one that makes sense to the public and to policy makers at this point in history.

The critical question, then, is: *Is there a similar narrative for how and why reentry should work?* In this paper, we will argue that a new narrative (which we refer to as a "strengths-based" or "restorative" narrative) is emerging in multiple fields that would fit nicely with the reentry court concept. Unfortunately, the current reentry proposals do not seem to reflect an explicitly restorative agenda and therefore may suffer the same fate as previous efforts to improve offender reentry processes.

Rentry: An Initiative in Need of a Narrative

> *"Bullets kill and bars constrain, but the practice of supervision inevitably involves the construction of a set of narratives which allows the kept, the keepers, and the public to believe in a capacity to control (crime) that cannot afford to be tested too frequently"*
> — Jonathan Simon (1993) *Poor Discipline: Parole and the Social Control of the Underclass*

In his tremendous history of parole in the United States, Simon (1993:9) writes, "One of the primary tasks of an institution that exercises the power to punish is to provide a plausible account of what it does and how it does what it does." This might be particularly important for community corrections, which, as Fogel (1984:85) notes, lacks the "forceful imagery that other occupations in criminal justice can claim: police catch criminals, prosecutors try to get them locked up, judges put them in prisons, wardens keep them locked up, but what do probation officers do?" Simon argues that a good correctional narrative needs some rather obvious components. It needs, first, a plausible theory of criminogenesis (what causes people to commit crime?), and second, a set of practices that appear capable of reversing this process.

Unlike the drug court model described by Gebelein, today's reentry system seems to have no such, compelling narrative for what it does or how it works. In fact, Rhine (1997:74) concludes that the lack of a "plausible narrative of community-based supervision" is "the most pressing and vexing problem facing probation and parole administrators today." The "growing conviction that the system no longer represents a credible response to the problem of crime" (Rhine 1997:71) has led to several new proposals to severely curtail or even abandon parole supervision[2] entirely (e.g., Austin 2001). One of the participants at a recent expert panel on the future of community corrections stated this matter quite bluntly: "Public regard for probation is dangerously low, and for the most part in most places, what passes for probation supervision is a joke. It's conceptually bankrupt and it's politically not viable.... We have to realize that we don't have broad public legitimacy" (Dickey & Smith 1998:3). Another participant described the public mood toward community corrections as a "malaise." He continued, "Even more importantly, there is a malaise in our own house [among probation professionals]" (Cited in Dickey & Smith 1998:5).

It is in this climate that the reentry court initiative has emerged with the promise of breathing new life into a much-maligned system of parole and community supervision. If instituted on a broad scale, the reentry court would represent a significant change in the structure of how the process of prison release works. It is not clear, however, that this important, new policy initiative is being accompanied by a new policy *narrative*. In fact, the discourse around these new reentry initiatives may sound eerily familiar to those who have followed the history of parole in the US. According to Reno (2000:3):

> The reentry court is modeled on the...theory of a carrot and stick approach, in using the strength of the court and the wisdom of the court to really push the issue...The message works with us: stay clean, stay out of trouble, and we'll help you get a job, we'll help you prepare in terms of a skill. But if you come back testing positive for drugs, if you commit a further crime, if you violate the conditions of your release, you're going to pay. This description unfortunately makes the new reentry court initiative sound suspiciously like "simply another word for parole supervision, which many have tried to discredit and dismantle" (Austin 2001:314).

Indeed, Reno's stick and carrot are key symbols of the two reigning paradigms in parole practice over the last 100 years, which can be broken down into the familiar dichotomy of punishment and welfare (Garland 1985), monitor and mentor, or cop and social worker. We refer to these as "risk-

based" and "need-based" narratives, respectively. Both are deficit models—
that is, they emphasize convicts' problems—but they require very different
technologies and connote different meanings.

Below, we briefly outline both narratives, discussing their plausibility as
explanatory accounts and their internal coherence. In addition, using a therapeutic jurisprudence lens, we will also evaluate each narrative in terms of its
fit with established psychological principles regarding sustained behavior
change (see Wexler 2001), and the empirical evaluation research referred to
as "what works" (Gendreau, Cullen, & Bonta 1994). Finally, whenever possible, we will also try to present the convicted person's own interpretation of
these narratives, as these subjective perceptions are also crucial in understanding the success or failure of correctional practice.

Control Narratives (Risk-Based)

The February 2000 press release from U.S. Senator Joseph Biden's office an-
nouncing the "first-ever" reentry court in Delaware began with the macho
headline "Biden Introduces Tough New Court Program for Released Inmates."
Getting "tough" on those who have already "paid their debt" to society has become a standard, if not always coherent reentry narrative. The basic story, here,
seems to be that ex-prisoners are dangerous, and they need to be watched carefully at all times. Indeed, this implication is clear in the new name given to the
Reentry Initiative in the United States. Originally titled, "Young Offender
Reentry Initiative"(OJP 2001), under the Clinton Administration, the Bush
Administration transformed the project into the "Serious and Violent Offender Reentry Initiative" (OJP 2002) and have "toughened" up the language of
control substantially in their version of the proposal. Whereas the Clinton Administration's call for proposals emphasized the problems of substance abuse,
mental illness and stigmatization, the Bush Administration's reworking focuses
on minimizing the risks posed by the "most predatory" ex-convicts.

This points out another important difference between drug courts and the
reentry courts. Whereas drug courts explicitly exclude violent offenders, the
reentry court plan would focus almost exclusively on persons thought to be at
risk for violence. Peyton and Gossweiler (2001) found that of 212 reporting
drug courts in their study, only seven of them include persons with violence in
their criminal histories. Indeed, drug courts that receive federal funding are
prohibited from admitting offenders with current violent charges or with prior
convictions of violent felony crimes. Because of the different public and professional assumptions about the differences between persons convicted of violent
versus non-violent crime (and in particular, drug-related non-violent crime),
treatment of these two populations probably require different narratives.

Underlying the "risk management" approach to violence is the assumption that returning ex-convicts will respond best to the constant threat of
sanctions (or, at any rate, if they do not, then they are too dangerous to be

out of prison). In terms of policy prescriptions, this narrative suggests the need for an "electronic panopticon" (Gordon 1991) or "pee 'em and see 'em" (Cullen 2002) approach to reentry involving electronic monitoring, intensive supervision (i.e., additional home and office visits), random drug testing, home confinement, extensive behavior restrictions, strict curfews, and expanded lengths of supervision. The basic idea is that these forms of tough community controls can reduce recidivism by thwarting an offender's criminal instincts.

Empirically, these prototypically "tough" community sanctions — intensive community supervision in particular — have failed to live up to the promise of the control narrative. Petersilia and Turner's (1993) nine-state, random-assignment evaluation found no evidence that the increased surveillance in the community deterred offenders from committing crimes. At the same time, their research quite conclusively showed that this additional control increased the probability that technical violations would be detected, leading to greater use of incarceration (and hence much higher costs).

Further, the control narrative has little support from the psychological literature on behavioral change. Specific deterrence in general has long been pronounced "dead" as a social scientific concept (see esp. McGuire 1995), and the literature is especially critical of the notion that prisons could serve as an effective deterrent. For instance, psychological research on effective punishment suggests that, to be effective, punishing stimuli must be immediate, predictable, and as intense as possible — none of which is possible in even the most Draconian correctional intervention (Gendreau, Goggin and Cullen 1999).

Research on effective planned change similarly suggests that power-coercive strategies are the least likely to promote internalization and long-term change (Chin and Benne 1976). Kelman (1958), for instance, discusses three means of changing behavior: change via compliance, change via identification, and change via internalization. The first strategy, utilizing power-coercive means, may achieve instrumental compliance, Kelman says, but is the least likely of the three to promote "normative re-education" and long-term transformation once the "change agent" has been removed (see also Bottoms 2000). This hypothesis is empirically supported in MacKenzie and De Li's (2001) rigorous study of intensive supervision probation. They write:

> The disappointing factor is the possibility that the offenders may be influenced only as long as they are being supervised.... When probation is over, these offenders may return to their previous levels of criminal activity because the deterrent effect of arrest may wear off when they are no longer under supervision (37–38).

Heavy-handed control tactics can undermine the perceived legitimacy in paroling authorities among clients (see Tyler, Boeckmann, Smith and Huo

1997). For instance, parole conditions that include prohibitions against asso-
ciating with fellow ex-convicts or entering drinking establishments (both of
which are nearly impossible to enforce) are often viewed as evidence that the
entire parole process is a joke. Persons returning from the trauma of prison
with few resources and little hope are likely to become "defiant" (Sherman,
1993) at the "piling up of sanctions" (Blomberg and Lucken 1994) involved
in such risk-based supervision. And, constant threats that are not backed up
can lead to a form of psychological inoculation. Colvin, Cullen and Vander
Ven (2002:22) write:

> Coercive interpersonal relations constitute the most aversive and
> negative forces individuals encounter. These are most likely to
> produce a strong sense of anger. The anger is only intensified if
> the individual perceives the coercive treatment as unjust or arbi-
> trary. Instead of producing conformity, such coercive treatment
> creates greater defiance of authority.

Ex-convicts often feel they have paid their debt to society already and
should therefore be left alone after release. Far from endorsing a "seamless"
transition from prison control to community control, ex-convict academics
Alan Mobley and Chuck Terry (2002) write, "No one wants the separation of
prison and parole more urgently than do prisoners. When people 'get out,'
they want to *be out.* Any compromise or half-measure, any 'hoops' or hassles
placed in their path, breeds resentment." The extent of this resentment is apparent in the fascinating, and apparently somewhat widespread, phenomenon of convicts choosing to "max out" of their sentence inside a prison
rather than be released early and face high levels of supervision (see also Petersilia and Deschenes 1994).

Most importantly, however, the control narrative suffers from the "deeply
entrenched view" that "equates punishment and control with incarceration,
and that accepts alternatives as suitable only in cases where neither punishment nor control is thought necessary" (Smith 1984:171). Essentially, if
parolees are such "dangerous men" and need so much supervision, then why
aren't they still in prison? The average US parole officer—who has a caseload of 69 parolees each averaging 1.6 face-to-face contacts per month
(Camp and Camp 1997)—simply cannot compete with the iron bars, high
walls and razor wire of the prison when it comes to securing constraint-
based compliance (see Bottoms 2000:92–93). Colvin and his colleagues
(2002:23) write, "Although in theory consistent coercion can prevent crime,
it is highly difficult to maintain consistent coercion in interpersonal relations, which requires nearly constant monitoring to detect noncompliance."
As a result, of course, those who truly support a risk-centered narrative traditionally oppose parole release altogether, supporting instead maximum use
of incapacitation.

Support Narratives (Need-Based)

The traditional counter to a risk-based parole system is a program of aftercare based on needs. Here the story is that ex-convicts are people with multiple deficits: some resulting from their incarceration (e.g., post-traumatic stress, disconnection from family, unfamiliarity with the world of work); some existing prior to incarceration (e.g., poor educational history, psychological problems, anger issues); and some attributable to societal forces outside of their control (e.g., discrimination, abuse, poverty, isolation). The most significant of these deficits, in the support narrative, are those deemed "criminogenic needs" or those problems that seem to be empirically related to offending (cognitive deficits are especially important here). In order to reduce crime, these needs must be "met" or at least "addressed." Specifically, released prisoners are thought to need access to programs in addiction counseling, cognitive therapy, life skills training, anger management and the like.

Like the control narrative, this account has intuitive appeal. Yet, unlike in the case of coercive strategies of control, there is a well-known body of research (the so-called "What Works" literature) that supports the notion that rehabilitative interventions can marginally reduce recidivism rates when treatment is correctly matched to a client's criminogenic needs (see Gendreau et al. 1994). Moreover, in the few studies that ask returning prisoners themselves what would help to keep them "straight," basic "survival" needs (i.e., concerns like housing and employment) are almost always mentioned prominently (e.g., Erickson, Crow, Zurcher, and Connet 1973).

The support narrative, however, is a difficult sell politically. As everyone has needs, can it make sense for the state to prioritize the needs of persons who have recently been punished by the criminal justice system? As Bazemore (forthcoming) argues, "The notion of someone who has hurt another citizen…getting help or service without making amends for what has been damaged flies in the face of virtually universal norms of fairness." This was recently illustrated vividly in New York State, where gubernatorial candidate Carl McCall suggested that ex-convicts should receive help getting into college programs. During a discussion with homeless shelter residents who complained of difficulties receiving federal assistance for education because of their criminal records, McCall stated, "Just because you're an ex-offender, you should not be denied education aid. In fact, if you're an ex-offender I think you ought to get a preference." This simple statement of the support position set off an eruption of protest from his gubernatorial opponents, both Democratic and Republican, one of whom said, "Now he wants ex-convicts to get preference over hard-working students. No wonder Carl McCall was such a failure as president of the N.Y.C. Board of Education" (Nagourney 2002:B1).

Indeed, if the State ever really tried to meet all of the needs of ex-convicts (including financial, social, esteem and self-actualization needs) and not just those needs deemed "criminogenic," the out-pouring of generosity would surely contradict all principles of justice — let alone the controversial notion of "less eligibility." Who would not want to go to prison if the reward awaiting them upon release was that all their needs would be met? Of course, the needs of ex-convicts are rarely met in the 1.6 monthly meetings with a parole officer, referral or placement orders, and social service access that are at the heart of the casework model. "Needs" in correctional terms have come to connote something quite different than the way the word was defined by Maslow (1970) (who left "pro-criminal attitudes" or "criminal associates" off his hierarchy). In their powerful essay contrasting criminogenic needs to human needs, Tony Ward and Claire Stewart (forthcoming:4) point out: "Even when the focus has been on offenders' needs, policy makers tend to be concerned with reducing further crimes or the incidence of disruptive behavior within prisons rather than the enhancement of their well being[3] and capabilities." In fact, needs have become synonymous with risk factors, and "meeting needs" can often equate to expanding the net of social control. So, for example, random mandatory drug testing for marijuana use gets framed as meeting a person's "need" to stop risky behaviors. It is unclear what is meant to represent the "carrot" in such treatment.

Combining Carrots and Sticks: An Odd Couple?

The traditional, middle-ground position, which appeals to Reno and many of the contemporary reentry reformers is to resolve the pendulous mentor-monitor debate by trying to do both. Basically, the idea is that if one combines a control approach (which does not really work, but is assumed to have public support) with a treatment approach (that works a little, but is thought to lack widespread support), the end result will be a program that is both popular and effective.

Instead, more often than not, the result of mixing such disparate goals is a "muddle" (Dickey & Smith 1998). David Fogel (1978:10–11) once quipped, "A parole officer can be seen going off to his/her appointed rounds with Freud in one hand and a .38 Smith and Wesson in the other.....Is Freud a backup to the .38? Or is the .38 carried to 'support' Freud?" The history of crime control in the 20th Century suggests that, when both tools (the therapeutic and the punitive) are available, the latter will almost always win out or at least undermine the former (Garland 1985). Although parents and parental guardians are comfortable combining a disciplinary role with a social support role, this cop-and-counselor combination may not be possible in the much more limited relationship between the reentry court judge and the ex-convict or the parole officer and parolee. Indeed, more often than not, interventions premised on a combination-deficit model end up becoming "almost all stick and no carrot" (Prison Reform Trust 1999).

Theoretically, control strategies are intended to encourage instrumental compliance during the supervisory period, while the treatment strategies are designed to help participants internalize new, moral values. That is, the therapy or the job training is what is really going to work, but without the heavy coercion, the ex-prisoners will not show up for the treatment. And, this hypothesis has some empirical support (MacKenzie and Brame 2001; Petersilia and Turner 1993). In particular, it has been well established that persons coerced into drug treatment programs fare equally well as those who enter voluntarily (Farabee, Prendergast, and Anglin 1998).

Nonetheless, coercing compliance is one thing, but coercing good behavior is quite another. Consistent coercion may produce minimal levels of criminal behavior but it also produces very low levels of prosocial behavior (Colvin, Cullen and Vander Ven 2002:28). Paul Gendreau and his colleagues (1999) argue this forcefully:

> Punishment only trains a person what not to do. If one punishes a behaviour what is left to replace it? In the case of high-risk offenders, simply other antisocial skills! This is why punishment scholars state that the most effective way to produce behavioural change is not to suppress "bad" behaviour, but to shape "good" behavior.

"Carrot and stick" models of reentry assign a largely passive role to the ex-prisoner and hence are unlikely to inspire intrinsically motivated self-initiative (Bazemore 1999). As such, critics argue that the operant conditioning implied in the "carrot and stick" metaphor confounds blind conformity with responsible behavior. Clark (2000:42) writes: "Compliance makes a poor final goal for drug courts. Obedience is not a lofty goal. We can teach animals to obey."

Moreover, coerced treatment is often resented by correctional consumers, who prefer self-help groups to state-sponsored reform programs (Irwin 1974; Mobley and Terry 2002). The eminent social psychologist George H. Mead (1918) explained the reason why combination control-support efforts are doomed to failure, almost a century ago:

> The two attitudes, that of control of crime by the hostile procedure of the law, and that of control through comprehension of social and psychological conditions, cannot be combined. To understand is to forgive and the social procedure seems to deny the very responsibility which the law affirms, and on the other hand the pursuit by criminal justice inevitably awakens the hostile attitude in the offender and renders the attitude of mutual comprehension practically impossible (592).

In a process evaluation of the experimental Reentry Partnership Initiative, Faye Taxman and colleagues (2002:8) found telling evidence in support for this view. They write: "Program designers assumed offenders would be willing to be under additional community supervision in exchange for access to free community-based services on demand. They were surprised when almost no one took them up on the offer." The authors conclude that the offenders' past experience with law enforcement, supervision agencies, and treatment providers had "left them dubious about the real intentions of these agencies and staff." Therefore, the authors decide that any further "efforts to find fault, increase revocations, or speed a return to the justice system will only undermine the reentry goals" (8; see also Tyler et al. 1997).

Finally, the carrot and stick model of reentry fails to assign a meaningful role to the community. Although the process of reintegration has always had as much to do with the community as it has with the individual, carrot and stick reintegration models focus almost exclusively on the individual ex-prisoner. If reentry is to be a meaningful concept, presumably it implies more than physically re-entering society, but also includes some sort of "relational reintegration" back into the moral community. Braithwaite and Braithwaite (2001:49) list four facets of what they call "reintegration":

- Approval of the person—praise
- Respectfulness
- Rituals to terminate disapproval with forgiveness
- Sustaining pride in having the offender included as a member of communities of care (families, the school, the law abiding community at large)

Reintegration, then, means full inclusion in and of a wider moral community. Social dependency and intensive supervision (or so-called carrots and sticks) seem to be the opposite of this sort of moral and social inclusion.

Strengths-Based Reentry: An Emerging Narrative

> "Nobody makes the critical point: We need these people. The country is missing something because a huge bulk of its population is not part of it. They have talents we need."
> —Mimi Silbert, Co-Founder of Delancey Street (Cited in Mieszkowski 1998).

An alternative paradigm is emerging (actually re-emerging) in social service areas related to corrections that may be useful in re-imagining reentry. For the sake of consistency (and not just to invent another new term), we will refer to this as a "strengths-based" paradigm[4] (see also Bazemore 1999; Nissen and Clark forthcoming; van Wormer 2001)—or else "restorative reentry."[5] Strengths-based or restorative approaches ask not what a person's deficits are, but rather what positive contribution the person can make. Nissen and Clark (forthcoming) caution that strengths (of youths, families, and communities) are believed to be the most commonly wasted resources in the justice system. Strengths need to be assessed and "targeted" in the same way that risks and needs traditionally have been. To do so, one simply asks "How can this person make a useful and purposeful contribution to society?" In Jeremy Travis's (2000:7) words: "Offenders are seen as assets to be managed rather than merely liabilities to be supervised." This shift represents a move away from the notion of entitlement to the principle of "social exchange" (Levrant, Cullen, Fulton, and Wozniak 1999:22) or to what Bazemore (1999) calls "earned redemption."

Importantly, we make no pretension to "discovering" (and most certainly not inventing) this paradigm. Strengths-based themes have been a staple of progressive criminal justice reforms at least since the time of Maconochie's Mark System. After a recent rejuvenation in the 1960's and 1970's under the guise of the "New Careers Movement" (Cressey, 1965; Grant 1968), however, this theme largely disappeared from correctional practice and rhetoric. The case being made in this section is only that there are signs that a "strengths" narrative seems to be coming back in multiple guises in the social services, and that this theme may be an appropriate one to introduce into the reentry debate.

In the reentry context, the strengths *narrative* begins with the assumption that ex-convicts are stigmatized persons, and implicitly that this stigma (and not some internal dangerousness or deficit) is at the core of what makes ex-convicts likely to re-offend. The "narrative of criminogenesis" that Simon (1993) calls for, then, is clearly based on a labeling/social exclusion story— on which, of course, the very idea of "reintegration" is also premised (Duffee and McGarrell 1990). Johnson (2002:319) writes, "released prisoners find themselves 'in' but not 'of' the larger society" and "suffer from a presumption of moral contamination." To combat this social exclusion, the strengths paradigm calls for opportunities for ex-convicts to make amends, demonstrate their value and potential, and make positive contributions to their communities. In the language of the New Careers movement, the goal is to "devise ways of creating more helpers" (Pearl & Riessman 1965:88). Strengths-based practice, like the New Careers movement before it would seek "to transform receivers of help (such as welfare recipients) into dispensers of help; to structure the situation so that receivers of help will be placed in roles requiring the giving of assistance" (Pearl & Riessman 1965:88–89).

These accomplishments are thought to lead to "a sense of hope, an orientation toward the future, and the willingness to take responsibility" (Richie 2001:385). Moreover, such demonstrations send a message to the community that the offender is worthy of further support and investment in their reintegration (Bazemore 1999). Ideally, these contributions can be recognized and publicly "certified" in order to symbolically "de-label" the stigmatized person (see Maruna 2001: chapter eight). Although this sort of reentry is always a challenge, it is far more likely to occur in a reciprocal situation: one needs "to do something to get something," (Toch 1994:71). A participant in the "Rethinking Probation" conference discussed the intuitive appeal of such a narrative:

> Let me put it this way, if the public knew that when you commit some wrongdoing, you're held accountable in constructive ways and you've got to earn your way back through these kinds of good works,...(probation) wouldn't be in the rut we're in right now with the public (Dickey & Smith 1998:36).

This symbolic appeal of transforming the probationer into a "giver rather than a consumer of help" is also evidenced by the enthusiasm around community service as a sanction in the 1970s, especially in Europe.

Strengths-based practices: A growing trend

Indeed, the narrative seems to have become somewhat contagious, at least among academics, over the last half-decade or so. Variations of "strengths-based" practice can now be found in every form of social work practice in the United States (Saleebey 1997) and are slowly making their way into traditional criminal justice practice (Clark 2000, 2001; Nissen and Clark forthcoming; van Wormer 2001). Identical paradigm shifts seem to be taking place across a variety of other disciplines including the focus on "positive psychology," developmental resilience, appreciative inquiry, wellness research, solution-focused therapy, assets-based community development, and narrative therapy. All of these new paradigms share an anti-pathologizing approach that focuses on building on strengths rather than correcting deficits.

In a criminal justice framework, strengths approaches would ask not what needs to be done to a person in response to an offense, but rather what the person can accomplish to make amends for his or her actions (e.g., in the form of community service contributions). In the last 30 years, virtually every US probation department has had some experience with community service as a sanction, and it has been widely viewed as a rare penal success story. Yet despite its origins as a rehabilitative panacea, community service is no longer uniformly justified using a strengths narrative. According to Bazemore and Maloney (1994), "punishment now appears to have become the dominant objective of service sanctions in many jurisdictions." Indeed, in the United Kingdom, this shift has been made explicit by the re-labeling of community service as a "community punishment order." When it is strengths-based, community service work is voluntarily agreed upon, and involves challenging tasks that could utilize the talents of the offender in useful, visible roles (McIvor 1998).

> Probation and parole projects in which offenders visibly and directly produce things the larger community wants, such as gardens, graffiti-free neighborhoods, less dangerous alleys, habitable housing for the homeless...have also helped build stronger communities, and have carved channels into the labor market for the offenders engaged in them (Dickey & Smith 1998:35).

These volunteer activities could take place both inside as well as outside the prison. In a partnership program with Habitat for Humanity, convicts from 75 prisons (working alongside volunteers from the community) built over 250 homes for low-income Americans in 1999 (Ta 2000). Prisoners in New York State have been involved in the crucial work of providing respite care to fellow inmates dying of AIDS and other illnesses in the prison system. In the year 2000, as part of a service learning curricula focused on "personal responsibility and reparation," prisoners in the state of Ohio performed more than 5 million hours of community service work, including rehabbing low-income homes, training pilot and companion dogs, and repairing computers to be donated to schools (Wilkinson 2001). Perhaps most impressive among the contributions made by prisoners is the little publicized, but essential work that teams of prisoners have voluntarily undertaken in fighting the forest fires ravaging America's national parks. Prisoners are routinely sent into areas struck by flooding or other natural disasters to provide support to relief efforts.

Prisoners also have initiated parenting programs—like the Eastern Fathers' Group (EFG) that was created "by" and "for" incarcerated fathers at a maximum-security New York State prison (Lanier and Fisher 1990). Consisting of mutual support meetings, monthly educational seminars, and a certified parenting education course, the EFG served to heighten participants' sense of accomplishment and responsibility. At the same time it helped fathers work through the grief they experienced over the loss or deterioration of family bonds. Surveys of prisoners in the United States show that 55 percent of State and 63 percent of Federal prisoners have children under the age of eighteen, and almost half of those parents were living with their children at the time they were incarcerated (Bureau of Justice Statistics 2000). Active engagement in parenting while incarcerated is thought to provide a "stability zone" for offenders that "softens the psychological impact of confinement" (Toch 1975), and may help reduce recidivism and "transmit prosocial attitudes to a future generation" (Lanier and Fisher 1990:164).

Another characteristically strengths-based role is that of the "wounded healer" or "professional ex-" (Brown 1991:219), defined as a person who desists from a "deviant career" by "replacing it" with an occupation as a paraprofessional,[6] lay therapist or counselor. Although it is impossible to measure the true extent of the "professional ex-" phenomenon, Brown (1991:219) estimated that around three-quarters of the counselors working in the over ten thousand substance abuse treatment centers in the United States are former substance abusers themselves. Describing female "wounded healers," Richie (2001:385) writes:

> Most services that are successful in helping women reintegrate into the community have hired (or are otherwise influenced by) women who have been similarly situated. The extent to which

women have a peer and/or mentoring relationship with someone
whom they perceive is 'like them' is critical.

In addition to such professional work, thousands of former prisoners and
addicts freely volunteer their time helping others in mutual aid groups like
Bill Sands' Seventh Step organization. Indeed, the "twelve steps" of Alcoholics Anonymous (AA) and Narcotics Anonymous (NA), are premised
around an explicit service orientation, codified in the Twelfth Step and the
Fifth Tradition, which encourages those who find sobriety to assist others in
taking this journey. According to O'Reilly (1997:128), "next to avoiding in-
toxicants," the therapeutic power of *helping* is "the major premise upon
which (AA) is built." AA and NA members, who have been sober for many
years often remain with the organization, not so much because they need to
receive any more counseling, but because the act of counseling *others* can itself be empowering and therapeutic. Members who stay connected to the
program eventually take on the role of "sponsors," and become the mentors
and teachers of the next generation of recovering addicts. AA's co-founder
Bill Wilson said that he felt that his own sobriety was dependent upon his
acting as a mentor in this way.

With little doubt, the best existing model for a strengths-based, mutual aid
society for ex-convicts outside prison is the Delancey Street program based in
San Francisco. Founded in 1971 by Mimi Silbert and ex-convict John Maher,
Delancey Street has grown from an organization consisting of ten recovering
addicts (and one criminal psychologist) living in an apartment to a thriving
organization with 1,500 full-time residents in five self-run facilities, more
than 20 businesses that double as training schools, and an annual operating
budget of close to $24 million (Boschee & Jones 2000; Mieszkowski 1998).
The program is self-supporting and has no professional staff. Instead, taking
an "each one teach one" approach, older residents teach and train newer ar-
rivals then utilize these new skills to sustain the organization once the more
senior residents "graduate" into private housing and independent careers. Silbert says residents "learn a fundamental lesson... that they have something to
offer. These are people who have always been passive....But strength and
power come from being on the giving end" (Boschee & Jones 2000:11).

Finally, in recent years there have been several efforts to coordinate the efforts and energies of a variety of such mutual aid groups in the name of creating lasting social change. In what is being called the "New Recovery Movement" (White 2001:16), wounded healers are also beginning to become
"recovery activists," turning their "personal stories into social action" (19),
and turning "recovery outwards" (19). Instead of working solely on their
own addiction problems, recovering persons and their supporters would
mobilize their strengths in order to change "the ecology of addiction and recovery" (White 2001:19). These and other mutual aid efforts are thought to

help transform individuals from being part of "the problem" into part of "the solution" as they give their time in the service of helping others.

Theoretical and empirical support for the "helper principle"
Although these activities can be justified on many grounds, one of the central, theoretical premises all of these strengths-based practices share is some faith in the "helper principle" (Pearl & Riessman 1965). Promoted in the 1960's New Careers Movement, the helper principle simply says that it may be better (that is, more reintegrative) to give help than to receive it (see also Cullen 1994:543–544). The alleged benefits of assuming the role of helper include a sense of accomplishment, grounded increments in self-esteem, meaningful purposiveness, and a cognitive restructuring toward responsibility (Toch 2000). Rather than coercing obedience, strengths-based practices are thought to develop intrinsic motivations toward helping behaviors—what Nissen and Clark (forthcoming:70) call the "difference between compliance and growth." Clients are supposedly "turned on" to prosocial behavior through involvement with activities that utilize their strengths. In the words of Alexis de Tocqueville (1835/1956:197), "By dint of working for one's fellow-citizens, the habit and the taste for serving them is at length acquired." In addition, as part of a helping collective, the "wounded healer" or community volunteer is thought to obtain "a sense of belonging and an esprit de corps" (Pearl & Riessman 1965:83). According to the helper principle, all these experiences should be related to successful reintegration and social inclusion.

Recent research on desistance from crime might provide some indirect empirical support for this claim. For instance, as is well known, Sampson & Laub (1993) found that one-time offenders who were employed and took responsibility for providing for their spouses and children were significantly more likely to desist from crime than those who made no such bonds. A less well known finding of their research was that desistance was strongly correlated with assuming financial responsibility for one's aging parents or siblings in need as well (Sampson & Laub 1993:219–220). One way to interpret these findings might be to hypothesize that nurturing behaviors may be inconsistent with a criminal lifestyle. Indeed, Lynne Goodstein speculates that women's traditional responsibility for other family and community members may be one reason that females are so dramatically under-represented in criminal statistics (cited in Cullen 1994).

Moreover, quasi-experimental evaluations of community service sentencing consistently show that it outperforms standard probation and other sanctions in reducing recidivism (Rex 2001; Schneider 1986). Further, McIvor (1998) found that people who viewed their experience of community service as "rewarding" had lower rates of recidivism than those who found it a chore, indicating that this impact is less about deterrence and more likely something to do with pro-social modeling or moral development (Van Voorhis 1985). McIvor (1998) writes, "In many instances, it seems, contact with the beneficiaries gave offenders an insight into other people, and an increased insight into themselves;...greater confidence and self-esteem;...(and) the confidence and appreciation of other people" (McIvor 1998:55–56; cite in Rex 2001).

More recently, longitudinal studies have tried to assess the long-term impact of volunteer work on life course trajectories. Uggen & Janikula (1999) investigated the question of whether involvement in volunteer work can induce a change in a person's likelihood of antisocial conduct. They found a robust negative relationship between volunteer work and arrest even after statistically controlling for the effects of antisocial propensities, prosocial attitudes, and commitments to conventional behavior. Uggen & Janikula (1999:355) conclude:

> What is it about the volunteer experience that inhibits antisocial behavior? We suggest that the informal social controls emphasized in social bond, social learning, and reintegrative theories are the mechanism linking volunteer work and antisocial behavior. Informal social controls are consonant with Tocquevillian conceptions of "self-interest, rightly understood," in which volunteers are gradually socialized or "disciplined by habit rather than will."

Finally, Maruna's (2001) research on the psychology of desistance from crime offers further evidence of a link between a "generative" identity and criminal reform. In a clinical comparison of successfully and unsuccessfully reformed ex-convicts, Maruna found that those who were able to "go straight" were significantly more care-oriented, other-centered and focused on promoting the next generation. They tried to find some meaning in their shameful life histories by turning their experiences into cautionary or hopeful stories of redemption, which they share with younger offenders in similar situations. Whereas active offenders characterized themselves as being doomed or predestined to failure, reformed offenders had an almost overly optimistic sense of control over their future and strong internal beliefs about their own self-worth. In short, their personal narratives (the stories they told about how they were able to "go straight") resembled "strength narratives" far more than control or support narratives. (Indeed, the latter seemed to characterize the narratives of active offenders.)

None of this research is firm evidence in favor of the "helper principle." In particular, although these studies may suggest a basic incompatibility between helping activities and criminal lifestyles, they tell us little about how to "create more helpers." Indeed, the lack of research on mutual aid organizations, self-help groups, and informal mentoring and parenting among convicts and ex-convicts is rather startling considering how much research is funded each year to examine the impact of greater controls and, less frequently, treatment programming (see Uggen and Piliavin 1998:1421–1422).

Still, as a narrative—that is, a theoretical premise—the restorative idea of "earned redemption" seems to have at least some plausibility from the limited research that exists.

A Strengths-Based Reentry Court

> *"Become future focused: the past, and the focus on past failures, can open the door to demoralization and resignation—hope is future based"*
> — Michael D. Clark (2001:23)

Strengths-based practices and principles may be uniquely suited to the new reentry court idea. First, unlike traditional jurisprudence, reentry courts would presumably be future-oriented rather than focused on the past. Determining guilt and devising a fair response to a criminal act are responsibilities that belong to other courts. The reentry court's role might more reasonably be understood as dispensing "reintegration"—not release from prison or supervision (as is the traditional role of the parole board), but rather a release from the stigma of the original conviction. The work of reentry, then, would be the facilitation of opportunities to make amends for what one has done, and the recognition of these contributions and accomplishments. True to its name, then, the reentry court could become a "court of redemption," through which a stigmatized person has the opportunity to formally "make good."

Rewarding positive achievements, rather than punishing violations, is an unusual role for the courts. Parole as it is currently practiced focuses almost entirely on detecting and punishing failure—even though the "what works" principles suggest that positive reinforcement should outweigh punishment by a 4:1 ratio (Gendreau et al. 1994). As conformity is all that is required of deficit-based parole, it makes little sense to commend or acknowledge persons simply for doing what they are supposed to and following the rules. Indeed, the primary "reward" available in parole today is to "get off" parole early, a particularly strange and unceremonious process.[7]

Alternatively, a strengths-based reentry court might be modeled on Braithwaite's (2001:11) notion of "active responsibility": "Passive responsibility means holding someone responsible for something they have done in the past. Active responsibility means the virtue of taking responsibility for putting things right for the future." The court would not be concerned with past offenses, misbehavior in prison or even violations of parole. All of these crimes and misdemeanors are properly punished by other authorities. The focus, instead, would be on monitoring, recording and judging what the individual has done to redeem him or herself through victim reparation, community service, volunteer work, mentoring, and parenting.[8] Witnesses would be called, testimony would be offered, tangible evidence would be produced—not in the name of establishing guilt or innocence, but rather in order to assess the contribution being made by the returning prisoner both in prison and afterwards. The reentry court could then be the setting for a "public recognition ceremony" acknowledging these contributions and accomplishments as "a milestone in repaying (one's) debt to society" (Travis 2000:9).

With no powers to punish, a strengths court, then, would be more a challenge to returning ex-convicts than a threat. That is, the ex-offender would be given an opportunity to be publicly and formally "reintegrated" if they were willing to pay a debt to society in terms of their service and contribution. Winick (1991:246) refers to this as "harnessing the power of the bet":

> Many people do not respond well when told to do so. Unless they themselves see merit in achieving the goal, sometimes even when the costs of non-compliance are high, they may well resent pressure imposed by others and refuse to comply, or act perversely in ways calculated to frustrate achievement of the goal. By contrast, the offer to wager can be accepted or rejected. The choice is up to the individual. The law strongly favors allowing such choice, rather than attempting to achieve public or private goals through compulsion.

Winick (1991:247) argues that, unlike coerced compliance, this challenge model is likely to mobilize "the self-evaluative and self-reinforcing mechanisms of intrinsic motivation" and effect "lasting attitudinal and behavioral change in the individual."

The notion of rewarding success, of course, is a key component of the reentry court idea. In drug treatment courts[9], "applause is common" and "even judicial hugs are by no means a rare occurrence" (Wexler 2001:21). Travis (1999:133) asserts that "the court should use positive judicial reinforcement by serving as a public forum for encouraging pro-social behavior and for affirming the value of individual effort in earning the privilege of successful reintegration." In the experimental Reentry Partnership Initiatives, successful "reentry graduates" may eventually move from being "recipients of services" to acting as role models and "guardians" for newly released offenders just entering the structured reentry phase of the process (Taxman, et al. 2002:18; similar recommendations were proposed by Erickson et al. 1973:103–105). Among other program requirements, each participant in Richland County, Ohio's new reentry court is required to complete 300 hours of community service work that commences upon incarceration (Wilkinson 2001). Finally, all reentry courts are required to outline milestones in the reentry process (such as the completion of this sort of volunteer work) that would trigger recognition and an appropriate reward (Office of Justice Programs 1999).

A strengths approach would probably take this further, and following Johnson (2002:328), would recast the reentry court process as "a mutual effort at reconciliation, where offender and society work together to make amends—for hurtful crimes and hurtful punishments—and move forward." Braithwaite and Braithwaite (2001:16) have argued that praise may work in the exact opposite form that shaming does. That is, while it is better to shame an individual act and not the whole person, it may be better to praise the whole person than the specific act.

> So when a child shows a kindness to his sister, better to say 'you are a kind brother' than 'that was a kind thing you did'.... (P)raise that is tied to specific acts risks counter productivity if it is seen as an extrinsic reward, if it nurtures a calculative approach to performances that cannot be constantly monitored....Praising virtues of the person rather than just their acts...nourishes a positive identity.

According to Makkai and Braithwaite (1993), such praise can have "cognitive effects on individuals through nurturing law-abiding identities, building cognitive commitments to try harder, encouraging individuals who face adversity not to give up...and nurturing belief in oneself."

As such, the strengths-based reentry court would need to go beyond the occasional rewarding of specific acts of service and instead build gradually to a more holistic "earned redemption" of the participant's character and reputation. This might take the shape of a "status elevation ceremony" that could "serve publicly and formally to announce, sell and spread the fact of the Actor's new kind of being" (Lofland 1969:227). In such rituals, "Some recognized member(s) of the conventional community must publicly announce and certify that the offender has changed and that he is now to be considered essentially noncriminal" (Meisenhelder 1977:329). These need not be once-off occasions. Just as Braithwaite and Braithwaite (2001) propose that reintegration ceremonies may need to be occur more than once, multiple certification rituals may be needed in multiple domains in order to counteract the stigma faced by former prisoners. If endorsed and supported by the same social control establishment involved in the "status degradation" process of conviction and sentencing, this public redemption might carry considerable social and psychological weight for participants and observers (Maruna 2001:chapter eight).

Most importantly, the reward would also involve the "expiration" of the individual's criminal history—allowing the person freedom from having to declare previous convictions to potential employers, licensing bodies, or other authorities and to resume full citizenship rights and responsibilities.[10] The ultimate prize, then, for (proactive) "good behavior" would be permission to legally move on from the past and wipe the slate clean. This, it seems, may better represent the definition of "reintegration."

Notes

1. The original Clinton agenda also involved a substantial new project referred to as the Reentry Partnership Initiative (RPI), which is beyond the scope of this paper, although similar in many ways to the reentry court. For instance, the stated goal of the RPI initiative is to "improve risk management of released offenders...by enhancing surveillance, risk and needs assessments, and pre-release planning" (RPI Report 2000: 1; see also Taxman, Young, Byrne, Holsinger, and Anspach 2002).

2. These should be seen as distinct from previous efforts to abolish parole *release* structures, which largely left post-incarceration supervision in tact.

3. Even in the most progressive versions of the support narrative, this level of need-fulfillment is difficult to achieve. For instance, Sullivan and Tifft (2001) point out that although there is much talk in restorative justice circles about "meeting the needs" of offenders as well as victims, the two are seen as significantly different. While crime victims are thought to need understanding, support and love from those around them, offenders are said to need a job, clothing and shelter. Sullivan and Tifft (2001:83) write, "By focusing on this level of needs alone, we do not show the same level of concern for them as we do for those who have been harmed."

4. This of course is an umbrella term that encompasses approaches that go by many other names (most notably Restorative Justice, the New Careers movement, relational rehabilitation, and the New Recover Movement).

5. "Restorative Reentry" is the preferred phrase of the Open Society Institute's remarkable array of strengths-based, advocacy projects sponsored as part of the After Prison Initiative (see <http://www.soros.org/crime/CJI_Guidelines.htm#tapi>)

6. Interestingly, the Clinton Administration's original Young Offender Initiative (OJP 2001:12) stated: "Applicants are encouraged to use ex-offenders as staff and those with a history of substance abuse or mental illness. Having some staff with these backgrounds helps the therapeutic process and builds the community's capacity to continue services after the grant ends." There is no mention of utilizing the strengths of ex-offenders in this way in the Bush Administration's initiative.

7. When one of this paper's authors earned his freedom after 56 months of parole supervision, he was offered not so much as a "congratulations" or a "good luck" from the officer who had such power over his life. In fact, he only found out that he had been released from parole supervision when he called his PO to get a travel pass to visit his family out of state. The memorable dialogue proceeded something as follows: "So, does that mean I'm

free?" "Yes, you don't need to report anymore." "Do I have all of my rights back?" "I don't know anything about that." "Thanks."

8. Research in the substance abuse field by Petry, Tedford, and Martin (2001:34) suggests that prosocial activity reinforcement (that is, rewarding positive behaviors) is more effective than reinforcement that is purely directed toward the absence of negative behaviors (e.g., drug abstinence). For instance, they found that prosocial activity reinforcement may result in improvements in psychosocial functioning (employment, medical, family problems) that are not apparent when drug abstinence alone is reinforced.

9. At their best, drug courts can epitomize the ideals of therapeutic jurisprudence, a clearly strengths-based approach (see Hora, Schma & Rosenthal 1999). Still, these ideals are not always realized in practice and one should be careful about exaggerating the role of praise in the actual practice of problem-solving courts. Ethnographers report that participants who successfully complete one large-scale drug court program, for instance, receive only "a congratulatory remark from the judge along with a T-shirt and key chain, claiming they are now "2 smart 4 drugs" (Miethe, Lu and Reese 2000:536). Burdon and colleagues (2001:78) write: "Descriptions of actual drug court operations reveal that most drug courts emphasize sanctions for noncompliance and few routinely use reinforcement of positive, desired behavior. [When used] rewards tend to be intermittent and, in contrast to sanctions, less specific, not immediately experienced, and based on a subjective evaluation of a defendant's progress in treatment."

10. Like many other observers, we would argue that ex-convicts should retain their full civil rights (voting, jury membership, etc.) regardless of reentry court participation. These rights are entitlements and should not be used as "rewards" even in a reciprocity based reentry program.

References

Austin, James. 2001. "Prisoner Reentry: Current Trends, Practices, and Issues." *Crime and Delinquency* 47:314–334.

Bazemore, Gordon. 1999. "After Shaming, Whither Reintegration: Restorative Justice and Relational Rehabilitation." Pp. 155–194 in *Restorative Juvenile Justice: Repairing the Harm of Youth Crime*, edited by G. Bazemore and L. Walgrave. Monsey, NY: Criminal Justice Press.

Bazemore, Gordon. Forthcoming. "Reintegration and Restorative Justice: Toward a Theory and Practice of Informal Social Control and Support." In *Ex-Offender Reintegration: Desistance from Crime After Prison*, edited by S. Maruna and R. Immarigeon. Albany, NY: SUNY Press.

Bazemore, Gordon and Dennis Maloney. 1994. "Rehabilitating Community Service: Toward Restorative Service Sanctions in a Balanced Justice System." *Federal Probation* 58:24–35.

Blomberg, Thomas and Karol Lucken. 1994. "Stacking the Deck by Piling Up Sanctions: Is Intermediate Punishment Destined to Fail?" *The Howard Journal* 33(1):62–80.

Booth, Maud B. 1903. *After Prison-What?* New York: Fleming H. Revell Company.

Boschee, Jerr & Syl Jones. 2000. "Recycling Ex-cons, Addicts and Prostitutes: The Mimi Silbert Story." [Online]. Available: <http://www.socialent.org/pubs.htm>

Bottoms, Anthony E. 2000. "Compliance and Community Penalties." Pp. 87–116 in *Community Penalties: Change and Challenges*, edited by A. Bottoms, L. Gelsthorpe, and S. Rex. Cullompton: Willan.

Braithwaite, John. 2001. "Intention Versus Reactive Fault." Pp. 345–357 in *Intention in Law and Philosophy*, edited by N. Naffine, R. Owens, and John Williams. Aldershot, UK: Ashgate.

Braithwaite, John and Valerie Braithwaite. 2001. "Part One." Pp 3–69 in *Shame Management Through Reintegration*, edited by E. Ahmed, N. Harris, J. Braithwaite, and V. Braithwaite. Cambridge: University of Cambridge Press.

Brown, David J. 1991. "The Professional Ex-: An Alternative for Exiting the Deviant Career." *The Sociological Quarterly* 32: 219–230.

Burdon, William M., John M. Roll, Michael L. Prendergast, and Richard A. Rawson. 2001.

"Drug Courts and Contingency Management." *Journal of Drug Issues* 31:73–90.

Bureau of Justice Statistics. 2000. *Incarcerated Parents and Their Children* (NCJ 182335). Washington, DC: U.S. Department of Justice.

Bureau of Justice Statistics. 2001, August 28. *Probation and Parole in the United States, 2000—Press Release* (NCJ 188208). Washington, DC: U.S. Department of Justice.

Camp, Camille G. and George M. Camp. 1997. *The Corrections Yearbook.* South Salem, N.Y.: Criminal Justice Institute, Inc.

Chin, Robert and Kenneth D. Benne. 1976. "General Strategies for Effecting Changes in Human Systems." Pp. 22–44 in *The Planning of Change*, 3rd ed., edited by W. G. Bennis, K. D. Benne, R. Chin, and K. Corey. New York: Holt, Rinehart and Winston.

Clark, Michael D. 2000. "The Juvenile Drug Court Judge and Lawyer: Four Common Mistakes in Treating Drug Court Adolescents." *Juvenile and Family Court Journal* 51(4):37–46.

Clark, Michael D. 2001. "Influencing Positive Behavior Change: Increasing the Therapeutic Approach of Juvenile Courts." *Federal Probation* 65(1):18–27.

Colvin, Mark, Francis T. Cullen, & Thomas M. Vander Ven. 2002. "Coercion, Social Support, and Crime: An Emerging Theoretical Consensus." *Criminology* 40:19–42.

Cressey, Donald R. 1965. "Social Psychological Foundations for Using Criminals in the Rehabilitation of Criminals." *Journal of Research in Crime and Delinquency* 2:49–59.

Cullen, Francis T. 1994. "Social Support as an Organizing Concept in Criminology: Presidential Address to the Academy of Criminal Justice Sciences." *Justice Quarterly* 11:527–559.

Cullen, Francis T. 2002. "Rehabilitation and Treatment Programs." Pp. 253–289 in *Crime: Public Policies for Crime Control,* edited by J. Q. Wilson and J. Petersilia. Oakland, CA: Institute for Contemporary Studies.

Dickey, Walter J. and Michael E. Smith. 1998. *Dangerous Opportunity: Five Futures for Community Corrections: The Report from the Focus Group.* Washington, DC: U.S. Department of Justice, Office of Justice Programs.

Duffee, David E. and Edmund F. McGarrell.1990. *Community Corrections: A Community Field Approach.* Cincinnati, Ohio: Anderson.

Erickson, Rosemary J., Wayman J. Crow, Louis A. Zurcher, and Archie V. Connet. 1973. *Paroled But Not Free.* New York: Human Sciences Press.

Farabee, David, Michael Prendergast, and M. Douglas Anglin. 1998. "The Effectiveness of Coerced Treatment for Drug-abusing Offenders." *Federal Probation* 62(1):3–10.

Fogel, David. 1978. "Foreword." Pp. 7–15 in *Dangerous Men: The Sociology of Parole* by Richard McCleary. Beverly Hills, CA: Sage Publications.

Fogel, David. 1984. "The Emergence of Probation as a Profession in the Service of Public Safety: The Next Ten Years." Pp. 65–99 in *Probation and Justice: Reconsideration of Mission,* edited by P. D. McAnany, D. Thompson, and D. Fogel. Cambridge, MA: Oelgeschlager, Gunn, and Hain.

Garland, David. 1985. *Punishment and Welfare: A History of Penal Strategies.* Brookfield, VT: Gower Publishing Company.

Gebelein, Richard S. 2000. *The Rebirth of Rehabilitation: Promise and Perils of Drug Courts.* Papers from the Executive Sessions on Sentencing and Corrections (NCJ 181412). Washington, DC: U.S. Department of Justice, National Institute of Justice.

Gendreau, Paul, Francis T. Cullen, & James Bonta. 1994. "Intensive Rehabilitation Supervision: The Next Generation in Community Corrections?" *Federal Probation* 58:173–84.

Gendreau, Paul, Claire Goggin, and Francis T. Cullen. (1999). *The Effects of Prison Sentences on Recidivism.* A Report to the Corrections Research and Development and Aboriginal Policy Branch, Solicitor General of Canada, Ottawa.

Gordon, Diana. 1991. *The Justice Juggernaut: Fighting Street Crime, Controlling Citizens.* New Brunswick, NJ: Rutgers University Press.

Grant, J. Douglas. 1968. "The Offender as a Correctional Manpower Resource." Pp. 226–234 in *Up from Poverty: New Career Ladders for Nonprofessionals,* edited by F. Riessman and H.L. Popper. New York: Harper and Row.

Hora, Peggy F., William G. Schma, and John T. A. Rosenthal. 1999. "Therapeutic Jurisprudence and the Drug Treatment Court Movement: Revolutionizing the Criminal Justice System's Response to Drug Abuse and Crime in America." *Notre Dame Law Review* 74:439–537.

Hughes, Timothy A., Doris. J. Wilson, and Allen J. Beck. 2001. *Trends in State Parole, 1990–2000.* Washington D.C.: U.S. Department of Justice, Bureau of Justice Statistics: Special Report.

Irwin, John. 1974. "The Trouble with Rehabilitation." *Criminal Justice and Behavior* 1(2): 139–149.

Johnson, Robert. 2002. *Hard Time,* 3rd ed. Belmont, CA: Wadsworth.

Kelman, Herbert C. 1958. "Compliance, Identification and Internalization: Three Processes of Opinion Change." *Journal of Conflict Resolution* 2:51–60.

Langan, Patrick A. and David J. Levin. 2002. *Recidivism of Prisoners Released in 1994* (NCJ 193427). Washington, D.C.: U.S. Department of Justice, Bureau of Justice Statistics.

Lanier, Charles S. and Glenn Fisher. 1990. "A Prisoners' Parenting Center (PPC): A Promising Resource Strategy for Incarcerated Fathers." *Journal of Correctional Education* 41:158–165.

Levrant, Sharon, Francis T. Cullen, Betsy Fulton, and John F. Wozniak. 1999. "Reconsidering Restorative Justice: The Corruption of Benevolence Revisited?" *Crime and Delinquency* 45:3–27.

Lofland, John. 1969. *Deviance and Identity.* Englewood Cliffs, NJ: Prentice-Hall.

MacKenzie, Doris L. and Robert Brame. 2001. "Community Supervision, Prosocial Activities, and Recidivism." *Justice Quarterly* 18(2):429–448.

MacKenzie, Doris L. and Spencer De Li. 2002. "The Impact of Formal and Informal Social Controls on the Criminal Activities of Probationers." *Journal of Research in Crime and Delinquency* 39:243–276.

Makkai, Toni and John Braithwaite. 1993. "Praise, Pride and Corporate Compliance." *International Journal of the Sociology of Law* 21:73–91.

Maruna, Shadd. 2001. *Making Good: How Ex-convicts Reform and Rebuild Their Lives.* Washington, D.C.: American Psychological Association Books.

Maslow, Abraham H. 1970. *Motivation and Personality,* 2nd ed. New York: Harper and Row.

McArthur, Verne A. 1974. *Coming Out Cold: Community Reentry from a State Reformatory.* Lexington, MA: Lexington Books.

McGuire, James. 1995. "The Death of Deterrence." In *Does Punishment Work? Proceedings of a Conference Held at Westminster Central Hall, London, UK,* edited by J. McGuire and B. Rowson. London: ISTD

McIvor, Gillian. 1998. "Pro-social Modelling and Legitimacy: Lessons from a Study of Community Service." In *Pro-social Modelling and Legitimacy: The Clarke Hall Day Conference,* edited by S. Rex and A. Matravers. Cambridge: Institute of Criminology, University of Cambridge.

Mead, George H. 1918. "The Psychology of Punitive Justice." *American Journal of Sociology* 23:577–602.

Meisenhelder, Thomas. 1977. "An Exploratory Study of Exiting from Criminal Careers." *Criminology* 15:319–334.

Mieszkowski, Katherine. 1998. "She Helps Them Help Themselves." *Fast Company* 15:54–56.

Miethe, Terrance D., Hong Lu, and Erin Reese. 2000. "Reintegrative Shaming and Recidivism Risks in Drug Court: Explanations for Some Unexpected Findings." *Crime and Delinquency* 46:522–541.

Mobley, Alan and Charles Terry. 2002. *Dignity, Resistance and Re-entry: A Convict Perspective*. Unpublished manuscript.

Nagourney, Adam. 2002, June 20. "McCall Urges Giving Help on Tuition to Ex-convicts." *New York Times*, B1.

Nissen, Laura B. and Michael D. Clark. Forthcoming. *Power of the Strengths Approach in the Juvenile Drug Court—Practice Monograph*. Washington, D.C.: U.S. Department of Justice, Office of Justice Programs, Juvenile Drug Court Programs Office.

O'Reilly, Edmund B. 1997. *Sobering Tales: Narratives of Alcoholism and Recovery*. Amherst, MA: University of Massachusetts Press.

Office of Justice Programs. 1999. *Reentry Courts: Managing the Transition from Prison to Community, A Call for Concept Papers*. Washington D.C.: U.S. Department of Justice, Office of Justice Programs.

Office of Justice Programs. 2001. *Young Offender Initiative: Reentry Grant Program*. Washington D.C.: U.S. Department of Justice, Office of Justice Programs.

Office of Justice Programs. 2002. *Serious and Violent Offender Reentry Initiative—Going Home*. Washington D.C.: U.S. Department of Justice, Office of Justice Programs.

Pearl, Arthur and Frank Riessman. 1965. *New Careers for the Poor: The Nonprofessional in Human Service*. New York: The Free Press.

Petersilia, Joan and Elizabeth P. Deschenes. 1994. "What Punishes? Inmates Rank the Severity of Prison vs. Intermediate Sanctions." *Federal Probation* 58:3–8.

Petersilia, Joan and Susan Turner. 1993. "Intensive Probation and Parole." Pp. 281–335 in *Crime and Justice: An Annual Review of Research, Vol. 19*, edited by M. Tonry. Chicago, IL: University of Chicago Press.

Petry, Nancy M., Jacqueline Tedford, and Bonnie Martin. 2001. "Reinforcing Compliance with Non-drug-related Activities." *Journal of Substance Abuse Treatment* 20:33–44.

Peyton, Elizabeth A. and Robert Gossweiler. 2001. *Treatment Services in Adult Drug Courts: Report on the 1999 National Drug Court Treatment Survey* (NCJ 188085). Washington, DC: U.S. Department of Justice, Office of Justice Programs.

Prison Reform Trust. 1999. *Prison Incentives Scheme.* London: Prison Reform Trust.

Reentry Partnerships Initiative Report 2000. "Reducing the Threat of Recidivism." *RPI Report: Newsletter of the Reentry Partnerships Initiative* 1:1–2.

Reno, Janet. 2000. *Remarks of the Honorable Janet Reno on Reentry Court Initiative,* John Jay College of Criminal Justice, New York, February 10, 2000. [Online]. Available: <http://www.usdoj.gov/ag/speeches/2000/doc2.htm>

Rex, Sue. 2001. "Beyond Cognitive-Behaviouralism? Reflections on the Effectiveness Literature." In *Community Penalties: Change and Challenges,* edited by A. E. Bottoms, L. Gelsthorpe, and S. Rex. Cullompton, UK: Willan.

Rhine, Edward E. 1997. "Probation and Parole Supervision: In Need of a New Narrative." *Corrections Management Quarterly* 1(2):71–75.

Richie, Beth 2001. "Challenges Incarcerated Women Face as They Return to Their Communities: Findings from Life History Interviews." *Crime and Delinquency* 47: 368–389.

Saleebey, Dennis. 1997. *The Strengths Perspective in Social Work Practice,* 2nd ed. New York: Longman.

Sampson, Robert J. and John Laub. 1993. *Crime in the Making: Pathways and Turning Points Through Life.* Cambridge, MA: Harvard University Press.

Schneider, Anne L. 1986. "Restitution and Recidivism Rates of Juvenile Offenders: Results from Four Experimental Studies." *Criminology* 24:533–552.

Sherman, Lawrence W. 1993. "Defiance, Deterrence, and Irrelevance: A Theory of the Criminal Sanction." *Journal of Research in Crime and Delinquency* 30:445–473.

Simon, Jonathan. 1993. *Poor Discipline: Parole and the Social Control of the Underclass, 1890–1990.* Chicago: The University of Chicago Press.

Smith. Micheael E. 1984. "Will the Real Alternatives Please Stand Up?" *New York University Review of Law and Social Change* 12:171–97.

Sullivan, Dennis and Larry Tifft. 2001. *Restorative Justice: Healing the Foundations of Our Everyday Lives.* Monsey, NY: Willow Free Press.

Ta, Christine. 2000, October. "Prison Partnership: It's About People." *Corrections Today* 62(6):114–123.

Taxman, Faye S., Douglas Young, James M. Byrne, Alexander Holsinger, and Donald Anspach. 2002. *From Prison Safety to Public Safety: Innovations in Offender Reentry.* University of Maryland, College Park, Bureau of Government Research.

Toch, Hans. 1975. *Men in Crisis: Human Breakdowns in Prisons.* Chicago: Aldine.

Toch, Hans. 1994. "Democratizing Prisons." *Prison Journal* 73:62–72.

Toch, Hans. 2000. "Altruistic Activity as Correctional Treatment." *International Journal of Offender Therapy and Comparative Criminology* 44:270–278.

Tocqueville, Alexis. 1835/1956. *Democracy in America.* New York: Knopf. (Original work published in 1835).

Travis, Jeremy. 1999. "Prisons, Work and Re-entry." *Corrections Today* 61(6):102–33.

Travis, Jeremy. 2000. *But They All Come Back: Rethinking Prisoner Reentry, Research in Brief—Sentencing and Corrections: Issues for the 21st Century* (NCJ 181413). Washington, DC: U.S. Department of Justice, National Institute of Justice.

Travis, Jeremy and Joan Petersilia. 2001. "Reentry Reconsidered: A New Look at an Old Question." *Crime and Delinquency* 47:291–313.

Tyler, Tom R., Robert J. Boeckmann, Heather J. Smith and Yuen J. Huo. 1997. *Social Justice in a Diverse Society.* Denver, CO: Westview Press.

Uggen, Christopher and Jennifer Janikula. 1999. "Volunteerism and Arrest in the Transition to Adulthood." *Social Forces* 78:331–362.

Uggen, Christopher and Irving Piliavin. 1998. "Asymmetrical Causation and Criminal Desistance." *Journal of Criminal Law and Criminology* 88:1399–1422.

Van Voorhis, Patricia. 1985. "Restitution Outcome and Probationers' Assessments of Restitution: The Effects of Moral Development. *Criminal Justice and Behavior* 12: 259–287.

van Wormer, Kathryn. 2001. *Counseling Female Offenders and Victims: A Strengths-Restorative Approach.* New York: Springer.

Ward, Tony and Claire Stewart. Forthcoming. "Criminogenic Needs and Human Needs: A Theoretical Model." *Psychology, Crime and Law.*

Wexler, David, B. 2001. "Robes and Rehabilitation: How Judges Can Help Offenders 'Make Good.'" *Court Review* 38:18–23.

White, William L. 2001. *The Rhetoric of Recovery Advocacy: An Essay on the Power of Language.* [Online]. Available: http://www.defeataddiction.org/grfx/LANGUAGE.pdf

Wilkinson, Reginald A. 2001. "Offender Reentry: A Storm Overdue." *Corrections Management Quarterly* 5(3):46–51.

Winick, Bruce J. 1991. "Harnessing the Power of the Bet: Wagering with the Government as a Mechanism for Social and Individual Change." Pp. 219–290 in *Essays in Therapeutic Jurisprudence,* edited by David B. Wexler and Bruce J. Winick. Durham, NC: Carolina Academic Press.

M. Structural and Administrative Principles

Implementing the reentry court proposed by Maruna & Le Bel in the previous selection would require a structural change in the way in which courts now typically function. In the most extensive section of Part II, we discuss several "structural and administrative" aspects of the therapeutic jurisprudence project.

For example, Winick discusses the rationale for a separate domestic violence court, while Professor Barbara Babb, the director of a family law institute at the University of Baltimore, explains the therapeutic rationale underlying a unified family court. And Judges Hora and Schma, together with attorney John Rosenthal, explain how a drug treatment court can capitalize on the therapeutic impact of a supportive judge-client relationship.

This section also includes a short selection by Hora, Schma, and Rosenthal on judicial monitoring of treatment provision and progress. Hora, Schma, and Rosenthal are also drawn upon to illustrate how case calendaring can be used to promote vicarious learning by clients—how cases can be ordered so as to give new clients a glimpse of the hard-work, but also of the opportunity and hope for real recovery, that lies ahead.

When judges and others start seeing the legal world through a therapeutic jurisprudence lens, many therapeutic opportunities will present themselves, as they do in the otherwise ordinary and routine area of the ordering of cases. Sociologist Thomas Scheff so saw the legal world, in the earlier reading on community conferences, Part II J, when he observed that the critical moment—or "core sequence"—of offender-victim "healing," when it occurred, often took place in the haphazard aftermath of the formal conference. Accordingly, Scheff suggested it "might be advantageous to build in a delay after the formal end of the conference, such as the signing of a written agreement." Such a built-in paperwork procedure "would allow the participants to complete their unfinished business of symbolic reparation."

Using the therapeutic jurisprudence lens to suggest reforms is the stuff of the final three selections in this section. In a snippet from his much longer work on domestic violence court, Winick draws on important psychological work on the therapeutic value of "opening up," and proposes the design of intake and other processing forms to enable domestic violence victims to write out a description of their victimization and associated trauma.

Then, Judge J. Richardson Johnson, of Kalamazoo, Michigan, explains how his court created a "duty judge" to handle matters that previously required the interruption of ongoing trials. Once these matters were, for efficiency, moved to the duty judge, they were no longer regarded as bothersome interruptions. Indeed, in a judicial climate already hospitable to therapeutic jurisprudence, these "matters" could now be seen not simply as "matters," but as real people with real problems, and the duty judge could now take on a more active, caring, problem-solving role.

In the final selection of the structural and administrative section, Connecticut Judge Carmen Lopez describes how a therapeutic jurisprudence approach enabled her to take an otherwise "legalistic" pretrial proceeding in the child welfare area and convert it into a therapeutically meaningful—and professionally rewarding—experience.

The Case for a Specialized
Domestic Violence Court
by Bruce J. Winick
(Excerpted from *Applying the Law Therapeutically in Domestic Violence Cases*, 69 UMKC L. REV. 33, 35–45, 87–90 (2000), Copyright 2000 by Bruce J. Winick, reprinted with permission).

Although police, prosecutorial, and judicial practices traditionally did not differentiate between stranger and domestic violence, there is an increasing tendency to treat domestic violence cases differently. Police and prosecutors often treated domestic violence complaints less seriously than incidents of stranger violence, declining to arrest or prosecute on the ground that these were private matters or on implicit sexist assumptions perpetuating the common law practice that husbands could beat their wives. Under the pressure of feminist reform efforts, which targeted domestic violence as an issue at or near the top of its political agenda, many of these practices have changed. Domestic violence is now taken more seriously by the legal system. There is increasing public awareness of domestic violence and its devastating consequences. Some jurisdictions have adopted mandatory arrest and mandatory prosecution policies. An increasing number of jurisdictions have established specialized domestic violence courts to deal with these cases. Virtually all jurisdictions now make domestic violence a crime, and many imposed penalties that are comparable to those available for serious criminal assaults.

Is it appropriate to treat domestic violence differently than stranger violence? Should these cases be dealt with in general criminal courts or specialized domestic violence courts? Are mandatory arrest or prosecution practices warranted for domestic violence, but not for stranger violence? Are comparable penalties warranted? I believe that it is appropriate to treat domestic violence differently. Even though there is evidence that people who commit domestic violence do not specialize, but rather commit a variety of other criminal offenses, the special repetitive nature of domestic violence and of the harm it brings warrants separate treatment. Unlike stranger violence, which tends to be a one-time incident from the victim's perspective, domestic violence tends to be an on-going course of behavior involving both violence and threats of violence. Stranger violence certainly can produce intense pain, terror, and psychological distress, but on-going domestic violence can have a significantly more serious impact on the victim. That the offender often lives with the victim presents an added level of danger that brings uniqueness to the crime. The possibility of subsequent abuse is ever present after the police have left the scene, after the defendant has been released from jail if arrested, and even after the issuance of a restraining order. Once stranger violence has occurred, it rarely will be repeated. With intimate violence, however, the victim may have to live under the constant fear of repeated abuse with ever escalating force, sometimes including deadly force.

In addition to its physical impact, domestic violence imposes significant psychological injuries to its victims that are long-lasting. Victims can develop a form of learned helplessness and experience the symptoms of post-traumatic stress disorder. Many experience diminished self-esteem and anxiety, depression, and despair. Moreover, intimate violence can often produce a shattering of the victim's ability to have future trusting relationships. These added psychological injuries justify treating domestic violence as an offense similar in severity to serious acts of stranger violence. They also justify adopting specialized police, prosecutorial, and judicial practices in this area. Treating domestic violence seriously provides a healthy signal to offenders that their conduct will not be tolerated and to victims that their suffering will not be ignored.

There are now more than 200 specialized domestic violence courts, and the number is growing. What are the benefits of such specialized courts? Because there is a high risk of repeated violence in domestic violence cases, dealing with these issues in a specialized domestic violence court can provide increased continuity, more effective monitoring, and a range of more flexible responses that can more effectively contain the risk of violence.

A specialized domestic violence court is an integrated system that can handle both civil protection orders and criminal domestic violence cases. In addition to its ability to allow for integrated adjudication of all issues related to the domestic violence occurring in a victim's environment, the court can address domestic violence from a community-wide perspective by incorporating into the judicial process referrals for counseling, batterers' intervention treatment programs, substance abuse programs, and other resources for victims, batterers, and their families. Domestic violence courts can thus constitute a comprehensive community response to domestic violence that integrates multiple services into a single court-based system. This multidisciplinary, comprehensive approach designed to promote both the rehabilitation of abusers and to assist victims to receive necessary services, can be seen as reflecting principles of therapeutic jurisprudence.

Such an integrated court can offer heightened responsiveness of the judicial system to individual domestic violence victims. For example, to attempt to alleviate the economic oppression that keeps many victims in an abusing relationship, the court can order and monitor the payment of child support. A fully integrated court can also deal with related issues such as paternity and divorce.

The intake unit of a specialized domestic violence court can effectively coordinate case management by linking the present case to any related case currently pending or subsequently filed. The availability of a central court able to process all issues related to the problem provides greater access to the judicial process for victims, particularly for the majority of them who will not have the assistance of counsel because of their economic status. Rather than dealing with issues on a piecemeal basis, specialized domestic violence court judges can develop expertise in dealing with all aspects of the domestic violence problem and can improve their ability in the adjudication and disposition of these difficult issues, a difficulty enhanced by the fact that many victims and perpetrators are unrepresented.

An integrated domestic violence court also can allow effective monitoring of conditions of probation for abusers and compliance with the terms of protection orders, including treatment orders. Judges who have entered orders restraining batterers or requiring them to do various things, accepted pleas that carry various conditions, or imposed sentences that include mandated treatment or other requirements can periodically monitor the perpetrator's compliance with the court's orders and make it clear to them that the court is serious and will enforce its rulings. This can greatly increase the ability of the court to hold perpetrators accountable and to increase their compliance with court orders and conditions.

Domestic violence court also allows a more timely response than is possible in the typically backlogged criminal court. Time often is of the essence in these cases, and the ability of the court to act quickly may make the difference between life and death. Moreover, specialized domestic violence courts can do much to raise community consciousness about the problem of domestic violence and to marshal community resources for dealing with its prevention and treatment. Having a domestic violence court can emphasize to the community both the seriousness with which the judicial process treats domestic violence and the dedication of the courts to dealing effectively with the problem. Rather than being merely adjudicatory, the domestic violence court can play a more proactive role, reaching out to both offenders and victims and stimulating community resources to deal with this devastating social problem. Instead of being merely a band-aid approach to the latest manifestation of violence, domestic violence court holds out the promise of dealing with the root of the problem, thereby avoiding what otherwise would be the high likelihood of repeated abuse. Moreover, the domestic violence court can function as an advocate for victims, assisting them in obtaining needed protective orders and to press criminal charges when appropriate and helping them to obtain access to needed services and resources.

In addition, a specialized domestic violence court can play an important role in the rehabilitation of offenders. Such an opportunity exists in cases in which offenders accept diversion or plead guilty and receive a probationary term that includes various conditions of probation, including participation in rehabilitative programs. The opportunity also exists in cases in which a variety of creative sentencing alternatives are utilized that include participation in rehabilitation.

* * *

Moreover, domestic violence courts can be structured in ways that can allow them to function as instruments of risk management. These courts can use tools like the Spousal Abuse Risk Assessment (SARA) Guide to collect information about the offender, and use this information in ways that facilitate police, prosecutorial, and judicial decision making and supervision and monitoring. These tools can increase the ability of the judicial process accurately to assess the risk of future violence, take appropriate steps to prevent it, and motivate the offender to learn ways of reducing the risk he presents.

* * *

Thus there are many advantages to the use of specialized domestic violence courts. These specialized courts are able to play a more effective role in the rehabilitation of offenders and the healing of their victims. The special role played by the judge in such courts, as well as the court's function in preventing future domestic violence and in dealing directly with the rehabilitation of abusers, makes these courts a more effective vehicle for dealing with the problem in a comprehensive way than would be possible in the criminal court. These courts thus can apply principles of therapeutic jurisprudence to deal more responsively and effectively with the problem of domestic violence.

Although there are many advantages to the use of specialized domestic violence courts rather than generalized criminal courts in the processing of domestic violence cases, there may be one disadvantage. Criminal court judges process a great variety of criminal matters, while domestic violence courts will only see domestic violence offenses. As a result, domestic violence court judges will develop an expertise in the area of domestic violence, reading the literature in this area, understanding the treatment approaches and how they work, and observing similarities in the thousands of victims and batterers that will come before them. Their institutional role also will often make such judges advocates for the plight of domestic violence victims at community meetings, schools, and government and legislative sessions. This expertise and institutional role is likely to produce in many domestic violence court judges an identification with the domestic violence victim that might adversely affect their ability to be fair and impartial adjudicators of cases in which the issue of domestic violence is contested.

While the overwhelming majority of domestic violence perpetrators will plead guilty or seek diversion, some will wish to contest their charges and to demand the fair trial that our Constitution guarantees. In such cases, domestic violence court judges will need to switch modes and remember and respect the presumption of innocence that attaches to all criminal defendants. In adjudicating criminal cases and civil disputes about restraining orders, domestic violence court judges must put aside their rehabilitative and advocacy roles and give fair and impartial consideration to the evidence presented. To the extent that a domestic violence court judge has become jaded and cynical about those accused of domestic violence or has over-identified with the perspective of the domestic violence victim in ways that prevent him or her from being a fair adjudicator, it may be time to request a transfer from domestic violence court to a court of general jurisdiction. Indeed, there may be some wisdom in rotating domestic violence court judges (and judges in other specialized courts) after a period of service in order to avoid these kinds of problems. With this caveat, however, one that most judges will be able to understand and respond to, the advantages of having specialized domestic violence courts rather than generalized criminal courts deal with domestic violence cases are significant.

* * *

Several important considerations suggest that domestic violence cases should be dealt with in specialized domestic violence courts rather than in generalized criminal courts. These courts can deal more effectively and efficiently with the range of problems presented by domestic violence, act with a heightened sensitivity to the needs of domestic violence victims, and stimulate community resources toward the prevention and treatment of battering and the increased provision of services to their victims, including their children who may have witnessed their abuse. They can play a more effective role in the monitoring and supervision of batterer's compliance with protective orders and attendance at treatment programs. Through increased use of risk assessment tools, they can become courts which manage and reduce the risk of violence that batterers present, thereby not merely punishing abuse, but preventing its reoccurrence.

A number of important considerations thus argue for the use of specialized domestic violence courts in this area. With more than 200 such courts now in existence, and the number growing, there seems to be a movement in the direction of domestic violence courts. But against their many advantages, including therapeutic jurisprudence considerations relating to the rehabilitation of the offender and the well-being of the victim, must be weighed the possible disadvantages of this approach. Because they use an expanded array of judicial personnel, and involved judges in the time-consuming business of monitoring compliance and rehabilitative efforts, they undoubtedly are more costly than generalized criminal courts. This article makes no attempt to assess the relative costs of these two approaches. How much more expensive are they, and are the added costs worth the benefits such specialized courts might bring? Do such courts increase the rehabilitation of offenders, decrease recidivism, and improve the healing of victims, as this article suggests? What is their impact on community attitudes and behavior concerning violence in the home? Do they respond more effectively and efficiently to domestic violence cases than would criminal courts? Will their approach help to prevent domestic violence more so than would the simple punishment approach of the criminal court? Can judges playing the new roles called for in domestic violence courts also be fair and impartial adjudicators in resolving contested issues in domestic violence cases? Can domestic violence court judges help offenders and victims without doing so in a paternalistic manner? These are all important empirical issues that need further examination. More studies should be funded of existing domestic violence courts so that we can better understand their operations and successes and failures. Thus, although strong arguments support specialized domestic violence courts, a number of questions remain that need further exploration.

To suggest that domestic violence courts should apply principles and practices of therapeutic jurisprudence is not to suggest that domestic violence courts should emphasize considerations of rehabilitation over those of punishment. It would be a mistake if domestic violence courts were thought of as "soft on crime." Domestic violence is a serious offense, more serious than many acts of stranger violence. As a result, both punishment and rehabilitation are appropriate. The traditional punishment approach applied to domestic violence "did little to discourage violence in the home." While traditional criminal courts could do little more than convict and punish offenders, domestic violence courts can play a significant role in the rehabilitation of abusers and in the management of the risk they present. There has been a traditional debate between those contending that courts should take a punitive approach in domestic violence cases and those advocating a rehabilitative approach. But this is a false dichotomy. Domestic violence courts should be both punitive, sentencing domestic violence offenders to incarceration when appropriate, and rehabilitative, motivating them to enter batterer's intervention programs and supervising and monitoring their compliance in ways that can more effectively produce positive results.

The debate over the propriety of diversion in the domestic violence context exemplifies this punishment versus rehabilitation debate. Should diversion be permitted in domestic violence cases? Some jurisdictions authorize diversion, in which charges ultimately will be dismissed upon successful completion of a batterer's intervention program, but others do not use diversion on the ground that it minimizes the seriousness of the offense. Because diversion allows the offender to avoid conviction and incarceration, it should be reserved for those cases in which the seriousness of the violence does not warrant criminal confinement. Prosecutors and judges should exercise discretion to limit diversion in this way. Diversion should not be considered altogether off limits. It can be a helpful tool to motivate offenders into accepting treatment who might not otherwise do so. This has been the experience in the Miami-Dade Domestic Violence Court. Many abusers who are indigent accept diversion to a batterer's intervention program at the court intake level and before counsel is assigned to represent them. Many of them benefit from treatment and become rehabilitated. Were diversion unavailable, however, these offenders would be appointed counsel, who might then encourage a plea of not guilty rather than acceptance of rehabilitation. Counsel who do so, without fully exploring with their clients the option of diversion and rehabilitation, would be making a mistake, at least in cases in which the client's guilt is not genuinely in question.

The diversion option holds out a good chance for rehabilitation for offenders motivated to change their attitudes and behavior. Not all clients will be so motivated, and those who, after consultation with counsel about their options choose to plead not guilty and take their chances at trial, have every right to do so, and counsel must and should respect such decisions. But those who are motivated for change can derive real benefits from a form of judicially supervised participation in a rehabilitation program. The reality of facing a trial for a domestic violence offense for which conviction and a prison sentence seem likely can cause a batterer to confront his cognitive distortions about his battering behavior and provide an opportunity for him to undergo a positive cognitive restructuring concerning his attitudes about violence in the home. Moreover, those who are not offered the diversion option and plead not guilty and stand trial may find the experience of doing so to reinforce their cognitive distortions. In addition, they may experience a form of cognitive dissonance that may make rehabilitation as part of their sentence more difficult.

Thus, diversion might allow many more abusers to enter into treatment and to benefit from it than might occur in a jurisdiction that does not permit diversion. If diversion is used judiciously in ways that do not diminish the seriousness of the offense or undermine the interests of the victim, it can be a useful tool in the fight against domestic violence. Even when diversion is not formally available in a jurisdiction, the trial judge can motivate defendants to accept an informal kind of diversion in which probation or more lenient sentences are made available for defendants who enter into treatment programs and succeed in their rehabilitative efforts.

Domestic violence courts present a blend of punitive and rehabilitative approaches for domestic violence, and hold out the hope of helping batterers to adopt more pro-social attitudes and behaviors. Their ability to supervise and monitor compliance with program attendance and performance provides a rich therapeutic opportunity for judge-offender interactions that themselves can help to reduce recidivism. Such courts can hold status conferences to monitor treatment progress, commending offenders who are doing well and sanctioning those who are not much in the way that drug treatment court judges act to assist substance abusers in ending their addictions. Such monitoring with judicial interaction can occur in cases in which the defendant accepts diversion, is sentenced to probation, or is sentenced to incarceration followed by attendance at a rehabilitative program. While more empirical work is needed to verify the effectiveness of such judicial supervision and encouragement in the treatment process, there is reason to believe that it holds great therapeutic value in the rehabilitation of the offender. In these ways, domestic violence courts can function as treatment courts, applying principles of therapeutic jurisprudence to assist both batterers and victims alike.

Domestic violence courts also increase the potential that the legal response to domestic violence can truly help the victim. By playing a leadership and coordinating role within the community, such courts increase the availability of resources for helping victims and rehabilitating offenders, and can have an important impact on the way that police, prosecutors, and court personnel act toward the victim. Whether or not jurisdictions adopt specialized domestic violence courts, they need to design processes that are more focused on the needs and interests of the victim. Police, prosecutors, and court officials need extra training in interpersonal skills, counseling skills, communication skills, and the ability to convey sympathy and empathy. In their interaction with victims in particular, these officials need to be more psychologically minded, conveying a sense of caring toward the victim that can have enormous therapeutic value for her.

* * *

Key References
Casey, Pamela and David B. Rottman, Therapeutic Jurisprudence and the Emergence of Problem Solving Courts, Nat'l Inst. Just. J. 13 (July 1999).

Fritzler, Randal B. and Leonore M. J. Simon, Creating a Domestic Violence Court: Combat in the Trenches, 37 Ct. Rev. 28 (Spring, 2000).

Karan, Amy et al., Domestic Violence Courts: What Are They and How Should We Manage Them?, Juv. & Fam. Ct. J. 71 (Spring, 1999).

Tsai, Betsy, Note, The Trend Toward Specialized Domestic Violence Courts: Improvements on an Effective Innovation, 68 Fordham L. Rev. 1285 (2000).

A Unified Family Court
by Barbara A. Babb

Family law cases focus on some of the most intimate, emotional, and all-encompassing aspects of parties' personal lives. The volume and scope of family law cases exacerbate the difficulty of their resolution. Family law cases comprise approximately thirty-five percent of the total number of civil cases handled by the majority of our nation's courts, and they constitute the largest and fastest growing part of the civil caseload. The situation is complicated due to the large volume of unrepresented family law litigants, most of whom cannot secure private counsel or free legal services, as well as the duplicative, time-consuming nature of the family court process. These problems have triggered the need for court reform in family law.

I have advocated for the creation of unified family courts, or courts that coordinate the work of independent agencies and tribunals, each with some limited role in resolving the controversies incident to a family's legal matters. I define a unified family court to consist of the following components: a specialized court structure that is either a separate court or a division of an existing court and that is established at the same level and receives the same resources and support as a generalist court; comprehensive subject-matter jurisdiction over the full range of family law cases, including juvenile delinquency and child welfare; a case management and case processing system that includes early and hands-on contact with each family law case and a judicial assignment system that results in the family appearing before one judge for the completion of the case or one case management team; an array of court-supplied or court-connected social services to address litigants' non-legal problems that contribute to the exacerbation of family law problems; and a user-friendly court that is accessible to all family law litigants, including the large volume of pro se litigants. In addition to these components, I have advocated that unified family courts embrace the notions of therapeutic jurisprudence and an ecological, holistic approach to the family's problems. By adopting the goal of therapeutic jurisprudence, I have sought to provide a model version or blueprint for a court which most accurately portrays the concept of and the purpose behind a unified family court.

To address the special needs of families who present themselves to the court system, therapeutic jurisprudence assists the court to understand how it must intervene in the lives of families. I have argued that it is intrinsic to the family law decision-making process that intervention ought to aim to improve the participants' underlying behavior or situation, a therapeutic consequence.

Resolving legal disputes with the aim of improving the lives of families and children requires structuring the court system to enhance the system's potential to maximize the therapeutic benefits of court intervention. To accomplish this goal, the court system must allow for the contemplation of alternative legal outcomes intended to produce more effective functioning on the part of families and children. As I have said before, in the field of family law, therapeutic jurisprudence should strive to protect families and children from present and future harms, to reduce emotional turmoil, to promote family harmony or preservation, and to provide individualized and efficient, effective family justice. Adopting therapeutic jurisprudence as the goal of a model family law adjudicatory system requires careful consideration of the therapeutic implications resulting from all aspects of the court process and encourages the discovery of creative ways to resolve family conflicts effectively.

I have argued that the field of family law appropriately lends itself to adjudication within a specialized court, either as a separate court or as an autonomous division or department of an existing trial court. In addition, judges assigned to specialized family courts must be informed about relevant social science literature, including child development and family dynamics, and about how that knowledge applies to family law decision-making. In this manner, resolutions should promote more effectively the well-being of families and children and should occur more efficiently, both therapeutic outcomes.

For the family court to coordinate multiple legal issues involving the same family and to monitor and enforce family court orders, a fundamental principle of any model unified family court must be the exercise of comprehensive subject-matter jurisdiction over the full range of family law matters. These often interrelated matters include divorce or dissolution, marital property, separation, annulment, child custody, visitation, child support, paternity, child abuse and neglect, termination of parental rights, adoption, domestic violence, juvenile delinquency, guardianships, mental health matters, legal-medical issues, emancipation, and name change. The potential to resolve completely a family's related legal problems becomes a therapeutic consequence; this outcome enables the participants to experience a sense of completion and to move forward with their lives, rather than remaining anchored to the court system by various unresolved legal issues.

Any delay in processing and resolving family law cases interferes with a therapeutic outcome for individuals and families, particularly in child-related cases, as the delay allows the families' problems to remain unresolved and potentially to escalate. Attempts must occur to decrease delay in case processing by focusing on improving the court's case management functions. Because parties in family law disputes generally seek a resolution of highly-charged, emotional matters, a therapeutic approach to structure court reform requires that these cases receive active, hands-on case management as early as possible. This type of case processing can result in more therapeutic outcomes for family law litigants by reducing the court's delay in attending to the families' problems and by linking the families as early as possible with appropriate social services.

Further, I have argued that one judge should preside over a family's case from start to finish. Ongoing involvement with a family's legal matters enables a judge to develop a more complete understanding of the comprehensive nature of the family's legal problems and permits judges to fashion more effective outcomes to resolve a family's problems, another therapeutic consequence.

A model unified family court also must have available an array of social services it can offer families to assist court professionals' understanding of the context of a family's legal problems and to address effectively social and psychological issues related to the family's functioning. Unified family courts must allow decision-makers the opportunity to understand the reasons for behavior underlying a particular family's situation, such as substance abuse involvement or mental health issues. This informed decision-making enables a judge to fashion a creative resolution to the family problem and contributes to a court system that is therapeutic in its treatment of the family. The nature of the services courts can offer varies widely and depends upon the needs of the community served by the court. Further, while the court can choose to offer some of the services itself, a more fiscally prudent option is to link the family with needed services that already exist within community agencies and organizations. Finally, the earlier participants in family law cases receive necessary services, the more likely it will be that the particular family experiences fewer problems later — another therapeutic outcome.

The final component critical to a unified family court blueprint is the notion that the court remain accessible to and user-friendly for the participants, including the large proportion of pro se family law litigants. The mechanisms to achieve this result range from new information technologies, such as computerized kiosks that disseminate prepared legal forms, to the creation of a new service paradigm in the justice system. Implementing this new paradigm involves designing court structures for the convenience of the users and training court personnel to treat litigants with courtesy and civility, all therapeutic outcomes.

While there is no one ideal court design adaptable for every jurisdiction engaged in addressing systemic family law adjudication problems, family law court reform must proceed with a specific vision. The application of a therapeutic framework to proposed family law adjudicatory system reform is a blueprint critical to the construction of any court, as this approach empowers courts to render family justice that promotes the participants' well-being. More effective resolution of family legal matters can strengthen individuals' and families' functioning, a benefit to the entire society.

References

Babb, Barbara A. "An Interdisciplinary Approach to Family Law Jurisprudence: Application of an Ecological and Therapeutic Perspective," 72 Indiana Law Journal 775 (1997).

Babb, Barbara A. "Fashioning an Interdisciplinary Framework for Court Reform in Family Law: A Blueprint to Construct a Unified Family Court," 71 Southern California Law Review 469 (1998).

Babb, Barbara A. "Where We Stand: An Analysis of America's Family Law Adjudicatory Systems and the Mandate to Establish Unified Family Courts," 32 Family Law Quarterly 31 (1998).

Babb, Barbara A. "Where We Stand Redux: Another Look at America's Family Law Adjudicatory Systems," 35 Family Law Quarterly 627 (2002).

A Unified Drug Court

by Judge Peggy F. Hora, Judge William G. Schma,
and John T. A. Rosenthal
(Excerpted from *Therapeutic Jurisprudence and the Drug
Treatment Court Movement: Revolutionizing the Criminal Justice
System's Response to Drug Abuse and Crime in America*,
74 Notre Dame L. Rev. 439, 471–477 (1999), Copyright 1999
by Judge Peggy F. Hora, Judge William G. Schma &
John T.A. Rosenthal, reprinted with permission).

In most jurisdictions, DTCs do not adjudicate other types of criminal cases, nor do they handle civil cases of any sort. This important feature allows a jurisdiction's DTC to concentrate its efforts on administering the treatment program in a hands-on manner. Those jurisdictions that do not have the caseload to support a full-time DTC have created DTCs that hold court less frequently. In Kalamazoo, Michigan, the DTC holds court every Friday, but reverts to a traditional court setting the rest of the week. This setup allows the court to administer and supervise treatment of addicts without devoting unnecessary assets to this method of adjudication. The common denominator among all of these variations of DTCs is the practice of only adjudicating DTC cases when the DTC is in session.

In accordance with their therapeutic focus, DTCs may operate as a single entity, a "unified drug court." In a unified drug court, "only one" means that only one court with one judge adjudicates and monitors all the cases screened and all the offenders admitted to the treatment program. This important component of the DTC concept provides the court with structural accountability, both to the agencies and personnel administering the court and treatment program, and to the offender in treatment. "In a structurally accountable system, participating agencies share program effectiveness, with each participant directly linked to, dependent on, and responsible to the others." Following this theme of structural accountability, the DTC "judge and court personnel [including the prosecutor and defense counsel] are [usually] assigned for at least a one-year term" to provide both the court and the defendant with continuity and accountability throughout the treatment process.

The personnel assignment process underscores the structural accountability of the DTC. Structural accountability means that DTC personnel and their respective agencies take responsibility for the success or failure of an offender to complete the treatment program. The DTC builds this accountability into the structure of the treatment process because the DTC is soley responsible for the defendant and the program. In utilizing a therapeutic approach to adjudicating certain drug-offense crimes, "[t]he court process actually becomes part of the treatment." "By the structure it provides—by establishing a separate [but connected]...specialized court," DTCs lead offenders "through the treatment process."

Through providing a single DTC, the system does not force defendants to shuttle from courtroom to courtroom and defense counsel to defense counsel over a period of months, attending hearing after hearing. Under the DTC system, the defendant confronts a single judge and DTC team who become intimately familiar with the defendant and her drug and other problems. This DTC team will hold the defendant accountable for her actions during the course of treatment and reinforce one another in actions taken to ensure that the defendant stays in treatment whenever possible and appropriate. DTCs abandon the traditional adjudication process which may slowly wind its way from arraignment to preliminary hearing, pretrial hearing, and trial, and involve many judges, defense counsel, and prosecutors. This traditional structure conflicts with the therapeutic foundation of the DTC, and * * * may actually reinforce or facilitate addictive behavior.

* * *

The fact that only one judge will deal with the offender's case through frequent, mandatory court appearances allows the judge and offender to develop "an ongoing, working relationship." This one-on-one relationship tends to facilitate honesty through familiarity and permits the DTC judge to become "a powerful motivator for the offender's rehabilitation." The judge, using the power and authority of the court, provides the addict with the incentive to stay in treatment, while the treatment provider concentrates on the treatment process itself. Without judicial leadership involving active monitoring of an offender's recovery, a DTC would not work. "Rather than moralize about an addict's character flaws, the judge must assume, according to [Judge] Tauber, 'the role of confessor, task master, cheerleader, and mentor.'"

Monitoring Treatment Provision and Progress
By Judge Peggy F. Hora, Judge William G. Schma,
and John T. A. Rosenthal
(Excerpted from *Therapeutic Jurisprudence and the Drug Treatment
Court Movement: Revolutionizing the Criminal Justice System's
Response to Drug Abuse and Crime in America*,
74 NOTRE DAME L. REV. 439, 524–525 (1999), Copyright 1999
by Judge Peggy F. Hora, Judge William G. Schma &
John T.A. Rosenthal, reprinted with permission).

Despite the fact that the DTC judge plays such a large part in the entire DTC process and represents the power of the court, tensions between the treatment providers and the DTC judge may erode the judge's ability to maintain control of a given case. Because DTC participants may have more frequent contact with treatment providers than the DTC judge, the judge may lack the requisite information to withdraw court support from a treatment program, modify an individual's program, or terminate someone's participation in the program. This problem requires a two-pronged solution consisting of (1) judicial oversight of treatment providers and treatment programs and (2) accurate, readily available information about an individual's "treatment progress status."

Judicial involvement is a cornerstone of the DTC process. The cooperative and collaborative nature of the relationship between the DTC judge and treatment providers is an essential component of the judge's oversight role. Without this kind of relationship, the DTC judge can easily lose control of the treatment process. * * * The Miami DTC has experienced the problem of ineffective judicial oversight of treatment providers and treatment programs.

For two years, state prosecutors…quietly conducted a criminal investigation of Drug Court. They looked into allegations that some court-approved halfway house operators stole money from Drug Court defendants and put them in substandard housing.

Although prosecutors did not have enough evidence to bring charges, they concluded that "prostitution and narcotics trafficking" took place at the halfway houses.

This chain of events in Miami may be an anomaly, but it represents a clear and ever present threat to the DTC concept. While a majority of the treatment process takes place outside of the courthouse, this situation does not relieve the judge of the responsibility of ensuring that the drug court participants receive proper treatment. One remedy may be to create an in-house treatment provider in the jurisdiction.

The second prong of the solution to implementing judicial control of the DTC process involves information management. The DTC judge who does not have up-to-date information about a participant's treatment progress cannot apply the proper smart punishment or rewards which the DTC process requires. The introduction of computers into the courtroom seems to provide the solution to the problem of accurate, timely information. Computer networking systems coupled with software specifically designed for DTCs give the judge and all the DTC participants near real-time information about a participant's treatment progress. Although existing software may be utilized, some jurisdictions have experienced problems sharing data between departments that have different software. Fortunately, this problem can and has been cured through new software.

Being at the center of the process, the DTC judge must attempt to overcome these administrative and supervisory problems in a manner that does not affect the quality of justice or treatment within her court—no simple task in an era of shrinking budgets and expanding dockets. But despite these problems, judges still find DTCs a more effective method of dealing with certain classes of drug abusers in our criminal justice system. In many instances, judges who previously suffered from "burnout" from the apparent futility of dealing with addicted criminal defendants by traditional methods of adjudication have found themselves rejuvenated as DTC judges. In the words of one DTC judge, "Just do it."

Promoting Vicarious Learning through Case Calendaring

by Judge Peggy F. Hora, Judge William G. Schma,
and John T. A. Rosenthal
(Excerpted from *Therapeutic Jurisprudence and the Drug
Treatment Court Movement: Revolutionizing the Criminal Justice
System's Response to Drug Abuse and Crime in America*,
74 Notre Dame L. Rev. 439, 474–475 (1999), Copyright 1999
by Judge Peggy F. Hora, Judge William G. Schma &
John T.A. Rosenthal, reprinted with permission).

DTCs (Drug Treatment Courts) design the courtroom process itself to reinforce the defendant's treatment. The court may set up its daily calendar so that "first-time participants appearing in Drug Court...are the last items on the session calendar. This gives them an opportunity to see the entire program in action, and know exactly what awaits them if they become a participant." The DTC may handle program graduates first in order to impart a sense of hope to the new and continuing program participants who may experience hopelessness at the beginning of the process. The court may then devote the next portion of the calendar to defendants who enter the court in custody. This procedure is designed to convey to all DTC participants the serious nature of the court and the gravity of the defendant's situation. This demonstrates that a violation of DTC rules may not get a defendant ejected from the program, but the court may use jail time as a form of "smart punishment" to get the defendant to conform to treatment protocol. Those DTCs that do not have treatment facilities in their jails recognize that incarceration represents a break in treatment for the individual. However, the shock of incarceration may serve to break down the person's denial of her addiction. Finally, the court handles the cases involving new defendants who wish to enter the DTC program. All of these procedures are founded on the therapeutic ideal that every aspect of a DTC can and does have a powerful impact on the success of the defendant in treatment.

The Healing Potential of Intake and Processing Forms

by Bruce J. Winick
(Excerpted from *Applying the Law Therapeutically in Domestic Violence Cases*, 69 UMKC L. Rev. 33, 64 (2000), Copyright 2000 by Bruce J. Winick, reprinted with permission).

To the extent that victims suffer from a form of post-traumatic stress disorder, police, judicial, and legal proceedings should encourage them to "open up" about their experiences and how they feel about them. This could be accomplished by designing intake and other processing forms to enable victims to write out a description of what occurred to them and what feelings they experienced. At a minimum, victims should be encouraged to do this on a voluntary basis and told that such descriptions will be helpful for improving police and judicial proceedings in these cases, for public understanding of these problems, and for helping other victims. Such written descriptions should be shared with other victims and the public on an anonymous basis, and the victim should be assured of privacy in this respect. Psychologist John Pennebaker, in his book *Opening Up*, has shown that people suffering a variety of traumas including war-trauma, natural disasters, or being victims of crime or accidental injury gain significant psychological benefits from telling their stories to others, particularly if in writing. Legal proceedings in the domestic violence context should thus encourage such opening up by the victim whenever possible. For example, when police, prosecutors, and court officials interview a victim who seems reluctant to tell her full story and ambivalent about her abuser, getting her to describe how she feels about him may assist her to begin the process of detaching from him or of reflecting critically on the relationship.

Key References

Pennebaker, James W., Opening Up: The Healing Power of Confiding in Others (1990).

Pennebaker, James W., *et al.*, *Disclosing and Sharing Emotion: Psychological, Social and Health Consequences, in* Handbook on Bereavement Research: Consequences, Coping, and Care (M.S. Stroebe, *et al*, eds., 2001).

Stephani, A.J., *Introduction-Symposium: Therapeutic Jurisprudence and the Importance of Expression in the Law,* 3 Fla. Coastal L.J. 113 (2002).

The Therapeutic Potential of a Duty Judge

by Judge J. Richardson Johnson

As a judge, one of the joys of the job is the serendipitous opportunity to help people and encourage a good outcome. The opportunities can arise at unexpected times and places. They can also be the unintended consequence of other changes. Therapeutic Jurisprudence can provide a framework to address such opportunities. Here is an example.

I was introduced to "therapeutic jurisprudence" by my colleague, Honorable William G. Schma, of the Kalamazoo County, Michigan Circuit Court. Bill was an early and enthusiastic convert. He is also adept at proselytizing, constantly encouraging others to use this approach. Bill recognizes each contact with a person in court is an opportunity. I have witnessed examples of him using an arraignment to directly address a defendant's serious addiction issues. This may be the best opportunity for an "intervention." My own approach leaned toward the more traditional, but I was also open to exploring a judge's therapeutic role.

As a traditional judge, one of my longstanding interests is case management. I sit in a court of general jurisdiction that, until several years ago, addressed civil, felony and domestic cases. Michigan courts have been going through a process of court consolidation. Through legislative change, our court and another were, in effect, merged to add a Family Court. One result was domestic cases moving into the Family Division, leaving civil and felony cases to be addressed in a Trial Division. As Presiding Judge of the Trial Division, I was involved in reworking our case management plan to address the changing case load. Out of this process, we adopted the "Duty Judge" concept. On a rotating basis, the duty judge handled a duty week, which involved arraignments, probation violation proceedings and other short matters — essentially the "walk-in" business that our courts had previously addressed during trial recesses. One disadvantage of addressing arraignments during recesses was they tended to be seen as interruptions and something to be quickly handled. In other words, the focus tended to be on the process, so we could get back to the jurors who were waiting and the litigants and attorneys who likewise viewed the delays for these activities as an intrusion on their trial.

The duty judge was instituted essentially to address scheduling concerns, but it turned out to yield unexpected, positive opportunities to provide a better quality of justice. Inadvertantly, we had created time for therapeutic jurisprudence. Duty week gave the duty judges an opportunity to interact with the people in front of them as fellow human beings who were worried, angry and often still coming down from their high or hangover. The judges began to comment favorably on their time spent during duty week. Judges in trial appreciated uninterrupted proceedings, just focusing on the trial at hand.

The following experience helps illustrate the type of opportunity that now presented itself. One duty morning, a defendant came in my courtroom to offer a guilty plea on a third drunk driving offense, a felony in Michigan. She had been scheduled to present her plea the day before, but did not show up. She was given until the next day to come in or a bench warrant would be issued for her arrest. She came in. As she was going through the plea taking process, I began to notice that she kept her hand by her mouth and her attorney was stepping a bit away from her. Suspicions started to percolate in my mind. Then the assistant prosecutor walked over to her vicinity and then to the judicial aide, who passed me a note that the prosecutor was suspicious the defendant had been drinking. Before duty week, I am not certain what I would have done with the information, but I may have chosen to "look the other way," recognizing that directly confronting the defendant was likely to significantly delay getting back to a trial (and a waiting jury). That morning I had the time and I asked the question: "Have you been drinking?" The answer was yes, and meant that she was in violation of a bond condition requiring that she not consume alcohol.

I believe the defendant's attorney recognized it was in his client's best interest to get in a treatment program. He could tell I would be supportive of such a result. Likewise, the assistant prosecutor was supportive. Judge Schma had initiated drug court programs in our court, so the Sheriff's Department, prosecutor, defense attorneys, probation agents and staff have a general understanding of the drug court process and philosophy. This helped set the stage for their willing assistance, and for a probationary sentence.

Thus far the defendant has been successful on probation. It is not possible to know what the course would have been if I, and others, had not seized an opportunity to intervene. I do know that the course we took brought about a result that was far more satisfying than going through the regular routines and "processing cases." Those involved in the effort have found some satisfaction in the results and are, I believe, more open to following that path in the future.

So, how do you get time to do therapeutic jurisprudence? Make a conscience decision to seize the therapeutic opportunity, but have a framework to utilize. Therapeutic jurisprudence need not be a "set aside" program like a drug court. The concepts can be applied during any regular proceeding. There can be unexpected opportunities for therapeutic jurisprudence based upon making other decisions on issues like case management.

Every day judges, and all who work with the courts, have opportunities to apply a type of justice that treats those who appear in court as persons: worthy of respect, in need of help and worth helping. Be alert—you never know when or how you will have the chance to make a difference in someone's life.

Judicial Pre-Trials in Child Protection Cases
by Judge Carmen L. Lopez

There is no question that the petition to terminate the parental rights a mother or father have to their child is one that is charged with an assortment of emotions as well as legal challenges. Because the Supreme Court has repeatedly held that the interest of parents in their children is a fundamental constitutional right that "undeniably warrants deference and, absent a powerful countervailing interest, protection,"[1] a petition to terminate this fundamental right is "a most serious and sensitive judicial action."[2]

When the state intrudes in the life of a family it must have a compelling reason. Certainly the protection of children from neglect and abuse has long been recognized as a compelling enough reason. However, before a court can permanently sever the parent child relationship, it must have "clear and convincing evidence"[3] that the State has made reasonable efforts to reunify the child with the parents and that one of the statutory grounds exists. In addition, the State must prove with clear and convincing evidence that the termination is in the child's best interests.

Once a petition to terminate parental rights has been filed in the Superior Court, the parties are expected to be ready to proceed with a trial. Given the enormous difficulties experienced by most of the players in this process, it may take over a year from the filing of a petition to reach the actual trial day. There are a myriad of reasons for the delay. In some instances the trial is delayed because the parents have not remained in touch with their attorneys and the attorneys have been unable to prepare for a trial. On other occasions the delay is due to the lack of preparation by one of the attorneys or parties in the case, resulting in an act of injustice should the trial proceed as scheduled without a continuance. In other instances, the parties have informed the court that settlement negotiations are in progress and should be allowed to proceed to conclusion. Factors that can also significantly contribute to the delay include congested court dockets and the need to effectively use judicial resources. And, unfortunately, some cases fall through the cracks.

If a case does proceed to a fully contested trial, it can and usually does take somewhere between one full day of trial to several weeks of trial. In addition, once the trial is concluded, the court must issue a written decision detailing the basis for its decision. This decision must be filed within 120 days after the close of evidence.[4] If an appeal is taken, the case proceeds through the appellate court which can also be a lengthy process. It is not unusual for a case that is tried to become final after the expiration of 18 to 24 months from the filing of the petition.

In addition to the use of the legal systems' limited resources, a fully contested trial uses the very limited resources of the child protection agency. Overworked and overburdened social workers are required to sit in court instead of tending to the needs of their clients. This usually means that many of the children in foster homes are not being visited by their workers and many of the necessary reports and studies which courts need to make timely decisions are not being filed. This of course compromises the best interests of many of the children in the system.

It is important that we not forget that the emotional resources of the parents are also tremendously used in these cases. Although it is not as easy to quantify the use of emotional resources as it is with monetary resources, it is still important that these resources be considered as the process of terminating parental rights is examined. The reported cases clearly show that many of the court involved families are suffering from untreated and/or under-treated mental illness, substance and alcohol abuse. Under these circumstances, it is clear that using the very limited emotional resources of parents to attempt to defend their "fundamental rights to their children" leaves most of them depleted, drained and at risk of further emotional and physical harm. Many of the parents involved with child protection services live at or below the poverty line. There is sufficient information and research to establish that living in poverty deprives a person of many of the basic opportunities available to those not living under the same circumstances.[5]

These are some of the reasons why finding alternative ways to resolve disputes in the child protection area is critical. Connecticut, like many other states has been searching for ways to improve this process so as to enhance the delivery of the product often referred to as justice. In its effort to better serve the people of the state, the court system has undergone significant changes within the last 25 years.

An area of change that has significantly impacted child protection cases is the merger of all courts into one court of original jurisdiction.[6] That court is known as the Superior Court.[7] "The Superior Court is divided into four divisions—Housing, Civil, Criminal, and Family. The court for Juvenile Matters is part of the Family Division. Juvenile Matters handles all proceedings involving juveniles who are delinquent, or from families with service needs. It also processes cases concerning neglect, dependency, emancipation and termination of parental rights."[8] The Juvenile Matters division of Connecticut processed over 5,000 cases in the year 2001.

For a variety of reasons, a tremendous backlog of cases has accumulated and has resulted in tremendous delays in resolving cases. In response to this backlog, a special session of the superior court known as the Child Protection Session was created. "In February, 1996, this special statewide session of the superior court for juvenile matters was established to provide for the timely trial of termination of parental rights cases from all regional juvenile matters sessions of the state. The impetus behind the session was to provide continuous trial dates for such cases and to ease the burden of the other sessions to handle their regular dockets.... The failure of the court system to provide for timely trials was highlighted in a court improvement study completed by the National Child Welfare Resource Center of the Muskie Institute in Maine as well as the fact that Connecticut was failing to finalize termination cases. At that time, less than 150 adoptions a year were being completed."[9]

The Judicial Department established this special session of the Superior Court in the Middlesex County Courthouse in the City of Middletown (literally in the middle of the state). The courthouse is a magnificent and very spacious building overlooking the Connecticut River. It has the space necessary to accommodate a judge to hear complex and lengthy termination of parental rights trials as well as cases involving the emergency removal of children. The idea was that one judge would be assigned to preside exclusively over these cases. As can be expected, the docket of cases grew so quickly that another judge was soon assigned to the session. It presently stands at four full time judges hearing only those cases that have already been determined (by a judge in the local referring court) to be long, complex and in need of a trial.

Notwithstanding the creation of a specialized session to hear complex and lengthy trials, cases are still pending for far longer than is desired, especially in view of the statutory mandate of protecting the best interests of children. One method that has addressed that issue and met with success in the child protection session is the judicial pre-trial incorporating and applying the legal theory known as Therapeutic Jurisprudence (TJ). TJ "is the study of the law as a therapeutic agent. It focuses on the law's impact on emotional life and on psychological well-being."[10] "It is a perspective that regards the law (rules of law, legal procedures, and roles of legal actors) itself as a social force that often produces therapeutic or anti-therapeutic consequences."[11]

Black's Law Dictionary defines a pre-trial as "an informal meeting at which opposing attorneys confer, usually with the judge, to work toward the disposition of the case by discussing matters of evidence and narrowing the issues that will be tried. The conference takes place shortly before trial and ordinarily results in a pretrial order." Connecticut Practice Book Sec. 35a-2, effective January 1, 2003, addresses judicial pre-trials within the child protection context. Subsection (c) of this section consists of a list of seven matters that attorneys and pro se parties must be prepared to discuss with the judge. They include, settlement; simplification and narrowing of the issues; amendments to the pleadings; the setting of firm trial dates; such other actions as may aid in the disposition of the case; identification of necessary arrangements for trial including, but not limited to, habeas for incarcerated parents, DCF transportation, interpreters and special equipment. In Subsection (d) of this section, the judicial authority is authorized "to issue a trial management order including, but not limited to, an order fixing a date prior to trial by which all parties are to exchange proposed witness and exhibit lists and copies of proposed exhibits not previously exchanged."

A judicial pre-trial utilizing TJ will discuss all of the matters as required by the practice book. It will, however, also include an invitation by the judge to the attorneys *and the parties*,[12] to meet with the judge outside of the presence of the opposing counsel and/or party. Since children who are the subject of the petitions are not present in court unless permission is granted by a judge,[13] the attorney representing the children appears at the judicial pre-trial on behalf of the children. If a guardian at litem has been appointed for the children, that person is required to appear at the judicial pre trial as well.[14] The judge meets first with the attorneys of record to discuss all of the outstanding legal issues in the case; for example, the need for discovery or amendments to the pleadings. At the conclusion of these discussions, the judge inquires of the attorneys regarding the appropriateness of including the parties in further discussions.

If the attorney for the parents, as well as the parents, agree to participate in a discussion with the pre-trial judge, everyone in the conference room is excused from the room. The parent's attorney is asked to escort the parent into the conference room and to remain alongside of his/her client while the discussions with the judge are taking place. After the judge is introduced to the respondent parent, the judge immediately extends her appreciation for the parent's willingness to participate in the pre-trial. The judge explains the voluntary nature of this part of the pre-trial, including the parent's right to leave at any time. The parent is also reminded that the trial judge is ready and available to begin the trial on the date on which it had previously been assigned. After explaining the confidential nature of all discussions and reassuring the parent that the trial judge will never be informed of the substance of any conversation with the pre-trial judge, the judge provides the parent with the background of the child protection session.

This is necessary because, as described above, the child protection session in Connecticut exists only to resolve fully contested matters referred to it by a court in one of the thirteen Superior Court Juvenile Matters locations around the state. The parents may wonder why they had to travel such a distance to get to court when previously their case was heard closer to their home. Because of the distance, parents may experience transportation difficulties in arriving to the court proceedings.

In what is often an anti-therapeutic occurrence, many times the parents are transported to the proceeding by the very social worker who will be testifying against the parent in the trial. In addition, parents involved in court proceedings are accustomed to having their cases heard in buildings which are far less majestic and grand than the Middletown courthouse. The contrast between the courts that work with the families while reunification efforts are being made and the court that enters termination orders, is striking.

This reality provides the background in which pre-trials are held and clarifies the reason why it is critical that the judge explain the nature of the proceedings to the parent. The judge should begin with informing the parent of what a review of the file, including, but not limited to the social study, the psychological evaluations, as well as the state's allegations, has revealed to the pre trial judge. The parent is encouraged to challenge the judge's conclusions and to point to errors in any of the court documents. When given this opportunity, many parents open up and speak freely as to why they believe they need to present their case in the formal setting of a trial or why they believe that an agreement may be reached. Many times parents explain the ineffectiveness of the reunification efforts made by the state. Since the state must prove by clear and convincing evidence that it has made reasonable efforts to reunify the family, this information is helpful to the pre trial judge as discussions are held with the social workers. There are times when this information alone is enough to postpone the case to allow meaningful reunification efforts to take place.

It is critical the judge be as prepared as possible for this meeting. This means knowing as much as possible about the procedural history of the file but, in addition, knowing as much as possible about the parents and their life experience. The overarching goal of a pre-trial is after all, an attempt to resolve the dispute between the parties without the need of a contested, hostile trial. Trials of this nature, leave the parents, even if they should prevail, with the sense that they are worthless human beings in addition to being unworthy parents. Contested termination of parental rights trials require parents to sit through expert testimony about the extent of their mental illness or of their substance abuse. And of course, since DCF must prove their case with clear and convincing evidence, the questions, as well as the responses, are never "mild."

Experiences of this type may push a parent who is struggling with issues of substance abuse and/or mental illness into the proverbial "dead end with no way out." In the pre-trial setting, the well prepared judge will know, for example, if the parent is himself or herself a "child of the system" or if the parent has been the victim of physical or sexual abuse, and what, if any, issues surrounding mental health exist. This information is useful in approaching the parent. It may help to explain the "attitude" with which the parent approaches this interaction. The judge must be careful to remember not to be judgmental or accusatory of the parent, but instead to listen with what has been described as "the third ear."[15] Most of the people involved in the child protection system are used to being treated as marginalized and un-empowered. Therefore it is extremely important that the judge make sure that respect and dignity permeate all discussions. The judge should be prepared to *listen* to the story so that he/she can identify and construct what the case is really about. Certainly the case is about abuse and neglect and of children in foster care. But listening also involves empathy. Real listening can be very difficult, it requires a kind of emptying out of one's self to create inner space to contain someone else's story. Once a better understanding of the social context in which the parent has lived their life can be obtained, this knowledge can better inform the judge's recommendations for settlement.

There is a point in time when the parent can be asked, respectfully, for his/her thoughts on what would be best for their child. Sometimes parents agree that, in fact, too much time has gone by and that the best that can be done is to allow their child to find some sense of belonging and happiness with an adoptive family. Sometimes they are convinced that they can effectively parent their child and they should be given another opportunity. But in either case, they have been listened to, with respect.[16]

During the meeting with the attorneys, the attorney for DCF is also asked whether or not there is any objection to a discussion between the Department's agents, usually the social worker and the supervisor with authority to settle, and the pre-trial judge. If there is no objection, the assistant attorney general representing the department is asked to bring in the social worker(s) and to remain in the room while the discussion with the judge is in process. When the judge meets with the social workers, it is equally important to frame the discussion in terms of a recognition of the difficulties and obstacles which face the workers on a daily basis.

A review of the actions taken and the reasons why they were taken, many times reveal systemic flaws rather than a lack of caring on the part of the worker. One can sense a willingness to discuss areas where perhaps other services should have been put in place or more creative approaches to working with the particular family could have been used. Sometimes, the department agrees that, in fact, reasonable efforts to reunify have not been made and sometimes they have overwhelming proof that every effort that could have been made, has been made. In either case, the workers have also been heard.

It is important to note that although the pre-trial judge does not meet with the children, their attorney is present at the pre-trial and is given every opportunity to participate in the discussions. Sometimes, when a child is desirous of formalizing his relationship with his foster parent through an adoption, the child's attorney will join the meeting between the judge and the parents to articulate the child's position. If the child wants to be reunited with his parents and opposes a termination, that position is also communicated to the parents. However, if the child's best interest is represented by a guardian ad litem who takes a position different than that of the child's attorney, the parent is also told of how such a conflict may be resolved in a trial setting.

Following the individual meetings, the judge gives the parties time to meet with their attorneys privately. The judge and clerk are waiting and available to assist the parties and their lawyers with copies of documents or answering questions to clarify the discussions. The judge then meets in conference with the attorneys and conveys the judge's settlement recommendation. These conferences are scheduled for no more that a three hour period. Sometimes, the parties are prepared to settle the case on that day, on other occasions, the judge grants the parties a continuance to think more carefully about the settlement proposal and return at a date prior to trial.

There are instances where the discussions are postponed to allow pre-adoptive foster parents, and their attorneys, an opportunity to attend the pre-trial and communicate their position on post-adoption contact between the child and the biological parent. And, of course, on other times, the case proceeds to trial. Even if they do not result in a settlement of the case, discussions such as these, are very productive. One outstanding reason is that all of the parties have been heard and informed of the process by a neutral judicial authority. Many times, this translates into a reduction of the mystery surrounding court proceedings and enhances public trust in the judicial process.

Another equally important reason is that this type of a setting provides a place where the parents and the child protection agency are on a more equal footing. "It must be acknowledged that in matters of termination of parental rights, the department occupies a superior position. As one court realistically noted, "[t]he parties are by no means dealing on an equal basis. The parent is by definition saddled with problems: economic, physical, sociological, psychiatric or any combination thereof. The agency in contrast is vested with expertise, experience, capital, manpower and prestige."[17] Because of the less restrictive nature of the judicial pre-trial, the differences between the parties are much less pronounced. There is parity of treatment within this setting that is not often appreciated within the structured trial setting.

This is a very brief overview of what the former presiding judge of the Child Protection Session, Hon. Bruce L. Levin, encouraged me to do in Middletown during the 2001–2002 term. Since October, 2001, I have pretried over 80 termination of parental rights cases to conclusion and at least 51 cases have settled either because DCF withdrew the petition or the parents voluntarily executed a consent to the termination of their parental rights. This translates into a 63% settlement rate during this twelve-month period.

Quite apart from the statistics, there is no effective way to measure the benefits of enabling a parent to leave a legal proceeding as an active and respected participant as opposed to a passive victim.

Notes

1. In re Jessica M., 217 Conn. 459,464 (1991), citing Stanley v. Illinois, 405 U.S. 645, 651 92 S.Ct. 120 831 L.Ed. 2d 551 (1972).

2. Anonymous v. Norton, 168 Conn. 421, 430 362 A2.532, cert. denied, 423 U.S. 935, 96 S. Ct. 294, 46 L. Ed. 268 (1975).

3. General Statutes §17a-112(j)

4. General Statutes §51-183b provides: "Any judge of the Superior Court and any judge trial referee who has the power to render judgment, who has commenced the trial of any civil cause, shall have power to continue such trial and shall render judgment not later than 120 days from the completion date of the trial of such civil cause. The parties may waive the provisions of this section."

5. In addition, the statistics establish that they are predominantly families of color. See, Dorothy Roberts, Shattered Bonds: The Color of Child Welfare, (Basic Civitas Books, 2002).

6. General Statutes §51-164w. Juvenile Court, Circuit Court and Court of Common Pleas construed to mean Superior Court as of July 1, 1978.

7. General Statutes §51-164s. Superior Court sole trial court. Jurisdiction transferred from Court of Common Pleas and Juvenile Court. The Superior Court shall be the sole court of original jurisdiction for all causes of action, except such actions over which the courts of probate have original jurisdiction, as provided by statute.

8. Juvenile Justice in Connecticut: Legislative Program Review and Investigations Committee, January 1989, page 33.

9. Hon. Barbara M. Quinn, Child Protection Session: Practice and Procedure (2001).

10. David B. Wexler & Bruce J. Winick, Law in a Therapeutic Key: Developments in Therapeutic Jurisprudence xvii(1996)

11. Id.

12. Practice Book §26-1(k) "Parties" includes: (1) the child or youth who is the subject of the proceeding and those additional persons as defined herein;(2) "Legal party": Any person, including a parent, whose legal relationship to the matter pending before the court is of such a nature and kind as to mandate the receipt of proper legal notice as a condition precedent to the establishment of the court's authority to adjudicate the matter pending before it; and (3) "intervening party": Any person whose interest in the matter before the court is not of such a nature and kind as to entitle legal service as a prerequisite ro the court's authority to adjudicate the matter pending before it but whose participation therein, at the discretion of the judicial authority, may promote the interests of justice. This definition may include but

is not limited to any father or mother, natural, adoptive or putative, or any defacto custodian. An "intervening party" may in any proceeding before the court be given notice thereof in any manner reasonably appropriate to that end, but no such "intervening party" shall be entitled, as a matter of right, to provision of counsel by the court.

13. Connecticut Practice Book §32a-4(b) provides in relevant part: Any party who intends to call a child as a witness shall first file a motion seeking permission of the judicial authority. See also, *In re Brandon W.* 56 Conn. App418 (2000). *In re Lauren R.* 49 Conn. App.763(1998); *In re Noel M.*, 23 Conn. App. 410, 421 (1990);

14. General Statutes §46b-129a provides in pertinent part: "In proceedings in the Superior Court under section 46b-129 (neglect petitions and emergency removal of children) (1)The court may order the child, the parents, the guardian, or other persons accused by a competent witness with abusing the child, to be examined by one or more competent physicians, psychiatrists or psychologists appointed by the court (2) a child shall be represented by counsel appointed by the court te represent the child whose fee shall be paid by the parents or guardian or the estate of the child, or, if such persons are unable to pay, by the court. In all cases in which the court deems it appropriate, the court shall also appoint a person, other than the person appointed to represent the child, as guardian-ad-litem for such child to speak on behalf of the best interests of the child, which guardian-ad-litem is not required to be an attorney at law but shall be knowledgeable about the needs and protection of children and whose fee, if any, shall be paid by the parents or guardian, or the estate of the child, or if such persons are unable to pay, by the court..."

15. Theodore Reik, Listening with the Third Ear (Doubleday, 1951).

16. Specific examples have not been provided to protect the confidential nature of the proceedings. See, Practice Book §32a-7(b): "Except as otherwise provided by statue, all records maintained in juvenile matters brought before the judicial authority, either current or closed, including the transcripts of hearings, shall be kept confidential."

17. *In Re Eden F. Et Al,* 48 Conn. App. 290, 311–312, 710 A. 2d 771, cert. Granted on other grounds, 245 Conn. 917, 717A.2d. 234(1998), citing, *Matter of Sheila G., 61 N.Y.2d 368, 381, 462 N.E.2d 1139, 474 N.Y.S.2. 421(1984), quoting Matter of Sydney, 84 Misc. 2d 932, 934 934, 377 N.Y.S.2d 908 (1975).*

N. Therapeutic Techniques in the Appellate Arena

Up to this point, all of the readings have related to trial level proceedings. But therapeutic jurisprudence is now entering the appellate arena as well, and we close the volume with some of the recent writings in that area. After a brief overview of the issues, by Wexler, we present a selection by Professor Amy Ronner (St. Thomas University School of Law in Miami), co-authored by Winick. Ronner has had considerable experience as an appellate lawyer and as director of an appellate advocacy clinic. In their short selection, Ronner and Winick draw on the psychology of procedural justice and on the importance to litigants of "voice" and "validation." They use that research to underscore the anti-therapeutic aspects of a *per curiam* affirmance, and propose in its stead a very brief opinion with reasons—in essence a "therapeutic affirmance".

Finally, the volume closes with a short essay by Wexler regarding the use of legal doctrine to reduce contentiousness, to promote dialogue, and to generally "lower the volume" in certain controversies. Appellate courts sensitive to the raw emotions underlying certain conflicts may be able to craft legal doctrines—such as a "duty to negotiate"—that may be preferable to declaring, by judicial fiat, a winner and a loser. The essay seeks to open up this area for future discussion and attention.

How Appellate Courts Can Use Therapeutic Jurisprudence
by David B. Wexler
(Excerpted from *Therapeutic Jurisprudence in the Appellate Arena*, 24 Seattle U. L. Rev. 217, 219–222 (2000), Copyright 2000 by David B. Wexler, reprinted with permission).

* * *

In this Introduction, I will briefly summarize Des Rosiers' *Court Review* article, entitled *From Telling to Listening: A Therapeutic Analysis of the Role of Courts in Minority-Majority Conflicts*, placing it in a framework that transcends minority-majority conflicts and encourages discussion regarding the use of therapeutic jurisprudence by appellate tribunals. * * *

Even though there was no immediate plan for a referendum regarding the independence of Quebec, the Canadian federal government, exercising its power to refer questions to the Canadian Supreme Court, asked the Court to rule on the constitutionality of a possible future unilateral Quebec secession. The Court held that Quebec did not have the right to unilaterally secede, but it nonetheless stated that a "clear" majority vote in Quebec on a "clear" question favoring secession "would confer democratic legitimacy on the secession initiative which all of the other participants in the Confederation would have to recognize."

Des Rosiers notes that both separatists and federalists applauded the Supreme Court decision. Using a therapeutic jurisprudence framework, she attempts to explain the favorable reaction. Basically, Des Rosiers claims that the members of the Canadian Supreme Court moved away from their past stance as "tellers of the truth," becoming "more process-oriented listeners, translators, educators, and, if possible, facilitators." She notes the therapeutic value of process—of telling one's story and being heard—and of a procedure that values the ongoing, continuous relationship between the parties. And, of course, she notes the sensitive use of language by the court. Finally, she commends the Canadian Supreme Court's doctrinal solution—the imposition of an "obligation to negotiate."

In these brief introductory remarks, I cannot even attempt to capture the nuances and texture of the case or Professor Des Rosiers' analysis. Those writings clearly deserve to be read in full.

Instead, I will race to Des Rosiers' conclusion, and through my own italics, try to set the stage for the [comments] that follow:

> It is true that it is easier for a court to be "therapeutic" when the case presented is "hypothetical", as the Secession Reference was. However, there is still a lesson to be learned in the approach adopted by the Supreme Court. Its attention to the language it used in order not to create a problem of legitimacy for itself in Quebec has been fruitful. Particularly welcome is the process-driven solution it offered, which called for respect for other minorities and defined the values which had to be taken into account.
>
> It could be that an inventory of process-driven solutions ought to be offered to courts. The imposition of an obligation to negotiate, as was done here, is one example. The creation of duties to consult, as was done in the Aboriginal context, may also be of value. Several mechanisms that exist in other fields, the obligation to negotiate in good faith in labor law or the obligation to inform in tort law, for example, could be explored. More must be done in this area. It could also be that lawyering will have to be done differently: if the process is to have the therapeutic benefits

argued for, it requires that the "true" story be told, that the groups' narratives be heard. It may require that lawyers relinquish control of the story told by the group-client. Again, the implications for lawyers of a judicial therapeutic approach will have to be examined further.

Des Rosiers' first point is structural: she posits a therapeutic advantage to the "hypothetical" nature of the case. Does the ability to issue advisory opinions enhance a court's ability to create "therapeutic" doctrines? Surely, this issue warrants discussion. Interestingly, Des Rosiers notes that asking the unilateral secession question in the absence of an immediate plan for another referendum was risky and "angered most Quebecois." Might a "reference power" judicial structure possible have antitherapeutic *pre*-decision consequences and therapeutic *post*-decision consequences?

Next, Des Rosiers speaks of language use, and elsewhere she speaks of opinion-writing as writing a "letter to the loser." If past opinions are read through this prism, we are likely to find admirable, abominable, and average illustrations. It may be useful to collect, classify, and use these illustrations in educational programs for judges, lawyers, and law students.

Des Rosiers is very much taken with the "obligation to negotiate" or, as she terms it, the "process-driven solution" shaped by the Supreme Court of Canada. In fact, she cites similar doctrinal devices found in labor and tort law, and makes the intriguing suggestion that "an inventory of process-driven solutions ought to be offered to the courts." We should indeed seek to collect examples from existing law (in various legal regimes), and perhaps begin to propose still other solutions.

* * *

By and large, dialogue-producing doctrines are likely to be helpful. Such doctrines may, in and of themselves, actually constitute the corpus of an emerging therapeutic and preventive law. In some instances, however, courts may eventually need to call a halt to endless and unproductive dialogue. When might that be the case? How might it best be accomplished?

Des Rosiers conclusion notes that, in some instances, perhaps "lawyering will have to be done differently," perhaps by giving more room to clients or group-clients to tell their own stories.

* * *

These are some of the many issues that can be healthy and appetizing food for thought in a therapeutic jurisprudence appellate project.

* * *

Key References

Des Rosiers, Nathalie, *From Telling to Listening: A Therapeutic Analysis of the Role of Courts in Minority-Majority Conflicts*, 37 Ct. Rev. 54 (2000).

Des Rosiers, Nathalie, Reference Re Secession of Quebec, 24 Seattle L. Rev. 217 (1998)

The Antitherapeutic Per Curiam Affirmance

By Amy D. Ronner & Bruce J. Winick

(Excerpted from *Silencing the Appellant's Voice: The Antitherapeutic Per Curiam Affirmance*, 24 Seattle U. L. Rev 499, 500–507 (2000), Copyright 2000 by Amy D. Ronner & Bruce J. Winick, reprinted with permission).

I. Introduction

* * *

When an appellate court issues a PCA (per curiam affirmance), it simply says one word: "affirmed."

PCA decisions are generally accepted and often justified. In cases warranting a PCA, the application of legal precedent to the facts of the case seems straightforward to the appellate court, justifying the saving of appellate resources that results from dispensing with the preparation of an appellate opinion. In addition, because the case makes no new law, further savings can be accomplished by dispensing with the publication of a full decision, which would further clutter the already voluminous official report of decisions and risk both lawyer and judicial confusion. Because it is generally thought that "[t]he parties themselves have no right to an opinion," considerations of appellate efficiency and economy are invoked to justify what appears to be an increasing practice. Since it contains no discussion of facts, no disclosure of the court's reasoning, and gives no sense of validation, the PCA is antitherapeutic. In this instance, not only has the appellant lost the appeal, but he or she is left with the feeling (correct or incorrect) that the court did not take the contentions made (at considerable expense) with any degree of seriousness. To the appellant, the contentions in the appeal deserve a reasoned response rather than a summary dismissal.

This Article will analyze the antitherapeutic impact of the PCA in two steps. First, delving into the psychology of procedural justice, this Article will explain how litigants value "voice," or the ability to tell their stories, as well as "validation," or the sense that the decision-maker has heard their words and taken them seriously. Second, this Article, through the use of narrative, will show how a PCA had a negative psychological impact on an actual appellant in a criminal case. The Article will conclude by proposing an alternative to the antitherapeutic PCA.

II. Voice and Validation

There are quite a few empirical studies dealing with how litigants experience the litigation process. These studies essentially agree that litigants place great importance on the process itself, as well as on the dignitary value of a hearing. When individuals feel that the system has treated them with fairness, respect, and dignity, they experience greater satisfaction. This basically boils down to the litigants' having a sense of "voice," or an opportunity to tell their story to a decision maker. Equal with voice is "validation," or the feeling that the tribunal has really listened to, heard, and taken seriously the litigants' stories.

* * *

Appellate courts can also be more effective by being good listeners. Even if they must, due to the constraints of the law, issue a decision adverse to a litigant, there are still ways to express empathy, let individuals know that they have been heard, and let individuals know that their arguments have been fairly and fully considered. The PCA does not accomplish this.

III. Being Without Voice and Validation

One of this Article's authors ran an in-house appellate clinic at her university in which third-year law students represented indigent clients on appeal. One such client, Ralph Walker, was convicted of conspiring to murder a South Florida trial judge. The appellate clinic, however, was not retained until after the conviction was affirmed and Walker had lodged an unsuccessful motion for a new trial based on ineffective assistance of counsel. Convinced that Mr. Walker had not received a fair trial, the clinic supervisor and the student team appointed to handle the appeal following the denial of the ineffectiveness of counsel motion spent numerous hours drafting a brief that told Mr. Walker's story. In this context, his story was that which happened to him at the trial itself.

The case against Mr. Walker ostensibly began when he befriended a cocaine-addicted felon with multiple convictions. This felon, who became the heart of the prosecution's case against Mr. Walker, testified at trial that Walker planned to murder a judge. Law enforcement had outfitted this informant with transmitting devices to obtain evidence of the supposed murder plans. Although the tapes were mostly inaudible and the police had erased the back-up set, the State introduced them into evidence; Walker's trial counsel failed to move to suppress them. Walker asserted that had the tapes been intelligible, the unredacted conversations between him and the informant would have established his innocence.

Further, Walker's defense counsel failed to call several exculpatory witnesses. Walker asserted that these individuals would have rebutted portions of the informant's testimony and shown that several of the alleged conversations between Walker and the informant simply did not occur.

Finally, Walker challenged both the failure of defense counsel to file a motion to disqualify the allegedly biased presiding judge and the exclusion of African Americans from the jury.

In the initial and reply briefs, the clinic students told Mr. Walker's story and gave him a voice. The court conducted an oral argument and shortly thereafter issued a decision. The opinion merely said, "per curiam affirmed."

Several scholars writing in the area of therapeutic jurisprudence have pointed out that when individuals participate in a judicial process, what influences them most is not the result, but their evaluation of the fairness of the process itself. As Tom Tyler, a social psychologist and one of the principal architects of the psychology of procedural justice, explains:

> Studies suggest that if the socializing influence of experience is the issue of concern (i.e., the impact of participating in a judicial hearing on a person's respect for the law and legal authorities), then the primary influence is the person's evaluation of the fairness of the judicial procedure itself, not their evaluations of the outcome. Such respect is important because it has been found to influence everyday behavior toward the law. When people believe that legal authorities are less legitimate, they are less likely to be law-abiding citizens in their everyday lives.

Professor Gould applies these insights to the process of criminal sentencing. Analyzing individuals involved in felony cases, she concludes that those who "experienced a legal procedure that they judged to be unfair... had less respect for the law and legal authorities and are less likely to accept judicial decisions." These feelings can seriously diminish the potential for rehabilitation. When litigants perceive the process as unfair, they do not feel like voluntary participants in it. Rather than being a part of a process that brings healing, they feel unfairly treated, ignored, powerless, and angry.

These therapeutic jurisprudence principles are illustrated by Mr. Walker's case. What struck Mr. Walker as unfair was that the appellate court had not given him any form of validation. For him, the court neither heard his story nor acknowledged his points. He essentially emerged from the experience feeling that the system was coercive and that he was not a voluntary participant in it. As such, the PCA diminished his respect for both the legal process and the law.

IV. Conclusion

* * *

What could replace the cold and silent per curiam affirmance is an order essentially reciting the salient facts of the case and mentioning some of the arguments. Even if the court feels bound by authority to decide a case adversely to a litigant, it could communicate this and still send out a message that the participants in the process have been heard. Such speaking (or therapeutic) affirmances would not consume considerably more time than a PCA, and could essentially be constructed from a law clerk's case summary or memorandum.

Moreover, speaking or therapeutic affirmances would not need to be published in the law books. They could simply be sent to the parties and their counsel. Therapeutic affirmances could be short documents that demonstrate the appellate court's understanding of the basic facts of the controversy and the contentions made by the appellant. After reciting the facts and summarizing the arguments, a therapeutic affirmance could simply conclude with a one-sentence statement enunciating the reasons why the judgment must be affirmed. For example, the court could say: "While we understand the contentions made by the appellant and that he or she feels that the decision below was erroneous, under our law we must defer to the discretion of the trial judge in matters such as these, and therefore, for the reasons set forth in the appellee's brief, we must affirm." The second portion of this sentence, explaining the basis for the affirmance, of course, could vary based upon the appellate issues presented.

While drafting a brief therapeutic affirmance would involve time and effort by an appellate court that a *per curiam* affirmance would render unnecessary, the therapeutic value of trying to satisfy the appellant's need for procedural justice more than justifies these additional expenses. Moreover, these expenses may also be justified by an additional consideration—increased accuracy in the appellate process.

* * *

Even if insufficient to change the result reached by the trial court, the therapeutic value of providing the appellant with the assurance that his or her story was heard and understood can be significant. It can help a criminal offender accept the court's conclusion that he has violated the law and is deserving of punishment, thereby increasing the potential for successful rehabilitation and reintegration into the community. It can help parties in civil disputes get past the bad feelings that such disputes inevitably inspire and that lawsuits frequently exacerbate; such resolution will ease the transition to post-litigation circumstances. It can enable parties who have experienced the physical or emotional trauma of an accident, an intentional tort, or a divorce, to begin the healing process. While these emotional and therapeutic dimensions of an appeal have not been regarded as a proper concern of an appellate court, they should be.

* * *

Key References

Tyler, Tom R., The Psychological Consequences of Judicial Procedures: Implications for Civil Commitment Hearings, 96 SMU L. Rev. 433 (1992).

Reducing Contentiousness through Legal Doctrine

by David B. Wexler
(Excerpted from Lowering the Volume Through Legal Doctrine:
A Promising Path for Therapeutic Jurisprudence Scholarship,
by 3 Fla. Coastal L.J. 123, 124–133 (2002), Copyright 2002
by David B. Wexler, reprinted with permission).

Introduction

* * *

Therapeutic jurisprudence is now moving into the world of practice, with literature addressed to practicing lawyers and law students and to the judiciary. The use of therapeutic jurisprudence by courts originally focused on the trial stage, but has now expanded to the appellate arena, principally due to an article written by Professor Nathalie Des Rosiers, now President of the Law Commission of Canada, entitled *From Telling to Listening: A Therapeutic Analysis of the Role of Courts in Minority-Majority Conflicts*.

Des Rosiers uses a therapeutic jurisprudence analysis to examine the opinion of the Supreme Court of Canada in the 1998 *Quebec Secession Reference* case. In contrast to prior cases, where the Court often took the traditional position of ruling with crisp authority, and justifying its ruling by minimizing the complexity or ambiguity of the issues, the Court here took a very different—and refreshing—approach. Using very sensitive language, the Court underscored the difficulty of the issue, emphasized the importance of process and negotiation, and recognized the importance of the continuing relationship between Quebec and the rest of Canada.

The Court held that Quebec did not have the right to unilateral secession, but nonetheless stated that a "clear" majority rule in Quebec on a "clear" question favoring secession "would confer democratic legitimacy on the secession initiative which all of the other participants in Confederation would have to recognize."

In other words, the Court established the circumstances under which a "duty to negotiate" would be triggered. Des Rosiers was particularly intrigued by this "process-driven solution." In fact, she suggests that "an inventory of process-driven solutions ought to be offered to courts." The duty to negotiate is one such doctrine. She notes the duty to "consult," employed in a case involving Aboriginal concerns, is still another. Others might be "the obligation to negotiate in good faith in labor law or the obligation to inform in tort law...."

The present essay uses Des Rosiers' suggestion as a springboard. It is my thesis that therapeutic jurisprudence scholarship can contribute to the formulation of legal doctrine—process-driven solutions or otherwise—that can contribute to preserving relationships, to promoting dialogue rather than debate, and, in general, to diffusing anger, to curtailing contentiousness, and to turning down the volume so that creative problem-solving might ensue. The remainder of this essay, then, will begin to examine certain legal doctrines from the therapeutic jurisprudence perspective.

II. Legal Doctrine in Therapeutic Context

Baker v. Vermont—While the *Quebec Secession Reference* case was a process-driven doctrine that apparently operated in the desired dialogue—producing direction, *Baker v. Vermont,*—the Vermont same-sex marriage case—was a process-driven result that took a rough and rocky road.

Construing the "common benefits" clause of the Vermont Constitution, the *Baker* case held squarely that same-sex couples could not be deprived of the statutory benefits and protections accorded to heterosexual married couples. While the court required the state to extend these benefits and protections to same-sex couples, it declined to specify a required route. Instead, it left to the legislature the decision whether to extend the marriage laws to gay couples or whether to create an alternative equivalent, such as a domestic partnership arrangement.

Concerned with avoiding disruptive consequences, the *Baker* court went on to "hold that the current statutory scheme shall remain in effect for a reasonable period of time to enable the legislature to consider and enact implementing legislation in an orderly and expeditious fashion." In the event of legislative inaction, the court noted that "plaintiffs may petition this Court to order the remedy they originally sought"—i.e., a marriage license. Concurring in the majority's holding, but dissenting from its process-driven remedy, Justice Johnson would have simply granted the requested relief and would have enjoined the defendants from "denying plaintiffs a marriage license based solely on the sex of the applicants."

The legislature eventually enacted, and the governor promptly signed, a "civil union" law. From all reports, however, the process was a deeply divisive one, with legislators in tears and at great risk of being ousted at the polls. Interestingly, the timing of the judicial decision—in mid-December—may have had something to do with the polarization of the issue: "It is self-selecting, of course," Dr. Dean [the Governor] said: "Look out your window. When it's snowing like this, you're not going to get up and out of your cozy armchair in the middle of the Vermont winter to take the moderate path."

Interesting timing issues aside, however, one wonders whether, in the particular context, the court's process-driven doctrinal solution simply backfired. If it did, we should explore whether there are lessons to be learned from the case, a matter I will return to during the discussion of *Miranda*, immediately following.

Miranda—The Supreme Court in *Miranda* employed a very interesting doctrinal technique apparently designed to take some of the sting out of its holding and to promote continued discussion and dialogue. The technique is to identify the crucial interest at stake—such as protection of the self-incrimination privilege during custodial interrogation—and to set down a default rule for satisfying the interest. A default rule ensures that the interest will be protected, but does not create a 'constitutional straightjacket', for it recognizes that alternative solutions may be devised to protect the interest at stake. The default rule technique therefore operates to insure interest protection while not cutting off discussion and dialogue. In many ways, the device heeds the advice of negotiation theorists to recognize the primacy of "interests" over "positions."

Elsewhere, I have written that I have long been fascinated with

> ...the Warren Court's invitation...to think through the true bases of *Miranda* and the line-up cases. Recall that the *Miranda* Court required specific warnings and waivers, including advice regarding appointed counsel during interrogation, 'unless other fully effective means are devised to inform accused persons of their right of silence and to assure a continuous opportunity to exercise it'....With lineups, the Court's right to counsel was not intended as a 'constitutional straightjacket.' Legislative or other regulations... which eliminate the risks of abuse and unintentional suggestion at proceedings and the impediments to meaningful confrontation at trial may...remove the basis for regarding the stage as 'critical.'

In its recent reaffirmation of *Miranda*, the Court in *Dickerson v. United States* reiterated *Miranda*'s default rule status, noting that Congress never availed itself of the opportunity to design an effective alternative means of protecting the self-incrimination privilege. Surely, the 1968 congressional enactment—permitting the admission of voluntary confessions—was in no way an effective alternative means for protecting the interest at stake; it was merely a feeble legislative attempt to turn back the constitutional clock to pre-*Miranda* days.

The *Miranda-Dickerson* discussion leads one to wonder whether the *Baker v. Vermont* gay marriage case might have produced a less angry atmosphere if the court had gone a small step further and cast its ruling *explicitly* as a default rule. After all, the *Baker* court was willing to serve as a lightening rod in ruling that same sex couples are entitled to the benefits accorded heterosexual couples. But its holding, without more explicit guidance, created a *legislative* lightening rod as well.

Perhaps the legislature would have been put in a less vulnerable posture by a rule falling somewhere between the *Baker* majority and Justice Johnson's dissent. For example, the court might have said that 1) same-sex couples are entitled to the same benefits as married couples, 2) there are various means of satisfying that legal interest, 3) in the interest of maintaining stability and promoting dialogue, the current legislation will remain in effect for a reasonable time (e.g., a full legislative session), and—the key—4) at the end of the given reasonable time period, the current marriage laws will be read to apply to same-sex couples, and ordinary marriage licenses will issue to them, unless by that date there is in place a legislative measure otherwise satisfying the legal interest of according equal benefits to same-sex couples.

In other words, perhaps if the legal situation *absent* legislative action were crystal clear, the legislature could have discussed the various options in an atmosphere freer of emotional frenzy.[1] A default doctrine, imposing a legal "position" unless policymakers otherwise creatively satisfy the underlying legal "interest," may be a particularly fruitful and effective "process-driven solution."

But using legal doctrine to turn down the volume and to diffuse anger need not necessarily take the form of "process-driven" solutions. Rules establishing firm legal positions—the ordinary fare of judicial decisionmaking—can also be cast with a hope of avoiding unnecessary friction, misunderstanding, and controversy, as the next two examples seek to illustrate.

Johnson v. New Jersey—By using the default doctrine discussed above, the Supreme Court sought to soften the impact of its controversial *Miranda* ruling. But the Court blundered badly when, a week later, it decided *Johnson v. New Jersey*, dealing with the prospective applicability of the *Miranda* ruling.

As expected, the Court in *Johnson* held that *Miranda* should not be applied retroactively. Observers were confident the Court would not create a furor and deal a deadly blow to the administration of justice by upsetting the convictions and sentences of all those whose confessions had been obtained in accordance with pre-*Miranda* law. In fashioning a prospective application of the *Miranda* requirements, the *Johnson* Court ruled that the *Miranda* standards would apply to "trials begun" after the date of the decision.

The Court's choice of that particular cut off date was unfortunate, for it in essence created a type of "limited retroactivity" that was purposeless and, at the same time, added salt to the wound. In the immediate aftermath of *Miranda*, with media attention focused squarely on the impact of the Court's new-fangled and far-reaching rule, judges across the country—presiding over trials that were just beginning—were forced to suppress confessions for police failure to read the *Miranda* warnings—even though the confessions were obtained before the *Miranda* ruling was announced. This anger, confusion, and controversy could have been avoided if the Court had "gone all the way and had made *Miranda* applicable only to confessions taken after June 13, 1966 [the date of the *Miranda* decision]."

Mapp v. Ohio—Anger, confusion, and controversy have, of course, been hallmarks of the fourth amendment exclusionary rule. The controversy—sparked by the 1961 *Mapp v. Ohio* decision applying the exclusionary sanction to the states—continues to this day. Allowing the criminal 'to go free because the constable has blundered' is simply too bitter a pill for many to swallow, especially when politicians often purposely provoke and precipitate attacks on the rule.

It is easy to see why the exclusionary sanction continually creates controversy: the many benefits of the rule are indirect and are taken for granted by the public (e.g., sleeping peacefully at night without fearing entry by curious police officers); but the considerable costs of the rule operate in a very visible "in your face" manner, leading to the granting of motions to suppress tangible, highly incriminating, and critical evidence. In John Kaplan's words, the exclusionary sanction "flaunts before us the costs we must pay for fourth amendment guarantees."

Because of the continuing controversy, policymakers have regularly proposed "alternatives" to the exclusionary rule, such as civil suits, criminal prosecution, civilian review boards, and the like. But commentators have generally been highly skeptical about the deterrent effectiveness of these alternative approaches.

The point I would like to make here, however, goes beyond questions of constitutional straightjackets versus default doctrines. It goes, instead, to how a court might, in the proper circumstance, look to satisfying crucial interests while at the same time minimizing anger, rage, misunderstanding, and contentiousness. The exclusionary rule is likely not the context in which to actually propose such a solution, but, given certain assumptions, it does provide a context for discussion of the approaches.

When critics of the exclusionary rule propose abandoning the rule in favor of some supposedly effective alternative to it, defenders of the rule have some stock retorts. One of them is that the proposed alternative is likely not as effective a deterrent to unwanted police conduct as is the exclusionary rule itself. Thus, accepting an alternative remedy would operate in practice not only to repeal the exclusionary remedy but also to weaken the fourth amendment itself.

Relatedly, as to the critics' complaints that the criminal should not go free because the constable has blundered, exclusionary rule defenders often respond that under a truly effective alternative approach to the exclusionary rule, just as many guilty persons would go free. The difference is that, under the exclusionary rule, the evidence is *acquired* in violation of the fourth amendment and *later* suppressed, whereas under an alternative approach that truly induces compliance with fourth amendment standards, wrongful apprehension and evidence acquisition will presumably never occur in the *first* place; the criminal will not be caught and released, but will instead not be caught at all. Simply put, the difference is between "convicting" the criminal and "catching" the criminal.

Writing as a law review commentator, Justice Stewart put it well. Supporting the exclusionary sanction, he described as a "consolation" the fact that "in many of the cases in which exclusion is ordered, police officers would not have discovered the evidence at all if they had originally complied with the fourth amendment."

My point flows from Justice Stewart's "consolation" remarks. For the purpose of discussion, let us assume an alternative remedy—a civil suit, for instance—that is empirically demonstrated to be *every bit* as effective as the exclusionary sanction itself in deterring fourth amendment violations. Instead of continued defense of the exclusionary rule, using as a "consolation" the fact that just as many criminals will go free under the civil suit alternative, courts and policymakers should perhaps *embrace* the thoroughly effective civil alternative, and bid farewell to the exclusionary doctrine that has been so misunderstood and difficult to defend over the decades.

Slobogin put it well: "[I]f we can avoid flaunting the costs of the Fourth Amendment and still achieve its goals, so much the better."

Courts interested in this approach to "lowering the volume" will need to be sensitive and careful. I am in no way suggesting that we "bury" controversial issues, or that we create legal doctrines that will minimize controversy by exacting burdens on the poor, the powerless, the inarticulate, the unorganized.[2] I suggest only that where the same legal interest can be fully satisfied by two alternative approaches, one of which will predictably cause anger, confusion, misunderstanding, and controversy, we might be well-advised to choose the other.

III. Conclusion

If courts wish to pursue the approach proposed here, how might they best do so? How can lawyers and academics assist in that task?

It is not clear at the moment how traditional appellate advocates can best propose these therapeutic and preventive doctrines. Of course, courts could create and shape these doctrines on their own, even if the doctrines are not served up to them in the briefs of appellate advocates. Such a course of action is, however, both burdensome and a bit risky.

Perhaps issues and proposals of the type suggested here might best be presented to courts by *amicus curiae*, prepared by lawyers and scholars attached to various emerging law school centers relating to therapeutic jurisprudence, preventive law, creative problem-solving, and the like. Such centers would be ideally suited to generating legal and interdisciplinary scholarship regarding therapeutic and preventive legal doctrine, and to introducing law students to professional roles as peacemakers and creative problem-solvers.

Notes

1. My colleague Barbara Atwood has a different view. In providing comments on an earlier draft, Atwood notes that the *Baker* court *did* "turn down the volume", especially by framing the issue not in terms of marriage itself, but rather in terms of the benefits and consequences of marriage. Moreover, Atwood makes an interesting observation that had not occurred to me: that had the court adopted my proposed default rule, that rule might itself have misfired, leading to an amendment of the state constitution. All of this, of course, is flavorful food for thought.

2. For instance, civil commitment codes that produce many "false positive" type errors—committing people who in fact may be able to survive safely in the community—are likely to generate less controversy than are those commitment codes that produce "false negative" decisions, releasing persons as safe who in fact will prove dangerous to themselves or others. David B. Wexler, *The Structure of Civil Commitment: Patterns, Pressures, and Interactions in Mental Health Legislation*, 7 Law and Hum. Behav. 1 (1983). While the first type of code will presumably generate less controversy, that is *not* the sort of controversy-reducing legal approach I am proposing.

Key References

Abrahamson, Shirley S., *The Appeal of Therapeutic Jurisprudence*, 24 Seattle U. L. Rev. 223 (2000).

Baker v. State, 744 S.2d 864 (Vt.1999).

Des Rosiers, Nathalie, *From Telling to Listening: A Therapeutic Analysis of the Role of Courts in Minority-Majority Conflicts*, 37 Court Rev. 54 (2000).

Dickerson v. United States, 530 U.S. 428 (2000).

Johnson v. New Jersey, 384 U.S. 719 (1966).

Mapp v. Ohio, 376 U.S. 643 (1961).

Miranda v. Arizona, 384 U.S. 436 (1966).

ABOUT THE EDITORS

Bruce J. Winick is a professor of law at the University of Miami School of Law in Coral Gables, Florida, where he has taught since 1974. He is the author, co-author, and co-editor of numerous books, the latest of which include *Protecting Society from Sexually Violent Offenders: Law, Justice, and Therapy* (American Psychological Association Books 2003), *Practicing Therapeutic Jurisprudence: Law as a Helping Profession* (Carolina Academic Press 2000), *The Essentials of Florida Mental Health Law* (W.W. Norton & Co. 2000), *The Right to Refuse Mental Health Treatment* (American Psychological Association Books 1997), *Therapeutic Jurisprudence Applied: Essays on Mental Health Law* (Carolina Academic Press 1997), and *Law in a Therapeutic Key: Developments in Therapeutic Jurisprudence* (Carolina Academic Press 1996). Winick also has been guest editor of numerous symposia issues in academic journals, and has authored over 80 articles in legal and interdisciplinary journals. He is the coeditor of the APA book series *Law and Public Policy: Psychology and the Social Sciences*. He is legal advisor and a founding member of the board of editors of *Psychology, Public Policy, and Law* and serves on the editorial board of *Law and Human Behavior*. Winick has received numerous awards, including the Thurgood Marshall Award of the Association of the Bar of the City of New York and the Human Rights Award of the American Immigration Lawyers Association. He previously served as New York City's Director of Court Mental Health Services and as General Counsel of its Department of Mental Health. Winick received his law degree from the New York University School of Law.

David B. Wexler is Professor of Law and Director of the International Network on Therapeutic Jurisprudence at the University of Puerto Rico in San Juan, Puerto Rico and John D. Lyons Professor of Law and Professor of Psychology at the University of Arizona in Tucson, Arizona. His other books include Therapeutic Jurisprudence: Law as a Helping Profession(with Dennis P. Stolle and Bruce J. Winick, Carolina Academic Press, 2000), Law in a Therapeutic Key: Developments in Therapeutic Jurisprudence (with Bruce J. Winick, Carolina Academic Press, 1996), Essays in Therapeutic Jurisprudence (with Bruce J. Winick, Carolina Academic Press, 1991), Therapeutic Jurisprudence: The Law as a Therapeutic Agent (Carolina Academic Press, 1990), and Mental Health Law: Major Issues (Plenum Press, 1981). He received the American Psychiatric Association's Manfred S. Guttmacher Forensic Psychiatry Award; received the National Center for State Courts Distinguished Service Award; chaired the American Bar Association's Commission on Mental Disability and the Law; chaired the Association of American Law Schools Section on Law and Mental Disability; chaired the advisory board of the National Center for State Courts' Institute on Mental Disability and Law; was a member of the Panel on Legal Issues of the President's Commission on Mental Health; was a member of the National Commission on the Insanity Defense; served as Vice President of the International Academy of Law and Mental Health; received the New York University School of Law Distinguished Alumnus Legal Scholarship/Teaching Award; and served as a member of the MacArthur Foundation Research Network on Mental Health and the Law. He is a consultant to the National Judicial Institute of Canada, and has served as a Fulbright Senior Specialist, lecturing on therapeutic jurisprudence in Australia and New Zealand.

Index